Practical Skills in
Environmental Science

ALLAN JONES
ROB DUCK
JONATHAN WEYERS
ROB REED

PEARSON
Prentice
Hall

Harlow, England • London • New York • Boston • San Francisco • Toronto
Sydney • Tokyo • Singapore • Hong Kong • Seoul • Taipei • New Delhi
Cape Town • Madrid • Mexico City • Amsterdam • Munich • Paris • Milan

Pearson Education Limited
Edinburgh Gate
Harlow
Essex CM20 2JE
England

and Associated Companies throughout the world

Visit us on the World Wide Web at:
www.pearsoned.co.uk

First published in 2000 by Prentice Hall

© Pearson Education Limited 2000

Typeset in 9.5 pt Times
by 32

Printed in Malaysia, VVP

British Library Cataloguing-in-Publication Data
A catalogue record for this book is available from the British Library

ISBN-10: 0-582-32873-X
ISBN-13: 978-0-582-32873-0

10 9 8 7 6 5
10 09 08 07 06

Practical Skills in
Environmental Science

We work with leading authors to develop the strongest educational materials in environmental science bringing cutting-edge thinking and best learning practice to a global market.

Under a range of well-known imprints, including Prentice Hall, we craft high quality print and electronic publications which help readers to understand and apply their content, whether studying or at work.

To find out more about the complete range of our publising please visit us on the World Wide Web at: www.pearsoned.co.uk

Contents

Contents

Boxes

Acknowledgements

The Publishers are grateful to the following for permission to reproduce copyright material:

Merck & Co., Inc. for Fig. 4.1 (Budavari *et al.*, 1996); Cambridge University Press for Fig. 11.2 (Tomkeieff, 1953); The University of Chicago Press for Tables 28.1 and 28.2 (Tables 17.6 and 17.9 in Leverlich and Levin, 1979); Microsoft Corporation for Fig. 42.1.

Preface

Knowledge and theory in Environmental Science have originated from practical observation and experimentation in a diverse range of component disciplines. Field and laboratory studies are fundamental components of undergraduate training in most aspects of Environmental Science. The skills required range from observation and recording accurately in the field to operating high-tech field or laboratory equipment. Students are expected to design practical investigations, keep records of their work, analyse data and present and communicate their work in writing and orally. While some of the skills are specific, many are transferable and will be valuable in subsequent careers.

The breadth of available courses in Environmental Science is very large and individual courses can have quite different emphases. However, practical aspects, in common with those of most sciences, are under increasing pressure both from within, as the knowledge base expands, and from without, as it competes with other subjects for time and resources. Moreover, students come into Environmental Science with increasingly diverse academic backgrounds as access to tertiary education is widened. They are often expected to acquire complex skills from limited practice at an early stage of their courses and, as a consequence, many under-perform in practical work.

The need for this volume grew out of the success of the two earlier volumes in this series, *Practical Skills in Biology* and *Practical Skills in Biomolecular Science*. Environmental Science integrates many sub-disciplines ranging from biology through aspects of chemistry and physics to the Earth sciences and geography. Clearly, no single book could adequately cover all of the practical skills and methods required for all of these disciplines, and so the authors have selected material for inclusion based upon their own teaching experiences. Since most students take a range of courses in their early years, we have tried to provide a generic approach to skills and have restricted topics to those that first- and second-year undergraduates are likely to require as part of their groundwork. We have not, therefore, attempted to go into detail about topics such as chemical analysis but have instead provided basic methodologies and attempted to guide students into the process of making strategic decisions based upon an understanding of the aims and objectives of their work and of the factors that may influence their choices. We are confident, however, that the book will remain valuable as a student progresses to Honours degree level and beyond.

The book's main emphasis is on fieldwork and taking field measurements and samples, but it also includes sections relating to basic laboratory procedures and to transferable skills such as computing and study skills. It is designed to provide support to students (and lecturers) before, during and after practical classes. With such a wide range of potential skills to cover, we could not hope to provide a detailed, recipe-like solution to every problem. We believe that learning general strategies and skills can result in a deeper understanding of the underlying rationale of methods. This approach recognizes the integrated and complex nature of environmental systems where generic methodologies for entire studies are not definable.

Advice on core skills and techniques is presented in a concise and user-friendly manner, and we have indicated in the text where more specialized texts should be consulted for particular methodologies. The text is supported by illustrations, tips and hints, worked examples, 'how to' boxes and checklists. Theory is given where required but the emphasis throughout is on practical applications and fieldwork. The authors plan to provide extra references and case study material on site which can be accessed via a link on the publisher's Web site at http://www.booksites.net..

To students who buy this book, we hope that you will find it useful in your fieldwork, practical classes and project work – this is not a book to be left on the bookshelf. Lecturers and teachers should find the text provides an effective means of supplementing the information provided for practical work.

Finally, we would like to acknowledge the support of our families and the help provided by colleagues who read and commented upon early drafts of revised material and new chapters. Special thanks are due to David Hopkins and Steve Hubbard who commented on an early outline of the book; Rachel Morris for assistance during the preparation of the text and figures; and Hester Parr who helped with the chapter on questionnaires. We would also like to thank the anonymous reviewers for their kind and helpful comments on the draft of this book.

ALLAN JONES (a.m.jones@dundee.ac.uk)
ROB DUCK (r.w.duck@dundee.ac.uk)
JONATHAN WEYERS (j.d.b.weyers@dundee.ac.uk)
ROB REED (rob.reed@unn.ac.uk)

Fundamental principles

(1) Basic principles

All knowledge and theory in science has originated from practical observation and experimentation: this is equally true for disciplines as diverse as geology and molecular genetics. Practical work is an important part of most courses and often accounts for a significant proportion of the assessment marks. This book aims to provide an easy-to-use reference source dealing with the basic practical techniques and skills of relevance to environmental science. The abilities developed in practical classes will continue to be useful throughout your course and beyond, some within science and others in any career you choose.

Being prepared

KEY POINT **You will get the most out of practicals if you prepare well in advance. Do not go into a practical session assuming that everything will be provided, without any input on your part.**

The main points to remember are:

- Read any handouts in advance: make sure you understand the purpose of the practical and the particular skills involved. Does the practical relate to, or expand upon, a current topic in your lectures? Is there any additional preparatory reading that will help?
- Take along appropriate textbooks, to explain aspects in the practical.
- Consider what safety hazards might be involved, and any precautions you might need to take, before you begin (p. 5).
- Listen carefully to any introductory guidance and note any important points: adjust your schedule/handout as necessary.
- During the practical session, organize your bench space – make sure your lab book is adjacent to, but not within, your working area. You will often find it easiest to keep clean items of glassware, etc. on one side of your working space, with used equipment on the other side.
- Write up your work as soon as possible, and submit it on time, or you may lose marks.
- Catch up on any work you have missed as soon as possible – preferably, before the next practical session.

Basic requirements

Recording practical results

An A4 loose-leaf ring binder offers flexibility, since you can insert laboratory handouts and lined and graph paper at appropriate points. The danger of losing one or more pages from a loose-leaf system is the main drawback. Bound books avoid this problem, although those containing alternating lined/graph or lined/blank pages tend to be wasteful – it is often better to paste sheets of graph paper into a bound book, as required.

A good quality HB pencil or propelling pencil is recommended for recording your raw data, making diagrams, etc. as mistakes are easily corrected. Buy a black, spirit-based (permanent) marker for labelling glassware, plastic containers, etc. Fibre-tipped fine line drawing/lettering pens are useful for preparing final versions of graphs and diagrams for assessment purposes. Use a clear ruler (with an undamaged edge) for graph drawing, so that you can see data points/information below the ruler as you draw. Fieldwork requirements are discussed in Chapter 5.

Calculators

These range from basic machines with no pre-programmed functions and only one memory, to sophisticated programmable minicomputers with many memories. The following may be helpful when using a calculator:

- Power sources. Choose a battery-powered machine, rather than a mains-operated or solar-powered type. You will need one with basic mathematical/scientific operations, including powers, logarithms (p. 206), roots and parentheses (brackets), together with statistical functions such as sample means and standard deviations (Chapter 39).
- Mode of operation. The older operating system used by e.g. Hewlett Packard calculators is known as the reverse Polish notation: to calculate the sum of two numbers, the sequence is 2 [enter] 4 + and the answer 6 is displayed. The more usual method of calculating this equation is as $2 + 4 =$, which is the system used by the majority of modern calculators. Most newcomers find the latter approach to be more straightforward. Spend some time finding out how a calculator operates, e.g. does it have true algebraic logic ($\sqrt{}$ then number, rather than number then $\sqrt{}$)? How does it deal with scientific notation (p. 206)?
- Display. Some calculators will display an entire mathematical operation (e.g. '$2 + 4 = 6$'), while others simply display the last number/operation. The former type may offer advantages in tracing errors.
- Complexity. In the early stages, it is usually better to avoid the more complex machines, full of impressive-looking, but often unused pre-programmed functions – go for more memory, parentheses, or statistical functions rather than engineering or mathematical constants. Programmable calculators may be worth considering for more advanced studies. However, it is important to note that such calculators are often unacceptable for exams.

Presenting more advanced practical work

In some practical reports and in project work, you may need to use more sophisticated presentation equipment. Computer-based graphics packages can be useful – choose easily-read fonts such as Arial or Helvetica for project work and posters and consider the layout and content carefully (p. 263). Alternatively, you could use fine line drawing pens and dry-transfer lettering/symbols, such as those made by Letraset®, although this approach can be more time-consuming than computer-based systems.

To prepare overhead transparencies for oral presentations, you can use spirit-based markers and acetate sheets. An alternative approach is to print directly from a computer-based package, using a laser printer and special acetates, or directly onto 35 mm slides. You can also photocopy onto special acetates. Advice on content and presentation is given in Chapter 51.

Presenting graphs and diagrams – ensure these are large enough to be easily read: a common error is to present graphs or diagrams that are too small, with poorly chosen scales.

Printing on acetates – standard overhead transparencies are not suitable for use in laser printers or photocopiers: you need to make sure that you use the correct type.

2 Health and safety

In the UK, the **Health & Safety at Work, etc. Act 1974** provides the main legal framework for health and safety. The **Control of Substances Hazardous to Health (COSHH) Regulations 1994 and 1996** impose specific legal requirements for risk assessment wherever hazardous chemicals or biological agents are used, with Approved Codes of Practice for the control of hazardous substances, carcinogens and biological agents, including pathogenic microbes.

Definitions

Hazard – the ability of a substance or environmental agent or condition to cause harm.

Risk – the likelihood that a substance or environmental agent or condition might be harmful under specific circumstances.

Distinguishing between hazard and risk – one of the *hazards* associated with water is drowning. However, the *risk* of drowning in a few drops of water is minimal!

Fig. 2.1 Warning labels for specific chemical hazards.

Health and safety law requires institutions to provide a working environment that is safe and without risk to health. Where appropriate, training and information on safe working practices must be provided. Students and staff must take reasonable care to ensure the health and safety of themselves and of others, and must not misuse any safety equipment.

KEY POINT All field and laboratory work must be carried out with safety in mind, to minimize the risk of harm to yourself and to others – safety is everyone's responsibility.

Risk assessment

The most widespread approach to safe working practice involves the use of risk assessment, which aims to establish:

1. The intrinsic chemical, biological and physical hazards, together with any maximum exposure limits (MELs) or occupational exposure standards (OESs), where appropriate. Chemical manufacturers provide data sheets listing the hazards associated with particular chemical compounds, while pathogenic (disease-causing) microbes are categorized according to their ability to cause illness.
2. The risks involved, by taking into account the amount of substance to be used, the way in which it will be used and the possible routes of entry into the body. In this regard, it is important to distinguish between the intrinsic hazards of a particular substance and the risks involved in its use in a particular exercise.
3. The persons at risk, and the ways in which they might be exposed to hazardous substances, including accidental exposure (spillage).
4. The steps required to prevent or control exposure. Ideally, a non-hazardous or less hazardous alternative should be used. If this is not feasible, adequate control measures must be used, e.g. a fume cupboard or other containment system. Personal protective equipment (e.g. lab coats, safety glasses) must be used in addition to such containment measures. A safe means of disposal will be required.

The outcome of the risk assessment process must be recorded and appropriate safety information must be passed on to those at risk. For most practical classes, risk assessments will have been carried out in advance by the person in charge: the information necessary to minimize the risks to students may be given in the practical schedule. Make sure you know how your Department provides such information and that you have read the appropriate material before you begin your practical work. You should also pay close attention to the person in charge at the beginning of the practical session, as they may emphasize the major hazards and risks. In project work, you will need to be involved in the risk assessment process along with your supervisor, before you carry out any practical work.

In addition to specific risk assessments, most institutions will have a safety handbook, giving general details of safe working practices, together with the names and telephone numbers of safety personnel, first aiders, hospitals, etc. Make sure you read this and abide by any instructions.

Table 2.1 Clothing and climate

Cold weather

Head Warm, waterproof wear in winter
Trunk Thick wool/fibre jumper over normal shirt & underwear. Waterproof, not showerproof, jacket/cagoule/macintosh which is also windproof
Legs Loose-fitting, heavy-duty trousers containing wool/cotton fibres. Tight jeans are *not* advisable
Feet Thick socks and stout boots giving ankle support. Wellington boots are not suitable for long walks

Hot weather

Head and trunk Keep covered with thin, light-coloured garments to avoid sunstroke
Exposed areas Use a high-factor sunblock lotion

Table 2.2 International distress signals

On land

1. SIX long whistle blasts, torch flashes, arm waves or shouts for help in succession. PAUSE for about 1 minute, then repeat, as necessary

On water

1. Using a whistle or torch

   The Morse code signal 'SOS' should be signalled, as follows:
        3 SHORT blasts/flashes
   then 3 LONG blasts/flashes
   then 3 SHORT blasts/flashes
   PAUSE, then repeat, as necessary

2. Raise and lower arms slowly and repeatedly

3. Wave an oar with a brightly coloured cloth tied to it, slowly from side to side

4. Fire RED flares or ORANGE smoke

Basic rules for laboratory work

- Make sure you know what to do in case of fire, including exit routes, how to raise the alarm, and where to gather on leaving the building. Remember that the most important consideration at all times is human safety: do not attempt to fight a fire unless it is safe to do so.
- All laboratories display notices telling you where to find the first aid kit and who to contact in case of accident/emergency. Report all accidents, even those appearing insignificant – your Department will have a formal recording procedure to comply with safety legislation.
- Wear appropriate protective clothing at all times – a clean lab coat (buttoned up), plus safety glasses if there is any risk to the eyes.
- Never smoke, eat or drink in any laboratory, because of the risks of contamination by inhalation or ingestion.
- Never work under the influence of alcohol or drugs other than prescribed medicines.
- Never mouth pipette any liquid. Use a pipette filler (see p. 7).
- Take care when handling glassware – see p. 11 for details.
- Know the warning symbols for specific chemical hazards (see Fig. 2.1).
- Use a fume cupboard for hazardous chemicals. Make sure that it is working and then open the front only as far as is necessary: many fume cupboards are marked with a maximum opening.
- Always use the minimum quantity of any hazardous materials.
- Work in a logical, tidy manner and minimize risks by thinking ahead.
- Always clear up at the end of each session. This is an important aspect of safety, encouraging a responsible attitude towards laboratory work.

Basic rules for fieldwork

- Make sure you understand the objectives of the fieldwork, the potential hazards and appropriate responses to such hazards, before you set out.
- Your work must be designed carefully, to allow for the experience of the participants and the locations visited. Don't overestimate what can be achieved – fieldwork is often more demanding than laboratory work.
- Any physical disabilities must be brought to the attention of the organizer, so that appropriate precautions can be taken.
- Never work under the influence of alcohol or drugs other than prescribed medicines.
- A comprehensive first aid kit must be carried: at least two participants should have training in first aid. Be alert for hypothermia or heat exhaustion.
- Never work alone without the permission of your organizer or leader.
- Make sure you can read a map and use a compass: your group should have both.
- Your clothing (Table 2.1) and equipment must be suitable for all of the weather conditions likely to be encountered during the work.
- Check the weather forecast before departure: look out for changes in the weather at all times and do not hesitate to turn back if necessary.
- Leave full details of your intended working locations, routes and times. Never change these arrangements without informing someone.
- Make sure that you know the international distress signals (Table 2.2).
- Always wear a life-jacket when working in or on water.
- Check tide times when working on the coast and try to work on a falling tide.

Working with liquids

Measuring and dispensing liquids

The equipment you should choose to measure out liquids depends on the volumes being dispensed, the accuracy required and the number of times the job must be done (Table 3.1).

Table 3.1 Criteria for choosing a method for measuring out a liquid

Method	Best volume range	Accuracy	Usefulness for repetitive measurement
Pasteur pipette	30 μl to 2 ml	Low	Very good
Measuring cylinder	5–2000 ml	Medium	Good
Volumetric flask	5–2000 ml	High	Good
Burette	1–100 ml	High	Very good
Pipette/pipettor	5 μl to 25 μl	High*	Very good
Microsyringe	0.5–50 μl	High	Good
Weighing	Any (depends on accuracy of balance)	Very high	Poor
Conical flask/beaker	25–5000 ml	Very low	Good

*If correctly calibrated and used properly (see p. 9).

Certain liquids may cause problems:

- High-viscosity liquids are difficult to dispense: allow time for all the liquid to transfer.
- Organic solvents may evaporate rapidly, making measurements inaccurate: work quickly; seal containers quickly.
- Solutions prone to frothing (e.g. detergent solutions) are difficult to measure and dispense: avoid forming bubbles; do not transfer quickly.
- Suspensions (e.g. river suspended sediment samples) may sediment: thoroughly mix them before dispensing.

Pasteur pipettes

Hold correctly during use (Fig. 3.1) – keep the pipette vertical, with the middle fingers gripping the barrel while the thumb and index finger provide controlled pressure on the bulb. Squeeze gently to dispense individual drops.

Pasteur pipettes should be used with care for hazardous solutions: remove the tip from the solution before fully releasing pressure on the bulb – the air taken up helps prevent spillage. To avoid the risk of cross-contamination, take care not to draw up solution into the bulb or to lie the pipette on its side. Plastic disposable 'Pastettes®' are safer and avoid contamination.

Measuring cylinders and volumetric flasks

These must be used on a level surface so that the scale is horizontal; you should first fill with solution until just below the desired mark; then fill slowly (e.g. using a Pasteur pipette) until the meniscus is level with the mark. Allow time for the solution to run down the walls of the vessel.

Reading any volumetric scale – make sure your eye is level with the bottom of the liquid's meniscus and take the reading from this point.

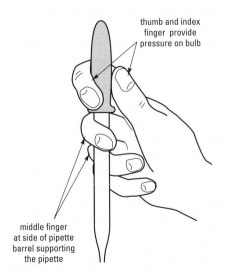

thumb and index finger provide pressure on bulb

middle finger at side of pipette barrel supporting the pipette

Fig. 3.1 How to hold a Pasteur pipette.

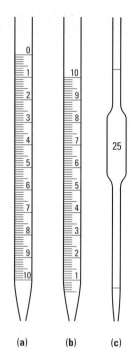

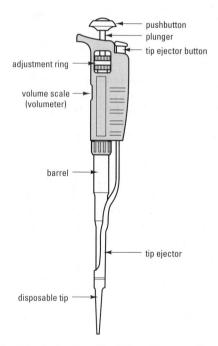

Fig. 3.2 Glass pipettes – graduated pipette, reading from zero to shoulder (a); graduated pipette, reading from maximum to tip, by gravity (b); bulb (volumetric) pipette, showing volume (calibration mark to tip, by gravity) on bulb (c).

Fig. 3.3 A pipettor – the Gilson Pipetman®.

Burettes

Burettes should be mounted vertically on a clamp stand – don't overtighten the clamp. First ensure the tap is closed and fill the body with solution using a funnel. Open the tap and allow some liquid to fill the tubing below the tap before first use. Take a meniscus reading, noting the value in your notebook. Dispense the solution *via* the tap and measure the new meniscus reading. The volume dispensed is the difference between the two readings. Titrations are usually performed using a magnetic stirrer to ensure thorough mixing.

Pipettes

These come in various designs, including graduated and bulb (volumetric) pipettes (Fig. 3.2). Take care to look at the volume scale before use: some pipettes empty from full volume to zero, others from zero to full volume; some scales refer to the shoulder of the tip, others to the tip by gravity or to the tip after blowing out.

KEY POINT **For safety reasons, it is no longer permissible to mouth pipette – various aids are available such as the Pi-pump®.**

Pipettors (Autopipettors)

These come in two basic types:

- Air displacement pipettors. For routine work with dilute aqueous solutions. One of the most widely used examples is the Gilson Pipetman® (Fig. 3.3). Box 3.1 gives details on its use.
- Positive displacement pipettors. For non-standard applications, including dispensing viscous, dense or volatile liquids, where an air displacement pipettor might create aerosols, leading to errors.

Air displacement and positive displacement pipettors may be:

- Fixed volume: capable of delivering a single factory-set volume.
- Adjustable: where the volume is determined by the operator across a particular range of values.
- Pre-set: movable between a limited number of values.
- Multi-channel: able to deliver several replicate volumes at the same time.

Whichever type you use, you must ensure that you understand the operating principles of the volume scale and the method for changing the volume delivered – some pipettors are easily misread.

A pipettor must be fitted with the correct disposable tip before use: each manufacturer produces different tips to fit particular models. Specialized tips are available for particular applications.

Syringes

Syringes should be used by placing the tip of the needle in the solution and drawing the plunger up slowly to the required point on the scale. Check the barrel to make sure no air bubbles have been drawn up. Expel slowly and touch the syringe on the edge of the vessel to remove any liquid adhering to the end of the needle. Microsyringes should always be cleaned before and after use by repeatedly drawing up and expelling pure solvent. The dead space in the syringe needle can occupy up to 4% of the nominal syringe volume. A way of avoiding such problems is to fill the dead space with an inert substance (e.g. silicone oil) after sampling. An alternative is to use a syringe where the plunger occupies the needle space (available for small volumes only).

Box 3.1   Using a pipettor to deliver accurate, reproducible volumes of liquid

A pipettor can be used to dispense volumes with accuracy and precision, by following this step-wise procedure:

1. **Select a pipettor that operates over the appropriate range.** Most adjustable pipettors are accurate only over a particular working range and should not be used to deliver volumes below the manufacturer's specifications. Do not attempt to set the volume above the maximum limit, or the pipettor may be damaged.

2. **Set the volume to be delivered.** In some pipettors, like the Finnpipette®, you 'dial up' the required volume, using a twisting motion to set the scale (take great care not to overtighten). Other types, like the Gilson Pipetman®, have a more complex system where the scale (or 'volumeter') consists of three numbers, read from top to bottom of the barrel, and adjusted using the black knurled adjustment ring (Fig. 3.3). This number gives the first three digits of the volume scale and thus can only be understood by establishing the maximum volume of the Pipetman®, as shown on the push-button on the end of the plunger (Fig. 3.3). The following examples illustrate the principle for two common sizes of Pipetman®:

P1000 Pipetman®
(maximum volume 1000 μl)
if you dial up

the volume is set at 1000 μl

P20 Pipetman®
(maximum volume 20 μl)
if you dial up

the volume is set at 10.0 μl

3. **Fit a new disposable tip to the end of the barrel.** Make sure that it is the appropriate type for your pipettor and that it is correctly fitted. Press the tip on firmly using a slight twisting motion – if not, you will take up less than the set volume and liquid will drip from the tip during use. Tips are often supplied in boxes, for ease of use: if sterility is important, make sure you use an appropriate sterile technique at all times. *Never, ever, try to use a pipettor without its disposable tip.*

4. **Check your delivery.** Confirm that the pipettor delivers the correct volume by dispensing volumes of distilled water and weighing on a balance,

assuming 1 mg = 1 μl = 1 mm^3. The value should be within 1% of the selected volume. For small volumes, measure several 'squirts' together, e.g. 20 'squirts' of 5 μl = 100 mg. If the pipettor is inaccurate (p. 41) giving a biased result (e.g. delivering significantly more or less than the volume set), you can make a temporary correction by adjusting the volumeter scale down or up accordingly (the volume *delivered* is more important than the value *displayed* on the volumeter), or have the pipettor recalibrated. If the pipettor is imprecise (p. 41), delivering a variable amount of liquid each time, it may need to be serviced. After calibration, fit a clean (sterile) tip if necessary.

5. **Draw up the appropriate volume.** Holding the pipettor vertically, press down on the plunger/push-button until a resistance (spring-loaded stop) is met. Then place the end of the tip in the liquid. Keeping your thumb on the plunger/push-button, release the pressure slowly and evenly: watch the liquid being drawn up into the tip, to confirm that no air bubbles are present. Wait a second or so, to confirm that the liquid has been taken up, then withdraw the end of the tip from the liquid. Inexperienced users often have problems caused by drawing up the liquid too quickly/carelessly. If you accidentally draw liquid into the barrel, seek assistance from your demonstrator or supervisor as the barrel will need to be cleaned before further use.

6. **Make a quick visual check on the liquid in the tip.** Does the volume seem reasonable? (e.g. a 100 μl volume should occupy approximately half the volume of a P200 tip). The liquid will remain in the tip, without dripping, as long as the tip is fitted correctly and the pipettor is not tilted too far from a vertical position.

7. **Deliver the liquid.** Place the end of the tip against the wall of the vessel at a slight angle (10–20° from vertical) and press the plunger/push-button slowly and smoothly to the first (spring-loaded) stop. Wait a second or two, to allow any residual liquid to run down the inside of the tip, then press again to the final stop, dispensing any remaining liquid. Remove from the vessel with the plunger/push-button still depressed.

8. **Eject the tip.** Press the tip ejector button if present (Fig. 3.3). If the tip is contaminated, eject directly into an appropriate container, e.g. a beaker of disinfectant, for microbiological work, or a labelled container for hazardous solutions (p. 5). For repeat delivery, fit a new tip if necessary and begin again at step 5 above. Always make sure that the tip is ejected before putting a pipettor on the bench.

Balances

These can be used to weigh accurately (p. 17) how much liquid you have dispensed. Convert mass to volume using the equation:

$$mass/density = volume \qquad [3.1]$$

e.g. 9 g of a liquid with a density of $1.2 \, g \, ml^{-1} = 7.5 \, ml$. Densities of common solvents can be found in Lide and Frederikse (1996). You will also need to know the liquid's temperature, as density is temperature dependent.

Holding and storing liquids

Test tubes

These are used for colour tests, small-scale reactions, holding samples, etc. The tube can be sterilized by heating and maintained in this state with a cap or cotton wool plug.

Beakers

Beakers are used for general purposes, e.g. heating a solvent while the solute dissolves, carrying out a titration, etc. They may have volume gradations on the side: these are often inaccurate and should only be used where approximations will suffice.

Conical (Erlenmeyer) flasks

These are used for storage of solutions: their wide base makes them stable, while their small mouth reduces evaporation and makes them easier to seal. Volume gradations, where present, are usually inaccurate.

Bottles and vials

These are used when the solution needs to be sealed for safety, sterility or to prevent evaporation or oxidation. They usually have a screw top or ground glass stopper to prevent evaporation and contamination. Many types are available, including 'bijou', 'McCartney', 'universal', and 'Winkler'.

You should clearly label all stored solutions (see p. 17), including relevant hazard information, preferably marking with orange hazard warning tape. Seal vessels in an appropriate way, e.g. using a stopper or a sealing film such as Parafilm® or Nescofilm® to prevent evaporation. To avoid degradation store your solution in a fridge, but allow it to reach room temperature before use. Unless a solution containing organic constituents has been sterilized or is toxic, microbes will start growing, so older solutions may not give reliable results.

Creating specialized apparatus

Glassware systems incorporating ground glass connections such as Quickfit® are useful for setting up combinations of standard glass components, e.g. for chemical reactions. In project work, you may need to adapt standard forms of glassware for a special need. A glassblowing service (often available in chemistry departments) can make special items to order.

Choosing between glass and plastic

Bear in mind the following points:

- Reactivity. Plastic vessels often distort at relatively low temperatures; they may be inflammable, may dissolve in certain organic solvents and may be affected by prolonged exposure to ultraviolet (UV) light. Some

Storing light-sensitive chemicals – use a coloured vessel or wrap aluminium foil around a clear vessel.

Table 3.2 Spectral cutoff values for glass and plastics (λ_{50} = wavelength at which transmission of EMR is reduced to 50%)

Material	λ_{50} (nm)
Routine glassware	340
Pyrex® glass	292
Polycarbonate	396
Acrylic	342
Polyester	318
Quartz	220

Special cleaning of glass – for an acid wash use dilute acid, e.g. 100 mmol l^{-1} (100 mol m^{-3}) HCl. Rinse thoroughly at least three times with distilled or deionized water. Glassware that must be exceptionally clean (e.g. for a micronutrient study) should be washed in a chromic acid bath, but this involves toxic and corrosive chemicals and should only be used under supervision.

plasticizers may leach from vessels and have been shown to have biological activity. Glass may adsorb ions and other molecules and then leach them into solutions, especially in alkaline conditions. Pyrex® glass is stronger than ordinary soda glass and can withstand temperatures up to 500 °C.

- Rigidity and resilience. Plastic vessels are not recommended where volume is critical as they may distort through time. Glass vessels are more easily broken than plastic, which is particularly important for centrifugation.
- Opacity. Both glass and plastic absorb light in the UV range of the EMR spectrum (Table 3.2) Quartz should be used where this is important, e.g. in cuvettes for UV spectrophotometry.
- Disposability. Plastic items may be cheap enough to make them disposable, an advantage where there is a risk of chemical or microbial contamination.

Cleaning glass and plastic

Beware the possibility of contamination arising from prior use of chemicals or inadequate rinsing following washing. A thorough rinse with distilled or deionized water immediately before use will remove dust and other deposits and is good practice in quantitative work, but ensure that the rinsing solution is not left in the vessel. 'Strong' basic detergents (e.g. Pyroneg®) are good for solubilizing acidic deposits. If there is a risk of basic deposits remaining, use an acid wash. If there is a risk of contamination from organic deposits, a rinse with Analar® grade ethanol is recommended. Glassware can be sterilized by washing with a sodium hypochlorite bleach such as Chloros® or with sodium metabisulphite – dilute as recommended before use and rinse thoroughly with sterile water after use. Alternatively, heat glassware to at least 121 °C for 15 min in an autoclave or 160 °C for 3 h in an oven.

Safety with glass

Many minor accidents in the laboratory are due to lack of care with glassware. You should follow these general precautions:

- Wear safety glasses when there is *any* risk of glass breakage, e.g. when using low pressures or heating solutions.
- If heating glassware, use a 'soft' Bunsen flame – this avoids creating a hot spot where cracks may start. Always use tongs or special heat-resistant gloves when handling hot glassware.
- Don't use chipped or cracked glassware – it may break under very slight strains and should be disposed of in the broken glassware bin.
- Never carry large bottles by their necks – support them with a hand underneath or, better still, carry them in a basket.
- Take care when attaching tubing to glass tubes and when putting glass tubes into bungs – wear a pair of thick gloves.
- Don't force bungs too firmly into bottles – they can be very difficult to remove. If you need a tight seal, use a screw top bottle with a rubber or plastic seal.
- Dispose of broken glass thoroughly and with great care – use disposable paper towels and wear thick gloves. Always put pieces of broken glass into the correct bin.

Using chemicals

Safety aspects

In practical classes, the person in charge has a responsibility to inform you of any hazards associated with the use of chemicals. In project work, your first duty when using an unfamiliar chemical is to find out about its properties, especially those relating to safety. For routine practical procedures, a risk assessment will have been carried out by a member of staff and relevant safety information will be included in the practical schedule: an example is shown in Table 4.1. Before you use any chemical you must find out whether safety precautions need to be taken and complete the appropriate forms confirming that you appreciate the risks involved. Your Department must provide the relevant information to allow you to do this. If your supervisor has filled out the form, read it carefully before signing.

Key safety points when handling chemicals are:

- Treat all chemicals as potentially dangerous.
- Wear a laboratory coat, with buttons fastened, at all times.
- Make sure you know where safety devices such as eye bath, fire extinguisher, first aid kit, are kept before you begin work in the lab.
- Wear gloves and safety glasses for toxic, irritant or corrosive chemicals and carry out procedures with them in a fume cupboard.
- Use aids such as pipette fillers to minimize risk of contact.
- Extinguish all naked flames when working with flammable substances.
- Never smoke, eat or drink where chemicals are handled.
- Label solutions appropriately (see pp. 5, 17).
- Report all spillages and clean them up properly.
- Dispose of chemicals in the correct manner.

The Merck Index (Budavari et al., 1996) and the CRC Handbook of Chemistry and Physics (Lide and Frederikse, 1996) are useful sources of information on the physical and biological properties of chemicals, including melting and boiling points, solubility, toxicity, etc. (see Fig. 4.1).

8544. Sodium Chloride. Salt; common salt. ClNa; mol wt 58.45. Cl 60.66%, Na 39.34%. NaCl. The article of commerce is also known as *table salt, rock salt* or *sea salt.* Occurs in nature as the mineral halite. Produced by mining (rock salt), by evaporation of brine from underground salt deposits and from sea water by solar evaporation: Faith, Keys & Clark's *Industrial Chemicals.* F. A. Lowenheim, M.K. Moran, Eds. (Wiley-Interscience, New York, 4th ed., 1975) pp 722-730. Comprehensive monograph: D. W. Kaufmann, *Sodium Chloride,* ACS Monograph Series no. 145 (Reinhold, New York, 1960) 743 pp.
Cubic, white crystals, granules, or powder; colorless and transparent or translucent when in large crystals. d 2.17. The salt of commerce usually contains some calcium and magnesium chlorides which absorb moisture and make it cake. mp 804° and begins to volatilize at a little above this temp. One gram dissolves in 2.8 ml water at 25°, in 2.6 ml boiling water, in 10 ml glycerol; very slightly sol in alcohol. Its soly in water is decreased by HCl and it is almost insol in concd HCl. Its aq soln is neutral. pH: 6.7-7.3. d of satd aq soln at 25° is 1.202. A 23% aq soln of sodium chloride freezes at − 20.5°C (5°F). LD$_{50}$ orally in rats: 3.75 g/kg, Boyd. Shanas, Arch. Int. Pharmacodyn. Ther. **144,** 86 (1963).
Note: Blusalt, a brand of sodium chloride contg trace amounts of cobalt, iodine, iron, copper, manganese, zinc is used in farm animals.
Human Toxicity: Not generally considered poisonous. Accidental substitution of NaCl for lactose in baby formulas has caused fatal poisoning.
USE: Natural salt is the source of chlorine and of sodium as well as of all, or practically all, their compds, e.g., hydrochloric acid, chlorates, sodium carbonate, hydroxide, etc.; for preserving foods; manuf soap, dyes - to salt them out; in freezing mixtures; for dyeing and printing fabrics, glazing pottery, curing hides; metallurgy of tin and other metals.
THERAP CAT: Electrolyte replenisher, emetic; topical anti-inflammatory.
THERAP CAT (VET): Essential nutrient factor. May be given orally as emetic, stomachic, laxative or to stimulate thirst (prevention of calculi). Intravenously as isotonic solution to raise blood volume, to combat dehydration. Locally as wound irrigant, rectal douche.

Fig. 4.1 Example of typical *Merck Index* entry showing type of information given for each chemical.

Table 4.1 Representative risk assessment information for some typical laboratory substances

Substance	Hazards	Comments
Sodium dodecyl sulphate (SDS)	Irritant Toxic	Wear gloves
Sodium hydroxide (NaOH)	Highly corrosive Severe irritant	Wear gloves
Isopropanol	Highly flammable Irritant/corrosive Potential carcinogen	No naked flames Wear gloves
Phenol	Highly toxic Causes skin burns Potential carcinogen	Use in fume hood Wear gloves
Chloroform	Volatile and toxic Irritant/corrosive Potential carcinogen	Use in fume hood Wear gloves

Selection

Chemicals are supplied in various degrees of purity and this is always stated on the manufacturer's containers. Suppliers differ in the names given to the grades and there is no conformity in purity standards. Very pure chemicals cost more, sometimes a lot more, and should only be used if the situation demands. If you need to order a chemical, your Department will have a defined procedure for doing this.

Preparing solutions

Solutions are usually prepared with respect to their molar concentrations (e.g. mmol l^{-1}, or mol m^{-3}), or mass concentrations (e.g. g l^{-1}, or kg m^{-3}): both can be regarded as an amount per unit volume, in accordance with the relationship:

$$\text{Concentration} = \frac{\text{amount}}{\text{volume}} \qquad [4.1]$$

The most important aspect of eqn 4.1 is to recognize clearly the units involved, and to prepare the solution accordingly: for molar concentrations, you will need the relative molecular mass of the compound, so that you can determine the mass of substance required. Further advice on concentrations and interconversion of units is given on p. 24.

Box 4.1 shows the steps involved in making up a solution. The concentration you require is likely to be defined by a protocol you are following and the grade of chemical and supplier may also be specified. Success may depend on using the same source and quality. To avoid waste, think carefully about the volume of solution you require, though it is always a good idea to err on the high side because you may spill some or make a mistake when dispensing it. Try to choose one of the standard volumes for vessels, as this will make measuring-out easier.

Use distilled or deionized water to make up aqueous solutions and stir to make sure all the chemical is dissolved. Magnetic stirrers are the most convenient means of doing this: carefully drop a clean magnetic stirrer bar ('flea') in the beaker, avoiding splashing; place the beaker centrally on the stirrer plate, switch on the stirrer and gradually increase the speed of stirring. When the crystals or powder have completely dissolved, switch off and retrieve the flea with a magnet or another flea. Take care not to contaminate your solution when you do this and rinse the flea with distilled water.

'Obstinate' solutions may require heating but do this only if you know that the chemical will not be damaged at the temperature used. Use a stirrer-heater to keep the solution mixed as you heat it. Allow the solution to cool down before you measure its volume or pH as these are affected by temperature.

Stock solutions

Stock solutions are valuable when making up a range of solutions containing different concentrations of a reagent or if the solutions have some common ingredients. They also save work if the same solution is used over a prolonged period (e.g. a nutrient solution). The stock solution is more concentrated than the final requirement and is diluted as appropriate when the final solutions are made up. The principle is best illustrated with an example (Table 4.2).

Box 4.1 How to make up an aqueous solution of known concentration from solid material

1. **Find out or decide the concentration of chemical required** and the degree of purity necessary.

2. **Decide on the volume of solution required.**

3. **Find out the relative molecular mass of the chemical (M_r).** This is the sum of the atomic (elemental) masses of the component elements and can be found on the container. If the chemical is hydrated, i.e. has water molecules associated with it, these must be included when calculating the mass required.

4. **Work out the mass of chemical that will give the concentration desired in the volume required.**
   Suppose your procedure requires you to prepare 250 ml of 0.1 mol l^{-1} NaCl.

   (a) Begin by expressing all volumes in the same units, either millilitres or litres (e.g. 250 ml as 0.25 litres).

   (b) Calculate the number of moles required from eqn 4.1: 0.1 = amount (mol) ÷ 0.25.
   By rearrangement, the required number of moles is thus $0.1 \times 0.25 = 0.025$ mol.

   (c) Convert from mol to g by multiplying by the relative molecular mass (M_r for NaCl = 58.44 g).

   (d) Therefore, you need to make up $0.025 \times 58.44 = 1.461$ g to 250 ml of solution, using distilled water.

   In some instances, it may be easier to work in SI units, though you must be careful when using exponential numbers (p. 204).
   Suppose your protocol states that you need 100 ml of 10 mmol l^{-1} KCl.

   (a) Start by converting this to 100×10^{-6} m³ of 10 mol m⁻³ KCl.

   (b) The required number of mol is thus $(100 \times 10^{-6}) \times (10)$.

   (c) Each mol of KCl weighs 72.56 g (M_r, the relative molecular mass).

   (d) Therefore you need to make up 72.56×10^{-3} g = 72.56 mg KCl to 100×10^{-6} m³ (100 ml) with distilled water.
   See Box 6.1 for additional information.

5. **Weigh out the required mass of chemical to an appropriate accuracy.** If the mass is too small to weigh to the desired degree of accuracy, consider the following options:

   (a) Make up a greater volume of solution.

   (b) Make up a stock solution which can be diluted at a later stage (p. 15).

   (c) Weigh the mass first, and calculate what volume to make the solution up to afterwards using equation 4.1.

6. **Add the chemical to a beaker or conical flask then add a little less water than the final amount required.** If some of the chemical sticks to the paper, foil or weighing boat, use some of the water to wash it off.

7. **Stir and, if necessary, heat the solution to ensure all the chemical dissolves.** You can determine when this has happened visually by observing the disappearance of the crystals or powder.

8. **If required, check and adjust the pH of the solution when cool.**

9. **Make up the solution to the desired volume.** If the concentration needs to be accurate, use a volumetric flask; if a high degree of accuracy is not required, use a measuring cylinder.

   (a) Pour the solution from the beaker into the measuring vessel using a funnel to avoid spillage.

   (b) Make up the volume so that the meniscus comes up to the appropriate measurement line (p. 7). For accurate work, rinse out the original vessel and use this liquid to make up the volume.

10. **Transfer the solution to a reagent bottle or a conical flask and label the vessel clearly.**

Making a dilution – use the relationship $C_1V_1 = C_2V_2$ to determine volume or concentration (see p. 24).

Preparing dilutions

Making a single dilution

In analytical work, you may need to dilute a stock solution to give a particular mass concentration, or molar concentration. Use the following procedure:

1. Transfer an accurate volume of stock solution to a volumetric flask, using appropriate equipment (Table 3.1).

Table 4.2 Use of stock solutions. Suppose you need a set of solutions 10 ml in volume containing differing concentrations of KCl, with and without reagent Q. You decide to make up a stock of KCl at twice the maximum required concentration (50 mmol l^{-1} = 50 mol m^{-3}) and a stock of reagent Q at twice its required concentration. The table shows how you might use these stocks to make up the media you require. Note that the total volumes of stock you require can be calculated from the table (end column).

Stock solutions	Volume of stock required to make required solutions (ml)						Total volume of stock required (ml)
	No KCl plus Q	No KCl minus Q	15 mmol l^{-1} KCl plus Q	15 mmol l^{-1} KCl minus Q	25 mmol l^{-1} KCl plus Q	25 mmol l^{-1} KCl minus Q	
50 mmol l^{-1} KCl	0	0	3	3	5	5	16
[reagent Q] × 2	5	0	5	0	5	0	15
Water	5	10	2	7	0	5	29
Total	10	10	10	10	10	10	60

2. Make up to the calibration mark with solvent – add the last few drops from a pipette or solvent bottle, until the meniscus is level with the calibration mark.

3. Mix thoroughly, either by repeated inversion (holding the stopper firmly) or by prolonged stirring, using a magnetic stirrer. Make sure you add the magnetic flea *after* the volume adjustment step.

For routine work using dilute aqueous solutions where the highest degree of accuracy is not required, it may be acceptable to substitute test tubes or conical flasks for volumetric flasks. In such cases, you would calculate the volumes of stock solution and diluent required, with the assumption that the final volume is determined by the sum of the individual volumes of stock and diluent used (e.g. Table 4.2). Thus, a two-fold dilution would be prepared using 1 volume of stock solution and 1 volume of diluent. The dilution factor is obtained from the ratio of the initial concentration of the stock solution and the final concentration of the diluted solution. The dilution factor can be used to determine the volumes of stock and diluent required in a particular instance. For example, suppose you wanted to prepare 100 ml of a solution of NaCl at 0.2 mol l^{-1}. Using a stock solution containing 4.0 mol l^{-1} NaCl, the dilution factor is $0.2 \div 4.0 = 0.05 = 1/20$ (a twenty-fold dilution). Therefore, the amount of stock solution required is 1/20th of 100 ml = 5 ml and the amount of diluent needed is 19/20th of 100 ml = 95 ml.

Using the correct volumes – it is important to distinguish between the volumes of the various liquids: a one-in-ten dilution is obtained using 1 volume of stock solution plus 9 volumes of diluent $(1 + 9 = 10)$.

Preparing a dilution series

Dilution series are used in a wide range of procedures, including the preparation of standard curves for calibration of analytical instruments (p. 169), where a range of dilutions of a particular sample is often required. A variety of different approaches can be used:

Linear dilution series
Here, the concentrations are separated by an equal amount, e.g. a series containing NaCl at 0, 0.2, 0.4, 0.6, 0.8, 1.0 μg ml^{-1}. Use $[C_1]V_1 = [C_2]V_2$ to determine the amount of stock solution required for each member of the series, with the volume of diluent being determined by subtraction.

Logarithmic dilution series
Here, the concentrations are separated by a constant proportion, often referred to as the step interval. This type of serial dilution is useful when a

Using diluents – various liquids are used, including distilled or deionized water, salt solutions, buffers, Ringer's solution, etc., according to the specific requirements of the procedure.

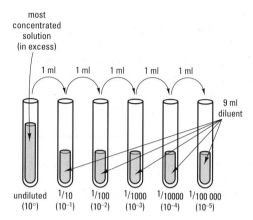

most
concentrated
solution
(in excess)

1 ml   1 ml   1 ml   1 ml   1 ml

9 ml
diluent

undiluted 1/10   1/100 1/1000 1/10000 1/100 000
(10^0) (10^{-1}) (10^{-2}) (10^{-3}) (10^{-4}) (10^{-5})

Fig. 4.2 Preparation of a dilution series. The example shown is a decimal dilution series, down to 1/100 000 (10^{-5}) of the solution in the first (left-hand) tube. Note that all solutions must be mixed thoroughly before transferring the volume to the next in the series.

> Preparing a dilution series using pipettes or pipettors – use a fresh pipette or disposable tip for each dilution, to prevent carry-over of solutions.

broad range of concentrations is required, or when an environmental process is logarithmically related to concentration.

The most common examples are:

- Doubling dilutions – where each concentration is half that of the previous one (two-fold step interval, $\log_2$ dilution series). First, make up the most concentrated solution at twice the volume required. Measure out half of this volume into a vessel containing the same volume of diluent, mix thoroughly and repeat, for as many doubling dilutions as are required. The concentrations obtained will be 1/2, 1/4, 1/8, 1/16 etc., times the original (i.e. the dilutions will be two, four, eight and sixteen-fold, etc.).
- Decimal dilutions – where each concentration is one-tenth that of the previous one (ten-fold step interval, $\log_{10}$ dilution series). First, make up the most concentrated solution required, with at least a 10% excess. Measure out one-tenth of the volume required into a vessel containing nine times as much diluent, mix thoroughly and repeat. The concentrations obtained will be 1/10, 1/100, 1/1000 etc., times the original (i.e. dilutions of 10^{-1}, 10^{-2}, 10^{-3}, etc.). To calculate the actual concentration of solute, multiply by the appropriate dilution factor.

When preparing serial doubling or decimal dilutions, it is often easiest to add the appropriate amount of diluent to several vessels beforehand, as shown in the worked example in Fig. 4.2. When preparing a dilution series, it is essential that all volumes are dispensed accurately, e.g. using calibrated pipettors (p. 8), otherwise any inaccuracies will be compounded, leading to gross errors in the most dilute solutions.

Harmonic dilution series

Here, the concentrations in the series take the values of the reciprocals of successive whole numbers, e.g. 1, 1/2, 1/3, 1/4, 1/5, etc. The individual dilutions are simply achieved by a stepwise increase in the volume of diluent in successive vessels, e.g. by adding 0, 1, 2, 3, 4 and 5 times the volume of diluent to a set of test tubes, then adding a constant unit volume of stock solution to each vessel. Although there is no dilution transfer error between individual dilutions, the main disadvantage is that the series is non-linear, with a step interval that becomes progressively smaller as the series is extended.

Solutions must be thoroughly mixed before measuring out volumes for the next dilution. Use a fresh measuring vessel for each dilution to avoid contamination, or wash your vessel thoroughly between dilutions. Clearly label the vessel containing each dilution when it is made: it is easy to get confused! When deciding on the volumes required, allow for the aliquot removed when making up the next member in the series. Remember to discard any excess from the last in the series if volumes are critical.

Mixing solutions and suspensions

Various devices may be used, including:

- Magnetic stirrers and fleas. Magnetic fleas come in a range of shapes and sizes, and some stirrers have integral heaters. During use, stirrer speed may increase as the instrument warms up.
- Vortex mixers. For vigorous mixing of small volumes of solution, e.g. when preparing a dilution series in test tubes. Take care when adjusting the mixing speed – if the setting is too low, the test tube will vibrate

rather than creating a vortex, giving inadequate mixing. If the setting is too high, the test tube may slip from your hand.

- Orbital shakers and shaking water baths. These are used to provide controlled mixing at a particular temperature.
- Bottle rollers. For culture work, ensuring gentle, continuous mixing.

Storing chemicals and solutions

Labile chemicals may be stored in a fridge or freezer. Take special care when using chemicals that have been stored at low temperature: the container and its contents must be warmed up to room temperature before use, otherwise water vapour will condense on the chemical. This may render any weighing you do meaningless and it could ruin the chemical. Other chemicals may need to be kept in a desiccator, especially if they are deliquescent.

KEY POINT Label all stored chemicals clearly with the following information: the chemical name (if a solution, state solute(s), concentration(s) and pH if measured), plus any relevant hazard warning information, the date made up, and your name.

Using balances

Electronic balances with digital readouts are now favoured over mechanical types: they are easy to read and their self-taring feature means the mass of the weighing boat or container can be subtracted automatically before weighing an object. The most common type offers accuracy down to 1 mg over the range 1 mg to 160 g, which is suitable for most biological applications.

To operate a standard self-taring balance:

1. Check that it is level, using the adjustable feet to centre the bubble in the spirit level (usually at the back of the machine). For accurate work, make sure a draught shield is on the balance.
2. Place an empty vessel on the balance pan and allow the reading to stabilize. *If the object is larger than the pan, take care that no part rests on the body of the balance or the draught shield as this will invalidate the reading.* Press the tare bar to bring the reading to zero.
3. Place the chemical or object carefully in the vessel (powdered chemicals should be dispensed with a suitably sized clean spatula).
4. Allow the reading to stabilize and make a note of the value.
5. If you add excess chemical, take great care when removing it. Switch off if you need to clean any deposit left on or around the balance.

Larger masses should be weighed on a top-loading balance to an appropriate degree of accuracy. Take care to note the limits for the balance: while most have devices to protect against overloading, you may damage the mechanism. In the field, spring or battery-operated balances may be preferred. Try to find a place out of the wind to use them. For extremely small masses, there are electrical balances that can weigh down to 1 μg, but these are very delicate and must be used under supervision.

Measuring length and area

When measuring linear dimensions, the device you need depends on the size of object you are measuring and the accuracy demanded (Table 4.3).

Weighing – never weigh anything directly onto a balance's pan: you may contaminate it for other users. Use a weighing boat or a slip of aluminium foil. Otherwise, choose a suitable vessel like a beaker, conical flask or aluminium tray.

Table 4.3 Suitability of devices for measuring linear dimensions

Measurement device	Suitable lengths	Degree of accuracy
Eyepiece graticule (light microscopy)	1 μm to 10 mm	0.5 μm
Vernier calipers	1–100 mm	0.1 mm
Ruler	10 mm to 1 m	1.0 mm
Tape measure	10 mm to 30 m	1.0 mm
Optical surveying devices	1 m to 100 m	0.1 m

See Box 4.2 for method of using Vernier calipers

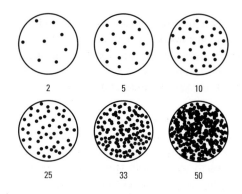

2 5 10

25 33 50

Fig. 4.3 Chart for estimating percentage of area in microscopic sections.

For many regularly shaped objects, area can be estimated from linear dimensions (see p. 219). The areas of irregular shapes can be measured with an optical measuring device or a planimeter. These have the benefits of speed and ease of use; instructions are machine specific. A simple 'low tech' method is to trace objects onto good quality paper or to photocopy them. If the outline is then cut round, the area can be estimated by weighing the cutout and comparing to the mass of a piece of the same paper of known area. Avoid getting moisture from the specimen onto the paper as this will affect the reading. Measuring area in microscopic sections (e.g. the area occupied by specific minerals in a rock slice) is made much easier by visual comparison with a percentage of area chart (Fig. 4.3).

Measuring and controlling temperature

Heating specimens

Care is required when heating specimens – there is a danger of fire whenever organic material is heated and a danger of scalding from heated liquids. Safety glasses should always be worn. Use a thermostatically controlled electric stirrer-heater if possible. If using a Bunsen burner, keep the flame well away from yourself and your clothing (tie back long hair). Use a non-flammable mat beneath a Bunsen to protect the bench. Switch off when no longer required. To light a Bunsen, close the air hole first, then apply a lit match or lighter. Open the air hole if you need a hotter, more concentrated flame: the hottest part of the flame is just above the apex of the blue cone in its centre.

Box 4.2   How to use Vernier calipers

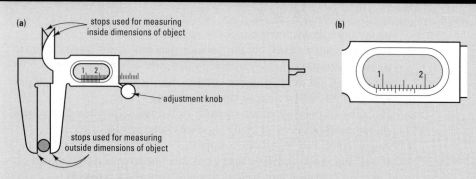

(a) stops used for measuring inside dimensions of object

adjustment knob

stops used for measuring outside dimensions of object

(b)

Fig. 4.4   (a) Vernier caliper.   (b) Vernier measurement scale.

Note that numbers on the scale refer to centimetres. Vernier scales consist of two numerical scales running side by side, the moving one being shorter with ten divisions compressed into the length for nine on the longer, static one. Use Vernier calipers to measure objects to the nearest 0.1 mm:

1. **Clamp the stops lightly over the object** as in Fig. 4.4(a), taking care not to deform it.

2. **Read off the number of whole millimetres** by taking the value on the fixed scale lying to the left of the first line on the moving (short) scale, i.e. 8 mm in Fig. 4.4(b).

3. **Read off 0.1 mm value** by finding which line in the moving scale corresponds most closely with a line on the fixed scale, i.e. 0.5 mm in Fig. 4.4(b). If the zero of the short scale corresponded to a whole number on the static scale, then record 0.0 mm as this shows fully the accuracy of the measurement.

4. **Add these numbers to give the final reading,** i.e. 8.5 mm in Fig. 4.4(b).

Ovens and drying cabinets may be used to dry specimens or glassware. They are normally thermostatically controlled. If drying organic material for dry weight measurement, do so at about 80 °C to avoid caramelizing the specimen. Always state the actual temperature used as this affects results. Check that all water has been driven off by weighing until a constant mass is reached.

Cooling specimens

Fridges and freezers are used for storing stock solutions and chemicals that would either break down or become contaminated at room temperature. Normal fridge and freezer temperatures are about 4 °C and −15 °C respectively. Ice baths can be used when reactants must be kept close to 0 °C. Most environmental science departments will have a machine which provides flaked ice for use in these baths. If common salt is mixed with ice, temperatures below 0 °C can be achieved. A mixture of ethanol and solid CO_2 will provide a temperature of −72 °C if required. To freeze a specimen quickly, immerse in liquid N_2 (−196 °C) using tongs and wearing an apron and thick gloves, as splashes will damage your skin. Always work in a well-ventilated room.

Maintaining specimens at constant temperature

Thermostatically controlled temperature rooms and incubators can be used to maintain temperature at a desired level. Always check with a thermometer or thermograph that the thermostat is accurate enough for your study. To achieve a controlled temperature on a smaller scale, e.g. for an oxygen electrode, use a water bath. These usually incorporate heating elements, a circulating mechanism and a thermostat. Baths for sub-ambient temperatures have a cooling element.

Controlling atmospheric conditions

Gas composition

The atmosphere may be 'scrubbed' of certain gases by passing through a U-tube or Dreschel bottle containing an appropriate chemical or solution.

For accurate control of gas concentrations, use cylinders of pure gas; the contents can be mixed to give specified concentrations by controlling individual flow rates. The cylinder head regulator allows you to control the pressure (and hence flow rate) of gas; adjust using the controls on the regulator or with spanners of appropriate size. Before use, ensure the regulator outlet tap is off (turn anticlockwise), then switch on at the cylinder (turn clockwise) – the cylinder dial will give you the pressure reading for the cylinder contents. Now switch on at the regulator outlet (turn clockwise) and adjust to desired pressure/flow setting. To switch off, carry out the above directions in reverse order.

Pressure

Many forms of pump are used to pressurize or provide partial vacuum, usually to force gas or liquid movement. Each has specific instructions for use. Many laboratories are supplied with 'vacuum' (suction) and pressurized air lines that are useful for procedures such as vacuum-assisted filtration. Make sure you switch off the taps after use. Take special care with glass items kept at very low or high pressures. These should be contained within a metal cage to minimize the risk of injury.

Heating/cooling glass vessels – take care if heating or cooling glass vessels rapidly as they may break when heat stressed. Freezing aqueous solutions in thin-walled glass vessels is risky because ice expansion may break the glass.

Using thermometers – some are calibrated for use in air, others require partial immersion in liquid and others total immersion – check before use. If a mercury thermometer is broken, report the spillage as mercury is a poison.

Example   Water vapour can be removed by passing gas over dehydrated $CaCO_3$ and CO_2 may be removed by bubbling through KOH solution.

5 Basic fieldwork procedures

Fieldwork should be one of the most enjoyable and rewarding aspects of Environmental Science, although it can also be difficult, especially in bad weather. It is very easy to waste a lot of time and effort carrying out field investigations if the objectives and preparations have been inadequate. You will need to think carefully in advance of any field exercise, with particular regard to three key areas: planning, preparation, and anticipation.

Planning and preparation

The key questions to ask yourself are:

- What are the aims of the fieldwork?
- How long and how many periods of fieldwork will this require?
- What are the safety implications of the work?
- Am I likely to encounter any difficult conditions/environments?
- What samples are needed and how will they be collected?
- How should samples be stored for transport to the laboratory?
- What equipment will be required?
- What transport will I need for personnel, equipment and samples?

The aims of your fieldwork must be realistic: most people overestimate what can be done in a given time period, especially if the weather is poor! Recognize your own limitations and those of others who might be involved. Plans should always be based upon a previous field site inspection and students should always discuss their aims and objectives with more experienced fieldworkers. Will your work require more than one visit? If so, what time interval is required between visits? This may affect the logistics and cost of the work.

Scheduling – most people underestimate the time needed to carry out a particular task in the field. Remember that you are more efficient in good weather conditions than in poor ones.

The number, frequency, nature and spatial or temporal distribution of samples or questionnaire responses (see also Chapter 21) must be consistent with the aims and objectives of the fieldwork and may require considerable pre-planning. Too many samples can be as much of a problem as too few, so determine the minimum required sample size with statistical evaluation in mind. Refer, according to your field activity, to Chapters 15–21. The sampling or environmental measurement/recording protocol you choose will influence your equipment requirements.

KEY POINT **Always construct a checklist of the required fieldwork equipment, paying attention to the smallest detail.**

It is frustrating (but not unknown) to arrive in the field without a notebook and pencil! If the work involves collecting physical samples, make sure your equipment list contains appropriate storage materials and identify temporary storage locations if necessary. Water samples may require refrigeration. Beware of spending a lot of time and effort collecting samples and then ruining them by inappropriate field storage!

Use laminated sheets for carrying important data to the field. This will prevent rain damage.

Having compiled your checklist, you may need to arrange for a vehicle or boat of appropriate size; do not overload! Choose a land vehicle appropriate for the terrain and only use an inflatable dinghy or shallow draft boat if working in shallow water. In deep water, make sure that the boat is capable of withstanding possible sea states.

Generic equipment checklist for fieldwork
- notebook and pencil, datasheets
- indelible marker pens
- camera
- food and drink (plus emergency rations)
- first aid equipment
- safety (protective) gear
- whistle
- watch or clock
- torch
- multi-purpose knife (e.g. Swiss Army knife)
- map/s and compass
- hand lens
- specialized measuring equipment
- sampling equipment (+ spares)
- specimen storage materials and labels
- rucksack or other carrying devices
- laminated guides and plans

Field site inspection

It is unlikely that you will be able to answer the questions listed if you or your instructor have not visited the field area. The terrain, for example, may be remote, rugged and dangerous; it may be intertidal and subject to problems of access; the area may have social hazards or be culturally sensitive. All fieldwork programmes, therefore, should be preceded by a scoping or orientation study in which an inspection of the area is undertaken. Access problems should be addressed at this stage and appropriate permissions obtained. Always make sure that landowners know explicitly who you are, what you intend to do, where you are from and when you are proposing to be on their land. Be open and honest with them and make them feel part of the project.

KEY POINT **Never enter private land without permission (this is trespass) and after your fieldwork, always thank the landowner.**

No sampling or survey work is carried out at this stage. However, the field area should be walked over, examined (with the aid of careful note taking) and photographed so that the strategy for subsequent sampling can be determined.

Safety

Safety in the field is always an important issue. Read and digest Chapter 2 on Health and safety before going into the field. Remember that although as a student you will normally be organized by someone else, this does not absolve you from a personal responsibility for your own and the group's safety. Never work alone irrespective of whether the environment is urban or rural, terrestrial or aquatic. Always wear appropriate clothing and safety equipment and let someone else know where you will be working and when you expect to return. Do not then vary from this plan without informing that person. Remember also that what may be a comfortable environment for one person may not be for another, depending on their outdoor experience and

Soft terrain – use a child's plastic sledge to transport equipment and samples across soft areas such as intertidal flats or bogs. Wear snow shoes or short skis when walking over expanses of soft mud – these are very dangerous habitats!

interests. Do not attempt to work from a boat or climb a rock face if you have no prior training for doing so. If your work requires specialist activities you must seek assistance from an appropriately qualified individual (e.g. rock climber or scuba diver).

Further tips for safe fieldwork

- Do not drink alcohol or take drugs (other than prescribed medication) in the field.
- Do not, in any way, annoy or antagonize the local population.
- Leave gates as you find them.
- Do not drop litter.
- Avoid fire risks, especially when working in wooded areas, sand dunes or heathlands.
- Do not frighten or disturb livestock or domestic animals.
- Do not attempt to carry too much. Keep rucksack loads below 14 kg. Make several trips rather than exhaust or even injure yourself by trying to carry too great a load.

Principles of solution chemistry

Preparing solutions – practical advice is given on p. 13.

A solution is a homogeneous liquid, formed by the addition of solutes to a solvent (usually water in biological systems). The behaviour of solutions is determined by the type of solutes involved and by their proportions, relative to the solvent. Many laboratory exercises involve calculation of concentrations, e.g. when preparing an experimental solution at a particular concentration, or when expressing data in terms of solute concentration. Make sure that you understand the basic principles set out in this chapter before you tackle such exercises.

Solutes can affect the properties of solutions in several ways, including:

Electrolytic dissociation

This occurs where individual molecules of an electrolyte dissociate to give charged particles (ions). For a strong electrolyte, e.g. NaCl, dissociation is essentially complete. In contrast, a weak electrolyte, e.g. acetic acid, will be only partly dissociated, depending upon the pH and temperature of the solution (p. 28).

> **Definition**
>
> **Electrolyte** – a substance that dissociates, either fully or partially, in water to give two or more ions.

Osmotic effects

These are the result of solute particles lowering the effective concentration of the solvent (water). These effects are particularly relevant to biological systems since membranes are far more permeable to water than to most solutes. Water moves across biological membranes from the solution with the higher effective water concentration to that with the lower effective water concentration (osmosis).

Ideal/non-ideal behaviour

This occurs because solutions of real substances do not necessarily conform to the theoretical relationships predicted for dilute solutions of so-called ideal solutes. It is often necessary to take account of the non-ideal behaviour of real solutions, especially at high solute concentrations (see Lide and Frederikse, 1996, for appropriate data).

Concentration

Expressing solute concentrations – you should use SI units wherever possible. However, you are likely to meet non-SI concentrations and you must be able to deal with these units too.

In SI units (p. 42), the concentration of a solute is expressed in $mol\,m^{-3}$, which is convenient for most biological purposes. The concentration of a solute is usually symbolized by square brackets, e.g. [NaCl]. Details of how to prepare a solution using SI and non-SI units are given on p. 14.

A number of alternative ways of expressing the relative amounts of solute and solvent are in general use, and you may come across these terms in your practical work, or in the literature:

Molarity

This is the term used to denote molar concentration, [C], expressed as moles of solute per litre volume of solution ($mol\,l^{-1}$). This non-SI term continues to find widespread usage, in part because of the familiarity of working scientists with the term, but also because laboratory glassware is calibrated in millilitres and litres, making the preparation of molar and millimolar solutions relatively straightforward. However, the symbols in common use for molar (M) and millimolar (mM) solutions are at odds with the SI system and many people

> **Example** A 1.0 molar solution of NaCl would contain 58.44 g NaCl (the molecular mass) per litre of solution.

Box 6.1 Useful procedures for calculations involving molar concentrations

1. **Preparing a solution of defined molarity.** For a solute of known relative molecular mass M_r, the following relationship can be applied:

$$[C] = \frac{\text{mass of solute/relative molecular mass}}{\text{volume of solution}} \quad [6.1]$$

So, if you wanted to make up 200 ml (0.2 l) of an aqueous solution of NaCl (M_r 58.44 g) at a concentration of 500 mmol l^{-1} (0.5 mol l^{-1}), you could calculate the amount of NaCl required by inserting these values into eqn [6.1]:

$$0.5 = \frac{\text{mass of solute/58.44}}{0.2}$$

which can be rearranged to

$$\text{mass of solute} = 0.5 \times 0.2 \times 58.44 = 5.844\,g$$

The same relationship can be used to calculate the concentration of a solution containing a known amount of a solute, e.g. if 21.1 g of NaCl were made up to a volume of 100 ml (0.1 l), this would give

$$[\text{NaCl}] = \frac{21.1/58.44}{0.1} = 3.61\,\text{mol l}^{-1}$$

2. **Dilutions and concentrations.** The following relationship is very useful if you are diluting (or concentrating) a solution:

$$[C_1]V_1 = [C_2]V_2 \quad [6.2]$$

where $[C_1]$ and $[C_2]$ are the initial and final concentrations, while V_1 and V_2 are their respective volumes: each pair must be expressed in the same units. Thus, if you wanted to dilute 200 ml of 0.5 mol l^{-1} NaCl to give a final molarity of 0.1 mol l^{-1}, then, by substitution into eqn [6.2]:

$$0.5 \times 200 = 0.1 \times V_2$$

Thus $V_2 = 1\,000$ ml (in other words, you would have to add water to 200 ml of 0.5 mol l^{-1} NaCl to give a final volume of 1 000 ml to obtain a 0.1 mol l^{-1} solution).

3. **Interconversion.** A simple way of interconverting amounts and volumes of any particular solution is to divide the amount and volume by a factor of 10^3: thus a molar solution of a substance contains 1 mol l^{-1}, which is equivalent to 1 mmol ml^{-1}, or 1 μmol μl^{-1}, or 1 nmol nl^{-1}, etc. You may find this technique useful when calculating the amount of substance present in a small volume of solution of known concentration, e.g. to calculate the amount of NaCl present in 50 μl of a solution with a concentration (molarity) of 0.5 mol l^{-1} NaCl:

   (a) this is equivalent to 0.5 μmol μl^{-1};

   (b) therefore 50 μl will contain $50 \times 0.5\,\mu$mol = 25 μmol.

   Alternatively, you may prefer to convert to primary SI units, for ease of calculation (see Box 9.1).

   The 'unitary method' (p. 206) is an alternative approach to these calculations.

now prefer to use mol l^{-1} and mmol l^{-1} respectively, to avoid confusion. Box 6.1 gives details of some useful approaches to calculations involving molarities.

Molality

This is used to express the concentration of solute relative to the *mass* of solvent, i.e. mol kg^{-1}. Molality is a temperature-independent means of expressing solute concentration, rarely used except when the osmotic properties of a solution are of interest (p. 26).

> **Example** A 0.5 molal solution of NaCl would contain $58.44 \times 0.5 = 29.22$ g NaCl per kg of water.

Per cent composition (% w/w)

This is the solute mass (in g) per 100 g solution. The advantage of this expression is the ease with which a solution can be prepared, since it simply requires each component to be pre-weighed (for water, a volumetric measurement may be used, e.g. using a measuring cylinder) and then mixed together. Similar terms are parts per thousand (‰), i.e. mg g^{-1}, and parts per million (ppm), i.e. μg g^{-1}.

> **Example** A 5% w/w sucrose solution contains 5 g sucrose and 95 g water ($= 95$ ml water, assuming a density of 1 g ml^{-1}) to give 100 g of solution.

Per cent concentration (% w/v and % v/v)

For solutes added in solid form, this is the number of grams of solute per 100 ml solution. This is more commonly used than per cent composition, since solutions can be accurately prepared by weighing out the required amount of solute and then making this up to a known volume using a volumetric flask. The equivalent expression for liquid solutes is % v/v.

The principal use of mass/mass or mass/volume terms (including $g l^{-1}$) is for solutes whose molecular mass is unknown (e.g. cellular proteins), or for mixtures of certain classes of substance (e.g. total salt in sea water). You should *never* use the per cent term without specifying how the solution was prepared, i.e. by using the qualifier w/w, w/v or v/v. For mass concentrations, it is simpler to use mass per unit volume, e.g. $mg l^{-1}$, $\mu g\, \mu l^{-1}$, etc.

Activity (a)

This is a term used to describe the *effective* concentration of a solute. In dilute solutions, solutes can be considered to behave according to ideal (thermodynamic) principles, i.e. they will have an effective concentration equivalent to the actual concentration. However, in concentrated solutions ($\geqslant 500\, mol\, m^{-3}$), the behaviour of solutes is often non-ideal, and their effective concentration (activity) will be less than the actual concentration [C]. The ratio between the effective concentration and the actual concentration is called the activity coefficient (γ) where

Table 6.1 Activity coefficient of NaCl solutions as a function of molality. Data from Robinson and Stokes (1970)

Molality	Activity coefficient at 25 °C
0.1	0.778
0.5	0.681
1.0	0.657
2.0	0.668
4.0	0.783
6.0	0.986

$$\gamma = \frac{a}{[C]} \qquad [6.3]$$

Equation [6.3] can be used for SI units ($mol\, m^{-3}$), molarity ($mol\, l^{-1}$) or molality ($mol\, kg^{-1}$). In all cases, γ is a dimensionless term, since a and [C] are expressed in the same units. The activity coefficient of a solute is effectively unity in dilute solution, decreasing as the solute concentration increases (Table 6.1). At high concentrations of certain ionic solutes, γ may increase to become greater than unity.

KEY POINT Activity is often the correct expression for theoretical relationships involving solute concentration (e.g. where a property of the solution is dependent on concentration). However, for most practical purposes, it is possible to use the *actual* concentration of a solute rather than the activity, since the difference between the two terms can be ignored for dilute solutions.

The particular use of the term 'water activity' is considered below, since it is based on the mole fraction of solvent, rather than the effective concentration of solute.

Equivalent mass (equivalent weight)

Equivalence and normality are outdated terms, although you may come across them in older texts. They apply to certain solutes whose reactions involve the transfer of charged ions, e.g. acids and alkalis (which may be involved in H^+ or OH^- transfer), and electrolytes (which form cations and anions that may take part in further reactions). These two terms take into account the valency of the charged solutes. Thus the equivalent mass of an ion is its molecular mass divided by its valency (ignoring the sign), expressed in grams per equivalent (eq) according to the relationship:

$$equivalent\ mass = \frac{molecular\ mass}{valency} \qquad [6.4]$$

For acids and alkalis, the equivalent mass is the mass of substance that will provide 1 mol of either H^+ or OH^- ions in a reaction, obtained by dividing the molecular mass by the number of available ions (n), using n instead of valency as the denominator in eqn [6.4].

Example A 0.5 N solution of sulphuric acid would contain $0.5 \times 49.04 = 24.52 \, g \, l^{-1}$.

Example Under ideal conditions, 1 mol of NaCl dissolved in water would give 1 mol of Na^+ ions and 1 mol of Cl^- ions, equivalent to a theoretical osmolarity of 2 osmol l^{-1}.

Example A 1.0 mol kg^{-1} solution of NaCl has an osmotic coefficient of 0.936 at 25 °C and an osmolality of $1.0 \times 2 \times 0.936 = 1.872$ osmol kg^{-1}.

Table 6.2 Osmotic coefficients of NaCl solutions as a function of molality. Data from Robinson and Stokes (1970)

Molality	Osmotic coefficient at 25 °C
0.1	0.932
0.5	0.921
1.0	0.936
2.0	0.983
4.0	1.116
6.0	1.271

Example A 1.0 mol kg^{-1} solution of NaCl at 25 °C has an osmolalilty of 1.872 osmol kg^{-1} and an osmotic pressure of $1.872 \times 2.479 = 4.641$ MPa.

Normality

A 1 normal solution (1 N) is one that contains one equivalent mass of a substance per litre of solution. The general formula is:

$$\text{normality} = \frac{\text{mass of substance per litre}}{\text{equivalent mass}} \qquad [6.5]$$

Osmolarity

This non-SI expression is used to describe the number of moles of osmotically active solute particles per litre of solution (osmol l^{-1}). The need for such a term arises because some molecules dissociate to give more than one osmotically active particle in aqueous solution.

Osmolality

This term describes the number of moles of osmotically active solute particles per unit mass of solvent (osmol kg^{-1}). For an ideal solute, the osmolality can be determined by multiplying the molality by n, the number of solute particles produced in solution (e.g. for NaCl, $n = 2$). However, for real solutes, a correction factor (the osmotic coefficient, ϕ) is used:

$$\text{osmolality} = \text{molality} \times n \times \phi \qquad [6.6]$$

If necessary, the osmotic coefficients of a particular solute can be obtained from tables (e.g. Table 6.2): non-ideal behaviour means that ϕ may have values > 1 at high concentrations. Alternatively, the osmolality of a solution can be measured using an osmometer.

Osmotic properties of solutions

Several inter-related terms can be used to describe the osmotic status of a solution. In addition to osmolality, you may come across the following:

Osmotic pressure

This is based on the concept of a membrane permeable to water, but not to solute molecules. For example, if a sucrose solution is placed on one side and pure water on the other, then a passive driving force will be created and water will diffuse across the membrane into the sucrose solution, since the effective water concentration in the sucrose solution will be lower. The tendency for water to diffuse into the sucrose solution could be counteracted by applying a hydrostatic pressure equivalent to the passive driving force. Thus, the osmotic pressure of a solution is the excess hydrostatic pressure required to prevent the net flow of water into a vessel containing the solution. The SI unit of osmotic pressure is the pascal, Pa $(= kg \, m^{-1} \, s^{-2})$. Older sources may use atmospheres, or bars, and conversion factors are given in Box 9.1 (p. 44). Osmotic pressure and osmolality can be interconverted using the expression 1 osmol kg^{-1} $= 2.479$ MPa at 25 °C.

The use of osmotic pressure has been criticized as misleading, since a solution does not exhibit an 'osmotic pressure', unless it is placed on the other side of a selectively permeable membrane from pure water!

pH

pH is a measure of the amount of hydrogen ions (H^+) in a solution: this affects the solubility of many substances and the activity of most biological systems, from individual molecules to whole organisms. It is usual to think of

Definitions

Acid – a compound that acts as a proton donor in aqueous solution.

Base – a compound that acts as a proton acceptor in aqueous solution.

Conjugate pair – an acid together with its corresponding base.

Alkali – a compound that liberates hydroxyl ions when it dissociates. Since hydroxyl ions are strongly basic, this will reduce the proton concentration.

Ampholyte – a compound that can act as both an acid and a base. Water is an ampholyte since it may dissociate to give a proton and a hydroxyl ion (amphoteric behaviour).

Example Human blood plasma has a typical H^+ concentration of approximately $0.4 \times 10^{-7}\,\text{mol}\,l^{-1}$ ($= 10^{-7.4}\,\text{mol}\,l^{-1}$), giving a pH of 7.4.

aqueous solutions as containing H^+ ions (protons), though protons actually exist in their hydrated form, as hydronium ions (H_3O^+). The proton concentration of an aqueous solution $[H^+]$ is affected by several factors:

- Ionization (dissociation) of water, which liberates protons and hydroxyl ions in equal quantities, according to the reversible relationship:

$$H_2O \rightleftharpoons H^+ + OH^- \qquad [6.7]$$

- Dissociation of acids, according to the equation:

$$H\text{–}A \rightleftharpoons H^+ + A^- \qquad [6.8]$$

where H–A represents the acid and A^- is the corresponding conjugate base. The dissociation of an acid in water will increase the amount of protons, reducing the amount of hydroxyl ions as water molecules are formed (eqn [6.7]). The addition of a base (usually, as its salt) to water will decrease the amount of H^+, due to the formation of the conjugate acid (eqn [6.8]).

- Dissociation of alkalis, according to the relationship:

$$X\text{–}OH \rightleftharpoons X^+ + OH^- \qquad [6.9]$$

where X–OH represents the undissociated alkali. Since the dissociation of water is reversible (eqn [6.7]), in an aqueous solution the production of hydroxyl ions will effectively act to 'mop up' protons, lowering the proton concentration.

Many compounds act as acids, bases or alkalis: those which are almost completely ionized in solution are usually called strong acids or bases, while weak acids or bases are only slightly ionized in solution.

In an aqueous solution, most of the water molecules are not ionized. In fact, the extent of ionization of pure water is constant at any given temperature and is usually expressed in terms of the ion product (or ionization constant) of water, K_w:

$$K_w = [H^+][OH^-] \qquad [6.10]$$

where $[H^+]$ and $[OH^-]$ represent the molar concentration (strictly, the activity) of protons and hydroxyl ions in solution, expressed as $\text{mol}\,l^{-1}$. At 25 °C, the ion product of pure water is $10^{-14}\,\text{mol}^2\,l^{-2}$ (i.e. $10^{-8}\,\text{mol}^2\,m^{-6}$). This means that the concentration of protons in solution will be $10^{-7}\,\text{mol}\,l^{-1}$ ($10^{-4}\,\text{mol}\,m^{-3}$), with an equivalent concentration of hydroxyl ions (eqn [6.7]). Since these values are very low and involve negative powers of 10, it is customary to use the pH scale, where:

$$pH = -\log_{10}[H^+] \qquad [6.11]$$

and $[H^+]$ is the proton activity (see p. 25).

KEY POINT While pH is strictly the negative logarithm (to the base 10) of H^+ activity, in practice H^+ concentration in $\text{mol}\,l^{-1}$ (equivalent to $\text{kmol}\,m^{-3}$ in SI terminology) is most often used in place of activity, since the two are virtually the same, given the limited dissociation of H_2O. The pH scale is not SI: nevertheless, it continues to be used widely in biological science.

The value where an equal amount of H^+ and OH^- ions are present is termed neutrality: at 25 °C the pH of pure water at neutrality is 7.0. At this temperature, pH values below 7.0 are acidic while values above 7.0 are

Principles of solution chemistry

Table 6.3 Effects of temperature on the ion product of water (K_w), H^+ ion concentration and pH at neutrality. Values calculated from Lide and Frederikse (1996)

Temp. (°C)	K_w (mol^2 l^{-2})	[H^+] at neutrality (nmol l^{-1})	pH at neutrality
0	0.11×10^{-4}	33.9	7.47
4	0.17×10^{-4}	40.7	7.39
10	0.29×10^{-4}	53.7	7.27
20	0.68×10^{-4}	83.2	7.08
25	1.01×10^{-4}	100.4	7.00
30	1.47×10^{-4}	120.2	6.92
37	2.39×10^{-4}	154.9	6.81
45	4.02×10^{-4}	199.5	6.70

Table 6.4 Properties of some pH indicator dyes

Dye	Acid-base colour change	Useful pH range
Thymol blue (acid)	red–yellow	1.2–6.8
Bromophenol blue	yellow–blue	1.2–6.8
Congo red	blue–red	3.0–5.2
Bromocresol green	yellow-blue	3.8–5.4
Resazurin	orange–violet	3.8–6.5
Methyl red	red–yellow	4.3–6.1
Litmus	red–blue	4.5–8.3
Bromocresol purple	yellow–purple	5.8–6.8
Bromothymol blue	yellow-blue	6.0–7.6
Neutral red	red–yellow	6.8–8.0
Phenol red	yellow–red	6.8–8.2
Thymol blue (alkaline)	yellow-blue	8.0–9.6
Phenol-phthalein	none–red	8.3–10.0

Definition

Buffer solution – one which resists a change in H^+ concentration (pH) on addition of acid or alkali.

alkaline. However, the pH of a neutral solution changes with temperature (Table 6.3), due to the enhanced dissociation of water with increasing temperature. This must be taken into account when measuring the pH of any solution and when interpreting your results.

Always remember that the pH scale is a logarithmic one, not a linear one: a solution with a pH of 3.0 is not twice as acidic as a solution of pH 6.0, but one thousand times as acidic (i.e. contains 1000 times the amount of H^+ ions). Therefore, you may need to convert pH values into proton concentrations before you carry out mathematical manipulations (see Box 39.2, p. 215). For similar reasons, it is important that pH change is expressed in terms of the original and final pH values, rather than simply quoting the difference between the values: a pH change of 0.1 has little meaning unless the initial or final pH is known.

Measuring pH

pH electrodes

Accurate pH measurements can be made using a pH electrode, coupled to a pH meter. The pH electrode is usually a combination electrode, comprising two separate systems: an H^+-sensitive glass electrode and a reference electrode which is unaffected by H^+ ion concentration. When this is immersed in a solution, a pH-dependent voltage between the two electrodes can be measured using a potentiometer. In most cases, the pH electrode assembly (containing the glass and reference electrodes) is connected to a separate pH meter by a cable, although some hand-held instruments (pH probes) have the electrodes and meter within the same assembly, often using an H^+-sensitive field effect transistor in place of a glass electrode, to improve durability and portability.

Box 6.2 gives details of the steps involved in making a pH measurement with a glass pH electrode and meter.

pH indicator dyes

These compounds (usually weak acids) change colour in a pH-dependent manner. They may be added in small amounts to a solution, or they can be used in paper strip form. Each indicator dye usually changes colour over a restricted pH range, typically 1–2 pH units (Table 6.4): universal indicator dyes/papers make use of a combination of individual dyes to measure a wider pH range. Dyes are not suitable for accurate pH measurement as they are affected by other components of the solution including oxidizing and reducing agents and salts. However, they are useful for:

- estimating the approximate pH of a solution;
- determining a change in pH, for example at the end-point of a titration or the production of acids during bacterial metabolism;
- establishing the approximate pH of intracellular compartments, for example the use of neutral red as a 'vital' stain.

Buffers

Rather than simply measuring the pH of a solution, you may wish to *control* the pH, e.g in experiments. In fact, you should consider whether you need to control pH in any experiment involving an environmental system, components or biomolecules. One of the most effective ways to control pH is to use a buffer solution.

Box 6.2 Using a glass pH electrode and meter to measure the pH of a solution

The following procedure should be used whenever you make a pH measurement: consult the manufacturer's handbook for specific information, where necessary. Do not be tempted to miss out any of the steps detailed below, particularly those relating to the effects of temperature, or your measurements are likely to be inaccurate.

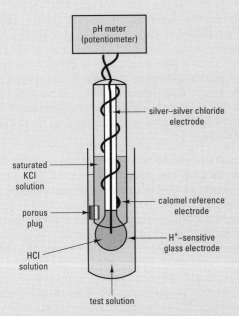

Fig. 6.1 Measurement of pH using a combination pH electrode and meter. The electrical potential difference recorded by the potentiometer is directly proportional to the pH of the test solution.

pH meter (potentiometer)

silver–silver chloride electrode

saturated KCl solution

porous plug

calomel reference electrode

HCl solution

H^+–sensitive glass electrode

test solution

1. **Stir the test solution thoroughly before you make any measurement:** it is often best to use a magnetic stirrer. Leave the solution for sufficient time to allow equilibration at lab temperature.

2. **Record the temperature of every solution you use,** including all calibration standards and samples, since this will affect K_w, neutrality and pH.

3. **Set the temperature compensator on the meter to the appropriate value.** This control makes an allowance for the effect of temperature on the electrical potential difference recorded by the meter: it does *not* allow for the other temperature-dependent effects mentioned elsewhere. Basic instruments have no temperature compensator, and should only be used at a specified temperature, either 20 °C or 25 °C, otherwise they will not give an accurate measurement. More sophisticated systems have automatic temperature compensation.

4. **Rinse the electrode assembly with distilled water** and gently dab off the excess water onto a clean tissue: check for visible damage or contamination of the glass electrode (consult a member of staff if the glass is broken or dirty). Also check that the solution within the glass assembly is covering the metal electrode.

5. **Calibrate the instrument:** set the meter to 'pH' mode, if appropriate, and then place the electrode assembly in a standard solution of known pH, usually pH 7.00. This solution may be supplied as a liquid, or may be prepared by dissolving a measured amount of a calibration standard in water: calibration standards are often provided in tablet form, to be dissolved in water to give a particular volume of solution. Adjust the calibration control to give the correct reading. Remember that your calibration standards will only give the specified pH at a particular temperature, usually either 20 °C or 25 °C. If you are working at a different temperature, you must establish the actual pH of your calibration standards, either from the supplier, or from literature information.

6. **Remove the electrode assembly from the calibration solution and rinse again with distilled water:** dab off the excess water. Basic instruments have no further calibration steps (single-point calibration), while the more refined pH meters have additional calibration procedures.

    If you are using a basic instrument, you should check that your apparatus is accurate over the appropriate pH range by measuring the pH of another standard whose pH is close to that expected for the test solution. If the standard does not give the expected reading, the instrument is not functioning correctly: consult a member of staff.

    If you are using an instrument with a slope control function, this will allow you to correct for any deviation in electrical potential from that predicted by the theoretical relationship (at 25 °C, a change in pH of 1.00 unit should result in a change in electrical potential of 59.16 mV) by performing a two-point calibration. Having calibrated the instrument at pH 7.00, immerse in a second standard at the same temperature as that of the first standard, usually buffered to either pH 4.00 or pH 9.00, depending upon the expected pH of your samples. Adjust the slope control until the exact value of the second standard is achieved (Fig. 6.2). A pH electrode and meter calibrated using the two-point method will give accurate readings over the pH range from 3 to 11: laboratory pH electrodes are not accurate outside this range, since the

Box 6.2 (continued)

theoretical relationship between electrical potential and pH is no longer valid.

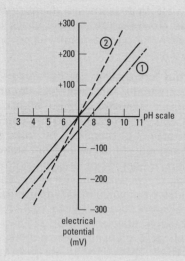

Fig. 6.2 The relationship between electrical potential and pH. The solid line shows the response of a calibrated electrode while the other plots are for instruments requiring calibration: 1 has the correct slope but incorrect isopotential point (calibration control adjustment is needed); 2 has the correct isopotential point but incorrect slope (slope control adjustment is needed).

7. **Once the instrument is calibrated, measure the pH of your solution(s)**, making sure that the electrode assembly is rinsed thoroughly between measurements. You should be particularly aware of this requirement if your solutions contain organic biological material, e.g. soil, tissue fluids, protein solutions, etc., since these may adhere to the glass electrode and affect the calibration of your instrument. If your electrode becomes contaminated during use, check with a member of staff before cleaning: avoid touching the surface of the glass electrode with abrasive material. Allow sufficient time for the pH reading to stabilize in each solution before taking a measurement: for unbuffered solutions, this may take several minutes, so do not take inaccurate pH readings due to impatience!

8. **After use, the electrode assembly must not be allowed to dry out.** Most pH electrodes should be stored in a neutral solution of KCl, either by suspending the assembly in a small beaker, or by using an electrode cap filled with the appropriate solution (typically $1.0 \, mol \, l^{-1}$ KCl buffered at pH 7.0). However, many labs simply use distilled water as a storage solution, leading to loss of ions from the interior of the electrode assembly. In practice, this means that pH electrodes stored in distilled water will take far longer to give a stable reading than those stored in KCl.

9. **Switch the meter to zero (where appropriate), but do not turn off the power:** pH meters give more stable readings if they are left on during normal working hours.

   Problems (and solutions) include: inaccurate and/or unstable pH readings caused by cross-contamination (rinse electrode assembly with distilled water and blot dry between measurements); development of a protein film on the surface of the electrode (soak in 1% w/v pepsin in $0.1 \, mol \, l^{-1}$ HCl for at least an hour); deposition of organic or inorganic contaminants on the glass bulb (use an organic solvent, such as acetone, or a solution of $0.1 \, mol \, l^{-1}$ disodium ethylenediamine-tetraacetic acid, respectively); drying out of the internal reference solutions (drain, flush and refill with fresh solution, then allow to equilibrate in $0.1 \, mol \, l^{-1}$ HCl for at least an hour); cracks or chips to the surface of the glass bulb (use a replacement electrode).

A buffer solution is usually a mixture of a weak acid and its conjugate base. Added protons will be neutralized by the anionic base while a reduction in protons, e.g. due to the addition of hydroxyl ions, will be counterbalanced by dissociation of the acid (eqn [6.8]); thus the conjugate pair acts as a 'buffer' to pH change. The innate resistance of most biological fluids to pH change is due to the presence of cellular constituents that act as buffers, e.g. proteins, which have a large number of weakly acidic and basic groups in their amino acid side chains.

The atmosphere contains a mixture of gases of which the main ones are nitrogen, oxygen and carbon dioxide. In addition, it contains water vapour in highly variable amounts. The gaseous composition of the atmosphere remains remarkably constant, although it has varied significantly over the lifetime of the planet. No discernible changes in the percentage composition have been found up to 100 km in altitude despite the pressure of the air being greatly reduced. This is due to the extensive mixing within this region. However, there may be significant variations in the composition of the air on a more local scale, e.g. in an animal's burrow or in a polluted city.

The ideal gas law and its significance

A gas which obeys the gas laws (Boyle's Law, Charles' Law and the pressure law) is termed 'ideal'. Non-ideal behaviour is generally exhibited only by gases close to liquefaction, and the atmosphere exhibits near-ideal behaviour at all times.

Boyle's Law states that the pressure (p) of a gas is inversely proportional to the volume (V) at constant temperature ($pV =$ constant). The modern equivalent of Charles' Law states that the volume is directly proportional to the thermodynamic temperature (T) at constant pressure (p) ($V/T =$ constant). The pressure law, a combination of Boyle's Law and Charles' Law, states that the pressure is directly proportional to the thermodynamic temperature for a gas at constant volume.

This can be summarized by the equation of state of an ideal gas:

$$\frac{pV}{T} = \text{constant} \tag{7.1}$$

in which p is the pressure, V the volume and T the absolute temperature in Kelvin. Any consistent units of pressure and volume can be used.

If specific conditions are defined by pressures p_1 and p_2 with corresponding volumes V_1 and V_2 and temperatures T_1 and T_2 for a given mass of gas, then:

$$\frac{p_1 V_1}{T_1} = \frac{p_2 V_2}{T_2} \tag{7.2}$$

This is useful when estimating the change in volume of a mass of air when atmospheric temperature and pressure are changed.

These three gas laws can be combined into the universal gas equation, expressed as

$$pV = nRT \tag{7.3}$$

where the constant of eqn 7.1 above has been replaced by the term nR. Here, $p =$ pressure (Pa or $J\,m^{-3}$); $V =$ volume (m^3); n is the number of moles of gas; R is called the universal gas constant ($8.314\,J\,mol^{-1}\,K^{-1}$) and $T =$ temperature (K). Both n and R are independent of the type of gas being considered. R may be expressed in a variety of units although the most useful in environmental chemistry relate to litres and atmospheres.

Avogadro's Law

This states that equal numbers of molecules of different gases will occupy the same volume at a given temperature and pressure. Whatever the gas, at STP one mole contains a specific number of molecules, namely 6.022×10^{23} mol^{-1}: this is known as Avogadro's constant.

Dalton's Law of Partial Pressures

This law applies to mixtures of gases and is particularly relevant to environmental chemistry. The partial pressure of a gas is defined as the pressure that the gas would exert if it alone occupied the whole volume of the mixture at that temperature. Therefore, the total pressure of a mixture of two or more gases is equal to the sum of the partial pressures of the constituent gases:

$$p = p_1 + p_2 + p_3 + \ldots p_n \tag{7.4}$$

where there are n constituent gases.

As a consequence of Dalton's Law of Partial Pressures, a complex mixture of gases like air may be treated as a single medium for analysis. Remember, however, that even trace amounts of water vapour must be taken into account.

Box 7.1 Worked examples of calculations using Dalton's Law of Partial Pressures

Example 1
If air at one atmosphere pressure is considered as a three-component mixture comprising 78% nitrogen, 21% oxygen and 1% argon (all by volume), calculate the partial pressure of each gas.
Since equal volumes of gases at a given temperature and pressure contain equal numbers of molecules, it follows that:
Nitrogen must contain 78% of the molecules and likewise of the moles. Nitrogen thus constitutes a mole fraction of 0.78 within the mixture. Thus for nitrogen at a pressure of 1 atm (101 325 Pa):

$$PN_2 = 0.78 \times 1 = 0.78 \text{ atm (79 033 Pa)}$$

Similarly for oxygen and argon the partial pressures are 0.21 (21 278 Pa) and 0.01 (1 013 Pa) atmospheres, respectively.

Example 2
What is a concentration of 1 ppm by volume of sulphur dioxide (SO_2) expressed in μg m^{-3} at 25 °C and 750 mmHg?

1 ppm SO_2 contains 1 ml SO_2 m^{-3}
At STP, 1 mol (64.1 g) SO_2 occupies 22.4 l.
Thus, at 25 °C and 750 mmHg, 1 mol SO_2 occupies

$$22.4 \times (298/273) \times (760/750) = 24.79 \text{ l}$$

Under these conditions, 1 ml SO_2 contains

$$64.1 \times 1 \times 10^{-3}/24.79 = 2.59 \times 10^{-3} \text{ g}$$

This is in 1 m^3 of polluted air, thus:
SO_2 concentration = 2590 μg m^{-3} = 2.59×10^3 μg m^{-3}

Definition

Saturated vapour pressure – the partial pressure of water vapour in saturated air at a given temperature.

Definition

Relative humidity – the ratio of the partial pressure of water vapour in air to the equilibrium vapour pressure of water over a liquid surface.

Definition

The law of buoyancy – states that any material or object immersed in a fluid will tend to rise through the fluid if the fluid density is greater than the material density.

Definition

The law of adiabatic expansion or compression (contraction) – states that any gas will cool that is allowed to expand freely from a higher pressure to a lower pressure without the transfer of external energy to the gas. Similarly, a gas will heat if compressed from a lower to a higher pressure in the absence of a transfer of energy from the gas.

The special case of water (moisture)

The mass concentration of water vapour in air is termed the absolute humidity and is expressed in $g\,m^{-3}$. This has an upper limit dependent on the air temperature: examples of saturated vapour pressure (SVP) are:

$0.611\,kPa$ at $0\,°C$ ($=$ a partial pressure of $0.006\,Pa\,Pa^{-1}$)
$3.166\,kPa$ at $25\,°C$ ($=$ a partial pressure of $0.031\,Pa\,Pa^{-1}$)

Other values can be looked up in tables (Jones, 1992) or calculated using the Bio/Chem Lab Assistant computer program (Parsons and Ogston, 1997).

Relative humidity is the actual water vapour pressure expressed as a percentage of the SVP.

Moist air is less dense than dry air at the same temperature and pressure because the molecular weight of water (18) is less than the average for air (29).

Buoyancy

The force associated with buoyancy is the difference between the weight of the displaced fluid and the weight of the immersed material. Air is a fluid with a low density at ground level of about $1\,kg\,m^{-3}$, while water is a much heavier fluid with a density of about $1000\,kg\,m^{-3}$. Buoyant support is, therefore, much more significant in water.

Temperature and altitude both affect the density of the atmosphere. Warm air becomes less dense and, therefore, more buoyant and unstable and rises in a process called convection: thunderclouds illustrate this well. The dynamics of the atmosphere and the hydrosphere can be considered to result from movement of discrete 'parcels' of atmosphere or water body, each subject to buoyant forces.

Adiabatic cooling and heating

The term adiabatic means 'without the gain or loss of heat' and in an adiabatic process involving a parcel of fluid, no energy in the form of heat is exchanged between the parcel and its surroundings – i.e. it is effectively thermally insulated under these circumstances. The pressure and temperature of the contained gases obey the adiabatic gas law and the process is termed adiabatic expansion or contraction. In general, as a gas expands by reduction of pressure, it cools (adiabatic cooling): compression results in adiabatic warming. Thus a parcel of air forced to rise will cool and *vice versa*.

Adiabatic expansion explains the overall decrease in temperature with increasing altitude in the troposphere. When the air is moist (high relative humidity), water may begin to condense as the air cools and clouds are formed.

The excess energy that is released (or absorbed) is called the latent heat of condensation (or latent heat of evaporation), a major source of the energy driving the Earth's weather systems.

Diffusion

In any situation where a concentration gradient exists, diffusion processes will operate to remove the gradient. In gases this process is driven by the kinetic energy of the substances and is referred to as molecular diffusion. In the atmosphere, molecular diffusion is too slow to cause significant mixing of gases on a large scale. Here turbulent mixing is the main process and this is termed eddy diffusion. Both processes can occur in liquids as well as gases and are important in both the atmosphere and the hydrosphere. The flux of material (F) across an interface from an area of high concentration to one of lower concentration is defined by Fick's Law as

$$F = -D\frac{\dot{d}c}{dx} \tag{7.5}$$

in which D is the diffusion coefficient (units of length^2 time^{-1}) and dc/dx is the concentration gradient. The equation applies to both molecular and eddy diffusion although the value of D differs markedly.

Solubility of gases

This is described by Henry's Law, which states that at constant temperature the solubility of a gas in a liquid is proportional to the partial pressure of the gas in contact with the liquid. Note, however, that this does not take account of the higher solubilities of gases which also react with water, e.g. ammonia and sulphur dioxide.

Henry's Law is expressed as

$$[X_{(aq)}] = KP_x \tag{7.6}$$

where $[X_{(aq)}]$ is the aqueous concentration of the gas; K is the Henry's Law constant applicable to a particular gas at a specified temperature and P_x is the partial pressure of the gas in contact with the liquid. For gas concentrations in units of moles per litre and gas pressures in atmospheres, the units of K are mol l^{-1} atm^{-1}.

In calculating the solubility of a gas in water, a correction must be made for the partial pressure of the water by subtracting it from the total pressure of the gas. Note also that gas solubility is affected by solute concentration.

The solubility of gases decrease with increasing temperature (see Fig. 7.1).

Table 7.1 Henry's Law constants for solubility of some environmental gases in water at 25 °C

Gas	K(mol l^{-1} atm^{-1})
O_2	1.28×10^{-3}
CO_2	3.38×10^{-2}
H_2	7.9×10^{-4}
CH_4	1.34×10^{-3}
N_2	6.48×10^{-4}
NO	2.0×10^{-4}

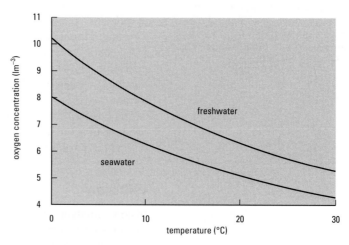

Fig. 7.1 The variation of dissolved oxygen concentration with temperature in seawater and fresh water.

Box 7.2 Worked example: calculating the solubility of a gas in water

Calculate the concentration of oxygen in water saturated with air at 1 atm and 25 °C.

Dry air contains 20.95% by volume oxygen. Factoring in the partial pressure of water at 25 °C (SVP = 3.166 kPa = 0.0313 atm):

$$P_{O_2} = (1.0000\ \text{atm} - 0.0313\ \text{atm}) \times 0.2095$$
$$= 0.2029\ \text{atm}$$

$$[O_{2(aq)}] = K \times P_{O_2}$$
$$= 1.28 \times 10^{-3}\ \text{mol} \times 1^{-1} \times \text{atm}^{-1} \times 0.2029\ \text{atm}$$
$$= 2.60 \times 10^{-4}\ \text{mol}\ 1^{-1}$$

The molecular weight of oxygen is 32, therefore, the concentration of dissolved oxygen in water at equilibrium with air under these conditions is 8.32 mg 1^{-1} or 8.32 parts per million (ppm).

The investigative approach

8

The principles of measurement

The term data (singular = datum, or data value) refers to items of information, and you will use different types of data from a wide range of sources during your practical work. Consequently, it is important to appreciate the underlying features of data collection and measurement.

Variables

Environmental variables (Fig. 8.1) can be classified as follows:

Quantitative variables

These are characteristics whose differing states can be described by means of a number. They are of two basic types:

- Continuous variables, such as length; these are usually measured against a numerical scale. Theoretically, they can take any value on the measurement scale. In practice, the number of significant figures of a measurement is directly related to the accuracy of your measuring system; for example, dimensions measured with Vernier calipers will provide readings of greater precision than a millimetre ruler (p. 18).
- Discontinuous (discrete) variables, such as the number of granite particles in a gravel sample; these are always obtained by counting and therefore the data values must be whole numbers (integers). There are no intermediate values – for example, you never find 25.8 granite pebbles in a gravel sample.

Ranked variables

These provide data which can be listed in order of magnitude (i.e. ranked). A familiar example is the abundance of an item in a sample, which is often expressed as a series of ranks, e.g. rare = 1, occasional = 2, frequent = 3, common = 4, and abundant = 5. When such data are given numerical ranks, rather than descriptive terms, they are sometimes called 'semi-quantitative data'. Note that the difference in magnitude between ranks need not be consistent. For example, regardless of whether there was a one-year or a five-year gap between offspring in a family, their ranks in order of birth would be the same.

Qualitative variables (attributes)

These are non-numerical and descriptive; they have no order of preference and therefore, are not measured on a numerical scale nor ranked in order of magnitude, but are described in terms of categories. Examples include viability (i.e. dead or alive) and shape (e.g. round, flat, elongated, etc.).

Variables may be independent or dependent. Usually, the variable under the control of the experimenter (e.g. time) is the independent variable, while the variable being measured is the dependent variable (p. 56). Sometimes it is not appropriate to describe variables in this way and they are then referred to as interdependent variables (e.g. the length and breadth of a fossil).

The majority of data values are recorded as direct measurements, readings or counts, but there is an important group, called derived (or computed), which result from calculations based on two or more data values, e.g. ratios, percentages, indices and rates.

Working with discontinuous variables – note that while the original data values must be integers, derived data and statistical values do not have to be whole numbers. Thus, it is perfectly acceptable to express the *mean* number of children per family as 2.4.

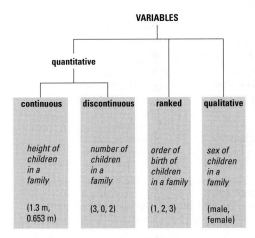

Fig. 8.1 Examples of the different types of variables as used to describe some characteristics of families.

Measurement scales

Variables may be measured on different types of scale:

- Nominal scale: this classifies objects into categories based on a descriptive characteristic. It is the only scale suitable for qualitative data.
- Ordinal scale: this classifies by rank. There is a logical order in any number scale used.
- Interval scale: this is used for quantitative variables. Numbers on an equal unit scale are related to an arbitrary zero point.
- Ratio scale: this is similar to the interval scale, except that the zero point now represents an absence of that character (i.e. it is an absolute zero).

The measurement scale is important in determining the mathematical and statistical methods used to analyse your data. Table 8.1 presents a summary of the important properties of these scales. Note that you may be able to measure a characteristic in more than one way, or you may be able to convert data collected in one form to a different form. For instance, you might measure light in terms of the photon flux density between particular wavelengths of the EMR spectrum (ratio scale), or simply as 'blue' or 'red' (nominal scale); you could find out the dates of birth of individuals (interval scale) but then use this information to rank them in order of birth (ordinal scale). Where there are no other constraints, you should use a ratio scale to measure a quantitative variable, since this will allow you to use the broadest range of mathematical and statistical procedures (Table 8.1).

Examples A nominal scale for temperature is not feasible, since the relevant descriptive terms can be ranked in order of magnitude.

An ordinal scale for temperature measurement might use descriptive terms, ranked in ascending order e.g. cold = 1, cool = 2, warm = 3, hot = 4.

The Celsius scale is an interval scale for temperature measurement, since the arbitrary zero corresponds to the freezing point of water (0 °C).

The Kelvin scale is a ratio scale for temperature measurement since 0 K represents a temperature of absolute zero (for information, the freezing point of water is 273.15 K on this scale).

Table 8.1 Some important features of scales of measurement

	Measurement scale			
	Nominal	Ordinal	Interval	Ratio
Type of variable	Qualitative (Ranked)* (Quantitative)*	Ranked (Quantitative)*	Quantitative	Quantitative
Examples	Species Gender Colour	Abundance scales Reproductive condition Optical assessment of colour development	Fahrenheit temperature scale Date (BC/AD)	Kelvin temperature scale Weight Length Response time Most physical measurements
Mathematical properties	Identity	Identity Magnitude	Identity Magnitude Equal intervals	Identity Magnitude Equal intervals True zero point
Mathematical operations possible on data	None	Rank	Rank Addition Subtraction	Rank Addition Subtraction Multiplication Division
Typical statistics used	Only those based on frequency of counts made: contingency tables, frequency distributions, etc. Chi-square test	Non-parametric methods, sign tests. Mann–Whitney U-test	Almost all types of test, t-test, analysis of variance (ANOVA), etc. (check distribution before using, p. 217)	Almost all types of test, t-test, ANOVA, etc. (check distribution before using, p. 217)

*In some instances (see text for examples)

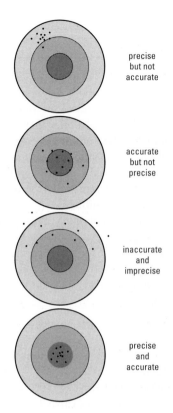

Fig. 8.2 'Target' diagrams illustrating precision and accuracy.

precise but not accurate

accurate but not precise

inaccurate and imprecise

precise and accurate

> Minimizing errors – determine early in your study what the dominant errors are likely to be and concentrate your time and effort on reducing these.

> Working with derived data – special effort should be made to reduce measurement errors because their effects can be magnified when differences, ratios, indices or rates are calculated.

Accuracy and precision

Accuracy is the closeness of a measured or derived data value to its true value, while precision is the closeness of repeated measurements to each other (Fig. 8.2). A balance with a fault in it (i.e. a bias, see below) could give precise (i.e. very repeatable) but inaccurate (i.e. untrue) results. Unless there is bias in a measuring system, precision will lead to accuracy and it is precision that is generally the most important practical consideration, if there is no reason to suspect bias. You can investigate the precision of any measuring system by repeated measurements of individual samples.

Absolute accuracy and precision are impossible to achieve, due to both the limitations of measuring systems for continuous quantitative data and the fact that you are usually working with incomplete data sets (samples, p. 71). It is particularly important to avoid spurious accuracy in the presentation of results; include only those digits which the accuracy of the measuring system implies. This type of error is common when changing units (e.g. inches to metres) and in derived data, especially when calculators give results to a large number of decimal places.

Bias (systematic error) and consistency

Bias is a systematic or non-random distortion and is one of the most troublesome difficulties in using numerical data. Biases may be associated with incorrectly calibrated instruments, e.g. a faulty pipettor, or with experimental manipulations, e.g. shrinkage during the preservation of a specimen. Bias in measurement can also be subjective, or personal, e.g. an experimenter's pre-conceived ideas about an 'expected' result.

Bias can be minimized by using a carefully standardized procedure, with fully calibrated instruments. You can investigate bias in 'trial runs' by measuring a single variable in several different ways, to see whether the same result is obtained.

If a personal bias is possible, 'blind' measurements should be made where the identity of individual samples is not known to the operator, e.g. using a coding system.

Measurement error

All measurements are subject to error, but the dangers of misinterpretation are reduced by recognizing and understanding the likely sources of error and by adopting appropriate protocols and calculation procedures.

A common source of measurement error is carelessness, e.g. reading a scale in the wrong direction or parallax errors. This can be reduced greatly by careful recording and may be detected by repeating the measurement. Other errors arise from faulty or inaccurate equipment, but even a perfectly functioning machine has distinct limits to the accuracy and precision of its measurements. These limits are often quoted in manufacturers' specifications and are applicable when an instrument is new; however, you should allow for some deterioration with age. Further errors are introduced when the subject being studied is open to influences outside your control. Resolving such problems requires appropriate experimental design (Chapter 12) and sampling procedures (Chapter 15).

One major influence virtually impossible to eliminate is the effect of the investigation itself: even putting a thermometer in a liquid may change the temperature of the liquid. The very act of measurement may give rise to a confounding variable (p. 56) as discussed in Chapter 12.

9

SI units and their use

When describing a measurement, you normally state both a number and a unit (e.g. 'the length is 1.85 metres'). The number expresses the ratio of the measured quantity to a fixed standard, while the unit identifies that standard measure or dimension. Clearly, a single unified system of units is essential for efficient communication of such data within the scientific community. The Système International D'Unités (SI) is the internationally ratified form of the metre-kilogram-second system of measurement and represents the accepted scientific convention for measurements of physical quantities.

Another important reason for adopting consistent units is to simplify complex calculations where you may be dealing with several measured quantities (see pp. 202 and 204). Although the rules of the SI are complex and the scale of the base units is sometimes inconvenient, to gain the full benefits of the system you should observe its conventions strictly.

The description of measurements in SI involves:

- seven base units and two supplementary units, each having a specified abbreviation or symbol (Table 9.1);
- derived units, obtained from combinations of base and supplementary units, which may also be given special symbols (Table 9.2);
- a set of prefixes to denote multiplication factors of 10^3, used for convenience to express multiples or fractions of units (Table 9.3).

Dimensionless measurements – some quantities can be expressed as dimensionless ratios or logarithms (e.g. pH), and in these cases you do not need to use a qualifying unit.

Table 9.1 The base and supplementary SI units

Measured quantity	Name of SI unit	Symbol
Base units		
Length	metre	m
Mass	kilogram	kg
Amount of substance	mole	mol
Time	second	s
Electric current	ampere	A
Temperature	kelvin	K
Luminous intensity	candela	cd
Supplementary units		
Plane angle	radian	rad
Solid angle	steradian	sr

Table 9.2 Some important derived SI units

Measured quantity	Name of unit	Symbol	Definition in base units	Alternative in derived units
Energy	joule	J	$m^2\,kg\,s^{-2}$	N m
Force	newton	N	$m\,kg\,s^{-2}$	$J\,m^{-1}$
Pressure	pascal	Pa	$kg\,m^{-1}\,s^{-2}$	$N\,m^{-2}$
Power	watt	W	$m^2\,kg\,s^{-3}$	$J\,s^{-1}$
Electric charge	coulomb	C	A s	$J\,V^{-1}$
Electric potential difference	volt	V	$m^2\,kg\,A^{-1}\,s^{-3}$	$J\,C^{-1}$
Electric resistance	ohm	Ω	$m^2\,kg\,A^{-2}\,s^{-3}$	$V\,A^{-1}$
Electric conductance	siemens	S	$s^3\,A^2\,kg^{-1}\,m^{-2}$	$A\,V^{-1}$ or Ω^{-1}
Electric capacitance	farad	F	$s^4\,A^2\,kg^{-1}\,m^{-2}$	$C\,V^{-1}$
Luminous flux	lumen	lm	cd sr	
Illumination	lux	lx	$cd\,sr\,m^{-2}$	$lm\,m^{-2}$
Frequency	hertz	Hz	s^{-1}	
Radioactivity	becquerel	Bq	s^{-1}	

Table 9.3 Prefixes used in the SI

Multiple	Prefix	Symbol	Multiple	Prefix	Symbol
10^{-3}	milli	m	10^3	kilo	k
10^{-6}	micro	μ	10^6	mega	M
10^{-9}	nano	n	10^9	giga	G
10^{-12}	pico	p	10^{12}	tera	T
10^{-15}	femto	f	10^{15}	peta	P
10^{-18}	atto	a	10^{18}	exa	E

Recommendations for describing measurements in SI units

Basic format

- Express each measurement as a number separated from its units by a space. If a prefix is required, no space is left between the prefix and the unit it refers to. Symbols for units are only written in their singular form and do not require full stops to show that they are abbreviated or that they are being multiplied together.

Example $10\,\mu g$ is correct, while $10\mu g$, $10\,\mu g$. and $10\mu\,g$ are incorrect. 2.6 mol is right, but 2.6 mols is wrong.

- Give symbols and prefixes appropriate upper or lower case initial letters as this may define their meaning. Upper case symbols are named after persons but when written out in full they are not given initial capital letters.
- Show the decimal sign as a full point on the line. Some metric countries continue to use the comma for this purpose and you may come across this in the literature: commas should not therefore be used to separate groups of thousands. In numbers that contain many significant figures, you should separate multiples of 10^3 by spaces rather than commas.

Compound expressions for derived units

- Take care to separate symbols in compound expressions by a space to avoid the potential for confusion with prefixes. Note, for example, that 200 m s (metre-seconds) is different from 200 ms (milliseconds).
- Express compound units using negative powers rather than a solidus (/): for example, write $mol\,m^{-3}$ rather than mol/m^3. The solidus is reserved for separating a descriptive label from its units (see p. 194).
- Use parentheses to enclose expressions being raised to a power if this avoids confusion: for example, a photosynthetic rate might be given in $mol\,CO_2\,(mol\,photons)^{-1}\,s^{-1}$.
- Where there is a choice, select relevant (natural) combinations of derived and base units: e.g. you might choose units of $Pa\,m^{-1}$ to describe a hydrostatic pressure gradient rather than $kg\,m^{-2}\,s^{-1}$, even though these units are equivalent and the measurements are numerically the same.

Use of prefixes

- Use prefixes to denote multiples of 10^3 (Table 9.3) so that numbers are kept between 0.1 and 1000.
- Treat a combination of a prefix and a symbol as a single symbol. Thus, when a modified unit is raised to a power, this refers to the whole unit including the prefix.
- Avoid the prefixes deci (d) for 10^{-1} and centi (c) for 10^{-2} as they are not strictly SI.
- Express very large or small numbers as a number between 1 and 10 multiplied by a power of 10 if they are outside the range of prefixes shown in Table 9.3.
- Do not use prefixes in the middle of derived units: they should be attached only to a unit in the numerator (the exception is in the unit for mass, kg).

KEY POINT For the foreseeable future, you will need to make conversions from other units to SI units, as much of the literature quotes data using imperial, c.g.s. or other systems. You will need to recognize these units and find the conversion factors required. Examples relevant to environmental science are given in Box 9.1. Table 9.4 provides values of some important physical constants in SI units.

Table 9.4 Some physical constants in SI terms

Physical constant	Symbol	Value and units
Avogadro's constant	N_A	$6.022\,174 \times 10^{23}\,\text{mol}^{-1}$
Boltzmann's constant	k	$1.380\,626\,\text{J K}^{-1}$
Charge of electron	e	$1.602\,192 \times 10^{-19}\,\text{C}$
Gas constant	R	$8.314\,43\,\text{J K}^{-1}\,\text{mol}^{-1}$
Faraday's constant	F	$9.648\,675 \times 10^{4}\,\text{C mol}^{-1}$
Molar volume of ideal gas at STP	V_0	$0.022\,414\,\text{m}^3\,\text{mol}^{-1}$
Speed of light *in vacuo*	c	$2.997\,924 \times 10^{8}\,\text{m s}^{-1}$
Planck's constant	h	$6.626\,205 \times 10^{-34}\,\text{J s}$

Box 9.1 Conversion factors between some redundant units and the SI

Quantity	SI unit/symbol	Old unit/symbol	Multiply number in old unit by this factor for equivalent in SI unit*	Multiply number in SI unit by this factor for equivalent in old unit*
Area	square metre/m^2	acre	$4.046\,86 \times 10^{3}$	$0.247\,105 \times 10^{-3}$
		hectare/ha	10×10^{3}	0.1×10^{-3}
		square foot/ft^2	$0.092\,903$	10.7639
		square inch/in^2	645.16×10^{-9}	$1.550\,00 \times 10^{6}$
		square yard/yd^2	$0.836\,127$	$1.195\,99$
Angle	radian/rad	degree/°	$17.453\,2 \times 10^{-3}$	$57.295\,8$
Energy	joule/J	erg	0.1×10^{-6}	10×10^{6}
		kilowatt hour/kWh	3.6×10^{6}	$0.277\,778 \times 10^{-6}$
		calorie/cal	4.1868	0.2388
Length	metre/m	Ångstrom/Å	0.1×10^{-9}	10×10^{9}
		foot/ft	$0.304\,8$	$3.280\,84$
		inch/in	25.4×10^{-3}	$39.370\,1$
		mile	$1.609\,34 \times 10^{3}$	$0.621\,373 \times 10^{-3}$
		yard/yd	$0.914\,4$	$1.093\,61$
Mass	kilogram/kg	ounce/oz	$28.349\,5 \times 10^{-3}$	$35.274\,0$
		pound/lb	$0.453\,592$	$2.204\,62$
		stone	$6.350\,29$	$0.157\,473$
		hundredweight/cwt	$50.802\,4$	$19.684\,1 \times 10^{-3}$
		ton (UK)	$1.016\,05 \times 10^{3}$	$0.984\,203 \times 10^{-3}$
Pressure	pascal/Pa	atmosphere/atm	$101\,325$	$9.869\,23 \times 10^{-6}$
		bar/b	$100\,000$	10×10^{-6}
		millimetre of mercury/mmHg	133.322	$7.500\,64 \times 10^{-3}$
		torr/Torr	133.322	$7.500\,64 \times 10^{-3}$
Radioactivity	becquerel/Bq	curie/Ci	37×10^{9}	$27.027\,0 \times 10^{-12}$
Temperature	kelvin/K	centigrade (Celsius) degree/°C	$°C + 273.15$	$K - 273.15$
		Fahrenheit degree/°F	$(°F + 459.67) \times 5/9$	$(K \times 9/5) - 459.67$
Volume	cubic metre/m^3	cubic foot/ft^3	$0.028\,316\,8$	35.3147
		cubic inch/in^3	$16.387\,1 \times 10^{-6}$	$61.023\,6 \times 10^{3}$
		cubic yard/yd^3	$0.764\,555$	$1.307\,95$
		UK pint/pt	$0.568\,261 \times 10^{-3}$	1759.75
		US pint/liq pt	$0.473\,176 \times 10^{-3}$	2113.38
		UK gallon/gal	$4.546\,09 \times 10^{-3}$	219.969
		US gallon/gal	$3.785\,41 \times 10^{-3}$	264.172

*In the case of temperature measurements, use formulae shown

Some implications of SI in environmental science

Volume

The SI unit of volume is the cubic metre, m^3. Whilst this is appropriate for expressing discharge of water by a stream (as $m^3\,sec^{-1}$, known as cumecs) it is rather large for many practical purposes. The litre (l) and the millilitre (ml) are technically obsolete, but are widely used and glassware is still calibrated using them.

Mass

The SI unit for mass is the kilogram (kg) rather than the gram (g): this is unusual because the base unit has a prefix applied.

Amount of substance

You should use the mole (mol, i.e. Avogadro's constant, see Table 9.4) to express very large numbers. The mole gives the number of atoms in the atomic mass, a convenient constant. Always specify the elementary unit referred to in other situations (e.g. mol photons $m^{-2}\,s^{-1}$).

Concentration

The SI unit of concentration, $mol\,m^{-3}$, is quite convenient for biological systems. It is equivalent to the non-SI term 'millimolar' (mM) while 'molar' (M) becomes $kmol\,m^{-3}$. Note that the symbol M in the SI is reserved for mega and hence should not be used for concentrations. If the solvent is not specified, then it is assumed to be water (see Chapter 6).

Time

In general, use the second (s) when reporting physical quantities having a time element (e.g. give photosynthetic rates in mol $CO_2\,m^{-2}\,s^{-1}$). Hours (h), days (d) and years should be used if seconds are clearly absurd (e.g., samples were taken over a 5-year period). Note, however, that you may have to convert these units to seconds when doing calculations.

The second is not an appropriate measure for the expression of geological time, which extends over billions, millions or thousands of years. A more suitable basis is the year, for which the conventional symbol is 'a', derived from *annum* (note the possible but unlikely confusion that could arise with the prefix 'a' as the symbol for atto, the multiple 10^{-18}). This is then prefixed by the appropriate multiple (Table 9.3), e.g. Ga, Ma or ka. Many authors continue to adopt the abbreviations m.y. (or My) and b.y. for millions of years and billions of years, respectively, a practice which must not be followed. You should express ages as, for example, 2 500 ka or age ranges as 315–290 Ma. Appropriate limits of uncertainty should be given as, for example, $451 \pm 6\,Ma$ or $451.6 \pm 6.4\,Ma$. Rates of geological processes should be expressed as per year, for example, 1.3–$1.4\,mm\,a^{-1}$, or as per Ma, for example, $2.6\,m\,Ma^{-1}$, etc.

Temperature

The SI unit is the kelvin, K. The degree Celsius scale has units of the same magnitude, °C, but starts at 273.15 K, the melting point of ice at STP. Temperature is similar to time in that the Celsius scale is in widespread use, but note that conversions to K may be required for calculations. Note also that you must not use the degree sign (°) with K and that this symbol must be in upper case to avoid confusion with k for kilo; however, you *should* retain the degree sign with °C to avoid confusion with the coulomb, C.

In this book, we use l and ml where you would normally find equipment calibrated in that way, but use SI units where this simplifies calculations. In formal scientific writing, constructions such as $1 \times 10^{-6}\,m^3$ ($= 1\,ml$) and $1\,mm^3$ ($= 1\,\mu l$) may be used.

Definition

STP – Standard Temperature and Pressure = 293.15 K and 0.101 325 MPa.

Light

While the first six base units in Table 9.1 have standards of high precision, the SI base unit for luminous intensity, the candela (cd) and the derived units lm and lx (Table 9.2), are defined in 'human' terms. They are, in fact, based on the spectral responses of the eyes of 52 American GIs measured in 1923! Clearly, few organisms 'see' light in the same way as this sample of humans. Also, light sources differ in their spectral quality. For these reasons, it is better to use expressions based on energy or photon content (e.g. $W\,m^{-2}$ or mol photons $m^{-2}\,s^{-1}$), in studies other than those on human vision. Ideally you should specify the photon wavelength spectrum involved.

10 Making observations

Observations provide the basic information leading to the formulation of hypotheses, the first step in the scientific method (see Fig. 12.1). Observations are obtained either directly by our senses or indirectly through the use of instruments which extend our senses and may be either:

- Qualitative: described by words or terms rather than by numbers and including subjective descriptions in terms of variables such as colour, shape and smell; often recorded using photographs and drawings.
- Quantitative: numerical values derived from counts or measurements of a variable (see Chapter 8), frequently requiring use of some kind of instrument.

KEY POINT **Although qualitative and quantitative observations are useful in environmental science, you should try to make numerical counts or measurements wherever possible, as this allows you to define your observations more rigorously and make objective comparisons using statistical tools.**

Factors influencing the quality of observations

Perception

Observation is highly dependent upon the perception of the observer. Perception involves both visual and intuitive processes, so your interpretation of what you see is very dependent upon what you already know or have seen before. Thus, two persons observing the same event may 'see' it differently, a good example of bias. This is frequently true in microscopy where experience is an important factor in interpretation.

When you start environmental science, your knowledge base will be limited and your experience restricted. Practical training in observation provides the opportunity to develop both aspects of your skills in a process which is effectively a positive feedback loop – the more you know/see as a result of practice, the better will your observations become.

Precision and error

Obviously very important for interpretive accuracy, with both human and non-human components. These are dealt with in Chapter 8.

Artefacts

These are artificial features introduced usually during some treatment process such as chemical fixation prior to microscopic examination. They may be included in the interpretive process if their presence is not recognized – again, prior experience and knowledge are important factors in spotting artefacts.

Developing observational skills

You must develop your knowledge and observational skills to benefit properly from your practical work. The only way to acquire these skills is through extensive practice.

Making observations

Make sure your observations are:

- relevant, i.e. directed towards a clearly defined objective;
- accurate, i.e. related to a scale whenever possible;
- repeatable, i.e. as error free (precise) as possible.

One of the best ways to develop observational skills is by making accurate drawings or diagrams, forcing you to look more carefully than is usual (see Chapter 11). An important observational skill to develop is the interpretation of two-dimensional images – such as sections through plant/animal/rock material, photographs (aerial and terrestrial) and satellite images – in terms of the three-dimensional forms from which they are derived. This requires a clear understanding of the nature of the image in terms of both scale and orientation (see Chapter 27). You will enhance your observational skills by asking yourself questions. When in the field, ask for example, 'Why is there no stream in that valley?' 'Why is that waterfall where it is?' 'Why is the vegetational pattern different along this side of the valley compared with the other?'

Counting

Counting is an observational skill that requires practice to become both accurate and efficient. It is easy to make errors or lose count when working with large numbers of objects. Use a counting aid whenever human error might be significant. There are many such aids such as tally counters, tally charts and specialized counting devices like colony counters. It is important to avoid counting items twice. For example, acetate sheets can be used as overlays for photographs, drawings and other images, then as each object is counted it can be marked off using a water-based marker pen. Remember to mark identification points in case the sheet slips!

Another valuable technique is to use a grid system to organize the counting procedure. Remember that you must decide on a protocol for sampling, particularly with regard to the direction of counting within the grid and for dealing with boundary overlaps to prevent double counting at the edges of the grid squares (see Fig. 15.4, p. 74).

Observation during examinations

Making appropriate observations during practical examinations often causes difficulty, particularly when qualitative observations are needed, e.g. when asked to identify a rock specimen, giving reasons. Answering such questions clearly requires geological knowledge but also requires a strategy to provide the relevant observations. Thus for the above example, observations relevant to determining each component mineral type should be made and recorded: set out your observations in a logical sequence so that you show the examiner how you arrived at your conclusions. Do not make irrelevant observations. For example, if comments on the distribution of erosional landforms in a field photograph are required, do not make observations on depositional structures. You will obtain maximum marks only if your answers are concise and relevant (Chapter 52).

Drawing and diagrams

Drawing has an important place in environmental science teaching because of its role in developing observation skills. You need to look at a specimen or structure very carefully to be able to draw it accurately, while labelling a diagram forces you to think about the component structures and their positions. If your observation of a specimen is poor, so too will be your diagram.

Strictly, a *drawing* is a detailed and accurate representation of a specimen, requiring no previous knowledge. This level of art work is never required for normal practical work. A *diagram*, on the other hand, needs to be accurate in its general proportions, but is otherwise very stylized, showing only the most important features. Specialist knowledge is required to select items for inclusion and to decide what detail to ignore. Diagrams are often called figures in formal scientific writing, but may sometimes be referred to loosely as drawings, since the above distinction is frequently ignored.

KEY POINT **You may not feel confident about being able to produce quality art work in practicals, especially when the time allowed is limited. However, the requirements of scientific drawing are not as demanding as you might think and the skills required can be learned. By following the guidelines and techniques explained below, most students should be able to produce good diagrams.**

> Figure numbering in reports – if producing several diagrams, graphs, etc., number them consecutively as Figure 1, Figure 2, etc., and use this system to refer to them in the text.

The main types of figure

Broadly there are two types of figure, line diagrams and continuous tone drawings. However, the distinction between the two is not always clear cut as what is essentially a line diagram may incorporate continuous tones (shading) to highlight specific features (e.g. a field sketch, see below).

Line diagrams

There are many types of line diagram, of which the commonest are:

- field sketches and field maps;
- apparatus diagrams;
- non-numerical charts, e.g. flowcharts;
- numerical charts, e.g. graphs and histograms;
- morphological diagrams.

Field sketches and field maps

When producing sketches and maps in the field, follow the general steps towards producing a good diagram (see below). Always try to work neatly; use a sharp HB pencil and carry a sharpener and eraser. Producing field sketches is often time-consuming so the golden rule is to draw carefully and systematically; do not rush. Never make a sketch just for the sake of it; in most situations a photograph (see Chapter 27) will provide you with a better level of detail and accuracy. There are four generic stages to field sketching and mapping:

> **Definitions**
>
> **Field sketch** – illustrates what a feature (e.g. a landform or a building) looks like from the ground surface.
> **Field map** – illustrates what a feature (e.g. a landform or a building) looks like from vertically above.

Drawing and diagrams

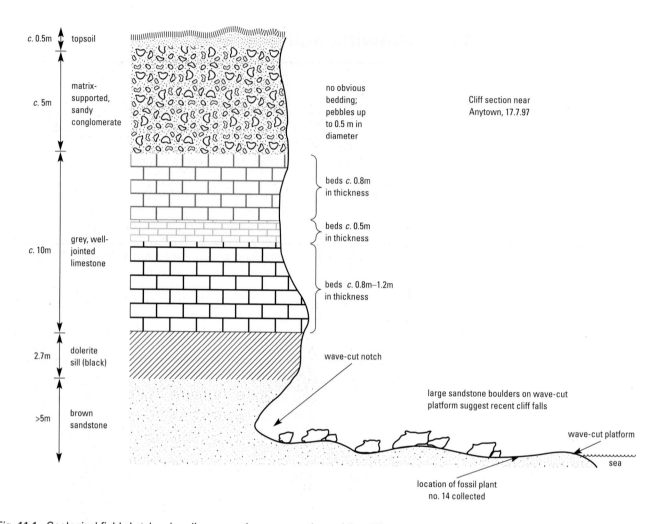

c. 0.5m — topsoil

c. 5m — matrix-supported, sandy conglomerate

no obvious bedding; pebbles up to 0.5 m in diameter

Cliff section near Anytown, 17.7.97

beds *c.* 0.8m in thickness

beds *c.* 0.5m in thickness

c. 10m — grey, well-jointed limestone

beds *c.* 0.8m–1.2m in thickness

2.7m — dolerite sill (black)

wave-cut notch

large sandstone boulders on wave-cut platform suggest recent cliff falls

>5m — brown sandstone

wave-cut platform

sea

location of fossil plant no. 14 collected

Fig. 11.1 Geological field sketch using diagrammatic representations of the different rock types present.

Using sketches – use sketches to indicate the locations from which specimens were collected (e.g. Fig. 11.1).

Field sketching – take advantage of elevated vantage points (e.g. cliff tops) for sketching 'maps' of features below.

1. Draw the broad outline of the feature(s), for example the outline of the cliff in Fig. 11.1.
2. Add the important details within the outline.
3. Add shading to indicate, for example, the slope of the land surface (if relevant).
4. Label the sketch or map and include a scale.

Geological field sketches may often include the use of diagrammatic symbols to indicate the presence of different rock types (e.g. Fig. 11.1). Others avoid diagrammatic representations and use shading to delineate the detail of rock structures (e.g. Fig. 11.2).

When drawing in the field it is very important to work in a comfortable posture since you may need to remain in that position for some time. Usually a sitting position is the most practical.

You will seldom produce a map onto a blank sheet of paper. Usually it is most practical to draw the feature of interest directly onto a copy of a 1:10 000 topographic map as a base (see Chapter 29). Note that geological and geomorphological mapping are specialist tasks beyond the scope of this book.

Fig. 11.2 Example of a geological field sketch using shading (Hutton's Unconformity, Isle of Arran). Whilst this is a good sketch, note that the original did not include a scale! (Reproduced from *Geological Magazine*, 90, p. 406, 1953.)

Apparatus diagrams

Here, your aim is to portray the components of some experimental set-up as a diagram (Fig. 11.3). Note that these figures are normally drawn as a section rather than a perspective drawing. Also, you may be more concerned with the relationship between parts than with showing them to a uniform scale. For example, in Fig. 11.3, the leaf clamp (LC) is exaggerated in size compared to other components so its internal detail can be shown.

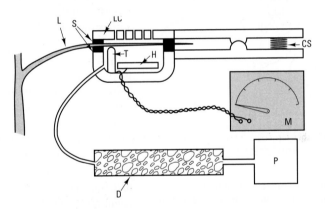

Fig. 11.3 Two-dimensional apparatus diagram of a diffusion porometer (not drawn to uniform scale). Note the use of letters to simplify labelling – these should be explained in the figure legend (e.g. L = leaf, P = pump).

Non-numerical charts

The main purpose of a non-numerical chart is to organize information (e.g. Fig. 11.4). You can use charts to communicate complex ideas, procedures or lists of facts by simplifying, grouping and appropriate layout. In environmental science, they are particularly useful for illustrating cycles and organizational hierarchies. Flowcharts (e.g. Fig. 15.6) are a specialized form. To be effective, charts must be logically organized. A good chart should clarify the parts and their relationships and its presentation should be simple, clear and visually pleasing. Make several rough sketches with different arrangements before deciding on the final version. You should use appropriate words or symbols to denote the components and link them with lines or arrows to show sequences or inter-relationships. Computer software packages can be used to enhance the quality of presentation.

Charts – the term 'chart' is often loosely applied to bathymetric maps as used for navigation purposes (see Chapter 29). Take care to avoid possible confusion.

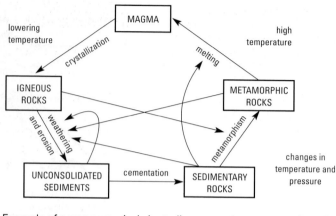

Fig. 11.4 Example of a non-numerical chart: diagrammatic representation of the rock cycle.

Numerical charts

These are used to display numerical information (data) in a form that is easily assimilated. Chapter 36 covers the main types of graph and how they should be constructed.

Morphological diagrams

The objective of a morphological diagram is to provide a stylized representation, typically of a living organism or a fossil, indicating the main surface features (Fig. 11.5). The use of shading should generally be avoided, unless it is essential to highlight a particular feature. Such diagrams should be fully labelled and notes added where relevant. The main problem you are likely to encounter is keeping the different parts in proportion to each other – using construction lines and frames (see below) can solve this. Remember that some 'artistic licence' is possible, allowing you to merge features seen on different specimens, or show, for example, the inside or underside of one of the parts.

Continuous tone drawings

Continuous tone drawings are more refined versions of morphological diagrams where shading is used to give a pictorial representation providing fine detail and realism (Fig. 11.6). These are generally used only for presentation work and are not normally expected from students. A properly taken photograph (Chapter 27) is often more appropriate and less time-consuming.

Steps towards drawing a good diagram

To produce good figures, both planning and careful execution are needed (Box 11.1).

Planning

The first stage of any drawing is to decide exactly what to draw – this may seem obvious, but until you have focused your thoughts, you will not be able to decide on the answers to the following questions:

- What is the purpose of the drawing?
- What type of drawing is required?
- What should go into it?
- What magnification or reduction is required?

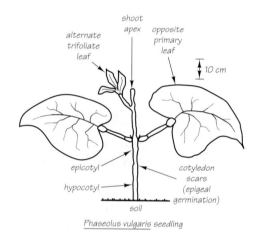

Fig. 11.5 Morphological diagram of a French bean seedling. *Phaseolus vulgaris* L. Note the lack of shading compared with Fig. 11.6.

Fig. 11.6 Continuous tone drawing of a French bean seedling, *Phaseolus vulgaris* L. Compare with Fig. 11.5.

Producing labels for diagrams in formal reports – create the text using a word processor and high-quality printer. This can then be stuck on your diagram using e.g. Prittstick®, taking care to keep all the text parallel. If the diagram is now photocopied or photographed with high contrast, the use of different pieces of paper cannot be detected.

Using construction lines – these are vital for producing well-proportioned drawings.

Once these decisions are made, you can determine the position and size of your diagram. Your diagram should be as large as possible, but remember to leave space for legends and labels.

Materials

Most diagrams for practicals are drawn in pencil, to allow corrections to be made. Propelling pencils are valuable for ensuring constant line thickness but they do not allow you the flexibility to vary line thickness as you can by changing the angle you hold an ordinary pencil. If you prefer to use an ordinary pencil, sharpen it frequently. Invest in a good quality eraser – those of poor quality tend to smudge badly – and frequently clean its working surface on a spare piece of paper. Always use plain paper for drawing, and if you are asked to supply your own, make sure it is of good quality. Use pen and ink to create line drawings for illustration purposes in posters, project reports, etc. Such diagrams should be in black and white only. Computer drawing programs can also provide good quality output suitable for these tasks.

(a)
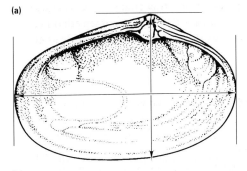

(b)
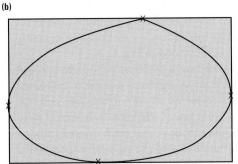

Fig. 11.7 How to draw an object in proportion: (a) determine linear dimensions; (b) construct a frame and outline, using reference points (x) determined from scaled measurements of the original specimen.

Constructing a diagram

1. Draw a faint rectangle in pencil to show the figure boundaries.
2. Draw very faint 'construction lines' using a 2H pencil with a sharp point to get the basic proportions and outlines correct before progressing. These should be erased once the basic drawing is complete. To lay in construction lines, use a ruler or pair of dividers to determine the actual proportions of the object to be drawn and then, using these dimensions, construct a scaled frame to allow further important reference points to be located (Fig. 11.7).
3. Draw the main outlines faintly with your 2H pencil. When satisfied, go over the lines with a sharp HB or 2B pencil. Draw firm, continuous lines, not hesitant, scratchy ones and make sure that junctions between lines are properly drawn. If you need to distinguish between different

Drawing and diagrams

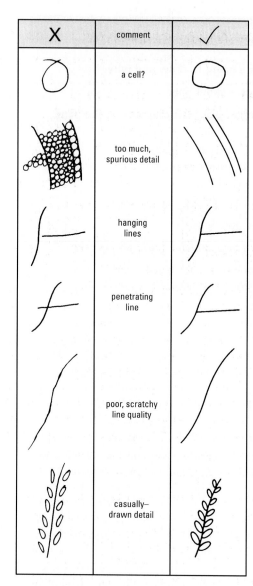

X	comment	✓
	a cell?	
	too much, spurious detail	
	hanging lines	
	penetrating line	
	poor, scratchy line quality	
	casually–drawn detail	

Fig. 11.8 Examples of common errors in drawings. Most of these mistakes are due to lack of care or attention to detail – easily solved!

regions within your drawing, use hatching or stippling (but not shading), and avoid drawing spurious detail (see Fig. 11.8). Always draw what you see, rather than what you think you should see, and seek advice at an early stage if you can't see a particular structure, or if you think your specimen is atypical. When drawing a specimen that is symmetrical or which contains repeated forms, it will save time if you draw its outline, and only provide detail in one of the replicated elements.

4. Complete your drawing by adding labels. This requires you to interpret your observations and helps you to remember what the structures look like. Careful and accurate labelling is as important as the drawing itself. It should be done clearly and neatly using either radiating or horizontal lines ending in arrowheads or large dots to indicate exact label references. The lines should not cross. Labels should be written clearly in one orientation, so that they can be read without needing to turn the paper. Annotations (short explanatory notes in brackets below the labels) are strongly recommended – regard them as notes to yourself about what you have seen, or what has been pointed out by tutors. For practical work, use a pencil for labelling in case your demonstrator or teacher corrects your work.

5. Add a title, a scale or magnification factor and a legend. The legend should provide all relevant information (see Box 11.1).

Drawing from the microscope

Begin by positioning the paper beside your drawing hand and use the 'opposite' eye for examining the specimen; thus for a right-handed person, the paper is placed on the right of the microscope and you use your left eye. With a binocular microscope, use only one of the eyepieces; if you keep both eyes open, it is possible with practice to learn to draw and see the page with one eye while observing the specimen with the other. For specimens that need to be drawn very accurately in project work, projection devices such as the *camera lucida* may be required.

Avoiding mistakes

There are four main categories of error in student diagrams:

- Incorrect positioning and proportions – solve these problems by following steps 1–3 above.
- Forgetting to add a title, scale or a full set of labels – use a checklist like that provided in Box 11.1 to ensure your diagram is complete.
- Untidiness in presentation – avoid this type of error by using the correct materials as discussed above and by taking care – untidiness is frequently due to lack of attention to detail, as illustrated in Fig. 11.8.
- Factual inaccuracies – this kind of mistake is the most important, and will lose you most marks. Avoiding these errors requires preparation before the practical, so that you know more about what you are drawing and, for instance, have a good idea which parts are which *before* you start. Try to focus clearly on the objectives of the practical, and listen carefully to any tips given by your tutors, which may relate to the particular specimen(s) available on that day rather than to those in your notes or texts.

Finally, it is important to realize that you cannot expect drawing skills to develop overnight. This skill, like any other, requires much practice. Try to learn from any feedback your tutor may provide, and if your marks are consistently low without explanation, seek advice.

12 Scientific method and experimental design

Definition

Hypothesis – One possible explanation for an observed event. A mechanistic hypothesis is one based on some intuition about the mechanism underlying a phenomenon.

Science is a systematized body of knowledge derived from observation and experiment. A scientist makes observations and attempts to explain them; these tentative explanations are called hypotheses and their validity is tested by systematically forming and rejecting alternative explanations.

Many branches of environmental science involve observational science. Here, structures and systems are usually investigated in as natural a condition as possible. This is an extremely valuable form of knowledge, but it rarely explains the mechanisms of the phenomena observed. The appropriate conditions with which to test a mechanistic hypothesis may take a long time to turn up or may only occur in a location that differs in other crucial ways. In experimental science, the process of obtaining relevant conditions is speeded up and controlled by the investigator.

An experiment is a contrived situation designed to test one or more hypotheses. Any hypothesis that cannot be rejected from the results of an experiment is provisionally accepted. This 'sieve' effect leaves us with a set of current explanations for our observations. These explanations are not permanent and may be rejected on the basis of a future investigation. A hypothesis that has withstood many such tests and has been shown to allow predictions to be made is known as a theory, and a theory may generate such confidence through its predictive abilities to be known as a law (Fig. 12.1).

Observations are a prelude to experimentation, but they are preconditioned by a framework of peripheral knowledge. While there is an element of luck in being at the right place and time to make important observations, as Pasteur stated, 'chance favours only the prepared mind'. A fault in scientific method is that the design of the experiment and choice of method may influence the outcome – the decisions involved may not be as objective as some scientists assume. Another flaw is that radical alternative hypotheses may be overlooked in favour of a modification to the original hypothesis, and yet just such leaps in thinking have frequently been required before great scientific advances.

No hypothesis can ever be rejected with certainty. Statistics allow us to quantify as vanishingly small the probability of an erroneous conclusion, but we are nevertheless left in the position of never being 100% certain that we have rejected all relevant alternative hypotheses, nor 100% certain that our decision to reject some alternative hypotheses was correct! However, despite these problems, experimental science has yielded and continues to yield many important findings.

KEY POINT The fallibility of scientific 'facts' is essential to grasp. No explanation can ever be 100% certain as it is always possible for a new alternative hypothesis to be generated. Our understanding of environmental systems changes all the time as new observations and methods force old hypotheses to be retested.

Quantitative hypotheses, those involving a mathematical description of the system, are very important in environmental science. They can be formulated concisely by mathematical models. Formulating models is often useful because it forces deeper thought about mechanisms and encourages simplification of the system. A mathematical model:

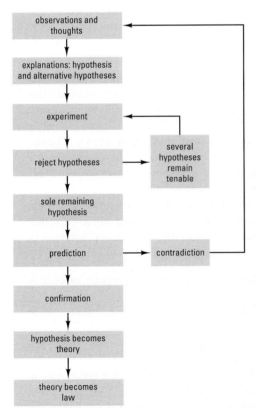

Fig. 12.1 How scientific investigations proceed.

- is inherently testable through experiment;
- identifies areas where information is lacking or uncertain;
- encapsulates many observations;
- allows you to predict the behaviour of the system.

Remember, however, that assumptions and simplifications required to create a model may result in it being unrealistic. Further, the results obtained from any model are only as good as the information put into it.

The terminology of experimentation

In many experiments, the aim is to provide evidence for causality. If x causes y, we expect, repeatably, to find that a change in x results in a change in y. Hence, the ideal experiment of this kind involves measurement of y, the dependent (measured) variable, at one or more values of x, the independent variable, and subsequent demonstration of some relationship between them. Experiments therefore involve comparisons of the results of treatments – changes in the independent variable as applied to an experimental subject. The change is engineered by the experimenter under controlled conditions.

Subjects given the same treatment are known as replicates (they are also called plots in some situations). A block is a grouping of replicates or plots. The blocks are contained in a field, i.e. the whole area (or time) available for the experiment (Fig. 12.2).

Why you need to control variables in experiments

Interpretation of experiments is seldom clear-cut because uncontrolled variables always change when treatments are given.

Confounding variables

These increase or decrease systematically as the independent variable increases or decreases. Their effects are known as systematic variation. This form of variation can be disentangled from that caused directly by treatments by incorporating appropriate controls in the experiment. A control is really just another treatment where a potentially confounding variable is adjusted so that its effects, if any, can be taken into account. The results from a control may therefore allow an alternative hypothesis to be rejected. There are many potential controls for any experiment.

The consequence of systematic variation is that you can never be certain that the treatment, and the treatment alone, has caused an observed result. By careful design, you can, however, 'minimize the uncertainty' involved in your conclusion. Methods available include:

- Ensuring, through experimental design, that the independent variable is the only major factor that changes in any treatment.
- Incorporating appropriate controls to show that potential confounding variables have little or no effect.
- Selecting experimental subjects randomly to cancel out systematic variation arising from biased selection.
- Matching or pairing individuals among treatments so that differences in response due to their initial status are eliminated.
- Arranging subjects and treatments randomly so that responses to systematic differences in conditions do not influence the results.

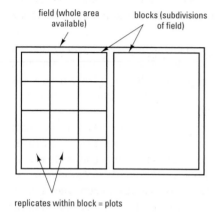

field (whole area available)

blocks (subdivisions of field)

replicates within block = plots

Fig. 12.2 Terminology and physical arrangement of elements in an experiment. Each block should contain the complete range of treatments (treatments may be replicated more than once in each block).

- Ensuring that experimental conditions are uniform so that responses to systematic differences in conditions are minimized. When attempting this, beware 'edge effects' where subjects on the periphery of the layout receive substantially different conditions from those in the centre.

> One way you can reduce edge effects is to incorporate a 'buffer zone' of untreated subjects around the experiment proper.

Nuisance variables

These are uncontrolled variables which cause differences in the value of y independently of the value of x, resulting in random variation. Environmental science is characterized by the high number of nuisance variables that are found and their relatively great influence on results: environmental data tend to have large errors! To reduce and assess the consequences of nuisance variables:

- incorporate replicates to allow random variation to be quantified;
- choose subjects that are as similar as possible;
- control random fluctuations in environmental conditions.

Constraints on experimental design

Box 12.1 outlines the important stages in designing an experiment. At an early stage, you should find out how resources may constrain the design. For example, limits may be set by availability of subjects, cost of treatment, availability of a chemical or bench space. Logistics may be a factor (e.g. time taken to record or analyse data).

> Evaluating design constraints – a good way to do this is by processing an individual subject through the experimental procedures – a 'preliminary run' can help to identify potential difficulties.

Your equipment or facilities may affect design because you cannot regulate conditions as well as you might desire. For example, you may be unable to ensure that temperature and lighting are equal within the experimental area or you may have to accept a great deal of initial variability if your material is collected from the wild. This problem is especially acute for experiments carried out in the field.

Use of replicates

Replicate results show how variable the response is within treatments. They allow you to compare the differences among treatments in the context of the variability within treatments – you can do this via statistical tests such as analysis of variance (Chapter 40). Larger sample sizes tend to increase the precision of estimates of statistical parameters and increase the chances of showing a significant difference between treatments if one exists. For statistical reasons (weighting, ease of calculation, fitting data to certain tests), it is best to keep the number of replicates even. Remember that the degree of independence of replicates is important: sub-samples cannot act as replicate samples – they tell you about variability in the measurement method but not in the quantity being measured.

> Deciding the number of replicates in each treatment – try to:
>
> - maximize the number of replicates in each treatment;
> - make the number of replicates even.

If the total number of replicates available for an experiment is limited by resources, you may need to compromise between the number of treatments and the number of replicates per treatment. Statistics can help here, for it is possible to work out the minimum number of replicates you would need to show a certain difference between pairs of means (say 10%) at a specified level of significance (say $P = 0.05$). For this, you need to obtain a prior estimate of variability within treatments (see Sokal and Rohlf, 1994).

Box 12.1 Checklist for designing and executing an experiment

1. **Preliminaries**

   (a) **Read background material** and decide on a subject area to investigate.

   (b) **Formulate a simple hypothesis to test.** It is preferable to have a clear answer to one question than to be uncertain about several questions.

   (c) **Decide which dependent variable you are going to measure and how:** is it relevant to the problem? Can you measure it accurately, precisely and without bias?

   (d) **Think about and plan the statistical analysis of your results.** Will this affect your design?

2. **Designing**

   (a) **Find out the limitations on your resources.**

   (b) **Choose treatments which alter the minimum of confounding variables.**

   (c) **Incorporate as many effective controls as possible.**

   (d) **Keep the number of replicates as high as is feasible.**

   (e) **Ensure that the same number of replicates is present in each treatment.**

   (f) **Use effective randomization and blocking arrangements.**

3. **Planning**

   (a) **List all the materials you will need.** Order any chemicals and make up solutions; grow, collect or breed any experimental subjects you require; check equipment is available.

   (b) **Organize space and/or time** in which to do the experiment.

   (c) **Account for the time taken to apply treatments and record results.** Make out a timesheet if things will be hectic.

4. **Carrying out the experiment**

   (a) **Record the results and make careful notes of everything you do.** Make additional observations to those planned if interesting things happen.

   (b) **Repeat experiment** if time and resources allow.

5. **Analysing**

   (a) **Graph data as soon as possible** (during the experiment if you can). This will allow you to visualize what has happened and make adjustments to the design (e.g. timing of measurements).

   (b) **Carry out the planned statistical analysis.**

   (c) **Jot down conclusions and new hypotheses** arising from the experiment.

Example If you knew that soil type varied in a graded fashion across a field, you might arrange blocks to be long thin rectangles at right angles to the gradient to ensure conditions within the block were as even as possible.

Randomization of treatments

The two aspects of randomization you must consider are:

- positioning of treatments within experimental blocks;
- allocation of treatments to the experimental subjects.

For relatively simple experiments, you can adopt a completely randomized design; here, the position and treatment assigned to any subject is defined randomly. You can draw lots, use a random number generator on a calculator, or use the random number tables which can be found in most books of statistical tables (see Box 12.2).

A completely randomized layout has the advantage of simplicity but cannot show how confounding variables alter in space or time. This information can be obtained if you use a blocked design in which the degree of randomization is restricted. Here, the experimental space or time is divided into blocks, each of which accommodates the complete set of treatments (Fig. 12.2). When analysed appropriately, the results for the blocks can be compared to test for differences in the confounding variables and these effects can be separated out from the effects of the treatments. The size and shape (or timing) of the block you choose is important: besides being able to accommodate the number of replicates desired, the suspected confounding variable should be relatively uniform within the block.

Box 12.2 How to use random number tables to assign subjects to positions and treatments

This is one method of many that could be used. It requires two sets of n random numbers – where n is the total number of subjects used.

1. **Number the subjects in any arbitrary order** but in such a way that you know which is which (i.e. mark or tag them).

2. **Decide how treatments will be assigned**, e.g. first five subjects selected treatment A; second five – treatment B, etc.

3. **Use the first set of random numbers in the sequence obtained to identify subjects and allocate them to treatment groups** in order of selection as decided in (2).

4. **Map the positions for subjects in the block or field. Assign numbers to these positions using the second set of random numbers**, working through the positions in some arbitrary order, e.g. top left to bottom right.

5. **Match the original numbers given to subjects with the position numbers.**

To obtain a sequence of random numbers

1. **Decide on the range of random numbers you need.**

2. **Decide how you wish to sample the random number tables** (e.g. column by column and top to bottom) and your starting point.

3. **Moving in the selected manner, read the sequence of numbers until you come to a group that fits your needs** (e.g. in the sequence 978186, 18 represents a number between 1 and 20). Write this down and continue sampling until you get a new number. If a number is repeated, ignore it. Small numbers need to have the appropriate number of zeros preceding (e.g. $5 = 05$ for a range in the tens, $21 = 021$ for a range in the hundreds).

4. **When you come to the last number required, you don't need to sample any more:** simply write it down.

Example: You find the following random number sequence in a table and wish to select numbers between 1 and 10 from it.

9059146823   4862925166   1063260345
1277423810   9948040676   6430247598
8357945137   2490145183   5946242208
6588812379   2325701558   3260726568

Working left to right and top to bottom, the order of numbers found is 5, 10, 3, 9, 4, 6, 2, 1, 8, 7 as indicated by bold type. If the table is sampled by working right to left from bottom to top, the order is 6, 10, 7, 2, 9, 3, 4, 8, 1, 5.

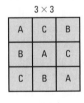
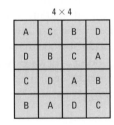

Fig. 12.3 Examples of Latin square arrangements for 3 and 4 treatments. Letters indicate treatments; the number of possible arrangements for each size of square increases greatly as the size increases.

A Latin square is a method of placing treatments so that they appear in a balanced fashion within a square block or field. Treatments appear once in each column and row (see Fig. 12.3), so the effects of confounding variables can be 'cancelled out' in two directions at right angles to each other. This is effective if there is a smooth gradient in some confounding variable over the field. It is less useful if the variable has a patchy distribution, where a randomized block design might be better.

Latin square designs are useful in serial experiments where different treatments are given to the same subjects in a sequence (e.g. Fig. 12.4). A disadvantage of Latin squares is the fact that the number of plots is equal to the number of replicates, so increases in the number of replicates can only be made by the use of further Latin squares.

Pairing and matching subjects

The paired comparison is a special case of blocking used to reduce systematic variation when there are two treatments. Examples of its use are:

- 'Before and after' comparison. Here, the pairing removes variability arising from the initial state of the subjects, e.g. weight loss of a crystal on dissolution, where the weight loss may depend on the initial weight.
- Application of a treatment and control to parts of the same subject or to closely related subjects. This allows comparison without complications

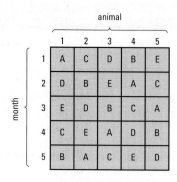

Fig. 12.4 Example of how to use a Latin square design to arrange sequential treatments. The experimenter wishes to test the effect of drugs A–E on weight gain, but only has five animals available. Each animal is fed on control diet for the first 3 weeks of each month, then on control diet plus drug for the last week. Weights are taken at start and finish of each treatment. Each animal receives all treatments.

Definition

Interaction – where the effect of treatments given together is greater or less than the sum of their individual effects.

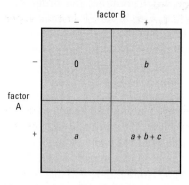

Fig. 12.5 Design of a simple multifactorial experiment. Factors A and B have effects *a* and *b* when applied alone. When both are applied together, the effect is denoted by $a + b + c$.

- If $c = 0$, there is no interaction (e.g. $2 + 2 + c = 4$).
- If c is positive, there is a positive interaction (synergism) between A and B (e.g. $2 + 2 + c = 5$).
- If c is negative, there is a negative interaction (antagonism) between A and B (e.g. $2 + 2 + c = 3$).

It is good practice to report how many times your experiments were repeated (in Materials and Methods); in the Results section, you should add a statement saying that the illustrated experiment is representative.

arising from different origin of subjects, e.g. drug or placebo given to sibling rats, virus-containing or control solution swabbed on left or right halves of a leaf.

- Application of treatment and control under shared conditions. This allows comparison without complications arising from different environment of subjects, e.g. rats in a cage, plants in a pot.

Matched samples represent a restriction on randomization where you make a balanced selection of subjects for treatments on the basis of some attribute or attributes that may influence results, e.g. age, sex, prior history. The effect of matching should be to 'cancel out' the unwanted source(s) of variation. Disadvantages include the subjective element in choice of character(s) to be balanced, inexact matching of quantitative characteristics, the time matching takes and possible wastage of unmatched subjects.

When analysed statistically, both paired comparisons and matched samples can show up differences between treatments that might otherwise be rejected on the basis of a fully randomized design, but note that the statistical analysis may be different.

Multifactorial experiments

The simplest experiments are those in which one treatment (factor) is applied at a time to the subjects. This approach is likely to give clear-cut answers, but it could be criticized for lacking realism. In particular, it cannot take account of interactions among two or more conditions that are likely to occur in real life. A multifactorial experiment (Fig. 12.5) is an attempt to do this; the interactions among treatments can be analysed by specialized statistics.

Multifactorial experiments are economical on resources because of 'hidden replication'. This arises when two or more treatments are given to a subject because the result acts statistically as a replicate for each treatment. Choice of relevant treatments to combine is important in multifactorial experiments; for instance, an interaction may be present at certain concentrations of a chemical but not at others (perhaps because the response is saturated). It is also important that the measurement scale for the response is consistent, otherwise spurious interactions may occur. Beware when planning a multifactorial experiment that the numbers of replicates do not get out of hand: you may have to restrict the treatments to 'plus' or 'minus' the factor of interest (as in Fig. 12.5).

Repetition of experiments

Even if your experiment is well designed and analysed, only limited conclusions can be made. Firstly, what you can say is valid for a particular place and time, with a particular investigator, experimental subject and method of applying treatments. Secondly, if your results were significant at the 5% level of probability (p. 217), there is still an approximately one-in-twenty chance that the results did arise by chance. To guard against these possibilities, it is important that experiments are repeated. Ideally, this would be done by an independent scientist with independent materials. However, it makes sense to repeat work yourself so that you can have full confidence in your conclusions. Many scientists recommend that experiments are done three times in total, but this may not be possible in undergraduate work!

13 Making notes of practical work

When carrying out advanced lab work or research projects, you will need to master the important skill of managing data and observations and learn how to keep a record of your studies in a lab book. This is important for the following reasons:

- An accurate and neat record helps when using information later, perhaps for exam purposes or when writing a report.
- It allows you to practise important skills such as scientific writing, drawing diagrams, preparing graphs and tables and interpreting results.
- Analysing and writing up your data as you go along prevents a backlog at the end of your study time.
- You can show your work to a future employer to prove you have developed the skills necessary for writing up properly; in industry, this is vital so that others in your team can interpret and develop your work.

KEY POINT **A good set of lab notes should:**

- **outline the purpose of your experiment or observation;**
- **set down all the information required to describe your materials and methods;**
- **record all relevant information about your results or observations and provide a visual representation of the data;**
- **note your immediate conclusions and suggestions for further experiments.**

Collecting and recording primary data

Individual observations (e.g. temperature) can be recorded in the text of your notes, but tables are the most convenient way to collect large amounts of information. When preparing a table for data collection, you should:

Recording primary data – never be tempted to jot down data on scraps of paper: you are likely to lose them, or to forget what individual values mean.

1. Use a concise title or a numbered code for cross referencing.
2. Decide on the number of variables to be measured and their relationship with each other and lay out the table appropriately:
   (a) The first column of your table should show values of the independent (controlled) variable, with subsequent columns for the individual (measured) values for each replicate or sample.
   (b) If several variables are measured for the same organism or sample, each should be given a row.
   (c) In time-course studies, put the replicates as columns grouped according to treatment, with the rows relating to different times.
3. Make sure the arrangement reflects the order in which the values will be collected. Your table should be designed to make the recording process as straightforward as possible, to minimize the possibility of mistakes. For final presentation, a different arrangement may be best (Chapter 37).

Designing a table for data collection – make sure there is sufficient space in each column for the values – if in doubt, err on the generous side.

4. Consider whether additional columns are required for subsequent calculations. Create a separate column for each mathematical manipulation, so the step-by-step calculations are clearly visible. Use a computer spreadsheet (p. 231) if you are manipulating lots of data.

5. Use a pencil to record data so that mistakes can be easily corrected.
6. Take sufficient time to record quantitative data unambiguously – use large clear numbers, making sure that individual numerals cannot be confused.
7. Record numerical data to an appropriate number of significant figures, reflecting the accuracy and precision of your measurement (p. 41). Do not round off data values, as this might affect the subsequent analysis of your data.
8. Record discrete or grouped data as a tally chart (see p. 191), each row showing the possible values or classes of the variable. Providing tally marks are of consistent size and spacing, this method has the advantage of providing an 'instant' frequency distribution chart.
9. Prepare duplicated recording tables if your experiments or observations will be repeated.
10. Explain any unusual data values or observations in a footnote. Don't rely on your memory.

Recording details of project work

The recommended system is one where you make a dual record.

Primary record

Choosing a notebook – a spiral-bound notebook is good for making a primary record – it lies conveniently open on the bench and provides a simple method of dealing with major mistakes!

The primary record is made at the bench or in the field. In this, you must concentrate on the detail of materials, methods and results. Include information that would not be used elsewhere, but which might prove useful in error tracing: for example, if you note how a solution was made up (exact volumes and weights used rather than concentration alone), this could reveal whether a miscalculation had been the cause of a rogue result. Note the origin, type and state of the chemicals and organism(s) used. Make rough diagrams to show the arrangement of replicates, equipment, etc. If you are forced to use loose paper to record data, make sure each sheet is dated and taped to your lab book, collected in a ring binder, or attached together with a treasury tag. The same applies to traces, printouts and graphs.

The basic order of the primary record should mirror that of a research report (see p. 257), including: the title and date, brief introduction, comprehensive materials and methods, the data and short conclusions.

Secondary record

You should make a secondary record concurrently or later in a bound book and it ought to be neater, in both organization and presentation. This book will be used when discussing results with your supervisor, and when writing up a report or thesis, and may be part of your course assessment. While these notes should retain the essential features of the primary record, they should be more concise and the emphasis should move towards analysis of the data. Outline the aims more carefully at the start and link the results to others in a series (e.g. 'Following the results of Expt. D24, I decided to test whether...'). You should present data in an easily digested form, e.g. as tables of means or as summary graphs. Use appropriate statistical tests (Chapter 40) to support your analysis of the results. The choice of a bound book ensures that data are not easily lost.

Points to note

The dual method of recording deals with the inevitable untidiness of notes taken at the bench or in the field; these often have to be made rapidly, in awkward positions and in a generally complex environment. Writing a second, neater version forces you to consider again details that might have been overlooked in the primary record and provides a duplicate in case of loss or damage.

The diary aspect of the record can be used to establish precedence (e.g. for patentable research where it can be important to 'minute' where and when an idea arose and whose it was); for error tracing (e.g. you might be able to find patterns in the work affecting the results); or even for justifying your activities to a supervisor.

If you find it difficult to decide on the amount of detail required in Materials and Methods, the basic ground rule is to record enough information to allow a reasonably competent scientist to repeat your work exactly. You must tread a line between the extremes of pedantic, irrelevant detail and the omission of information essential for a proper interpretation of the data – better perhaps to err on the side of extra detail to begin with. An experienced worker can tell you which subtle shifts in technique are important (e.g. batch numbers for an important chemical, or when a new stock solution is made up and used). Many important scientific advances have been made because of careful observation and record taking and because coincident data were recorded that did not seem of immediate value.

When creating a primary record, take care not to lose any of the information content of the data: for instance, if you only write down means and not individual values, this may affect your ability to carry out subsequent statistical analyses.

There are numerous ways to reduce the labour of keeping a record. Don't repeat Materials and Methods for a series of similar experiments; use devices such as 'method as for Expt. B4'. A photocopy might suffice if the method is derived from a text or article (check with supervisor). To save time, make up and copy a checklist in which details such as chemical batch numbers can be entered.

Always analyse and think about data immediately after collecting them as this may influence your subsequent activities. Particularly valuable is a graphical indication of what has happened. Carry out statistical analyses before moving on to the next procedure because apparent differences among variables may not turn out to be statistically significant when tested. Write down any conclusions you make while analysing your data: sometimes those which seem obvious at the time of doing the work are forgotten when the time comes to write up a report or thesis. Likewise, ideas for further studies may occur to you and a note of these may prove valuable later. Even if your study appears to be a failure, suggestions as to the likely reasons might prove useful.

Special requirements for fieldwork

The main problems you will encounter in the field are the effects of the weather while taking a primary record and the distance you might be from a suitable place to make a neat secondary record. Wind, rain and cold temperatures are not conducive to neat note-taking and you should be prepared for the worst possible conditions at all times. Make sure your clothing allows you to feel comfortable while recording data (see Chapter 2).

Making notes of practical work

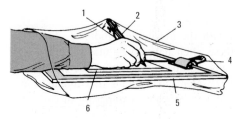

Fig. 13.1 Simple but effective method for keeping notes dry in the field.

1. string attaching pencil to clip
2. pencil (not pen) writes on damp paper
3. transparent plastic bag
4. bulldog clip
5. hardboard (at least 31 × 22 cm for A4 paper)
6. record sheet.

Waterproof notebooks – notebooks with waterproof paper are available (for example the 'Aquascribe' brand supplied by Hawkins and Mainwaring, Ltd, Newark, Notts). These are relatively expensive, but you can re-use them by rubbing out.

The simplest method of protecting a field notebook is to enclose it in a clear polythene bag large enough for you to take notes inside (Fig. 13.1). Alternatively, you could use a clipboard with a waterproof cover to shield your notes or a special notebook with a waterproof cover. When selecting a field notebook, choose a small size – the dimensions of outside pockets may dictate the upper size limit.

If recording results and observations outdoors:

- Use a pencil as ink pens such as ball-points smudge in wet conditions, are temperamental in the cold and may not work at awkward angles. Don't forget to take a sharpener.
- Prepare well to enhance the speed and quality of your field note-taking – the date and site details can be written down before setting out and tables can be made out ready for data entry.
- Transcribe field notes to a duplicate primary record at your base each time you return there. There is a very real risk of your losing or damaging a field notebook. Also, poor weather may prevent full note-taking and the necessary extra details should be written up while fresh in your memory.
- Consider using a tape recorder rather than a notebook, in which case transcription into written form should also take place while your memory is fresh in case the sound quality is poor.
- Use photographs to set data in context, when appropriate. Develop photographs as soon as possible to check their suitability. Consider using a Polaroid® or digital camera when the suitability of a record must be guaranteed.

Field data may be logged automatically, stored temporarily in the instrument's electronic memory, and downloaded to a portable computer ('data logger') when convenient. The information is then transferred to a data bank back at base. If you are using this system, make back up copies of each period's data as soon as possible – if the recording instrument's memory is cleared or overwritten after reading there may be no recourse if the logging machine fails.

Using communal records

If working with a research team, you may need to use their communal databases. These avoid duplication of effort and ensure uniformity in techniques. They may also form part of the legal safety requirements for lab work. You will be expected to use the databases carefully and contribute to them properly. They might include:

- a shared notebook of common techniques (like how to make up media or solutions);
- a set of simplified step-by-step instructions for use of equipment. Manuals are often complex and poorly written and it may help to redraft them, incorporating any differences in procedure adopted by the group;
- an alphabetical list of suppliers of equipment and consumables (perhaps held on a card index system);
- a list of chemicals required by the group and where they are stored;
- the risk assessment sheets for dangerous procedures (p. 5);
- the record book detailing the use of radioisotopes and their disposal.

14 Project work

Research projects are an important component of the final year syllabus for most degree programmes in environmental science, and shorter projects may also be carried out during courses in earlier years. Project work presents difficulties at many stages but can be extremely rewarding. The assessment of your project is likely to contribute significantly to your degree grade, so all aspects of this work should be approached in a thorough manner.

Deciding on a topic to study

Assuming you have a choice, this important decision should be researched carefully. Make appointments to visit possible supervisors and ask them for advice on topics that you find interesting. Use library texts and research papers to obtain further background information. Perhaps the most important criterion is whether the topic will sustain your interest over the whole period of the project. Other things to look for include:

- Opportunities to learn new skills. Ideally, you should attempt to gain experience and skills that you might be able to 'sell' to a potential employer.
- Ease of obtaining valid results. An ideal project provides a means to obtain 'guaranteed' data for your report, but also the chance to extend knowledge by doing genuinely novel research.
- Assistance. What help will be available to you during the project? A busy lab with many research students might provide a supportive environment should your potential supervisor be too busy to meet you often; on the other hand, a smaller lab may provide the opportunity for more personal interaction with your supervisor.
- Impact. It is not outside the bounds of possibility for undergraduate work to contribute to research papers. Your prospective supervisor can alert you to such opportunities.

Planning your work

As with any lengthy exercise, planning is required to make the best use of the time allocated. This is true on a daily basis as well as over the entire period of the project. It is especially important not to underestimate the time it will take to write and produce your thesis (see below). If you wish to benefit from feedback given by your supervisor, you should aim to have drafts in his/her hands in good time. Since a large proportion of marks will be allocated to the report, you should not rush its production.

If your Department requires you to write an interim report, look on this as an opportunity to clarify your thoughts and get some of the time-consuming preparative work out of the way. If not, you should set your own deadlines for producing drafts of the introduction, materials and methods section, etc.

Project work can be very time-consuming at times. Try not to neglect other aspects of your course – make sure your lecture notes are up to date and collect relevant supporting information as you go along.

The Internet as an information source – since many university departments have home pages on the World Wide Web, searches using relevant key words may indicate where research in your area is currently being carried out. Academics usually respond positively to e-mailed questions about their area of expertise.

Asking around – one of the best sources of information about supervisors, laboratories and projects is past students. Some of the postgraduates in your department may be products of your own system and they could provide an alternative source of advice.

Liaising with your supervisor(s) – this is essential if your work is to proceed efficiently. Specific meetings may be timetabled e.g. to discuss a term's progress, review your work plan or consider a draft introduction. Most supervisors also have an 'open-door' policy, allowing you to air current problems. Prepare well for all meetings: have a list of questions ready before the meeting; provide results in an easily digestible form (but take your lab or field notebook along); be clear about your future plans for work.

Project work

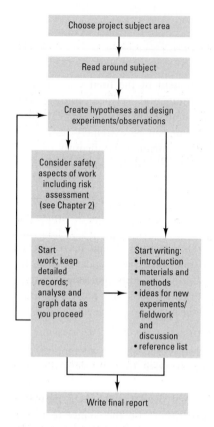

Fig. 14.1 Flowchart showing a recommended sequence of events in carrying out an undergraduate research project.

Getting started

Fig. 14.1 is a flowchart illustrating how a project might proceed; at the start, don't spend too long reading the literature and working out a lengthy programme of research. Get stuck in and do some practical work. There's no substitute for 'getting your hands dirty' for stimulating new ideas:

- even a 'failed' experiment will provide some useful information which may allow you to create a new or modified hypothesis;
- pilot studies may point out deficiencies in techniques that will need to be rectified;
- the experience will help you create a realistic plan of work.

Designing experiments or sampling procedures

Design of experiments is covered in Chapter 12, while sampling procedure is dealt with in Chapters 15–21. Avoid being too ambitious at the start of your work! It is generally best to work with a simple hypothesis and design your experiments or sampling around this. A small pilot experiment or test sample will highlight potential stumbling blocks including resource limitations, whether in materials or time or both.

Working in the laboratory or field

During your time as a project student, you are effectively a guest in your supervisor's laboratory.

- Be considerate – keep your 'area' tidy.
- Use instruments carefully – they could be worth more than you'd think. Careless use may invalidate calibration settings and ruin other people's work as well as your own. Do not use electronic equipment in wet weather unless manufacturers instructions specifically permit it.
- Do your homework on techniques you intend to use – there's less chance of making costly mistakes if you have a good background understanding of the methods you will be using.
- Always seek advice if you are unsure of what you are doing.

KEY POINT It is essential that you follow all the safety rules applying to the laboratory or field site. Make sure you are acquainted with all relevant procedures – normally there will be prominent warnings about these. If in doubt, ask!

Keeping notes and analysing your results

Tidy record keeping is often associated with good research, and you should follow the advice and hints given in Chapter 13. Try to keep copies of all files relating to your project. As you obtain results, you should always calculate, analyse and graph data as soon as you can (see Fig. 14.1). This can reveal aspects that may not be obvious in numerical or readout form. Don't be worried by negative results – these can sometimes be as useful as positive results if they allow you to eliminate hypotheses – and don't be dispirited if things do not work first time. Thomas Edison's maxim 'Genius is one per cent inspiration and ninety-nine per cent perspiration' certainly applies to research work!

Writing the report

The structure of scientific reports is dealt with in Chapter 48. The following advice concerns methods of accumulating relevant information.

Introduction This is a big piece of writing that can be very time-consuming. Therefore, the more work you can do on it early on, the better. You should allocate some time at the start for library work (without neglecting benchwork), so that you can build up a database of references (Chapter 45). While photocopying can be expensive, you will find it valuable to have copies of key reviews and references handy when writing away from the library. Discuss proposals for content and structure with your supervisor to make sure your effort is relevant. Leave space at the end for a section on aims and objectives. This is important to orientate readers (including assessors), but you may prefer to finalize the content after the results have been analysed!

Brushing up on IT skills – word processors and spreadsheets are extremely useful when producing a thesis. Chapters 42 and 43 detail key features of these programs. You might benefit from attending courses on the relevant programs or studying manuals or texts so that you can use them more efficiently.

Materials and methods You should note as many details as possible *when doing the experiment or making observations*. Don't rely on your memory or hope that the information will still be available when you come to write up. Even if it is, chasing these details might waste valuable time.

Results Show your supervisor graphed and tabulated versions of your data promptly. These can easily be produced using a spreadsheet (p. 231), but you should seek your supervisor's advice on whether the design and print quality is appropriate to be included in your thesis. You may wish to access a specialist graphics program to produce publishable-quality graphs and charts: allow some time for learning its idiosyncrasies! If you are producing a poster for assessment (Chapter 50), be sure to mock up the design well in advance. Similarly, think ahead about your needs for any seminar or poster you will present.

Using drawings and photographs – these can provide valuable records of sampling sites or experimental set-ups and could be useful in your report. Plan ahead and do the relevant work at the time of carrying out your research rather than afterwards. Refer to Chapters 11 and 27 for tips on technique.

Discussion Because this comes at the end of your thesis, and some parts can only be written after you have all the results in place, the temptation is to leave the discussion to last. This means that it can be rushed – not a good idea because of the weight attached by assessors to your analysis of data and thoughts about future experiments. It will help greatly if you keep notes of aims, conclusions and ideas for future work *as you go along* (Fig. 14.1). Another useful tip is to make notes of comparable data and conclusions from the literature as you read papers and reviews.

Acknowledgements Make a special place in your notebook for noting all those who have helped you carry out the work, for use when writing this section of the report.

References Because of the complex formats involved (p. 244), these can be tricky to type. To save time, process them in batches as you go along.

KEY POINT Make sure you are absolutely certain about the deadline for submitting your report and try to submit a few days before it. If you leave things until the last moment, you may find access to printers, photocopiers and binding machines is difficult.

Obtaining samples

15 Sampling strategies and statistics

The four main reasons for sampling are:

- economy, of time, finance and effort;
- the large size of many populations;
- the inaccessibility of some components of the population;
- the destructiveness of making the measurements.

Definitions

Sample – a finite part of a statistical population whose properties are studied to gain information about the whole.

Population – any specified, discrete collection of objects (units).

Do not include samples for which the appropriate data are not specified or available.

When working in the field, you are unlikely to be able to observe or measure all of the possible components of any population of variables in which you are interested. In practice, inferential statistics determined from a sub-set (sample) of the population are used to estimate relevant parameters for the entire population. Samples comprise data values for a particular variable (e.g. height), each recorded from an individual sampling unit (e.g. a person), the total sample comprising n units (e.g. $n = 50$ people) from the population under investigation (e.g. people from Dundee). The term 'replicate' can be applied to the measurements within a sample or to repeat samples (e.g. three samples of 50 people from Dundee).

Symbols are used to represent each type of sample statistic: these are given Roman character symbols, e.g. Y for the sample mean, while the equivalent population parameter is given a Greek symbol, e.g. μ for the population mean. When estimating population parameters from simple statistics, the sample size is important, larger sample sizes allowing greater statistical confidence. However, the optimum sample size is normally a balance between statistical and practical considerations.

Sampling has a number of dangers and the purpose of designing a sampling programme should be to minimize these. However, some potential error is the price we must pay for the convenience and savings that samples provide. A sample is intended to reflect the population from which it is drawn but this is subject to both error and bias (see also Chapter 8).

Sampling error is due solely to the particular units that happen to have been selected to comprise the sample. There are two basic causes for this:

- Chance. The only protection against this is to use a large enough sample so that the probability of any result occurring by chance is low enough to be considered insignificant.
- Bias – usually the result of poor sampling design or the personal prejudices/habits of the study designer or the data collector.

KEY POINT Non-sampling errors can also occur, due to inaccurate measurements resulting from malfunctioning instruments or poor procedures.

This chapter deals mainly with sampling in fieldwork situations but the same principles may also apply in a laboratory context (see Chapter 12).

Specifying the population being sampled

From the outset, it is important to provide a complete description of the population of data being sampled. Failure to do this will make your results difficult to interpret or to compare with other observations, including your own. Relevant factors you should specify include:

- geographical location;
- type of habitat;
- sample location and/or number, e.g. 4 of 20;
- date and time of sampling;
- name of collector;
- specifics relating to the condition of the sample, etc;
- note on method of preservation if relevant.

Such information might apply to the entire population or to the particular sampling unit. When populations of data are to be compared, ideally only the variable under consideration should differ if maximum significance is to be placed upon the analysis.

Deciding on a sampling strategy

Selecting a sample involves the formulation of rules and procedures, the sampling protocol, by which members of the population are included in the sample. The chosen sample is then measured using defined procedures to obtain the relevant data. Finally the information obtained is processed to calculate the appropriate sample and/or population statistics. Good sampling design takes into account all of these procedures to provide valid estimates of the features of the population(s) of data you are investigating.

There are two primary types of sampling appropriate for environmental science:

- Random sampling: the most important type of sample used for most scientific work.
- Purposeful sampling: selecting information-rich cases for in-depth study, primarily applicable to the study of human population behaviour.

Truly representative samples should normally be:

- Taken at random, or in a manner that ensures that every member of the population has an equal chance of being selected.
- Large enough to provide sufficient precision in estimating population parameters.
- Unbiased by the sampling procedure or equipment.

These requirements may well conflict, and there is rarely any unique answer to a sampling problem. You should, however, take great care to minimize bias and error otherwise the population parameters inferred from your samples will be unrealistic and this will invalidate your work and its conclusions.

KEY POINT Sampling involves choices on the part of the investigator. A 'sampling strategy' should allow you to obtain reliable and useful information about your particular population(s) while using your resources efficiently.

KEY POINT Sampling using questionnaires has its own set of sampling criteria, which are considered in Chapter 21.

The sampling protocol

You should decide on a sampling protocol before any investigation proceeds. The main aspects to be determined are:

- the positions of the sample points;
- the size and shape of the sample area;
- the number of sampling units in each sample.

Before this can be done, information is required about the likely distribution of the units under investigation. This can be random, uniform (homogeneous), patchy (contagious), stratified (homogeneous within sub-areas) or present as a gradient (Fig. 15.1). You might decide which type applies from a pilot study, published research or by analogy with other systems.

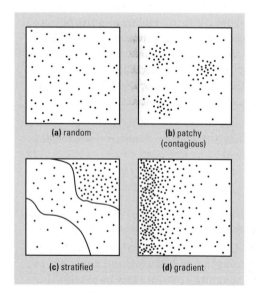

(a) random   (b) patchy (contagious)

(c) stratified   (d) gradient

Fig. 15.1 Types of distribution.

Definitions

Homogeneous – evenly distributed.

Patchy – showing clustered (contagious) distribution (e.g. numbers of parasites within hosts).

Gradient – a distribution that varies smoothly over the sampling area.

Stratified – showing a distribution with discrete levels or strata (e.g. algae on a rocky shore).

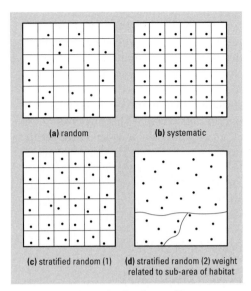

(a) random   (b) systematic

(c) stratified random (1)   (d) stratified random (2) weight related to sub-area of habitat

Fig. 15.2 Basic methods of sampling.

Locating your samples

The positions where sampling takes place can be determined either randomly, systematically or in some stratified manner (Fig. 15.2).

In simple random sampling (Fig. 15.2a), a 2-D co-ordinate grid is superimposed on the area to be investigated. The required number of grid reference data pairs is then obtained using random numbers (p. 59) and samples taken at these points. Every unit in the population thus has an equal chance of selection, but the area may not be covered evenly. This method is best if the distribution of units is homogeneous.

Systematic sampling (Fig. 15.2b) involves selecting the location of the first sampling position at random and then taking samples at fixed distances/ directions from this. This method has the advantage of simplicity and is often used where the intention is to map the data. The disadvantages are firstly, that the results can be biased if the interval between sampling positions coincides with some periodic distribution of the population, and secondly, that there is no reliable method of estimating the standard error of the sample mean.

Stratified random sampling may be preferable if you wish to avoid these disadvantages yet still ensure that each part of the area is represented (e.g. where you suspect there to be stratified microhabitats, as on a tidal seashore). The area is divided into sub-areas within which random sampling is carried out. These can be either constant in size (Fig 15.2c) or related to known features in the sampling area (Fig. 15.2d). If the latter, strata are normally sampled in proportion to their area. 'Weighting' is the general term applied to sampling procedures that allow the calculated statistics to represent the population better by accounting for differences in the distribution of the chosen character. You can analyse data from different strata by a one-way analysis of variance (see Chapter 40).

The dimensions of the sampling areas (units)

The main options when choosing a sampling regime are:

- point sampling (Fig. 15.3a);
- quadrat sampling (Fig. 15.3b);
- transect (traverse) sampling (Fig. 15.3c).

Quadrats are usually either circular or square. A circular quadrat has the advantage that its position (see Chapter 16) can be marked as a single point and the area defined by use of a tape measure, whereas a square quadrat may require marking at each corner. Transects (traverses) are generally used when it is difficult to move through the site to position quadrats. If a defined path is present, transects taken at right angles to the path (Fig. 15.3d) will save time in reaching the sites.

The problems involved in defining a sampling unit are illustrated by the selection of a quadrat for fieldwork sampling. Note first that the maximum number of independent sampling units (quadrats) is equal to the area occupied by the population under study (total theoretical sampling area) divided by the area of the sampling unit (quadrat area). The distribution and size of the units must be considered: it is obvious that you would require different-sized quadrats for trees in a forest than for daisies on a lawn. When the distribution is truly random, then all quadrat sizes are equally effective for estimating population parameters (assuming the total number of individual elements sampled is equal). If the distribution is patchy, a smaller quadrat size may be more effective than a larger one: too large an area might

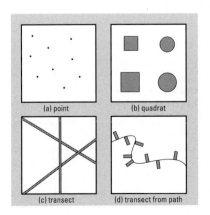

(a) point   (b) quadrat

(c) transect   (d) transect from path

Fig. 15.3 Methods of positioning samples.

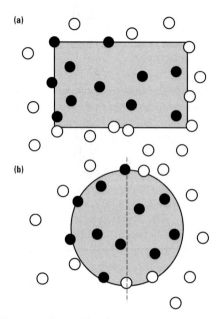

Fig. 15.4 Examples of sampling protocols for reducing edge effects. Filled circles represent objects to be counted or measured, open circles those to be ignored. (a) Rectangular area. All objects touching the top and left hand sides including the top left hand corner are included, as well as those clearly within the perimeter. (b) Circular area. All objects clearly within the perimeter are included as well as those touching the perimeter on the left hand side. In the bottom half, those that would touch both the perimeter and the imaginary plane of symmetry are ignored.

obscure the true nature of the clumped distribution. Alternatively, you might wish to exclude a patchy distribution from your investigation and you should thus choose a relatively large sampling area. If the distribution is stratified or graded (e.g. sediment grain sizes on a beach), then sampling area is generally less important than sampling position.

Small sample areas have the advantage that more small samples can usually be taken for the same amount of labour. This may result in increased precision, and many small areas will cover a wider range of the study area than a few large ones, so the samples may be more representative. However, sampling error at the edge of quadrats is proportionately greater as sample area diminishes, increasing as the scale of the quadrat and the sampled item become closer. To avoid such effects, you need to establish a protocol for dealing with items that overlap the edge of the quadrats (Fig. 15.4). These protocols are also valid when sampling objects in, for example, microscope fields.

Number of sampling units per sample (sample size)

When small numbers of sampling units are used it can lead to imprecise estimates of population parameters because the values of the sample statistics will be susceptible to the effects of random variation. This is especially true if the underlying spatial distribution is patchy, as is often the case. You may then be unable to demonstrate statistically that there are differences between the populations from which the samples were drawn. On the other hand, measuring large numbers of units to provide a large sample size may represent an impractical workload!

To estimate appropriate numbers of sampling units, you can use data from a pilot study to work out the probability of detecting a specified difference in the measured variable at a specified confidence level (see Elliott, 1977 or Sokal and Rohlf, 1994). However, the formulae are complex. A simpler method, usually performed as a pilot study, is as follows:

1. Take five sampling units at random and calculate the arithmetic mean of the measured variable for this sample.
2. Take five more units and calculate the mean for the ten units you have now collected.
3. Continue sampling in five-unit steps and plot the cumulative mean value against the number of samples. When the mean fluctuates within acceptable limits, say ±5%, a suitable number of sampling units has been reached (Fig. 15.5).

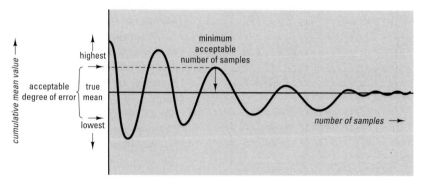

Fig. 15.5 Determination of the number of sampling units required.

Example To estimate mean density in a population with an accuracy of ± 100 per square m using a 95% confidence interval when the standard deviation for the population is ± 1600, the required sample size (N) is

$$N = \left[1.96 \times \left(\frac{1600}{100}\right)\right]^2$$

$$= 983$$

Alternatively, the sample size (N) required to estimate a population mean with a given level of precision can be calculated as:

$$N = [(1.96) \times (sd/p)]^2 \qquad [15.1]$$

where sd is the population standard deviation for the variable being estimated and p is the width of the variation one is willing to tolerate. The value 1.96 reflects the confidence level.

The sequence of events in creating a sampling strategy is shown in Fig. 15.6.

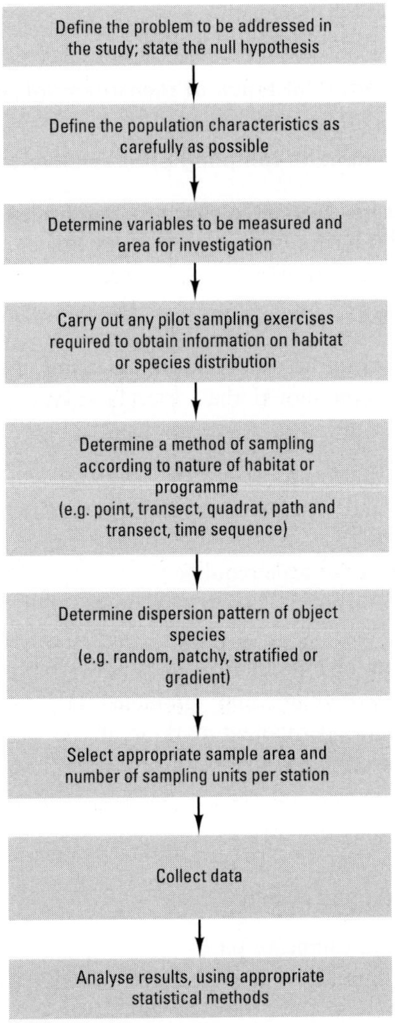

Fig. 15.6 Flowchart outlining decisions required for field sampling studies.

Definitions

Geodetic surveying – takes into account the curvature of the Earth. This is important only over a very large area, e.g. a whole country, so is not usually of significance to environmental science.

Planimetric surveying – assumes that the area under consideration approximates to a horizontal plane.

Surveying is an important aspect of many field studies in environmental science and it is important that you know both some of the basic and some of the increasingly used techniques. Surveying involves making measurements of both natural and man-made features on the Earth's surface and plotting these measurements at a suitable scale to form a map, a plan or a cross-section. For example, you may wish to determine the cross-profile of a beach, the spatial distribution of vegetation types in an area or the locations of soil sampling sites.

KEY POINT There are two fundamental types of measurement in environmental science:

1. The location of a point (e.g. a sediment sampling site) relative to other points of known positions.
2. The measurement of differences in vertical elevation (height) between two or more points (e.g. the long profile of a river reach).

Organizing and planning surveys

The key to successful and accurate surveying lies in sound organization and planning: begin by reading Chapter 5. You should then select a surveying method or methods. To do this, ask yourself:

Plotting survey data onto a pre-existing map – make certain that the scale of the map (see Chapter 29) is consistent with the accuracy of surveying required.

- What are the purposes of your survey?
- What features are to be surveyed and what is the accuracy required? These will determine the method(s) used.
- Is a map to be produced? If so, what is the scale required?

Marking points in the field

Always make a sketch of the locations of your station points with measurements relative to other nearby features. It is not uncommon for pegs or pins to be removed from an area overnight!

For the temporary marking of the points of interest in your survey (station points) use ranging rods, typically of aluminium and graduated in 0.5 m alternating red and white sections. For more permanent marking, if you wish to return to these points over a period of time, use a wooden peg, steel pin or painted 'X'.

Recording data in the field

When recording surveying data in the field you should:

For the marking of permanent stations a steel pin may be set in concrete, flush with the ground surface. Even if it becomes overgrown it can be located by a metal detector.

- Use a hard-backed notebook, ideally of rainproof paper.
- Write legibly and neatly so that the data are systematic and intelligible to others.
- Record the following:
    purpose of survey;
    personnel involved, noting their specific tasks (e.g. booker of data);
    survey method(s);
    instruments used;
    time and date;
    weather conditions;
    a sketch map of the survey area;
    all measurements taken (in tabular form);
    any other relevant information.

In the field, Snedecor's Rule may be used to provide a rapid estimate of standard deviation (s) based on the number of observations and their range (difference between highest and lowest = R).

No. observations	Approx. value of s
5	R/2
10	R/3
25	R/4
50	R/4.5
100	R/5

Errors and checks

Before commencing a survey you should read Chapter 8 and decide on the maximum permissible error which will, in turn, depend on the methods and instruments used. Beware of instrumental bias: if you suspect that systematic errors are being recorded (e.g. if a tape measure is incorrectly calibrated), check the readings of one instrument against another. Random or accidental errors also occur as a result of small differences in the reading of scales of an instrument by the same person or by different individuals. By taking, e.g., 10 readings of the same distance or angle you can record the range in readings arising from random errors and thus work out your own personal standard deviation (Chapter 39) with a particular instrument.

You should always incorporate *independent* check measurements of angles and distances in all surveying operations to minimize errors. This does not mean simply taking the same reading twice. For example:

- When locating the position of an unknown point, using the methods described below, do so in relation to more than one known point.
- When carrying out a levelling survey (see Boxes 16.3 and 16.4), the change in ground level from a known to an unknown point must be checked by recording the change in level in the opposite direction.

Basic procedures for locating points (position fixing) in the field

Angle and distance measurement

You can locate the position of an unknown point (X) relative to that of a known one by the 'radial line and distance method', which involves measuring two parameters:

1. The compass bearing (θ, Fig. 16.1) to the unknown point (see also Box 16.1) using either:

   - a good quality hand-held sighting compass (accuracy $\pm 0.5°$; see Box 16.2 and Fig. 16.2); or
   - a tripod mounted compass (accuracy $\pm 0.05°$).

   Note that a theodolite (see below) measures horizontal angles *by difference* and not relative to north.

2. The horizontal distance (H) between the two points. This may be determined directly, using a surveyor's chain or a tape, or by other methods of distance measurement (see below). Note that the distance measured will be parallel with the ground slope. Therefore, if a significant gradient is present, a correction must be made by measuring the slope angle. The horizontal or projected distance between the two points (H) is given by:

$$H = L \cos \alpha \qquad [16.1]$$

where: $L =$ distance measured parallel with ground slope; and
$\alpha =$ slope angle.

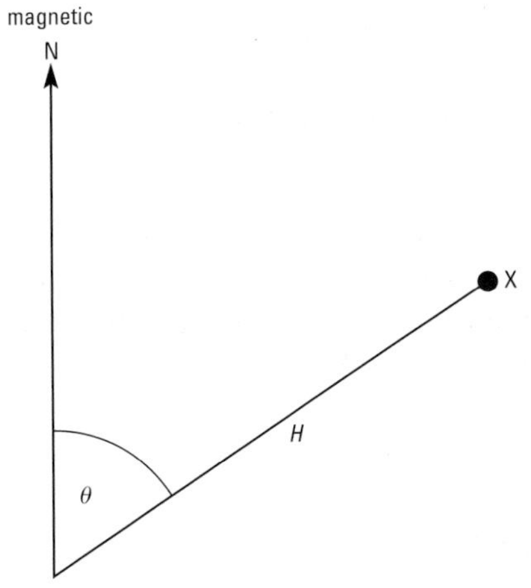

A series of connected lines, for which bearing (usually measured using a theodolite) and distance are measured, allows several points to be located and is known as traverse surveying or traversing. There are two types of traverse:

Fig. 16.1 Point location using the radial line and distance method.

Definitions

Traverse – a series of straight lines between successive points at which their bearings (or the angles between them) have been measured together with the distances between them.
Traverse leg – one line in a traverse.

Box 16.1 Reference directions in surveys: what is meant by north?

All surveys must be related to a reference direction, or meridian, which is normally the north–south direction. Many environmental scientists find the relationships among the north–south grid lines shown on a map, the direction that a compass needle points and so-called 'true north' confusing.

Definitions

- **True north** The direction of the North Pole along a true meridian.
- **True meridian** A great circle on the Earth's surface passing through both poles, i.e. a line of longitude.
- **Magnetic north or magnetic meridian** The direction indicated by a freely floating compass needle at a point on the Earth's surface. At any time the difference between the true meridian and the magnetic meridian is the magnetic declination. This varies with locality and time.
- **Grid lines (grid line meridian)** A system of straight lines at right angles constructed in squares, typically at 1 km intervals, which form the basis of the mapping systems for different countries (e.g. Ordnance Survey National Grid for the UK), hence the term **grid north** which is, by convention, towards the top edge of the map.
- **Arbitrary meridian** The direction from one station to another, or to some well-defined position, which may be used as the meridian of a small-scale survey (e.g. an agricultural plot).

- **Bearing** The direction of a particular line relative to a meridian.

Remember that a compass measures bearings relative to magnetic north, which is not coincident with grid north used on Ordnance Survey (OS) maps, nor is the difference between the two constant in time and space. All OS maps contain information in the legend of the form:

'magnetic north about $8\frac{1}{2}°$ W of grid north in 1976 decreasing by about $\frac{1}{2}°$ in five years.'

When plotting points you must make the appropriate correction for the bearing measured relative to magnetic north and convert it to grid north for the map you are using. Some types of compass allow declination adjustments to be made, enabling bearings to be measured directly relative to grid north. Many do not, so the corrections must be applied manually. For the above example, a survey in 1996 would have required a correction of $6\frac{1}{2}°$. Remember to check the adjustment of your compass according to the area you are working in and always use the most up-to-date maps available.

By convention:

- North (N) $= 000°$
- East (E) $= 090°$
- South (S) $= 180°$
- West (W) $= 270°$

- **Open** i.e. ending at an unknown point (Fig. 16.3). This is not recommended since there is no check on the accuracy of the work. Errors are likely to accumulate as the number of traverse legs increases.
- **Closed** i.e. ending at the start point (loop traverse, Fig. 16.4) or at another known point (connecting traverse, Fig. 16.3). This is recommended, as any accumulated error will be observed at the closing station.

A special case of the radial line and distance method is when one distance is measured along a line *at right angles* to AB, e.g. A and B may be points along a road and C is at some distance to the side of the road, in which case the distance from the line AB to C is known as the 'offset' (Fig. 16.5). This method is used in chain surveying (see below).

The location of C can also be determined by triangulation using a compass or a theodolite to measure the two angles BAC and ABC, provided that the horizontal distance AB is known. Always measure the angle ACB as a check to ensure that the three add up to 180°.

Distance–distance measurement

If you do not have a compass or theodolite you can locate the position of an unknown point (C) if you know the positions of two others (A and B), provided that the site is flat and slope corrections are not necessary:

Definition

Theodolite – a rotating telescope, mounted on a tripod, which measures angles in the horizontal and vertical planes to an accuracy of 1 minute to 0.1 second of arc.

Fig. 16.2 Using a hand-held sighting compass (see Box 16.2).

Using a compass – beware of magnetic anomalies caused by overhead power lines, nearby iron or steel fences, pocket knives, belt buckles etc. Remember that nearby iron-bearing rocks (e.g. basalt) can cause a compass needle to deflect from the true bearing.

Box 16.2   How to use a hand-held sighting compass

Sighting a bearing or aiming a compass at an object (e.g. a church spire) differs from one type of instrument to another. The best models have:

- A rectangular base.
- A north-seeking arrow which is free-floating in a liquid.
- A rotating dial ring, graduated in degrees, which contains a reference arrow which rotates with the ring.
- A mirror and a sighting mechanism, such as a v-sight.

To take a bearing to a distant object:

1. **Raise the compasss to eye level.**
2. **Align the sight with the object** and at the same time observe the compass housing in the mirror.
3. **Rotate the ring** so that the reference arrow and north-pointing arrow (see Box 16.1) are perfectly coincident.
4. **By using the mirror, read the bearing to the object** from the point on the scale of the dial which lies against the reference point marked outside the dial and which is directly beneath the line of sight (Fig. 16.2).

1. Using, e.g. a tape or one of the methods described below, measure the horizontal distance from A to B = AB.
2. Plot AB to an appropriate scale.
3. Measure the horizontal distances AC and BC.
4. Fix the position of the unknown point (C) by the intersection of the axes AC and BC.

So-called distance–distance position fixing systems are also available for surveying over water. These comprise two onshore transmitters, known as slaves, which transmit VHF radio signals and are located at precisely surveyed onshore locations. Signals are received by an omni-directional aerial on board the survey boat and the control system converts them to distances from the two known points. Typical accuracy is ±2 m with a maximum range of 20 km.

Global Positioning System (GPS)

The Global Positioning System (GPS) is being increasingly used for surveying, both on land and over water where it is currently an ideal method of position fixing. The GPS consists of a constellation of 24 satellites (four in

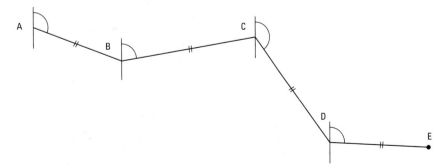

Fig. 16.3 Traverse from A to E by radial line and distance method. If E is an unknown point this is an open traverse, if E is known it is a connecting traverse.

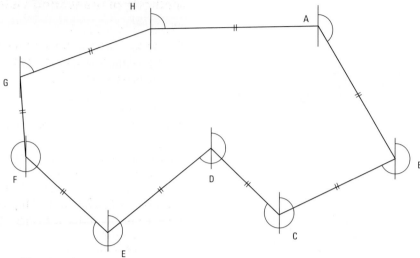

Fig. 16.4 A loop traverse, A–A. Angles shown are bearings relative to N. For a loop traverse with *n* legs, the external angle sum = $(2n + 4)$ right angles and the internal angle sum = $(2n - 4)$ right angles.

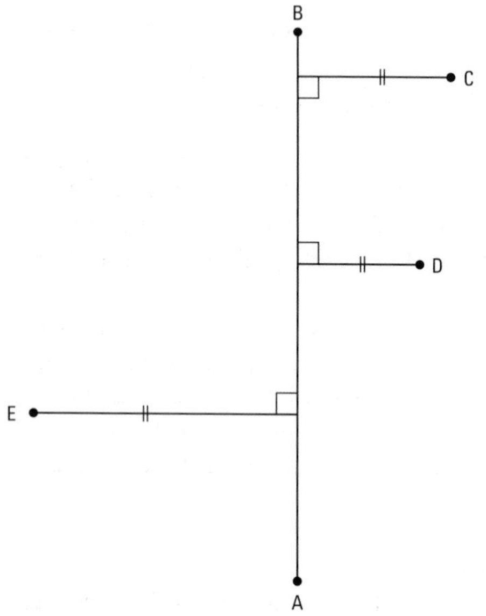

Fig. 16.5 Measurement of offsets (as used in chain surveying) to line AB.

each of six orbital planes), controlled and funded by the United States Department of Defense. This provides between five and eight satellites visible from any point on the Earth's surface. GPS receivers convert signals from the satellites into estimates of velocity and position, expressed as latitude, longitude and elevation (i.e. *x*, *y* and *z* co-ordinates), and can be used for navigation or for position fixing.

KEY POINT The Standard Positioning Service (SPS), available to civil users world-wide, has an intentionally degraded accuracy compared with the Precise Positioning Service (PPS), available only to the US military and government. During times of sensitive military activity, e.g. the Gulf War, the degradation is switched off resulting in higher positional accuracy.

Differential GPS (DGPS) provides a means of correcting errors in position (which arise from several sources, see e.g. Leick, 1995) and uses a reference receiver (base station) to compute corrections for each satellite signal. GPS receivers vary in cost depending on their capabilities but they continue to fall in price. Hand-held receivers, about the size of a mobile telephone, can be obtained relatively cheaply and some can now accept differential corrections. Positional accuracy varies from ±100 m for low cost, single receivers to ±1–10 m for medium cost differential systems. You are unlikely to use the very high accuracy (±1 mm–1 cm) differential systems which currently cost many thousands of pounds. Though affordable systems are less accurate than conventional surveying techniques, DGPS is particularly suited to rapid position fixing in difficult terrain where conventional methods would be much slower or impractical. For example it can be used in sequential surveys to quantify changes in the extent of flood waters, soil erosion, vegetation cover, etc.

KEY POINT GPS receivers are not always suited to working in narrow, deep valleys as high ground may impede the requisite direct line of sight of satellite signals. If signals from fewer than four satellites are received, the instrument will not be able to compute a position. Always check that the receiver is updating positions and not displaying a previous one.

Methods of measuring distance

Chain or tape measure

The simplest method of measuring distance is by means of a surveyor's chain or, more commonly, a tape measure. Further details are given below in the section on chain surveying.

Roadmeter

If you need to measure over long distances on flat surfaces (up to 10 km) a heavy duty measuring wheel or 'roadmeter' may be used. This measures distance according to the number of revolutions of the wheel as the device is pushed over the ground. Always use one with a counter which can be run backwards, to accurately subtract any overrun, and a broad tyre thickness (>20 mm) to prevent tilting from side to side. Superior models are equipped with folding stand, brake (for stop/start measuring) and dirt remover.

Ultrasonic distance measuring

Battery-powered, hand-held ultrasonic measuring instruments, as used by property surveyors, are ideal for rapid measurements of distances to an accuracy of ±5 mm in still air. They measure distance on the basis of the time taken for an emitted ultrasonic sound pulse to travel to and be reflected from a target, assuming a constant velocity of sound in air (*cf.* EDM, see below). High quality instruments permit measurements in two modes:

- Echo mode (one person required): requires the use of a solid target (e.g. a wall or a rock face) from which the echo is reflected. This method is suited to measuring the dimensions of enclosed spaces (e.g. caves). Depending on the instrument, maximum operating distance is usually in the range 15–20 m.
- Electronic target mode (two people required): requires the use of a hand-held electronic target (supplied) from which the echo is reflected. This method is especially suited to measuring the widths of streams and in areas where the use of tapes is made difficult by tall vegetation, or the heights of cliffs. Depending on the instrument, maximum operating distance is usually about 75 m.

Tacheometric levelling

This involves using the stadia wires (Fig. 16.6) of a surveyor's level (see below) to measure the horizontal distance from the level to the staff. Read the level on the staff of both stadia wires and the central cross wire. Check that the difference in reading between the upper stadia wire and the central cross wire equals that between the lower stadia wire and the cross wire. The horizontal distance (H) from the level to the staff is given by:

$$H = a + bd \qquad\qquad [16.2]$$

where d = difference in reading between the two stadia lines, a and b are instrument constants. Typically, a = 0 and b = 100, in which case $H = 100d$.

Electromagnetic distance measuring

There are many types of electromagnetic distance measuring (EDM) devices. Those used principally in surveying are tripod-mounted and emit infrared radiation, which is reflected from one or more prisms, located at the point of

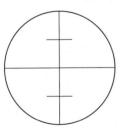

Fig. 16.6 View through the telescope of a level showing cross wires and stadia wires.

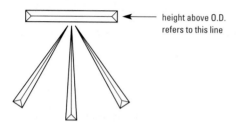

height above O.D. refers to this line

Fig. 16.7 An Ordnance Survey bench mark.

Chart Datum – for areas of Britain where the Hydrographer of the Navy is the surveying authority, Chart Datum is the level of the Lowest Astronomical Tide (LAT), i.e. the lowest possible tide under average meteorological conditions. Note that charts of waters outside the authority of the Hydrographer of the Navy may use another definition of Chart Datum.

Definitions

Level line – a line at a constant height relative to mean sea level, i.e. a curved line which follows the Earth's surface.

Horizontal line – a line which is tangential to a level line at any given point, i.e. perpendicular to gravity at the point in question.

Reading levels – many older levels have inverted images and it is necessary to read the scale on the staff upside down.

interest. The horizontal distance from the instrument to the reflector (H) is computed instantly according to the relationship:

$$H = vt/2 \qquad [16.3]$$

where v = velocity of the emitted radiation in the atmosphere, and
t = two-way travel time (i.e. time for radiation to travel to and from the reflector).

Such instruments are simple and quick to operate, highly accurate, reliable and can measure over distances of 1–2 km depending on the model. They are commonly combined with electronic theodolites to form electronic total stations (see below).

Basic procedures for determining heights: levelling

Levelling is the process of determining the heights of pairs of points on the Earth's surface relative to each other or, more normally, relative to that of a datum plane. In Britain, the datum to which heights are expressed is the mean sea level at Newlyn, Cornwall (as calculated from observations made between May 1915 and April 1921), known as Ordnance Datum (O.D.). Bench marks (Fig. 16.7), marked ground points, whose height is measured precisely, are usually engraved near to the ground in walls or close to the corners of buildings. Their locations can be determined by reference to 1 : 10 000 or 1 : 10 560 (6 inches to one mile) scale Ordnance Survey maps. The latter also give the heights of the bench marks but the more modern 1 : 10 000 maps do not. In this case it is necessary to contact the Ordnance Survey for the height information you require but note that a charge is levied for the service. Beware that some very old (pre-1920s) 1 : 10 560 scale Ordnance Survey maps give bench mark heights relative to a former datum of the mean sea level at Liverpool, which is not the same as O.D. Newlyn.

Do not confuse the term 'Chart Datum', the datum to which water depths are reduced on Admiralty Charts of the British Isles, with Ordnance Datum. Unlike O.D., Chart Datum is not constant; the difference in level between O.D. and Chart Datum varies from place to place depending on the local tidal range.

For most levelling surveys in environmental science, the curvature of the Earth is ignored and, over short distances, it can be assumed that there is no distinction between a level line and a horizontal line.

Two items of equipment are required for levelling:

- Tripod-mounted surveyor's level consisting of a telescope which pivots around a vertical axis. Several varieties are available (e.g. Dumpy, tilting and autoset levels) each with different methods of levelling to ensure a horizontal line of sight. Always use a high quality, modern level which gives good magnification and optical resolution.
- Levelling staff up to 4 m in height (in 1 m interconnecting sections) and graduated from the bottom upwards in m and cm divisions. This gives the height of a point *below* a horizontal line of sight. Readings should be taken to the nearest mm by estimating between divisions.

A horizontal line of sight is established using a level and used to determine the height at which this line intersects a graduated staff held *vertically* over a point on the ground (Boxes 16.3 and 16.4). Two people are required: one to operate the level and the other to hold the staff. Care must be taken to ensure that:

- the level is aligned horizontally with the aid of the levelling bubble;
- the tripod is stable (in soft earth push the feet firmly into the ground).

Box 16.3   How to determine the difference in level between two points

1. **Set up the level** *horizontally* **roughly half-way between the two points**, A and B (note that it need not be on the line AB).

2. **Focus the telescope on the staff held at A** (a levelling bubble aids vertical alignment of the staff by the holder) and take the reading, e.g. 2.27 m. You will, with most instruments, see cross wires and two short lines, known as stadia lines, positioned above and below (Fig. 16.6). Make certain that the central cross wire is used for reading the staff, otherwise large errors will result.

3. **Rotate the level and take the reading with the staff at B**, e.g. 1.79 m.

4. **The difference in level between A and B** = (2.27 − 1.79) m, = 0.48 m.

Remember that the smaller the reading on the staff, the higher the point is on the Earth's surface.

If point A is a bench mark, its height relative to O.D. (e.g. 102.53 m above O.D.) is known as the reduced level and therefore the reduced level of point B can also be determined as (102.53 + 0.48) m, = 103.01 m above O.D.

You can establish a known reference point (e.g. marked with a steel pin or a notch carved in a fence post) known as a **'temporary bench mark'** or TBM to which all levels are reduced during a survey. This can subsequently be related to O.D. (and therefore all levels) once a suitable bench mark has been located.

Electronic total stations

Electronic total stations with digital readouts and the ability to store many hundreds of readings for downloading to a computer are a combination of a theodolite and an EDM. They enable accurate angle (horizontal and vertical), distance and co-ordinate measurement relative to a base station. Although costly, they have virtually superseded traditional theodolites and should be available in all environmental science departments. It will take you a considerable amount of time to become familiar with all the functions and types of measurements possible with an electronic total station, but this is amply rewarded by the speed of field data acquisition.

Basic procedures for mapping

The production of maps from field survey data may be carried out by chain and offset surveying or plane table surveying (Box 16.5).

Chain surveying

Chain surveying is accurate for simple work over small (about 0.25 km²), flat areas. It is a low-cost method based entirely on measurements of length and got its name because the basic piece of equipment was traditionally a surveyor's chain. A metric chain has a length of 20 m and consists of a series of linked steel sections each measuring 200 mm from central link to central link. With the

Protecting equipment – carry a golf umbrella or a plastic sheet to hold over a level, theodolite or plane table during light rain. If the rain becomes heavy, stop work as delicate instruments could become damaged. Also use an umbrella to protect an electronic total station against direct sunlight.

Ropes – if you use a graduated rope to measure lengths make certain that it does not stretch or shrink when wet. Always check the accuracy of graduations painted on a rope against a ruler or tape.

Box. 16.4 How to carry out series levelling

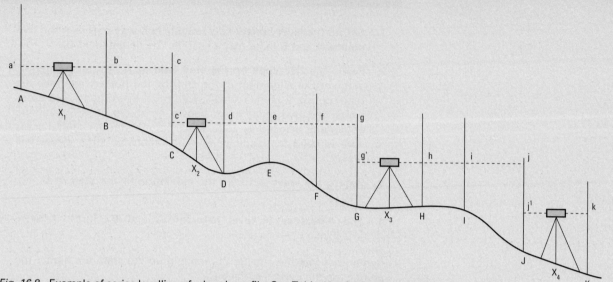

Fig. 16.8 Example of series levelling of a beach profile. See Table 16.1 for booking of data.

Most levelling surveys entail more than two height measurements and require several level stations and staff points to be established. Such surveys are known as series levelling, e.g. the determination of a beach profile, as shown in Fig. 16.8 from A to K. In this example, in which the level is located at four positions, X_1–X_4:

- Back sights = Aa′, Cc′, Gg′ and Jj′
- Fore sights = Cc, Gg, Jj and Kk
- Intermediate sights = Bb, Dd, Ee, Ff, Hh and Ii
- Change points = C, G and J

Definitions

- **Back sight**: the first sight taken from a new position of the level.
- **Fore sight**: the last sight taken from a position of the level.
- **Intermediate sight**: any sight between the back sight and the fore sight.
- **Change point (turning point)**: a point at which the staff remains while the level is being moved.

The difference in level between A and K:

$$= Aa′ - Cc + Cc′ - Gg + Gg′ - Jj + Jj′ - Kk$$
$$= (Aa′ + Cc′ + Gg′ + Jj′) - (Cc + Gg + Jj + Kk)$$
$$= (\Sigma \text{ back sights}) - (\Sigma \text{ fore sights})$$

A positive result indicates a rise in level, a negative result indicates a fall.

In undulating terrain, such as sand dunes, make certain that the level position is appropriate for both uphill and downhill sightings, i.e. the horizontal line must intersect the staff, not the ground surface in front of it or the air above it. **Never move the level and the staff at the same time during a survey!**

Data should be recorded systematically in a surveying notebook using the 'rise and fall method'. As an example, the results of the survey shown in Fig. 16.8 are given in Table 16.1. Always include the arithmetic checks on your work as shown at the bottom of Table 16.1. If the results go over the page in your notebook, enter the last reading at the foot of the page as a fore sight (even if it is an intermediate sight) and repeat it over the page in the back sight column.

Tapes – use tapes of plastic or glass fibre in preference to linen or steel. These are tougher and less likely to fray, rust or break when kinked.

chain extended on the ground it is possible to measure to the nearest 200 mm or estimate to the nearest 100 mm or 50 mm by eye. Normally yellow tags are attached at every fifth link (i.e. 1 m apart) and red tags at every 5 m to facilitate length measurement. Chains were formerly used in preference to tape measures because they were more durable. Modern tapes are tougher and are therefore more commonly used today. Typically 30 m in length, graduated in m and cm, they provide greater accuracy in length measurements.

Chain surveying is not suited to wooded terrain. Accuracy is lost if many changes in survey line direction are needed and measuring offsets is made difficult by obstacles.

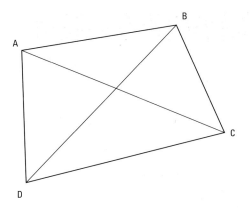

Fig. 16.9 Cross-braced quadrilateral as the basis for a simple chain survey. AC and BD provide check lines.

Always make sure that station points on the same line are visible from each other.

There are five basic stages in a chain survey:

1. Reconnaissance of the area involves walking the site and assessing how many lines will be needed to survey it. If the site is linear, e.g. parallel with a road, one line only may be adequate. If several lines are required it is important that all the relevant features in the area should be close to them. Survey lines should define a geometrical figure and always include at least one check line, e.g. a cross-braced quadrilateral which gives a series of four near-equilateral triangles (Fig. 16.9).

2. Selection and marking of station points which define the ends and intersections of the survey lines and should be clearly marked on the ground. Mark these as described above or use well-defined features existing in the area, e.g. a gate post or a tree. If you propose to return to the site over a period of years it will be necessary to mark station points with steel pins concreted into the ground. Always seek permission to do this.

3. Measurement of main survey lines, requiring two people, the 'leader' and the 'follower', to lay out the chain or tape. If the line is longer than the chain or tape, mark the ends of it with vertical ranging poles which will permit a straight line to be sighted by the follower, who directs the leader to the correct position. Intermediately positioned ranging poles, inserted by the leader, may be needed for sighting over long lines. As each successive length of chain or tape is laid out, mark the end by driving a peg or pin into the ground.

Table 16.1 Booking of data obtained in the levelling survey in Fig. 16.8 using the rise and fall method

Back sight	Intermed. sight	Fore sight	Rise	Fall	Reduced level	Remarks	
0.53					4.22	TBM top of steel peg tape = 0.0m	A
	1.02			0.49	3.73	tape = 15.7m	B
0.48		1.61		0.59	3.14	change point tape = 26.6m	C
	1.07			0.59	2.55	tape = 36.2	D
	0.80		0.27		2.82	tape = 44.3m	E
	1.33			0.53	2.29	tape = 51.8m	F
0.95		1.69		0.36	1.93	change point tape = 60.2m	G
	0.94		0.01		1.94	tape = 71.7m	H
	0.95			0.01	1.93	tape = 79.3m	I
0.84		1.82		0.87	1.06	change point tape = 88.0m	J
		1.27		0.43	0.63	sea level @ 18.15 BST tape = 98.9m	K
2.80		6.39	0.28	3.87	4.22		
−6.39				−0.28	−0.63	*Checks*	
−3.59				3.59	3.59		

Date	28.6.97	Time	18.00 BST
Location	A beach	Weather	Bright and sunny
Booker	RWD	Staffman	AMJ

KEY POINT It is best practice to make measurements along main survey lines in both directions (e.g. C to D and D to C) as a check on field accuracy. For long lines, do not forget to sum all the lengths of chain or tape required for measurement of a particular line.

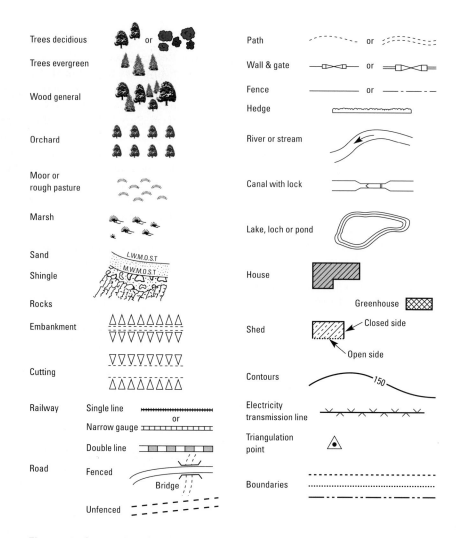

Fig. 16.10 Conventional surveying symbols.

Measuring longer offsets (> 5 m) – check the right angle as follows: one person should hold the zero end of the tape at the feature to be positioned while the other swings the tape in an arc over the marked survey line. The smallest offset distance will coincide with the tape at right angles to the survey line: record this and the corresponding chain measurement.

4. Measurement of detail by offsets is carried out by tape measuring offsets (Fig. 16.5) at 90° from a main survey line. For short offsets (< 5 m), judgement of the right angle by eye is adequate.

5. Record observations and measurements clearly and systematically, and in a way that can be understood by someone who has not seen the field area. The standard format for recording chain and offset measurements is in a note book with a central column, defined by two parallel lines, trending from the foot to the top of each page (Fig. 16.11). The pages should be printed with a square grid to allow measurements to be plotted approximately to scale. Distances of features along a survey line (e.g. denoted as CD, Fig. 16.11) are written in the central column and offset distances to either side. By convention, information is recorded from the bottom of the page working upwards, thus offsets to the left and right of the survey line are noted on the left and right sides of the page.

KEY POINT   Always make sketches of the site using conventional symbols (Fig. 16.10); never simply record chain survey data as 'words and numbers'. Examples of good and bad practice of data recording for the same area are given in Figs 16.11 and 16.12.

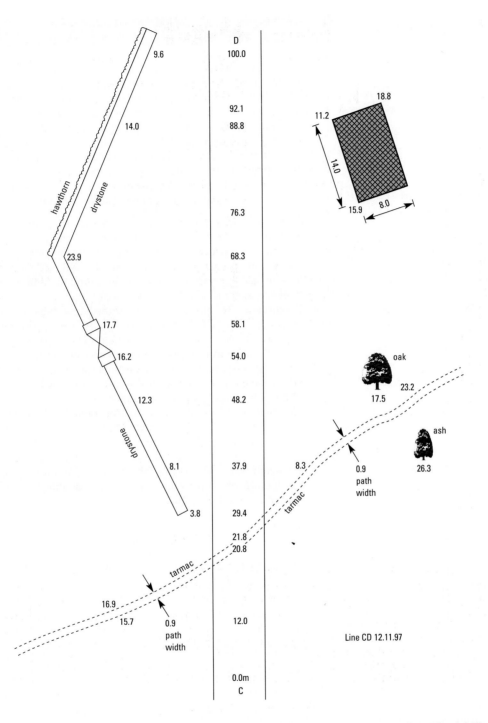

Fig. 16.11 Example of recording of observations and measurements in a chain survey, showing good practice (cf. Fig. 16.12).

Further reading

There are many good texts on surveying which will provide you with more details of the methods and equipment described in this chapter (e.g. Ritchie *et al.*, 1988; Wright, 1982).

	D	
hedge + wall 9.6	100.0	
	92.1	18.8 greenhouse corner
hedge + wall 14.0	88.8	11.2 greenhouse corner
	76.3	15.9 greenhouse corner
wall corner 23.9	68.3	
gate post 17.7	58.1	
gate post 16.2	54.0	
wall 12.3	48.2	17.5 tree, 23.2 path
wall 8.1	37.9	8.3 path, 26.3 tree
end of wall 3.8	29.4	
	21.8	path crosses line ⎫
	20.8	path crosses line ⎭
sides of path 16.9, 15.7	12.0	
	0.0m	
	C	

Fig. 16.12 Example of recording of observations and measurements in a chain survey, showing bad practice (cf. Fig. 16.11).

Box 16.5 How to carry out plane table surveying

In plane table surveying, field observations and plotting proceed simultaneously. It is a simple and inexpensive method. A plane table consists of a drawing board mounted on a tripod (Fig. 16.13) *via* a ball and socket joint so it can be made horizontal and clamped. Also required is an alidade – a sight rule either with folding sights or a telescopic variety (Fig. 16.14) where the sight is directly above the drawing edge. This is placed on a sheet of strong paper on the table, sighted on the target (often marked by a ranging rod) and a pencil line is drawn on the paper representing the line of sight. There are three principal methods of plane table surveying:

- **Radiation** This involves measurements to points requiring to be fixed. To fix A, B, C and D relative to the plane table station (X), sight each point in turn. Then draw the lines of sight (Fig. 16.15) and measure the distances XA, XB, XC and XD with a tape or tacheometry (using a tacheometric alidade) and plot each distance to scale (Xa, Xb, Xc and Xd).
- **Traversing** This involves moving the plane table from station to station. To fix A, B, C and D (Fig. 16.16) set up the table over A and sight to two adjacent stations using the alidade. Measure AD and AB and plot to scale as ad and ab. Move the table to B such that b is directly over the station. Sight to C, measure BC and plot to scale as bc. Move to C, check sight back to B and D and, as a double check, sight back to A.
- **Intersection** This is used to fix points of detail, e.g. the configuration of a river bend. Mark the point you wish to fix using a series of ranging rods. From A (Fig. 16.17) sight each point in turn and draw in rays. Note no distance measurements are taken. Move the plane table to B and sight the same points. The points of intersection of the rays enable the detail of the plan to be fixed (Fig. 16.17).

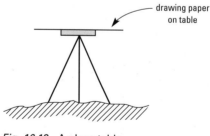

drawing paper on table

Fig. 16.13 A plane table.

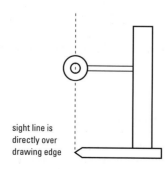

sight line is directly over drawing edge

Fig. 16.14 A telescopic alidade.

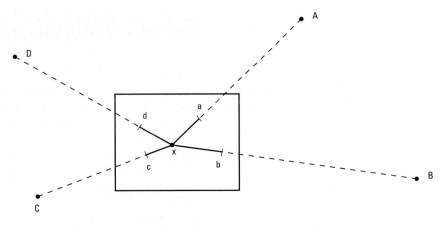

Fig. 16.15 Radiation using a plane table.

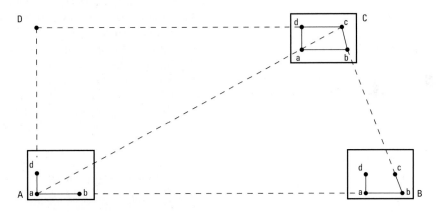

Fig. 16.16 Traversing using a plane table.

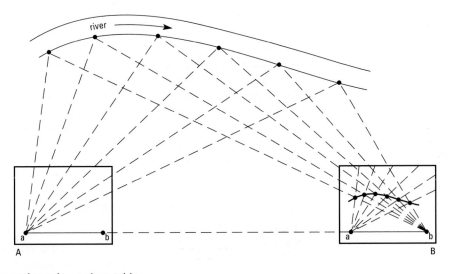

Fig. 16.17 Intersection mapping using a plane table.

17 Sampling biological materials

If you need to collect living material for observational/experimental investigations, this may require the use of a formal sampling procedure (see Chapter 15) or simple qualitative collecting. Once material is collected, you must take precautions to prevent destructive interactions between organisms within your sample.

Your choice of collecting equipment and subsequent treatment of the organisms will depend upon your objectives. Some of the main reasons for collecting include:

- Collecting for subsequent laboratory experimentation or observation: this requires that minimum stress and damage are caused to the specimens.
- Making measurements/estimations of population and community parameters: this can be destructive (requiring killing of specimens) or non-destructive, depending upon the objectives of the study and any requirements for subsequent laboratory work, e.g. sorting and identification.
- Collecting for museum-type collections of preserved specimens: here the main objective is to obtain undamaged and representative specimens, usually in a preserved form.
- Collecting for subsequent laboratory analysis: this may require formal sampling procedures to be used. This objective requires care in both the method of collection and of subsequent storage to avoid inducing or allowing changes that are artifacts of the collection and storage processes. Deep freezing is usually the preferred storage method when subsequent chemical analysis is likely.

The main 'rules' for collecting are:

- Collect only enough for your purposes.
- Be aware of any legislation relating to the species or habitats you are intending to use. Obtain any permits required and obey any regulations strictly.
- Treat animals with respect at all times: do not cause unnecessary stress or suffering. There are formal rules for the handling of many vertebrate species but the same attitude should be taken towards all living organisms.
- Minimize damage and stress during collection and transport: stressed organisms are of little use for realistic experimentation.
- Be aware of the limitations and bias of your collecting equipment: this is particularly important for formal sampling procedures where collecting devices almost always have such problems. This may require specific testing for your particular usage.
- Keep good records of collection details.

Collecting equipment and methods

There is an immense variety of collecting and sampling devices available, varying from the simple to complex mechanical devices. In general, collecting remote and/or animal samples presents the greatest problems. The more remote the operator is from the point of sampling, the more difficult it is to evaluate the quality of the sample in terms of its representativeness. Animal collection can be difficult because of factors such as mobility, size and complications introduced when allowing for phenomena such as avoidance behaviour.

Collecting formal samples

Here the objective is to obtain specimens that both qualitatively and quantitatively represent some well-defined habitat(s). Some of the more obvious practical considerations are listed below:

- Are there 'edge effects' associated with the sampling method? Because of such effects you may need to adopt a special protocol, e.g. to determine whether or not a specimen falling on a boundary is included or excluded from the sample (p. 74).
- Will the sample be uniform? For example, remote sampling of marine sediments of different texture using grabs often results in 'bites' of different depth being taken.
- Does the method sample all components of the biota equally well? This may not be important as long as it adequately samples those components in which you are interested.
- How accurately can the location of the sample be defined, especially with regard to other samples intended as replicates? This is particularly important in remote sampling.
- Is the size of the sampling unit adequate for the size and distribution of the object, species or communities being sampled? (See Chapter 15.) In remote sampling, this can often be a problem and frequently the method used is a compromise.
- Can inter-species interactions affect the integrity of the sample after collection but before processing? Factors such as predation can be prevented by fixing (Table 17.1) or narcotizing (Table 17.2) the sample in an appropriate chemical solution. Freezing is a poor option here since, upon thawing, most animal tissues tend to disintegrate and the specimens are in poor condition for subsequent identification, etc.

Microbiological sampling

Microbial diversity is enormous and, although samples may be taken relatively simply, subsequent extraction, isolation and quantification of meaningful data on diversity and abundance is complex. Generally, microbes can be studied by taking samples for analysis, usually in one of the following ways:

- By direct examination of individual cells of a particular microbe, e.g. using fluorescence microscopy (p. 116).
- By isolating/purifying a particular species or related individuals of a particular group, e.g. the faecal indicator bacterium *Escherichia coli* in seawater.
- By studying microbial processes, rather than individual microbes, either *in situ* or in the laboratory.

Sampling techniques include the use of swabs, Sellotape strips and agar contact methods for sampling surfaces; bottles for aquatic habitats; and plastic bags and corers for soils and sediments. A wide range of complex apparatus is available for accurately sampling water or soil at particular depths.

Definition

Edge effect – in this context, any phenomenon associated with the sampling procedure at the edge of a sampling device.

Defining location – for greatest precision, use the co-ordinates obtained from a large-scale map; for less precise measurements, co-ordinates given by satellite – or radio-based position-fixing may be appropriate (see Chapter 16).

See Chapter 16 of *Practical Skills in Biology* (2nd edn) for detail of narcotizing, fixing and preserving biological materials.

See Chapter 17 of *Practical Skills in Biology* (2nd edn) for information on techniques for isolating bacteria.

Sampling biological materials

Table 17.1 Some of the most widely used fixatives/preservatives and their properties

Substance	Fixation	Usage	Notes
Formaldehyde	+	4% v/v	Comes as 40% v/v solution (= formalin): normal dilution 1 + 9. Make up with sea water for marine specimens; buffer for calcareous specimens. Use in a fume cupboard – health hazard
Ethanol	+	70% v/v aqueous	Highly volatile; inflammable; containers must be well sealed to prevent evaporation; causes shrinkage and decolorization as well as loss of lipids
Acetic acid	+	In mixtures	Pungent vapour
Picric acid	+	In mixtures	Risk of explosion; detonates readily on contact with some metals. Not recommended for routine student use (significant health risk)
Mercuric chloride	+	In mixtures	Extremely poisonous; corrosive to metal implements; tissue will contain mercuric salt deposits
Osmium tetroxide	+	1% v/v in buffer or vapour	Both fluid and vapour highly toxic; use in fume cupboard only. Excellent for cytological detail but is expensive and can only be used for very small specimens due to poor penetration speed. Vapour good for protozoa
Propylene phenoxetol	–	1–2% v/v aqueous	Relatively expensive but innocuous and effective preservative: needs pre-fixation stage
Glutaraldehyde	+	2–4% v/v in buffer	Must be used cold

Table 17.2 Narcotizing agents and their characteristics

Agent	Usage	Notes
Cold (chilling)	Cold-blooded animals (Ectotherms)	Effective form of relaxing many animals such as tropical and sub-tropical invertebrates
Heat (warming)	Slow heat	Works for some animals. Start from ambient but keep time period as short as possible
Magnesium sulphate or	7% w/v in water	Quite effective for many invertebrates but beware of osmotic problems if made up in sea water: keep exposure times fairly short (1–2 h)
Magnesium chloride	20% w/v in water	
Menthol crystals	Float on water	Slow but effective for many aquatic animals
Chloral hydrate	1% w/v in sea water	General narcotizing agent
Ethanol	10% v/v dropwise	Slow and rather tedious process for all but very small specimens
MS-222 (Tricaine)	Use as 0.05% w/v aqueous solution	Good for marine and freshwater fish: very rapid effect (15 s–1 min)
Chloretone	0.1–0.5% w/v in water	General narcotizing agent
Ethyl acetate	Vapour	Effective for most insects (kills as well); highly volatile
Ether	Vapour	Effective for vertebrates
Chloroform	Vapour	Effective for vertebrates

KEY POINT An important feature of all sampling protocols is that the sampling apparatus must be sterile; strict aseptic technique must be used throughout the sampling process.

The sampling method must:

- Mimimize the chance of contamination with microbes from other sources, especially the exterior of the sampling apparatus and the operator. For example, if you are sampling an aquatic habitat, stand downstream of the sampling site. A portable gas burner or spirit lamp can be used to achieve sterile technique during field sampling.
- Ensure rapid processing after collection to minimize any changes in microbiological status. As a general guideline, many procedures require samples to be analysed within 6 h of collection. Changes in aeration, pH and water content may occur after collection. Some microbes are more susceptible than others to such effects, e.g. anaerobic bacteria may not survive if the sample is exposed to air.
- Keep samples cool (0–5 °C) during transport to the laboratory. However, some microbes may be affected by such procedures, particularly if coming from a warm environment, e.g. association with warm-blooded animals. An alternative approach is to keep the sample near the ambient sampling temperature by using a thermostatic vessel (e.g. Thermos flask).

General collecting strategies

For qualitative collecting, where a representative sample of the population or habitat is not the objective, then the effectiveness of equipment may be of less significance. Here, suitability for capturing living and undamaged specimens is the principal criterion in choosing your equipment. For mobile animals, this often involves nets or traps of various kinds, combined with narcotizing agents such as smoke for insects. If specimens can be killed before capture, then spray insecticides can be a useful aid.

The following general points are useful for all collections:

- Think ahead and be prepared. Your collecting equipment must be appropriate for the task!
- Keep good records of collection details: this is particularly important if the collection is for museum or herbarium purposes.
- Keep collected plants in humid atmospheres to ensure good condition. The vasculum originally designed for this purpose has largely been replaced by the polythene bag in most circumstances, except where mechanical damage is likely.
- Keep all living animals in conditions as similar as possible to the environment from which they were collected. Aquatic specimens are usually particularly temperature-sensitive and should be kept in a Thermos flask to prevent rapid temperature changes.
- If mechanical damage is likely during transport, use rigid containers. Plastic containers are usually preferable to glass. Make sure that the container seals properly to avoid losing specimens and to prevent water loss.

> Recording information – the following details should be recorded upon collection: date, time, location, habitat details, collecting technique, preservation technique.

18 Sampling soils and sediments

These substrates are characterized by their particulate nature and by the diversity of potential components, both organic and inorganic. However, the distinction between soils and sediments is not clear-cut (see Chapter 26 for details).

Soils

Soils are conventionally sampled using hand-dug pits. These enable the soil profile to be exposed and materials to be collected from the various horizons which are recognizable on the basis of colour differences (see Chapter 26). Ideally pits should extend to the level of bedrock but this is not always possible or safe (see below). Take advantage of sampling from soil sections exposed in ditches and other cuttings. The basic tools required for soil sampling are:

- a spade;
- a builder's trowel;
- a durable plastic sheet (for grassland);
- a tape measure;
- sample bags.

Once you have selected your sampling sites (see Chapter 15) on the basis of vegetation and geomorphology, mark out the rectangular outline of each pit with the tip of the spade. A spade with a pointed blade (Fig. 18.1) is the most effective for digging as it cuts through tough roots and stiff, cohesive materials. Ensure that the long axis of the marked rectangle is in a west–east orientation permitting optimum illumination of the base of the pit by sunlight. Normal pit dimensions are 0.5–0.6 m × 0.7–0.8 m with a depth of about 1 m.

If working on grassland, carefully cut out and remove the sods of grass and place them grass-side downwards on the plastic sheet, which should be spread out on the ground close to the site of the pit. Soil dug from the pit should also be placed on the plastic sheet to keep the grassland sampling area tidy. If working in woodland, scrape away leaf litter and other organic debris before starting to dig. Always keep one face of the pit (or cutting section) as 'clean' (i.e. unsmeared) as possible by trimming it using the builder's trowel or an old kitchen knife. Ideally this should be south facing to maximize sunlight illumination. Beware of shiny smearing effects, which can obscure or confuse the soil stratigraphy, especially in clay-rich soils.

If you aim to trace soil (or sediment) layers laterally in an area, trenches (elongated pits) may be excavated using a mechanical digger. There is a danger of wall collapse in cohesionless, sandy soils if a pit or trench is dug too deep.

KEY POINT Never dig or stand in a soil pit or trench that is greater than your height without the walls being shored up with supports.

How you collect soil materials from the profile exposed in a pit depends on what you want them for (Table 18.1). Use a tape to measure the depths of your sampling positions in the profile. Note that it is conventional to

Fig. 18.1 A pointed-blade spade.

Using spades – keep the pointed blade of your spade sharp to make it more effective at cutting through roots and compacted soils. Use a spade with a steel rather than a wooden shaft to prevent breakage.

Do not make your pit too big – remember that 1 m³ of soil weighs over 1 tonne and that this material has not only to be dug out, it has to be put back!

Do not place the plastic sheet in a place which will prevent you standing to see the cleaned, south-facing wall of the pit.

Take a Polaroid® colour photograph of the pit and mark your sampling positions directly on it. The tape should be in the frame to provide a scale.

Table 18.1 Some key reasons for sampling soils and sediments

Determination of physical properties	Determination of chemical and biological properties
Bulk density	Mineralogy
Particle density	Elemental analysis
Particle size distribution	Cation exchange capacity (CEC)
Aggregate size distribution	Concentration of soluble salts
Porosity	pH
Permeability	Concentration of organic matter and organic carbon
Penetrability	Concentration of pesticides
Compressibility	Microbial biomass
Water content	

When sampling soils in pits always be on the lookout for archaeological remains such as pottery, coins and shaped stones.

Samples for microbiological study – these must be kept cool. Use a domestic cool box with ice packs to keep them at <10°C during transport to the laboratory.

Always inform the local police that you have been sampling soils in an area. The discovery of the site of a large soil pit with newly replaced sods could easily be mistaken for something more sinister by a member of the public and might needlessly trigger a police alert.

measure downwards (in positive numbers) from the top of the mineral layers and upwards (in negative numbers) for the organic litter layers.

There are two types of sample, disturbed and undisturbed (intact):

- Disturbed materials may be collected from the various horizons simply using a trowel and then placed in sealed polythene bags, each clearly labelled with indelible marker pen.
- Undisturbed box cores, needed for bulk density determinations, for example, may be collected using commercially available sampling boxes. As a cheaper alternative you can use clean, empty food tins with a volume of no more than 10 cm^3. Make a hole with a nail in the base of the tin to allow air to escape before the tin is pushed carefully and slowly (to avoid compaction) horizontally into the soil at the appropriate level in the side of the pit. Make certain that the top of the tin is indelibly marked to avoid confusion when the sample is retrieved. Withdraw the tin from the side of the pit and seal inside a labelled polythene bag for transport to the laboratory.

On completion of your sampling and observations, carefully return the dug soil into the pit and replace any grass sods. Stamp the soil and sods down to compact them, leaving the site as close as possible to its original state. It is important that you leave the minimum of mess and disturbance behind.

As an alternative to digging pits, numerous types of auger (Fig. 18.2) are available for sampling soils, the commonest being the twin blade and corkscrew varieties. Both return disturbed samples to the surface, the degree of disturbance being greater with the corkscrew auger. Twin blade augers obtain larger samples and are easier to use but are liable to break if they hit a large stone; corkscrew augers are generally more robust. Sampling by auger is ideal for quick reconnaissance surveys and for filling in 'gaps' between soil pits. They can also be used in the base of a pit to extend the sampling depth if you are unable to dig the pit any deeper.

The shaft of an auger should be marked in 0.1 m intervals with tape so you know the depth of penetration into the soil profile. When pulling an auger out of the ground, take care not to hurt or injure your back: keep your legs together and do not bend your back.

Sediments

Sampling sediments on land is done in much the same way as for soils. Many sediments, however, accumulate under water and therefore other techniques are necessary. In intertidal areas, samples may be collected by

Fig. 18.2 A corkscrew soil auger.

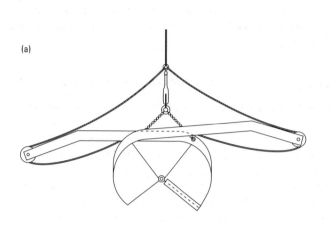
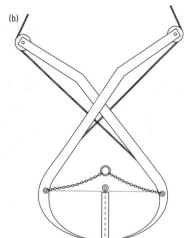

Fig. 18.3 A van Veen grab: (a) open position; (b) closed position.

Grabs and corers – these work best in fine sediments, i.e. muds to sands. They are not suitable for sampling coarse materials.	hand at low water: however, remember the safety implications of working in such environments (see Chapters 2 and 5). In subtidal waters and lakes, unless the assistance of divers is available, samples are obtained by various devices operated remotely from a boat. It is not appropriate here to describe the numerous specialist instruments (grabs and corers) that have been designed over many years (see Mudroch and MacKnight, 1991).

Grabs collect a bulk sediment sample using a scoop or bucket lowered to the bed either by hand or by a winch. According to design, either impact with the bed releases a restraining mechanism and sampling occurs with withdrawal (e.g. van Veen grab, Fig. 18.3), or a messenger dropped down a wire from the surface triggers the mechanism that closes the sampling bucket (e.g. Ekman grab). Note that the shape of sample collected, known as the 'bite shape', varies with the type of instrument, from a cube or rectangular prism (Ekman) to a prism of semi-circular cross-section (van Veen).

If a grab closes with a pebble in its jaws, fine sediment will wash out as it is lifted to the surface and your sample will be unrepresentative. Always check that this has not happened and, if it has, resample.

KEY POINT Grabs tend to disturb sediments. If undisturbed samples are required a box corer (e.g. Reineck box corer) must be used, but note that they are large and cumbersome, being designed for deep water use.

Analysing cores – take a photograph of cores immediately after sampling with a scale alongside. Clearly label the top. Changes in sediment colour may occur soon after retrieval which may rapidly obscure internal structures.

Corers are designed to be operated from a winch and penetrate vertically into sediment so that theoretically undisturbed samples of circular or square cross-section (box core) can be obtained. This permits the observation of vertical changes, internal laminations, sedimentary structures, etc., and sub-sampling of sediments at selected depths below the bed. The simplest is the gravity corer (Fig. 18.4) which penetrates the bed after free fall through the water column. The sample passes through a core cutter into a weighted metal corer tube containing a plastic core liner in which the core is withdrawn for subsequent analysis. Note that loose surface sediments are usually lost when sampling with a gravity corer because they become disturbed by the bow wave created on its descent into the bed.

Be aware that nearly all corers will cause some compaction/shortening of a sample, especially gravity corers in soft sediments. If you want to know more about the reliability of core sampling of soft underwater sediments see Blomqvist (1985).

Piston corers are used mainly for deep water work. Impact with the bed releases a piston which produces a vacuum within the core liner and draws the corer into the sediment. This method helps to reduce internal friction and results in improved penetration.

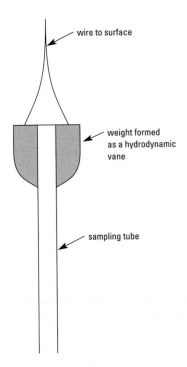

wire to surface

weight formed as a hydrodynamic vane

sampling tube

Fig. 18.4 Cross-section through a gravity corer.

For further details of the various techniques of sampling sediments underwater refer to Holme and McIntyre (1984) and Mudroch and MacKnight (1991).

Sampling pore waters and air from soils and sediments

Collecting samples of pore waters and pore air from soils and sediments is a specialist task involving the use of a modified hypodermic syringe. This should be of the large gauge, broad tip variety, with an opening of *c.* 4–5 mm in diameter. A piece of metal tubing, *c.* 15 cm in length, is attached to the tip. This should have a sealed end and be bored with several small holes around its perimeter at a specified sampling distance. Thus, if one or more holes become blocked the others will still allow water or air to be drawn into the syringe. Samples of *c.* 5 ml in volume may be collected in this way.

19

Sampling minerals, rocks and fossils

The first questions to ask yourself prior to collecting specimens from *in situ* solid geological materials are:

- Why am I sampling?
- Do I really need to sample?
- How do I sample?

These are important questions because you should never forget that such materials are irreplaceable once you have removed them. It is a form of vandalism to hammer off a piece of rock or mineral which may have taken hundreds of millions of years to form, give it a cursory glance and then throw it aside or assign it to a box from which it is never to emerge again.

KEY POINT Unless you need a sample for analytical purposes (e.g. a rock sample for major element geochemistry, an orientated specimen for structural geological analysis, or a fossil for palaeontological study) then do not remove it from the outcrop.

Observations should, as far as practicable, be made on *in situ* rock faces, by non-destructive means, e.g. the naked eye, a ×10 hand lens or photography.

Take full advantage of debris left behind by weathering or the indiscriminate hammering of previous 'collectors'. These materials have already been extracted from outcrops and may be freely collected. Fossils often 'weather out' from rock masses, making them show up clearly. Always look for newly exposed *in situ* surfaces and compare the appearance of fresh rock with that of naturally weathered surfaces. If samples are required for chemical analysis it is important that only fresh materials are collected rather than those which have been altered by chemical weathering.

If you need to collect samples from rock outcrops, do it using a good quality geological hammer, the head of which has a flat-faced end and a chisel end (Fig. 19.1). Sometimes a separate cold chisel is useful. Several weights of hammer head are available but for most purposes one of *c.* 2 kg is appropriate. Always use the flat end of the hammer for hand-sized specimens. To extract small fossils from highly friable rocks such as shales, it may be necessary to use the chisel end of a 2 kg hammer or perhaps a much smaller hammer. For very hard rocks, when a bulk sample is required, use a sledge hammer, *c.* 7 kg in weight. Do not hammer indiscriminately at rock outcrops causing damage to other features such as well-formed crystals, as this prevents them from being observed by others in the future.

KEY POINT Always wear a helmet when working beneath rock faces and wear shatter-proof safety glasses, to protect your eyes from splinters of rock, whenever you are hammering. Do not hammer in close proximity to other people where either the action of hammering or the sudden, violent release of a piece of rock may cause injury.

For many purposes a single sample from a site will suffice and then it is important that it is representative of the site. Do not attempt to hammer at the centre of large, flat rock faces: instead select a 'corner' bounded by joint planes or other discontinuities which will facilitate sample extraction by hammering/chiselling. When searching for and collecting fossils, split

Using a hand lens correctly – hold it very close to one eye with one hand and use your other hand to bring the sample into focus whilst looking through the lens.

Fig. 19.1 A geological hammer.

No hammering of rocks is permitted in Sites of Special Scientific Interest (SSSIs) and other protected areas in the UK. If in doubt about the status of a site, consult the appropriate authority (e.g. English Nature or Scottish Natural Heritage).

Collecting fossils – it is frequently best practice to remove a piece of rock containing a fossil to the laboratory for careful trimming and cleaning, rather than attempt to do this in the field. Remember that complete fossil specimens are rare. Collect identifiable fragments which can be discarded later if better specimens are discovered.

Marking sampling points – do not paint indelible marks on an outcrop to indicate where you propose to collect samples. Use chalk, which will wash off and not cause disfigurement of the site.

sedimentary rocks along their bedding planes (a chisel may be useful here), on which fossils may be preserved in various forms: indiscriminate hammering may destroy any fossils present.

Sometimes several samples are needed from one site, for example to examine the chemical variation through the thickness of an igneous rock body such as a lava flow or a sill. Then you should sample along a transect through the rock at measured intervals (see also Chapter 15). The spacing between samples will vary according to the scale of the outcrop and the degree of detail needed in the final analysis. Visible variations in grain size or mineralogy may clearly determine the necessary sampling points in the rock mass, but if the rock appears homogeneous, it is appropriate to sample at equidistant points.

Always make a careful and thorough description of the site (ideally incorporating a sketch – see Chapter 11) in your field note book. This should include its map reference and the stratigraphic level from which the sample was collected. Notes can be greatly aided by a photograph of the sampling point or points.

All samples must be carefully labelled, usually with a number corresponding with that used in your field notes and on an accompanying map. If you are collecting for geochemical analysis, do not write on specimens using a felt-tipped pen: the inks may penetrate porous rocks and contaminate them. Samples generally should be placed in strong, durable polythene bags. A label, clearly and boldly written in waterproof felt pen or pencil on a piece of strong paper, should be placed in the bag, and the bag itself should also be indelibly labelled with the same number. The bag should then be securely tied. Specimens of friable rocks and fossils are best stored in small cardboard boxes rather than polythene bags, and packed with cotton wool or other synthetic packaging material to prevent damage in transit to the laboratory.

KEY POINT **Careful labelling and packaging is vital to prevent misidentification of and damage to mineral, rock and fossil specimens.**

Once in the laboratory, more permanent labels may, if required, be applied to specimens using a small area of white paint (household gloss paint is ideal for this purpose) bearing the sample number subsequently written in indelible black ink.

Sampling air and water

There are many types of sampling device commercially available for sampling air and water. However, before you choose a particular sampler you must be clear about why you are sampling, what your samples will be used for and from what type of environment they are to be collected. Begin by reading Chapter 15 on sampling strategies and statistics.

KEY POINT Selection of an appropriate sampling device depends on:

1. **The nature of the body of air or water being sampled (see Table 20.1);**
2. **The aims of your sampling programme.**

Before embarking on any air or water sampling programme ask yourself the following questions:

- What level(s)/depth(s) in the water or air column should be sampled?
- How many samples are required and how many replicates?
- Are the samples to be used for (a) qualitative or (b) quantitative physical or chemical analyses?
- What types of instrument and analytical method are to be used (see Chapters 31, 32 and 34).
- What volume of sample is required for the chosen analysis?
- What types of container should be used to store the samples?
- Do the containers require any form of pre-treatment to prevent chemical changes?
- How should the samples be preserved?

KEY POINT The analytical method to be used influences the number of samples required, the volume of sample required and the method of sample preservation.

Table 20.1 Sources from which air and water samples may commonly be collected

General
Point sources, e.g. an effluent discharge pipe or a natural spring
Non-point sources, e.g. a lake that receives the drainage from a large catchment area.

Air
Outdoors (ambient)
Indoor environments   Vehicle exhaust emissions
Industrial emissions   Interstitial (e.g. soil) atmospheres

Water
Earth surface water environments   Precipitation
  oceans and seas   rainfall
  rivers and streams   ice, snow and sleet
  estuaries   fog
  lakes and ponds   dew
  glacial melt waters   Leachates from landfill sites
Groundwater   Mine drainage
  confined aquifers   Effluent discharges
  unconfined aquifers   Industrial wastewater
  springs

Table 20.2 Some key properties determined when sampling water

Suspended sediment/total particulate matter (TPM)
Total dissolved solids (TDS)
pH
Salinity/electrical conductivity
Colour
Dissolved oxygen
Biological oxygen demand (BOD)
Chemical oxygen demand (COD)
Total organic carbon (TOC)
Major anions and cations
Volatile and semi-volatile organic compounds
Metals
Pesticides

Table 20.3 Some key materials sampled from the air

Determination of the concentration of gases
Basic gases, e.g. O_2 and CO_2
Toxic gases, e.g. SO_2, NO, NO_2
Volatile and semi-volatile organic compounds, e.g. CH_4

Determination of the concentration of particulates
Inorganic particles, e.g. smoke, diesel
Organic particulates as aerosols
Biological materials, e.g. spores, pollen, insects
Dust
Fibres
Asbestos

Some of the most common materials you might need to sample from air and/or water are presented in Tables 20.2 and 20.3.

KEY POINT Remember that the composition of air and water in most environments varies significantly both temporally and spatially. You must take this into account when planning your sampling programme.

Sampling air

The ideal atmospheric analysis techniques are those that work successfully without sampling, but for most analyses, various types of sampling are required. The analytical result from a sample can only be as good as the method used to obtain that sample and for most substances, sampling methods are substance specific: you will need to consult appropriate texts.

The simplest technique for the collection of particles is passive sedimentation but the most common quantitative method is aspirated (pumped) filtration. Filters may be composed of sintered (porous) glass, porous ceramics, paper fibres, cellulose fibres, fibreglass, asbestos, mineral wool or plastic. Membrane filters are also useful since they allow relatively high flow rates through small, fairly uniform pores.

Sampling for vapours and gases ranges from methods designed to collect one specific substance to those designed to collect batch samples for all materials. Gases are then either measured in the gas phase directly or absorbed into a solvent or other sorbent. Sorbent tube sampling (Fig. 20.1) is the normal method for collecting volatile and semi-volatile compounds from the air. A sample is obtained by drawing a measured volume of air (<10–$500 \, m^3$) through an open tube that is connected to a pump. Airborne chemicals are trapped on the surface of the sorbent (e.g., silica gel, a glass fibre filter or a polyurethane plug) which is contained within the tube. The tube is then sealed with stoppers and transported to the laboratory for analysis, the trapped chemicals being removed from the sorbent using solvent extraction or heat (usually a specialist laboratory will undertake this).

Whole air samples may be collected in special bags and using a pump. Such bags are typically made of material which is inert to a wide range of chemicals, e.g. Tedlar®/Teflon®. When collecting such samples:

- Always check air sample bags for leaks before use.
- Avoid filling a bag to more than 75–80% of its maximum volume.
- For transit to the laboratory, pack air sample bags carefully to avoid puncturing.

As a control, use two different sorbents to compare analytical results and to determine if contamination reactions between sample and sorbent are occurring.

Labelling – always ensure that water sampling bottles or air sampling bags are clearly labelled in indelible ink.

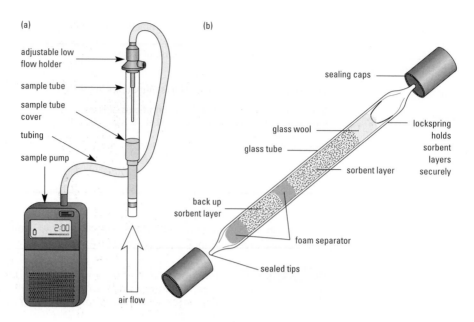

Fig. 20.1 (a) Basic system for sorbent tube sampling; (b) detail of a typical sorbent tube.

You may be able to reuse air sampling bags if you flush them with clean air or nitrogen after evacuation.

• Do not transport air sample bags by air unless the aircraft is pressurized: a decrease in pressure may cause them to burst.

Wind speed and direction must be continuously monitored when sampling ambient air. A change in direction can cause large variations in the concentration of airborne pollutants.

Sampling water

Water samplers are either automatic or manual in operation. Automatic samplers collect at fixed time intervals (usually, but not necessarily, uniform) and retain samples in separate bottles for subsequent analysis. They are suitable for use in rivers and at point sources, e.g. effluent discharges. Composite automatic samplers combine several samples into a single bottle, thereby permitting collection of a time-averaged sample. Automated samplers are also available for collecting precipitation samples. These are designed to trigger and open when precipitation commences.

KEY POINT From the instant a water sample is collected from a site, microbiological, chemical and physical processes that alter its composition may occur.

KEY POINT If any physical or chemical analyses of water samples are to be carried out, make certain that sampling equipment (i.e. samplers and sample containers) is thoroughly rinsed with distilled water immediately prior to field use.

Manually operated water samplers (e.g. Fig. 20.2) are commonly used in large bodies of open water and are essentially open tubes/chambers of fixed volume (usually from 1 to 30 litres), usually made of stainless steel or PVC. For sampling at specific depths in a water column the sampler should be attached to a calibrated line that neither shrinks nor expands in contact with water. A release mechanism, either a messenger weight dropped down the

Sampling close to the bottom of the water column in a lake or in the sea – make certain not to disturb (resuspend) the bed sediments and draw particles into the sampler, since these may contaminate your sample.

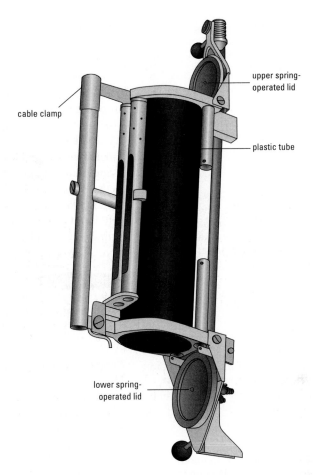

cable clamp

upper spring-
operated lid

plastic tube

lower spring-
operated lid

Fig. 20.2 A universal water sampler.

line or a tug on the line, triggers to seal the tube at the desired sampling depth, typically with two tightly closing rubber stoppers. A good quality water sampler (e.g. NIO Bottle, Niskin Bottle, LaMotte Water Sampler) should be sufficiently heavy to:

- guarantee rapid descent through the water column;
- provide minimal drift from the vertical.

The diameter of the openings should be the same as that of the body of the tube to ensure good flushing (through flow) characteristics on descent to the required sampling depth. Samplers that do not permit unimpeded flow of water through the tube (e.g. bottle and cork) should be avoided other than for surface samples. There are many varieties of tube or bottle type water samplers available on the market. When considering which to use, key attributes are:

- appropriate sample volume;
- efficiency and tightness of closure mechanism;
- ease of operation and handling;
- lack of sample contamination from component parts.

Do not use an elaborate sampler if a simple one will do the intended task. For example, if you need samples of *surface* waters for the determination of variables such as pH, electrical conductivity/salinity, colour, dissolved oxygen or suspended sediment concentration, a bucket attached to a length of rope will often suffice.

Take advantage of bridges to obtain surface water samples from the central, fastest flowing and least accessible parts of rivers and streams.

Pollutant concentrations in snow – these often change significantly as the snow lies on the ground. If you want to determine contemporary pollutant levels in snow, sampling should be carried out as the snow is falling.

Contamination – glass storage bottles can lead to silicon and boron contamination and stainless steel containers can cause contamination by nickel, iron, chromium and molybdenum.

Analysis of volatile organic compounds – store samples in glass bottles preferably with Teflon® caps. Plastics and PVC tend to adsorb organic compounds. Make certain the bottle is completely filled, with no air remaining.

Analysis of metals – store samples in polypropylene or glass bottles. Add a constant amount of 1M HNO_3 to prevent adsorption of metal species onto the bottles. Wash the bottles beforehand with 1M HNO_3.

If you require a very large (hundreds of litres) water sample this can be achieved either by repeated use of a tube sampler or a bucket, or by pumping the water *via* a hose from a specified depth.

Groundwater sampling is a specialist task for which various types of pump sampler are available. There are particular problems in obtaining uncontaminated samples of groundwater from boreholes which are lined with casings of PVC plastics. These can be a source of various organic leachates. Water flowing through steel pipes with soldered joints may become contaminated with lead and zinc.

Snow and ice can be sampled in a series of layers using much the same methods as for soils (see Chapter 18) if analyses of e.g. chemical variations through the sequence as a function of time are required.

It is vital that your samples do not become contaminated in any way during the sampling process, their containment, their transport to the laboratory and their possible period of storage prior to analysis.

KEY POINT The problem of sample contamination by leaching from water sampling devices and sample containers is inversely proportional to the concentration levels of the species (e.g. heavy metals) you are analysing.

Preserving and storing water samples

The mode of preservation and storage of water samples depends on the nature of the analyses to be performed on them. Questions that must be taken into consideration when storing and preserving water samples prior to analysis include:

- Should they be protected from sun or artificial light (e.g. by means of dark glass bottles)?
- Should they be stored at a controlled temperature (either above or below freezing point)?
- Should they be stored with no air remaining in the containers?
- Should they be treated with chemical additives (e.g. formaldehyde to preserve biota)?
- How long can they be stored (maximum storage time) without impairing the analytical results?

21 Sampling using questionnaires

Table 21.1 Some types of information about people that can be obtained from questionnaire surveys

Attitudes
Awareness
Background
Behaviour
Beliefs
Feelings
Ideas
Motives
Opinions
Perceptions
Plans

Questionnaire surveys are an important means of acquiring data in those branches of environmental science that relate to human and social issues, e.g. in gauging public opinion about the environmental impact of a proposed development. Indeed they can provide a broad range of up-to-date data about individuals not normally available from published sources, as summarized in Table 21.1.

KEY POINT If you are contemplating a questionnaire survey you must have clear aims and objectives. The mere wish to undertake such a survey is no justification for doing so.

Populations and sampling

You should initially establish the precise target population (e.g. the student population of your university) from which your sample of individuals is to be selected. How then do you determine which individuals make up your sample population? Begin by reading Chapter 15 on Sampling strategies and statistics. Sample selection may be either random (i.e. relatively unbiased and, therefore, preferable) or non-random (i.e. less representative), each category having various sub-methods.

Random sampling

- Simple random sampling involves obtaining a list of the names of all those in your target population (e.g. the students in your class) and assigning each a number, say 01–50. To select 12 names at random, use random number tables and select the first 12 numbers between 01 and 50. The corresponding individuals form your sample.
- Systematic random sampling is appropriate for very large target populations. Divide the total number of individuals in the target population list by the desired sample size. This will determine a sampling interval. Select a start point using a random number generator or by throwing a dice to determine the first name on the list. Add the sampling interval to this to determine the second individual, and so on until the total sample population has been identified. If your target population is people passing by in a certain street, you can perform systematic random sampling by questioning, for example, every 50th person.
- Stratified random sampling involves division of your target population into sub-groups (strata), e.g. on the basis of age ranges and/or gender, and the selection of a random sample from each sub-group. Full details are given in Fink (1995).
- Cluster sampling is similar to stratified random sampling but the target population is a natural 'cluster', e.g. a university or a school, and is often used for large questionnaire surveys.

Non-random sampling

- Convenience or accidental sampling involves questioning those individuals who are readily available and willing to take part in your survey.

Questioning every *n*th person in the street – this is easier said than done. It is virtually impossible to count in a crowded street, especially when you are concentrating on an individual's responses! If you aim to survey like this it is important to have someone to help you.

Convenience sampling – this is often ideal for undergraduate student projects/ dissertations. It is relatively simple and inexpensive if face-to-face questionnaire sampling is adopted.

- Snowball sampling means that you initially question a small group of individuals who each subsequently identify other participants for the survey and so on. Thus the sample population 'snowballs'.
- Quota sampling is similar to stratified random sampling but the selection of individuals from each stratum is non-random (see Fink, 1995 for further details).

Sample size

> Remember that the bigger the sample population, the higher the cost of the survey.

What size should your sample population be? The answer is the bigger the better in order to make your interpretations more statistically significant (see Chapter 40). Thirty respondents is usually considered as the absolute minimum.

Questionnaire design

KEY POINT Good questionnaire design is essential: questionnaires must be structured and systematic. All component questions must be relevant and unambiguous.

Good questionnaire design is not easy and you will be unlikely to get it right first time. Therefore you should always do at least one pilot study using your friends, family or colleagues as the sample population before embarking on the actual survey. This will allow you to remove unnecessary questions and modify ambiguous questions, and is likely to save you both time and money.

Types of question

There are many types of question which may be used in questionnaires. Some of the commonest are:

- Closed questions – questions simply requesting a 'yes' or 'no' response.
- Attitude battery – questions requesting a response according to a range of positive to negative feelings, e.g. on a five point scale: strongly agree, agree, neutral, disagree, strongly disagree.
- Open questions – questions requesting a detailed response in words, e.g. 'What do you think will be the main environmental problem of the next decade?'

At this stage you must think about how you propose to analyse your data. It is much easier to statistically analyse yes/no type or 'ticked box' responses than 'wordy' answers. However, remember that open questions often reveal more in-depth information about attitudes, beliefs, etc., probably the original reason for carrying out the questionnaire survey.

Some errors to avoid include:

> Always use plain language in questionnaires – avoid jargon.

> Never make questionnaires too long – people get bored quickly!

- Do not ask questions that may potentially cause embarrassment or offence, e.g. 'what is your annual income?' Instead provide the respondent with several income ranges, e.g. less than £9999; £10 000–£19 999; £20 000–£29 999, etc.
- Do not ask leading questions, e.g. 'Why do you think the creation of a local nature reserve is a good idea?' Replace with: 'Do you think that a local nature reserve should be created?' This could have a follow-up question to determine the reasons.
- Do not ask two questions in one, e.g. 'Have you ever seen a badger or a fox in this area?' Replace with two separate questions so that the respondent is absolutely clear which part he or she is answering.

- Do not use double negatives, e.g. 'Don't you think that eating non-organic produce is not good for your health?' Replace with: 'Do you think that eating non-organic produce is bad for your health?'
- Do not use imprecise wording, e.g. 'Have you seen a deer in this area recently?' Replace with: 'Have you seen a deer in this area during the last [insert number] months?'

Survey methods

There are several different questionnaire survey methods. Your choice should be guided by your aims and available financial resources.

Self-completion questionnaires, which must always include a clear set of instructions on how they should be completed, may be delivered to people and collected at a later date or sent out by post. In the latter case a stamped addressed envelope, in which to return the response, should be included. Increasing use is being made of the Internet to transmit such questionnaires and you should consider this as a cost-effective alternative to the post. Always have a much larger sample size than required for self-completion questionnaires to take account of non-responses.

Interviewer administered questionnaire surveys can be conducted face-to-face with individuals in the field or over the telephone. Always prepare an estimate of the costs of carrying out your survey and seek your supervisor's approval before proceeding. These should include photocopying, postage and telephone charges. Do not undertake telephone surveys from your university without the permission of your Head of Department.

To maximize the responses from all types of questionnaire survey you can offer rewards to respondents. These might be a small cash payment or the entry of the respondent's name into a prize draw (e.g. to win a book token). However, if you adopt this practice, make certain that you have adequate funds available to cover the costs.

Some rules for face-to-face questionnaire surveys

- Carry an identification card that can easily be seen and that contains a recent photograph of yourself.
- Dress smartly.
- Do not wear badges, emblems, etc. indicating affiliations which may cause offence to certain sections of the community.

Some rules for both face-to-face and telephone questionnaire surveys

- Speak clearly.
- Give your name and affiliation (e.g. Department of Environmental Science, University of Anytown).
- Explain concisely the purpose(s) of your survey.
- Assure respondents that their answers will be kept confidential and used only for statistical purposes.
- Be patient: do not hurry people into responses, make them feel at ease in conversation with you.

If you want to know more about sampling using questionnaires, refer to Fink and Kosecoff (1985) and the nine volume *Survey Kit* (Fink, 1995).

Layout – make sure that boxes or spaces to be used for 'ticked' responses on questionnaire forms are large enough and well spaced so there is no confusion about which box has been ticked.

Consider using a 'FREEPOST' facility as an alternative to sticking large numbers of postage stamps onto envelopes.

Do not use postal surveys if you need rapid responses.

Be polite, but do not necessarily expect people to be polite in return!

Manipulating and identifying sampled materials

Naming and classifying organisms

The use of scientific names is fundamental to all aspects of the study of living and fossil organisms since it aims to provide a system of identification which is precise, fixed and of universal application. Without such a system, comparative studies would be impossible.

The hierarchical system

KEY POINT The classification of organisms into kingdoms is somewhat arbitrary and no scheme has yet been universally adopted.

One approach is to recognize six kingdoms if the viruses are included:

- Virales. The viruses: very simple in structure, obligate parasites of prokaryotic or eukaryotic cells.
- Prokaryotae (Monera). The bacteria and cyanobacteria: prokaryotic, non-enucleate and lacking mitochondria, plastids, endoplasmic reticulum, Golgi apparatus.
- Protista. Includes algae, protozoans and slime moulds: eukaryotic, mainly unicellular and often autotrophs. A heterogeneous group.
- Plantae. The plants: eukaryotic, walled, mainly multicellular and usually photoautotrophs.
- Fungi. Eukaryotic, usually syncytial, walled and saprotrophic.
- Animalia. The animals: eukaryotic, multicellular and heterotrophs.

Six other levels of taxa are generally accepted: phylum, class, order, family, genus and species, although in botany and microbiology division is used instead of phylum. The levels of taxa above genus are rather subjective and may vary among authorities, but the use of genus and species are governed by strict, internationally agreed conventions called Codes of Nomenclature. There are three such Codes, the Botanical, Zoological and Bacteriological Codes, which operate on similar but not identical principles.

The basis of classification

The basic unit of classification is the species, which represents a group of recognizably similar individuals, clearly distinct from other such groups. No simple definition of a species is possible, but there are two generally used definitions:

- A group of organisms capable of interbreeding and producing fertile offspring – this, however, excludes all asexual, parthenogenetic and apomictic forms!
- A group of organisms showing a close similarity in phenotypic characteristics – this would include morphological, anatomical, biochemical, ecological and life history characters.

When species are compared, groups of species may show a number of features in common; they are then arranged into larger groupings known as genera (singular genus). This process can be repeated at each taxonomic stage to form a hierarchical system of classification whose different levels are known

---

Definitions

Systematics – the study of the diversity of living organisms and of the evolutionary relationships between them.

Classification (taxonomy) – the study of the theory and methods of organization of taxa and therefore, a part of systematics.

Taxon (plural taxa) – an assemblage of organisms sharing some basic features.

Nomenclature – the allocation of names to taxa.

Identification – the placing of organisms into taxa (see Chapter 25).

Alternative classifications – new classifications have been proposed on the basis of studies of e.g. molecular genetics. One such arrangement divides organisms into three major groups: Bacteria, Archaea and Eucarya. As yet, no one of these new systems has been widely adopted.

Definitions

Parthenogenesis – reproduction of a sexually reproducing organism without fertilization.

Apomixis – reproduction without fertilization in plants, akin to parthenogenesis but including development from cells other than gametes.

Table 22.1 Example of taxonomies for a plant, an animal and a bacterium

Common name	English oak	Honey-bee	Pseudomonas
Kingdom	Plantae	Animalia	Monera
Phylum/Division	Anthophyta	Arthropoda	Gracilicutes
Class	Dicotyledonae	Insecta	Scotobacteria
Order	Fagales	Hymenoptera	Pseudomonadales
Family	Fagaceae	Apidae	Pseudomonadaceae
Genus	*Quercus*	*Apis*	*Pseudomonas*
Species	*Q. robur*	*A. mellifera*	*P. aeruginosa*

as taxonomic ranks. The number of levels in this system is arbitrary and based upon practical experience – the seven levels normally used have been found sufficient to accommodate the majority of the variation observed in nature.

When a generic or specific name is changed as a result of further study, the former name becomes a synonym; you should always try to use the latest name. Where a generic name has been changed recently, the old name is occasionally given in parentheses to allow easy reference to the extensive use of the old name. Thus when the cockle *Cardium edule* was renamed *Cerastoderma edule*, it was commonly referred to in textbooks as *Cerastoderma (Cardium) edule*: this is strictly not correct practice but can be helpful for non-specialists. There are taxonomic reference works available for each discipline or sub-discipline, such as the *Flora Europea* (for plants) and the *Plymouth Marine Fauna* (for British marine animals) which can provide the current versions of a name and often its synonyms.

Nomenclature in practice

The scientific name of an organism is effectively a symbol or cipher which removes the need for repeated use of descriptions. It normally comprises two words and is, therefore, called a binomial term. The name of the genus is followed by a second term which identifies the species, e.g. *Quercus robur*, *Apis mellifera*, or *Pseudomonas aeruginosa* (Table 22.1). Common names are often interesting, but totally unsatisfactory for use in biological nomenclature because of the lack of consistency in their use: the Codes of Nomenclature were established to prevent any ambiguities.

The Codes require that all scientific names are either Latin or treated as Latin, written in the Latin alphabet and subject to the rules of Latin grammar. Consequently, you must be very precise in your use of such names. In some cases, the Codes stipulate a standardized ending for the names of all taxa of a given taxonomic rank, e.g. names of all animal families must end in -idae while plant, fungal and bacterial families end in -aceae. When used in a formal scientific context, you should follow the specific name by the authority on which that name is based, i.e. the name of the person describing that species and the date of the description.

Box 22.1 summarizes the basic rules for writing taxonomic names.

Writing taxonomic names – always underline or italicize generic and species names to avoid confusion: thus bacillus is a descriptive term for rod-shaped bacteria, while *Bacillus* is a generic name.

Taxa below the rank of species

Some use is made of taxa below the rank of species. Within zoology, this is confined to the term subspecies, so the names of subspecies have three components, e.g. *Mus musculus domesticus*, no rank name being necessary.

In bacteriology, the use of subspecies is again acceptable although a word

Box 22.1 Basic rules for the writing of taxonomic names

- Names of the seven levels of taxa should take lower case initial letters, e.g. class Mollusca or kingdom Fungi.
- The Latin forms of all taxon names except the specific name take initial capital letters, e.g. 'the Arthropoda ...' but anglicized versions do not, e.g. 'the arthropods...'.
- The names of the higher taxa are all plural, hence 'the Mollusca are...' while the singular of the anglicized version is used for a single member of that taxon, hence 'a mollusc is...'.
- The binomial system gives each species two terms, the first being the generic name and the second the specific name, which must never be used by itself. The generic and species names are distinguished from the rest of the text either:
  (a) by being underlined (when handwritten or typed), e.g. Patella vulgata; or
  (b) by being set in italics (in print or on a word processor), e.g. *Patella vulgata*.
- The generic name is singular and always takes an initial capital letter. If you use the generic name this implies that the point being made is a generic characteristic unless the specific name is present. Write the generic name in full when first used in a text, e.g. *Patella vulgata*, but subsequent references can be abbreviated to its initial letter, e.g. *P. vulgata*, unless this will result in confusion with another genus also being considered.
- The abbreviation 'sp.' should be used in place of the specific name if a single unspecified species of a genus is being referred to, e.g. *Patella* sp.; it is not underlined or italicized. If more than one unspecified species is meant, then the correct form is 'spp.', e.g. *Patella* spp.
- Common names should not normally be written with a capital letter, e.g. limpet.
- Each species name should be followed by the authority: on first usage in formal reports and in titles, the name or names of the person(s) to whom that name is attributed and the date of that description should be quoted. These names may sometimes be abbreviated, e.g. L. for Linnaeus and the standard abbreviations must be used. If the species was first described under its current generic name, the authority's name, often in abbreviated form is added, e.g. *Quercus robur* L. If, however, the species was first described under a different genus, the name of the author of the original description is presented in parentheses, e.g. *Quercus petraea* (Mattuschkal) Liebl. Note that in zoology and palaeontology, the date the description was published is also included, e.g. *Ischnochiton kermadecensis* Iredale, 1914. The use of authorities should be confined to formal papers, final year project reports, etc.; they would not normally be used in practical reports, short assignments or examinations.

indicating rank is usually inserted, e.g. *Bacillus subtilis* subsp. *niger*. The Bacteriological Code considers ranks from the level of subspecies up to, and including, class: the use of the term variety is discouraged, as the term is synonymous with subspecies. However, other terms are in widespread use for taxa below the species level, especially in medical microbiology and plant pathology, when a particular strain of bacterium has been identified.

Strains – the term 'strain' is now more widely used, particularly in the context of the practice of lodging microbiological strains with culture collections.

In botany, several categories below the rank of species are recognized and a term of rank is used before the name, e.g. *Salix repens* var. *fusca*: the term var. is short for the Latin word *varietas* and is subordinate to the term sub-species in the Botanical Code. The term cultivar (cv.) is an important modern term frequently used in experimental work and refers to cultivated varieties of plants.

The special case of viruses

The classification and nomenclature of viruses is less advanced than for cellular organisms and the current nomenclature has been arrived at on a piecemeal, *ad hoc* basis. Recently, the International Committee for Virus Taxonomy proposed a unified classification system, dividing viruses into fifty families on the basis of:

- host preference;
- nucleic acid type (i.e. DNA or RNA);
- whether the nucleic acid is single or double stranded;
- the presence or absence of a surrounding envelope.

Example The virus that causes tobacco mosaic disease belongs to the genus *Tobamovirus* and can be referred to as tobacco mosaic tobamovirus, tobacco mosaic virus or TMV.

Virus family names end in -viridae and genus names in -virus. (Note that these names are *not* latinized and the genus-species binomial is not now approved.) However, this system has not yet been adopted universally and many viruses are still referred to by their trivial names or by code-names, e.g. the bacterial viruses ϕX174, T4, etc. Many of the names used reflect the diseases caused by the virus. Often, a three-letter abbreviation is used, e.g. HIV (for human immunodeficiency virus), TMV (for tobacco mosaic virus).

23 Using microscopes

Many features of interest in environmental systems are too small to be seen by the naked eye and can only be observed with a microscope. All microscopes consist of a coordinated system of lenses arranged so that a magnified image of a specimen is seen by the viewer (Fig. 23.1). The main differences are the wavelengths of electromagnetic radiation used to produce the image, the nature and arrangement of the lens systems and the methods used to view the image.

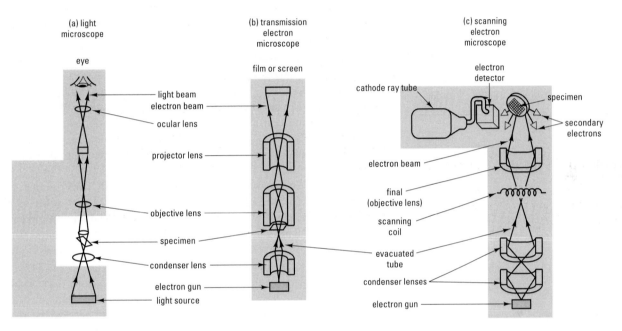

Fig. 23.1 Simplified diagrams of light and electron microscopes. Note that the electron microscopes are drawn upside-down to aid comparison with the light microscope.

Microscopes allow objects to be viewed with increased resolution and contrast. Resolution is the ability to distinguish between two points on the specimen – the better the resolution, the 'sharper' the image. Resolution is affected by lens design and inversely related to the wavelength of radiation used. Contrast is the difference in intensity perceived between different parts of an image. This can be enhanced (a) by the use of stains, and (b) by adjusting microscope settings, usually at the expense of resolution.

The three main forms of microscopy are light microscopy, transmission electron microscopy (TEM) and scanning electron microscopy (SEM). Their main properties are compared in Table 23.1.

Light microscopy

Two forms of the standard light microscope, the binocular (compound) microscope and the dissecting microscope, are described later: both forms are now available as field microscopes but they are of limited magnification and effectiveness. The laboratory versions are the instruments most likely to be used in routine practical work. In more advanced project work, you may use

Using microscopes

Table 23.1 Comparison of microscope types. Resolution is that obtained by a skilled user. LM, light microscope; SEM, scanning electron microscope; TEM, transmission electron microscope

Property	Type of microscope		
	LM	SEM	TEM
Resolution	200 nm	10 nm	1 nm
Depth of focus	Low	High	Medium
Field of view	Good	Good	Limited
Specimen preparation (ease)	Easy	Easy	Skilled
Specimen preparation (speed)	Rapid	Quite rapid	Slow
Relative cost of instrument	Low	High	High

one or more of the following more sophisticated variants of light microscopy to improve image quality:

- Dark field illumination involves a special condenser which causes reflected and diffracted light from the specimen to be seen against a dark background. The method is particularly useful for near-transparent specimens and for fresh aquatic materials. Care must be taken with the thickness of slides used – air bubbles and dust must be avoided and immersion oil must normally be used between the dark field condenser and the underside of the slide.

- Ultraviolet microscopy uses short-wavelength UV light to increase resolution. Fluorescence microscopy uses radiation at UV wavelengths to make certain naturally fluorescent substances (e.g. chlorophyll) or fluorescent dyes emit light of visible wavelengths. Special light sources, lenses and mountants are required for UV and fluorescence microscopy and filters must be used to prevent damage to users' eyes.

- Phase contrast microscopy is useful for increasing contrast when viewing transparent specimens. It is superior to dark field microscopy because a better image of the interior of specimens is obtained. Phase contrast operates by causing constructive and destructive interference effects in the image, visible as increased contrast. Adjustments must be made for each objective lens and the microscope must be set up carefully to give optimal results.

- Nomarski or Differential Interference Contrast (DIC) microscopy gives an image with a three-dimensional quality. However, the relief seen is optical rather than morphological, and care should be taken in interpreting the result. One of the advantages of the technique is the extremely limited depth of focus which results: this allows 'optical sectioning' of a specimen.

- Confocal microscopy allows 3-dimensional views of cells or thick sections. A finely focused laser is used to create electronic images of layered horizontal 'slices', usually after fluorescent staining. Images can be viewed individually or reconstructed to provide a 3-D computer-generated image of the whole specimen.

Polarized light microscopy

Most crystalline substances are anisotropic, i.e. their physical properties differ if measured in different directions. The petrological or polarizing microscope makes use of the effect of crystalline lattices on transmitted polarized light and is used for study of the optical properties of minerals in thin section. To achieve this, the polarizing microscope requires two additional features to those found on an ordinary light microscope:

- a light polarizing system;
- a rotating stage.

The polarizing system consists of two parts, the polarizer and the analyser. The polarizer is located at the base of the microscope sub-stage condenser system. It is a disc of polarizing film orientated to allow passage of only the east–west vibrating light from the light source through the condenser to the specimen.

The analyser, a second disc of polarizing film that permits passage of north–south vibrating light, mounted between the objective lens and the eyepiece, may be inserted into the optical path. This permits observation of thin sections of specimens in two modes:

Table 23.2 Some key points when examining thin sections of rocks by polarizing microscopy

- Isotropic crystals appear transparent in PPL but black in XPL.
- Anisotropic crystals transmit light in both PPL and XPL modes.
- Opaque crystals (e.g. oxides and sulphides) do not transmit light in either PPL or XPL modes.
- Some minerals change in colour in PPL on rotation of the stage; this is known as **pleochroism**.
- In PPL, minerals of higher refractive index stand out in contrast relative to those of lower refractive index. This is known as **relief**.
- Many minerals alter to chemically related species (e.g. feldspars alter to clay minerals). This generally results in a 'dusty' appearance in PPL known as **alteration**.
- Owing to the regular geometric arrangement of the atoms making up the crystal lattice, many minerals possess one, two or three planes along which they cleave preferentially. These **cleavage planes** appear as parallel lines in specimens observed in PPL.
- On rotation of the stage, anisotropic minerals show, in XPL, four positions, 90° apart, at which they become dark. These are known as **extinction positions** and relate to some definite direction in the crystal. The **extinction angle** of a given mineral is the angle between an extinction position and a crystallographic feature, e.g. a cleavage. Graduations on the stage permit determination of this angle, which can be an important diagnostic character for different minerals.
- **Interference colours** are determined by mineral type, thickness of the section and orientation of the crystal lattice cut by the plane of the section. They vary through low, medium and high orders:
    - Low order: grey and yellow
    - Medium order: deep yellow, red, blue and green
    - High order: brighter shades of the same colours.

- Plane polarized light (PPL). In this mode the analyser is removed from the light path and the following features are examined: opacity/transparency, colour, pleochroism, relative refractive index, alteration, cleavage (Table 23.2) and crystal shape.
- Cross polarized light (XPL). In this mode the analyser is inserted into the light path allowing observation of isotropy/anisotropy, extinction, interference colours (Table 23.2).

The rotating stage allows a crystal lattice to be rotated in the beam of polarized light; its axis of rotation is coincident with the light path of the microscope. Isotropic minerals (those belonging to the cubic system) always appear black in XPL but anisotropic minerals display different colours, known as interference colours, that change as the stage is rotated, i.e. according to the orientation of the crystals. For example, quartz may vary from grey to white. The identification of minerals in thin section may well be beyond the scope of your course but some key points are listed in Table 23.2. If you require further information see, for example, Gribble and Hall (1985).

KEY POINT   Interference colours also depend on the thickness of the section, so a constant thickness, by convention 30 μm, must be used.

Polarized light microscopy can also be used to reveal the presence and orientation of optically active components within biological specimens (e.g. starch grains, cellulose fibres), showing brightly against a dark background.

Electron microscopes

Electron microscopes offer an image resolution up to 200 times better than light microscopes (Table 23.1) because they utilize radiation of shorter wavelength in the form of an electron beam. The electrons are produced by a tungsten filament operating in a vacuum and are focused by electromagnets. TEM and SEM differ in the way in which the electron beam interacts with the specimen: in TEM, the beam passes through the specimen (Fig. 23.1b), while in SEM the beam is scanned across the specimen and is reflected from the surface (Fig. 23.1c). In both cases, the beam must fall on a fluorescent screen before the image can be seen. Permanent images ('electron micrographs') are produced after focusing the beam on photographic film.

You are unlikely to use either type of electron microscope as part of undergraduate practical work because of the time required for specimen preparation and the need for detailed training before these complex machines can be operated correctly.

Setting up and using a light microscope

The light microscope is an important instrument widely used in practicals and its correct use is one of the basic and essential skills of laboratory technique. A standard undergraduate binocular microscope (Fig. 23.2) consists of three main types of optical unit: eyepiece, objective and condenser. These are attached to a stand which holds the specimen on a stage. A monocular microscope is constructed similarly but has one eyepiece lens rather than two.

Setting up a binocular light microscope

Before using any microscope, familiarize yourself with its component parts.

KEY POINT Never assume that the previous person to use your microscope has left it set up correctly: apart from differences in users' eyes, the microscope needs to be properly set up for each lens combination used.

The procedures outlined below are simplified to allow you to set up microscopes like those of the Olympus CH series (Fig. 23.2). For monocular microscopes, disregard instructions for adjusting eyepiece lenses in (5).

1. Place the microscope at a convenient position on the bench. Adjust your seating so that you are comfortable operating the focus and stage controls. Unwind the power cable, plug in and switch on after first ensuring that the lamp setting is at a minimum. Adjust the lamp setting to about two-thirds of the maximum.
2. Select a low-power (e.g. $\times 10$) objective. Make sure that the lens clicks home.
3. Set the eyepiece lenses to your interpupillary distance; this can usually be read off a scale on the turret. You should now see a single circular field of vision. If you do not, try adjusting in either direction.
4. Put a prepared slide on the stage. Examine it first against a light source and note the position, colour and rough size of the specimen. Place the slide on the stage (coverslip up!) and, viewing from the side, position it with the stage adjustment controls so that the specimen is illuminated.
5. Focus the image of the specimen using first the coarse and then the fine focusing controls. The image will be reversed and upside-down compared to that seen by viewing the slide directly.
   (a) If both eyepiece lenses are adjustable, set your interpupillary distance on the scale on each lens. Close your left eye, look through the right eyepiece with your right eye and focus the image with the

Using binocular eyepieces – if you do not know your interpupillary distance, ask someone to measure it with a ruler. You should stare at a fixed point in the distance while the measurement is taken. Take a note of the value for future use.

Fig. 23.2 Diagram of the Olympus binocular microscope model CH.

- The lamp (1) in the base of the stand (2) supplies light; its brightness is controlled by an on–off switch and voltage control (3). Never use maximum voltage or the life of the bulb will be reduced – a setting two-thirds to three-quarters of maximum should be adequate for most specimens. A field–iris diaphragm may be fitted close to the lamp to control the area of illumination (not present on this model).

- The condenser control (4) focuses light from the condenser lens system (5) onto the specimen and projects the specimen's image onto the front lens of the objective. Correctly used, it ensures optimal resolution.

- The condenser–iris diaphragm (6) controls the amount of light entering and leaving the condenser; its aperture can be adjusted using the condenser–iris diaphragm lever (7). Use this to reduce glare and enhance image contrast by cutting down the amount of stray light reaching the objective lens.

- The specimen (normally mounted on a slide) is fitted to a mechanical stage or slide holder (8) using a spring mechanism. Two controls allow you to move the slide in x and y planes. Vernier scales (see p. 18) on the slide holder can be used to return to the same place on a slide. The fine and coarse focus controls (9) adjust the height of the stage relative to the lens systems. Take care when adjusting the focus controls to avoid hitting the lenses with the stage or slide.

- The objective lens (10) supplies the initial magnified image; it is the most important component of any microscope because its qualities determine resolution, depth of field and optical aberrations. The objective lenses are attached to a revolving nosepiece (11). Take care not to jam the longer lenses onto the stage or slide as you rotate the nosepiece. You should feel a distinct click as each lens is moved into position. The magnification of each objective is written on its side; a normal complement would be ×4, ×10, ×40 and ×100 (oil immersion).

- The eyepiece lens (12) is used to further magnify the image from the objective and to put it in a form and position suitable for viewing. Its magnification is written on the holder (normally ×10). By twisting the holder for one or both of the eyepiece lenses you can adjust their relative heights to take account of optical differences between your eyes. The interpupillary distance scale (13) and adjustment knob allow compensation to be made for differences in the distance between users' pupils.

- The turret clamping screw (14) allows the eyepiece turret (15) to be rotated so a demonstrator can view your specimen without exchanging position with you. If loosened too much, the turret can come off, so take care and always re-tighten after use.

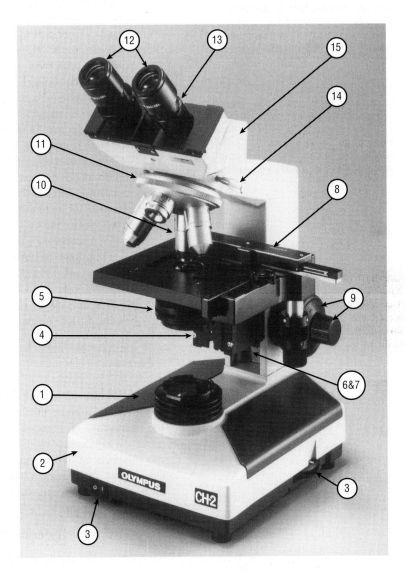

Problems with spectacles – those who wear glasses can remove them for viewing as microscope adjustments will accommodate most deficiencies in eyesight (except astigmatism). This is more comfortable and stops the spectacle lenses being scratched by the eyepiece holders. However, it creates difficulties in focusing when drawing diagrams.

Adjusting a microscope with a field–iris diaphragm – adjust this *before* the condenser–iris diaphragm: close it until its image appears in view, if necessary focusing its image with the condenser controls and centring it. Now open it so the whole field is just illuminated.

High-power objectives – *never remove a slide while a high power objective lens (i.e. ×40 or ×100) is in position. Always turn back to the ×10 first. Having done this, lower the stage and remove the slide.*

normal controls. Now close your right eye, look through the left eyepiece with your left eye and focus the image by rotating the eyepiece holder. Take a note of the setting for future use.

(b) If only the left eyepiece is adjustable, close your left eye, look with the right eye through the static right eyepiece and focus the image with the normal controls. Now close your right eye, look through the left eyepiece with your left eye and focus the image by rotating the eyepiece holder. Take a note of the setting for future use.

6. Close the condenser–iris diaphragm (aperture–iris diaphragm), then open it to a position such that further opening has no effect on the brightness of the image (the 'threshold of darkening'). The edge of the diaphragm should not be in view. Turn down the lamp if it is too bright.

7. Focus the condenser. Place an opaque pointed object (the tip of a mounted needle or a sharp pencil point) on the centre of the light source. Adjust the condenser setting until both the specimen and needle tip/pencil point are in focus together. Check that the condenser–iris diaphragm is just outside the field of view.

8. For higher magnifications, swing in the relevant objective (e.g. ×40), carefully checking that there is space for it. Adjust the focus using the fine control only. If the object you wish to view is in the centre of the field with the ×10 objective, it should remain in view (magnified, of course) with the ×40. Adjust the condenser–iris diaphragm and condenser as before – the correct setting for each lens will be different.

9. When you have finished using the microscope, remove the last slide and clean the stage if necessary. Turn down the lamp setting to its minimum, then switch off. Clean the eyepiece lenses with lens tissue. Check that the objectives are clean. Unplug the microscope from the mains and wind the cable round the stand and under the stage. Replace the dust cover.

If you have problems in obtaining a satisfactory image, refer to Box 23.1; if this doesn't help, refer the problem to the class supervisor.

Procedure for observing transparent specimens

Some stained preparations and all colourless objects are difficult to see when the microscope is adjusted as above. Contrast can be improved by closing down the condenser–iris diaphragm. Note that when you do this, diffraction haloes appear round the edges of objects. These obscure the image of the true structure of the specimen and may result in loss of resolution. Nevertheless, an image with increased contrast may be easier to interpret.

Care and maintenance of your microscope

Microscopes are delicate precision instruments. Handle them with care and never force any of the controls. Never touch any of the glass surfaces with anything other than clean, dry lens tissue. Bear in mind that a replacement would be very expensive.

If moving a microscope, hold the stand above the stage with one hand and rest the base of the stand on your other hand. Always keep the microscope vertical (or the eyepieces may fall out). Put the microscope down gently.

Clean lenses by gently wiping with clean, dry lens tissue. Use each piece of tissue once only. Try not to touch lenses with your fingers as oily fingerprints are difficult to clean off. Do not allow any solvent (including water) to come into contact with a lens; sea water is particularly damaging.

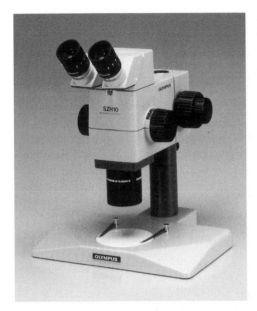

Fig. 23.3 A dissecting microscope.

Box 23.1   Problems in light microscopy and possible solutions

- No image; very dark image; image dark and illuminated irregularly
    Microscope not switched on (check plug and base)
    Illumination control at low setting or off
    Objective nosepiece not clicked into place over a lens
    Diaphragm closed down too much or off centre
    Lamp failure
- Image visible and focused but pale and indistinct
    Diaphragm needs to be closed down further
    Condenser requires adjustment
- Image blurred and cannot be focused
    Dirty objective
    Dirty slide
    Slide in upside-down
    Slide not completely flat on stage
    Eyepiece lenses not set up properly for user's eyes
    Fine focus at end of travel
- Dust and dirt in field of view
    Eyepiece lenses dirty
    Slide dirty
    Dirt on lamp glass or upper condenser lens

Measuring specimens using a dissecting microscope – because of the low magnification, sizes can generally be estimated by comparison with a ruler placed alongside the specimen, but if more accurate measurements are required, eyepiece graticules can be used.

The dissecting (stereoscopic) microscope

The dissecting microscope (Fig. 23.3) is a form of stereoscopic microscope used for observations at low total magnification ($\times 4$ to $\times 50$) where a large working distance between objectives and stage is required, perhaps because the specimen is not flat or dissecting instruments are to be used. A stereoscopic microscope essentially consists of two separate lens systems, one for each eye. Some instruments incorporate zoom objectives. The eyepiece–objective combinations are inclined at about 15° to each other and the brain resolves the compound image in three dimensions as it does for normal vision. The image is right side up and not reversed, which is ideal for dissections. Specimens are often viewed in a fresh state and need not be placed on a slide – they might be in a Petri dish or on a white tile. Illumination can be from above or below the specimen, as desired.

Most of the instructions for the binocular microscope given above apply equally well to dissecting microscopes, although the latter do not normally have adjustable condensers or diaphragms. With stereoscopic microscopes, make specially sure to adjust the eyepiece lenses to suit your eyes so that you can take full advantage of the stereoscopic effect.

24 Preparing specimens for light microscopy

Preparative techniques are crucial to successful microscopical investigation because the chemical and physical processes involved have the potential for making the material difficult to work with and for producing artefacts. The basic steps (Fig. 24.1) are similar in most cases, but the exact details (e.g. timing, chemicals used and their concentrations) differ according to the material being examined and the purpose of the investigation. It is usually best to follow a recipe that has worked in the past for your material (see, for example, Grimstone and Skaer, 1972). Some materials, e.g. rocks and minerals, do not require chemical fixation (preservation) before sectioning.

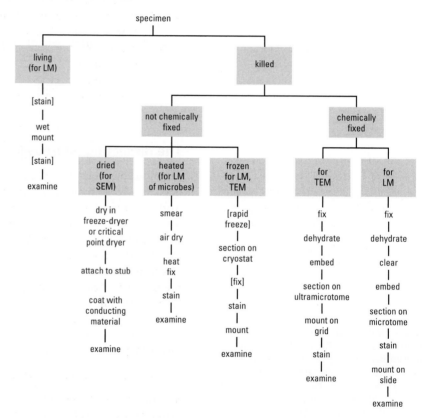

Fig. 24.1 Flowchart of procedures necessary to prepare specimens for different forms of microscopy. Steps enclosed in brackets are optional. LM, light microscope; SEM, scanning electron microscope; TEM, transmission electron microscope.

Chemical fixation

The main purpose of fixation is to preserve material in a life-like manner. The process of fixation for microscopy is much more critical than for whole specimens and only small pieces of material should be used. The fixation solutions used for microscopy are intended to:

- penetrate rapidly to prevent post-mortem changes in biological materials;
- coagulate organic contents into insoluble substances;
- protect material against shrinkage and distortion during subsequent processing;
- allow parts to become selectively and clearly visible when stained.

Fixative solutions are usually mixtures of chemicals selected for their combined properties (see Chapter 17). Your choice of fixative from the numerous recipes available in reference texts will depend upon both the type of investigation and the nature of the material.

KEY POINT Poor fixation can produce artefacts, particularly where coagulant fixatives are used.

When using a fixative for microscopy, observe the following points:

- Use fresh solutions: some of the fluids are unstable and do not keep well. Do not re-use fixative.
- Always use plenty of fixing fluid compared with the volume of material to be fixed (not less than a 10:1 fixative:sample volume ratio).
- Avoid under-fixation or over-fixation: in general the optimum time will be a function of several factors including:
  (a) Penetration capacity of the fixative.
  (b) The size of the piece of material: this should always be small and have as large a surface:volume ratio as possible.
  (c) The type of material to be fixed: uniform materials fix more quickly than complex ones, where one component may form a barrier to others. Materials filled with air can be difficult to submerge and infiltrate; this can be overcome by fixation in a partial vacuum.
  (d) The temperature: increased temperature results in increased penetration rate, but also tends to make organic materials brittle.
- Wash the specimen thoroughly after fixation: residues of fixative can interfere with subsequent processes. The washing may be in water or another appropriate solution. Biological materials may then require further processing by dehydration and cleaning and, for thin sections, embedding and sectioning (see *Practical Skills in Biology*, 2nd edn, Chapter 23).

Staining

The purpose of staining in microscopy is to:

- add contrast to the image;
- identify chemical components of interest;
- locate particular types of component.

This is achieved in different ways for different types of microscopy. In standard light microscopy, contrast is achieved by staining the structure of interest with a coloured dye; in UV microscopy, contrast is obtained using fluorescent stains. Physico-chemical properties of the stain cause it to attach to certain structures preferentially or be taken up across cell membranes.

Stains for light microscopy are categorized according to the charge on the dye molecule. Stains like haematoxylin, whose coloured part is a cation (i.e. basic dyes), stain acidic, anionic substances like nucleic acids: such structures are termed basophilic. Stains like eosin, whose coloured part is an anion (i.e. acid dyes), stain basic, cationic substances: such structures are termed acidophilic. Acid dyes tend to stain all tissue components, especially at low pH, and are much used as counterstains. Staining is progressive if it results in some structures taking up the dye preferentially. Staining is regressive if it involves initial over-staining followed by decolorization (differentiation) of those structures which do not bind the dye tightly.

Certain 'vital' stains (e.g. neutral red) are used to determine cell viability or the pH of cell compartments such as plant vacuoles. 'Mortal' stains (e.g. Evans' blue) are excluded from living cells but diffuse into dead ones and are used to assay cell mortality. For a list of stains and staining procedures, see *Practical Skills in Biology*, 2nd edn, Chapter 23.

Mounting material for microscopy

Wet mounts

These are used for observing fresh specimens. The following steps are involved:

1. Isolate the specimen or material.
2. Place the specimen in a small droplet of the relevant fluid (fresh water, sea water, etc.) on a microscope slide.
3. Gently lower a coverslip onto the droplet, using forceps or two needles and avoiding bubbles.
4. Remove any excess water on or around the coverslip with absorbent paper.

Entire specimens can be examined under the light microscope providing they are small enough to be mounted on a glass slide. They may be mounted in cavity slides or using ring mounts.

Temporary mounts

These essentially involve wet mounting in a mountant with a short useful life, e.g. for identification purposes. It may be desirable to clear the specimen first and a dual purpose substance such as lactophenol, which will clear from 70% (v/v) ethanol, is recommended.

Permanent mounts

These protect sections during examination and allow storage without deterioration. A permanent mount involves sealing your section under a coverslip in a mountant. The mountants used are clear resins dissolved in a slowly evaporating solvent. A good mountant has a similar refractive index to the tissue being mounted, remains clear through time, is chemically inert and will harden quickly. Natural resins like Canada balsam take a long time to dry, are variable in quality and tend to colour-up and crack in time. The newer synthetic resins and plastics such as DPX® mountant are superior: they dry quickly, are available in a range of refractive indices, and do not yellow with age. For tissue components soluble in organic solvents, aqueous mounting media based on, for example, gelatine or glycerol should be used. Find out which mountant is recommended for your particular sections.

The recommended procedure when mounting thin sections on a slide is:

1. Apply a little mountant to a coverslip of appropriate size.

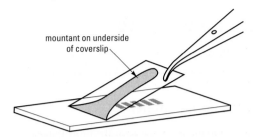

mountant on underside of coverslip

Fig. 24.2 How to lower a coverslip painted with mountant on its underside onto sections on a slide.

2. Turn the coverslip over and place on its edge to one side of the sections as in Fig. 24.2.
3. Lower the coverslip slowly down onto the sections so as to displace all the air and sandwich the sections between the slide and the coverslip.
4. Press firmly from the centre outwards to distribute the mounting medium evenly.
5. Allow the solvent to evaporate – best results come from slow drying when time allows, but many synthetic mountants will tolerate brief heating when speed is essential.

Thin sections of rocks

It is highly unlikely that you will ever have to make thin sections of geological materials since this is a specialist task involving:

- Cementing a thin slice of rock (cut with a diamond saw) onto a glass slide.
- Mechanical grinding and hand finishing using carborundum powder to produce a layer of rock with a standard thickness of $30\,\mu$m.
- Cementing a cover slip on top of the thin layer of rock.

The standard thickness of a rock section is estimated using the interference colours of known minerals in the specimen (see Chapter 23).

Squash preparations

These may be required for any type of mount. The smallest specimens can be squashed after mounting by applying gentle pressure on the coverslip with your forceps. Larger specimens can be squashed between two slides before fixing and mounting – this ensures that higher pressures are applied evenly.

Identifying organisms and using identification keys

Macroscopic organisms (plants and animals)

The normal way to identify plants or animals is to use identification guides. These consist of two parts:

> Observing rare specimens – take special care not to collect, disturb or destroy rare plants and animals in the course of your observations.

1. Written and pictorial descriptions of organisms, which you compare with your unknown specimen to aid in its identification. Good descriptions direct you to the crucial diagnostic features for the relevant taxon, explain the range of variability found and point out biological and ecological characteristics of importance.
2. Keys, which help you find the likely description for your specimen rapidly and simply. Most keys are arranged to present you with a series of choices, usually dichotomous (dividing in two). The paired statements of each 'couplet' are framed to be contrasting and mutually exclusive. Each choice you make narrows down the possibilities for your specimen until you find the appropriate description.

The authors of identification guides assume that you have a live or preserved specimen to hand and the means to observe it closely and measure it. The terminology in guides is designed to combine precision with brevity.

KEY POINT To use an identification guide properly, you need to know enough of the vocabulary to understand the choices presented to you, but all identification guides provide both a glossary and a list of abbreviations to help with this.

The best identification guides are those which lead you in the simplest way to a correct identification. If you need to choose one for your area of interest, think about the following questions:

- What degree of prior knowledge is assumed? Some guides are written for novices, while others assume an expert's command of terminology. If tempted to go for the former type, consider whether it will always be suitable for your needs.
- What is the scope of the guide? Guides may be restricted in the taxa they consider or in the geographical region that is covered; this will suit you if your interests are similarly narrow. However, if your interests are wide, the relevant guide may be so large as to be unwieldy in the field.
- How well is the guide illustrated? Good quality illustrations enhance the ease of use of a guide – features can be shown pictorially that might involve an off-putting specialized vocabulary to describe. Accurately coloured illustrations can be helpful, but note that colour can be a variable character: look for good line diagrams that highlight the critical diagnostic points.
- Is the guide divided into parts? Good guides are arranged in short parts dealing with different levels of the taxonomic hierarchy. This speeds up identification by allowing you to skip initial material when you have a fair idea of the specimen's identity.
- Do you like the style of the key? As discussed below, there are several ways in which a key can be presented, one of which may suit you more

> Out-of-date guides – taxonomists frequently change the names of taxa and update their classification. An up-to-date identification requires an up-to-date guide!

than the others. If you can't actually test out a key yourself on real specimens, the next best thing is to ask for the opinion of someone who has used it.

Types of key

Bracketed keys

Here, numbered pairs of adjacent lines in the key present you with a choice and either 'send' you to a new couplet or provide the tentative identification (Box 25.1).

Box 25.1   Example of a bracketed key

Part of key to ragworts, modified after Stace (1997):

1. Ligules <8 mm or 0; capitula cylindrical, about 2× as long as
    wide 2
    Ligules >8 mm; capitula bell-shaped in flower, about 1.5× as
    long as wide 3
2. Ligules usually 0; achenes ⩽ 2.5 mm   *Senecio vulgaris*
    Ligules usually present; achenes <3 mm   *Senecio cambrensis*

If there are no ligules on your specimen or they are less than 8 mm in length, you should proceed to choice 2, but if they are present and greater than 8 mm in length, you should proceed to choice 3.

In this case, the choice at 2 is sufficient to pin down the species; sometimes quite early in a key a distinctive characteristic may allow the specimen to be 'identified' to species level, while for the other options the specimen's identity remains open. Note the use of more than one comparison in each couplet to provide confirmation.

Indented keys

In this method, the pairs of choices are indented and given the same number. They are separated by other choices further down the sequence. Having made a choice, you look at the next couplet below which will be one indent level further in. When a choice is sufficiently distinctive, the tentative identity of your specimen will be given (Box 25.2).

KEY POINT   Bracketed keys have the advantage that they keep the couplets close together for ready comparison, but indented keys show the relationships between taxa more clearly and allow you to back-track more easily if an error has been made.

Flowchart keys

In this form of key, the choices are laid out in the form of a flowchart (Fig. 25.1), which allows easier cross-checking of options but is only feasible where there is a small number of choices. To use this type of key, follow the arrows after making each choice in the sequence; this will lead you on to another choice and eventually to the tentative identification.

Multi-access keys

These allow you to choose the characters used in the key according to the state of your specimen (Box 25.3). They are useful in situations where:

Box 25.2   Example of an indented key

Part of key for common species of true bumblebee, modified after Prys-Jones and Corbet (1987):

1. Thorax with black area(s)
    2. Thorax all black
        3. Pollen baskets with red hairs   *Bombus rudarius*
        3. Pollen baskets with black hairs   *Bombus lapidarius*
    2. Thorax black with yellow or brown patches
        4. Tail white, buff or brown
            5. Scutellum black   *Bombus terrestris*
            5. Scutellum yellow   *Bombus hortorum*
        4. Tail red or orange   *Bombus pratorum*
1. Thorax without any black   *Bombus pascuorum*

If your bumblebee has a black thorax with yellow patches, proceed to choice 4; if its tail is brown, carry on to choice 5, etc.

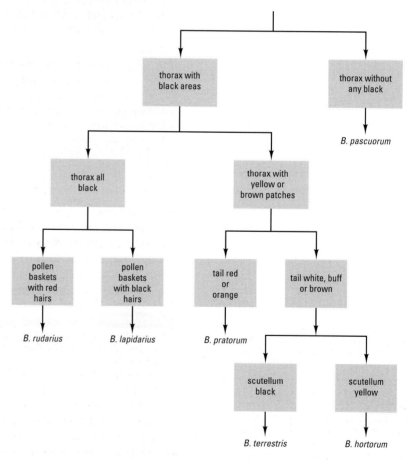

Fig. 25.1 A key for bumblebees (*Bombus* spp.) laid out in the form of a flowchart.

- important characters are difficult to observe;
- characters are likely to be misinterpreted;
- a single character would be unreliable in isolation;
- a part is missing or seems abnormal.

Box 25.3 Example of a multi-access key

Part of key to species of willowherbs, modified after Stace (1997):

Stigma 4-lobed	A
Stigma club-shaped	B
Seeds minutely uniformly papillose	C
Seeds with longitudinal papillose ridges	D
Stems erect or erect at apex	E
Stems trailing on ground	F

ACE	Petals 10–16 mm, purplish pink	*Epilobium hirsutum*
	Petals 5–9 mm, paler	*Epilobium parviflorum*
BCE	Petioles 4–15 mm, plant perennating by rosettes	
		Epilobium roseum
	Petioles ≤ 4 mm, plant perennating by stolons ending in tight bud	*Epilobium palustre*

If your specimen had a 4-lobed stigma and erect stems, but no seeds were available to examine, you could 'identify' it as either *E. hirsutum* or *E. parviflorum* and distinguish between these choices on the basis of petal size and colour.

Another way of presenting a multi-access key is in the form of a table. For instance, the taxa to be distinguished could make up the rows of the table and relevant characteristics the columns. Like the flowchart, this type of key is limited to a small number of choices.

Computerized keys

These simplify the initial stages of identification by providing a series of menu-like choices for the user. They can rapidly provide a list of tentative identifications on even a few positive choices from these menus, ranking these in likelihood of being correct. You can then work down the list, comparing your specimen to a description of the proposed species (see below). At present, computerized keys are more likely to be used in a laboratory or field station than in the field.

Advice for using keys

- Note down the route taken (i.e. the numbering system for the decision tree): this makes it easier to trace back your path through the key.
- At each step, read the full description for both choices before arriving at a decision about which one to take.
- Never guess if you do not know the precise meaning of the terms used – consult the key's glossary and list of abbreviations. Where measurements are required, use a ruler – do not guess sizes.
- If features are very small, use an appropriate lens to inspect them clearly.
- If the key is a multi-part one, look carefully at the descriptions for higher levels of taxa before progressing to the species key: this not only acts as a check that you are correct up to this stage, but may also provide definitions of useful terminology.
- If both of a pair of choices seem reasonable, try out each route – one will usually prove to be unsuitable at a later stage.

Problems of identification – sometimes your best attempts to identify the specimen will be confronted by the existence of confounding variables such as sexual dimorphism or polymorphism, juvenile and adult phases (e.g. gametophyte and sporophyte phases for certain plants), local forms, non-native taxa, etc. A good guide will point out these problems where they occur.

Comparing specimens with descriptions

KEY POINT When you arrive at the end of a key's path, *do not simply accept this as a reliable identification of your specimen.* Compare your specimen with the full description of the species.

If the specimen doesn't fit the description properly, follow the instructions outlined below:

- Compare the specimen with neighbouring descriptions: in a well-organized guide those of similar species will be together.
- Go back along the path of the key and re-examine each decision you have made. Try going down the alternative route for any that might have been questionable.
- Check to see whether you inadvertently went down the wrong pathway even though you made the correct diagnosis.
- Bear in mind the possibility that your specimen is not typical. A good key will use characteristics that are constant, but biological variation will often throw up an oddity to confuse you. Try to obtain another specimen, preferably not genetically related to the original.
- Consider the possibility that it could be outside its normal geographical range or even new to science!

The ultimate check on an identification is a comparison of the specimen with an authentically named specimen in a museum or herbarium. The ultimate comparison would be with the type specimen, the specimen used when the species or sub-species was first described and named. If this is the only specimen collected by the author(s) who named the species, it is called a holotype. Other 'type' specimens include:

- paratypes – those other than the type specimen also used by the author(s) at the time of the original description;
- syntypes – a collection of specimens used for the original collection, but from which no one specimen was defined as the type specimen;
- lectotype – a particular syntype subsequently chosen and designated through publication to act as the type specimen.

Microscopic organisms

The identification of environmental microbes such as bacteria, protozoa, fungi and algae may require either or both of:

- Microscopic examination and use of keys as above.
- Isolation and culture of (mainly) bacterial species followed by observation and laboratory testing of biochemical properties.

The study of these groups would not normally fall within the compass of environmental science courses but are covered in *Practical Skills in Biology*, 2nd edn (Chapters 17, 20 and 27).

The identification of minerals and rocks, soils or sediments is a specialist task. However, you should be able to recognize and distinguish the common minerals and major rock/sediment types on the basis of physical properties, both in the field and as hand specimens in the laboratory. Primary tools required are a ×10 hand lens and careful observation.

Minerals

Minerals, the fundamental building blocks of rocks, are naturally occurring, solid, inorganic compounds with well defined chemical compositions and atomic structures. The ions within a particular mineral are arranged according to a fixed geometrical pattern which is the same for all minerals of a particular group. This regular internal structure is often reflected in the outward form; whereby minerals tend to occur as crystals bounded by regularly arranged planar surfaces. Unfortunately, minerals from the field are usually far from perfect and do not compare with the quality of specimens housed in museums. There are many hundreds of naturally occurring minerals (most of which can be identified only by their optical or X-ray diffraction properties) but only a few are important in forming the bulk of rocks. These are the 'rock-forming minerals', so-called to distinguish them from economic minerals.

Twelve elements collectively make up over 99% of the mass of the Earth's crust, of which oxygen (45.2%) and silicon (27.2%) are the most abundant. Consequently, all but one of the nine common rock-forming minerals are silicates (Table 26.1), i.e. contain silicon and oxygen in the form of the silicate anion $(SiO_4)^{4-}$, with greater or lesser proportions of the next most abundant elements: Al (crystal abundance 8%), Fe (5.8%), Ca (5.1%), Mg (2.8%), Na (2.3%) and K (1.7%).

The most important physical properties used in mineral identification are:

- cleavage and fracture;
- hardness;
- density;
- colour and lustre;
- crystal form.

Table 26.1 The nine common rock-forming minerals

Mineral name	Chemical composition
Quartz	SiO_2
Feldspar group	
Orthoclase	$KAlSi_3O_8$
Plagioclase	$NaAlSi_3O_8 - CaAl_2Si_2O_8$
Olivine group	$(Mg, Fe)_2SiO_4$
Amphibole group	
(representative mineral Hornblende)	$(Ca, Mg, Fe, Na, Al)_{7-8}(Al, Si)_8O_{22}(OH)_2$
Pyroxene group	
(representative mineral Augite)	$(Ca, Mg, Fe, Al)_2(Al, Si)_2O_6$
Mica group	
Muscovite	$KAl_2(AlSi_3)O_{10}(OH, F)_2$
Biotite	$K(Mg, Fe)_3(AlSi_3)O_{10}(OH, F)_2$
Calcite	$CaCO_3$

Identifying Earth materials

Table 26.2 Mohs' scale of mineral hardness

1. Talc
2. Gypsum
3. Calcite
4. Fluorite
5. Apatite
6. Orthoclase feldspar
7. Quartz
8. Topaz
9. Corundum
10. Diamond

Estimating hardness – most environmental scientists do not normally carry a set of the minerals of Mohs' scale! However, readily available materials can aid in the determination of mineral hardness: your finger nail (H = 2+), a copper coin (H = 3), a steel knife blade, hammer head or a nail (H = 5).

Determining streak – make certain that the specimen is not harder than the streak plate otherwise white powdered porcelain could be mistaken for the streak of the mineral.

Table 26.3 Varieties of non-metallic lustre of minerals

Vitreous	– the lustre of broken glass (e.g. quartz)
Resinous	– the lustre of resin (e.g. opal)
Pearly	– the lustre of pearl (e.g. talc)
Silky	– the lustre of silk (e.g. gypsum)
Dull	– possessing no lustre (e.g. bauxite)

Some minerals break (cleave) along one, two or three definite planar surfaces (planes of cleavage), a consequence of weak planes in the crystal lattice. Minerals which do not break along a cleavage plane show irregular or curved fracture (e.g. quartz). The presence, number, angular relationship or absence of cleavage planes are important diagnostic properties.

Hardness refers to the resistance of a mineral to scratching and is expressed according to Mohs' scale of relative hardness. This consists of a set of ten minerals with increasing hardness from 1 to 10 (Table 26.2). For example a mineral which will scratch fluorite but is scratched by apatite is assigned a hardness (H) of 4.5.

Mineral density is a function of chemical composition and atomic packing. The rock-forming minerals show little variation in density and it is seldom necessary to measure the absolute density of a mineral. If required, this is done by one of several methods including water displacement, or use of a steelyard, pycnometer or heavy liquids (see Gribble, 1988 for details). It is generally adequate to estimate relative density as 'high' or 'low' in terms of the feel to the hand of the mass of samples of approximately equivalent volumes. Thus density is best used in conjunction with other physical properties as a means of mineral identification.

Mineral colour varies with chemical impurities and depends on both composition and crystal lattice structure. The colour of a powdered mineral (streak) is determined by scratching a sample across a piece of unglazed porcelain known as a streak plate, and is commonly more characteristic and distinctive than mineral colour.

Lustre refers to the appearance of a mineral in reflected light. Those that are highly reflective (typically sulphides) are described as having metallic lustre. Rock-forming and many other minerals are generally less reflective and have non-metallic lustres which may be sub-divided into vitreous, resinous, pearly, silky and dull varieties (see Table 26.3).

Where minerals have had space during growth, the internal crystal lattice is expressed by the development of crystal faces. On the basis of elements of symmetry (planes, axes and centre) minerals are grouped into six systems: cubic, tetragonal, orthorhombic, monoclinic, triclinic and hexagonal. The subject matter of crystallography is usually beyond the scope of most non-specialists but further details may be found in Gribble (1988). The uniqueness of the crystal lattice of minerals is important for the identification of microscopic samples, since the effects of the lattice on transmitted light (polarized light microscopy) and X-rays (X-ray diffraction spectroscopy) produce distinctive patterns.

Fig. 26.1 is a flowchart for identification of the nine common rock-forming minerals. There are many texts which aid in mineral identification by means of comparison of unknown samples with photographs. Also useful are the detailed wall charts, *Minerals of the World* (Lof, 1983), *Mineral and Rock Table* (Lof, 1982) and the *Multimedia Mineral CD-ROM* (BTL Publishing).

Rocks

Rocks are aggregates of one or more minerals (usually more than one). There are three major groups of rocks, primarily created as follows:

- Crystallization from the molten state (magma derived from the Earth's interior) to produce **igneous rocks**. If magma rises to the Earth's surface under gravity it becomes lava giving rise to extrusive rocks (e.g. rhyolite,

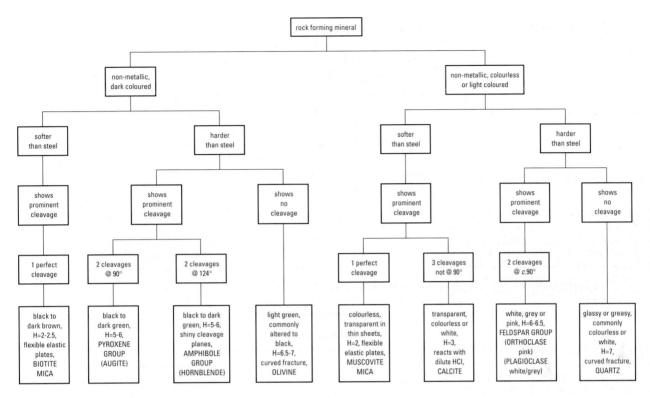

Fig. 26.1 Flowchart for identification of the rock-forming minerals.

basalt). Cooling beneath the surface leads to bodies of intrusive rocks (e.g. granite, gabbro).

- Physical and chemical breakdown at the Earth's surface of any pre-existing rocks or organic materials and the subsequent transport, accumulation and cementation of the fragments, or precipitation of soluble products, to produce **sedimentary rocks** of three categories:
  - fragmental or clastic (e.g. sandstone, shale);
  - biogenic (e.g. bioclastic limestone; coal);
  - chemical (e.g. oolitic limestone, evaporites such as NaCl, $CaSO_4$).
- Alteration within the Earth of any pre-existing rocks at temperatures and/or pressures above those characteristic of their original formation to produce **metamorphic rocks**. The effects of metamorphism may be localized or regional in extent.

There are no simple and readily applicable rules to aid rock identification, largely because there are so many different rock types in each of the above major groups. First, using the information given below, try to determine whether a rock is of igneous, sedimentary or metamorphic origin. Then, using the flow charts of Figs 26.2–26.4 you should be able to assign a broad name to a rock.

Igneous rocks

KEY POINT Igneous rocks typically have a compact, crystalline texture which is isotropic (uniform, non-laminated). Extrusive rocks (lavas) have small crystals (<1 mm) due to rapid cooling, intrusive rocks have coarser crystals (1->5 mm) as they cooled more slowly within the Earth. Look for contacts between intrusive bodies and the older rocks into which they were emplaced.

Distinguishing between the 'rock' and the 'rock mass' – a hand specimen of, e.g., an igneous rock in the laboratory may appear homogeneous and isotropic, whereas the same rock in field outcrop may be anisotropic, i.e. sub-divided by discontinuities such as joints, faults and bedding planes.

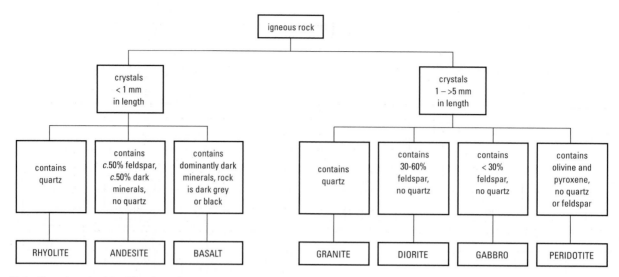

Fig. 26.2 Flowchart for identification of some common igneous rocks.

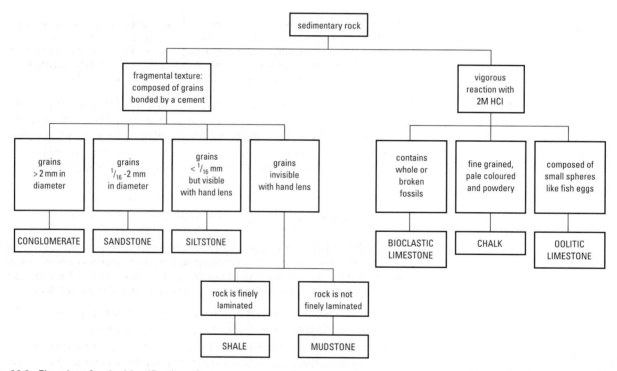

Fig. 26.3 Flowchart for the identification of some common sedimentary rocks.

Sequences of lava flows are usually layered – do not confuse with sedimentary rocks.

Acid igneous rocks have crystallized from magmas rich in Si, Na and K and poor in Fe, Mg and Ca. They are light coloured (leucocratic), containing less than 25% dark minerals. Characteristic minerals are orthoclase, quartz, plagioclase, micas and hornblende. Basic rocks have crystallized from magmas rich in Fe, Mg and Ca and poor in Si, Na and K. They are dark coloured (melanocratic), being dominated by dark minerals. Characteristic minerals are plagioclase, augite and olivine. They generally contain no quartz. Igneous rocks with compositions transitional between acid and basic are termed intermediate. They are medium coloured (mesocratic), containing 25–50% dark minerals of which hornblende is usually dominant.

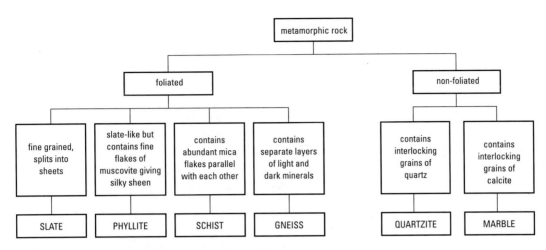

Fig. 26.4 Flowchart for identification of some common metamorphic rocks.

Sedimentary rocks

KEY POINT Sedimentary rocks are characterized by layering or bedding, a reflection of the discontinuous accumulation of sediment. This may vary from the sub-mm scale to the m scale. Look for evidence of mineral grains (especially quartz) or rock fragments held together by a precipitated cement, and for fossils.

Fragmental sedimentary rocks are sub-divided on the basis of particle size. Conglomerate is made of particles predominantly >2 mm in diameter, sandstone 0.0625–2 mm, siltstone 0.004–0.0625 mm and shale or mudstone <0.004 mm. Use a few drops of 2M HCl to test for calcite (effervescence as CO_2 is given off) as a means of identifying limestones and calcareous cements (see also Table 26.6).

HCl – use with care to avoid burning skin or clothing.

Metamorphic rocks

KEY POINT Metamorphic rocks are often anisotropic (foliated) with plate-like crystals of micas aligned parallel with planes along which preferential splitting occurs. Look for 'uncommon' minerals which may have crystallized in response to changed environmental conditions.

Slate and phyllite have a close-spaced laminar texture (foliated) with very fine grain size. Phyllite has shiny laminae due to the development of fine mica, but individual flakes are indistinguishable. The texture of schist is coarser: individual mica flakes are clearly seen. Gneiss has a banded texture with a clear tendency for dark minerals (biotite and hornblende) to separate from the light-coloured minerals (quartz and feldspars) into separate bands or lenses. Quartzite and marble are produced by the metamorphism of pure quartz sandstone and limestone, respectively. Both have non-foliated, 'sugary' textures.

For further information on the field identification of rocks the following should be consulted: Thorpe and Brown (1985) for igneous rocks, Tucker (1996) for sedimentary rocks and Fry (1984) for metamorphic rocks.

Soils and sediments

The distinction between sediments and soils is not clear-cut as both are the products of weathering of pre-existing rocks and contain inorganic and

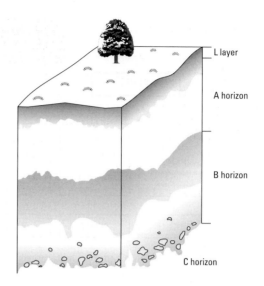

Fig. 26.5 A typical soil profile.

organic matter in varying proportions. The choice of terminology depends largely on one's scientific training. To the environmental scientist soils usually develop *in situ* whereas sediments are normally considered as accumulations of debris, transported by water (including dissolved products of chemical weathering), ice or the wind, which have been deposited (or precipitated) in an appropriate environment (e.g. a lake, a river bed, a sea, a desert). Peat, partially decomposed vegetation which builds up without transport and is the precursor of coal, is considered a soil by the soil scientist but a sediment by the geologist, since coal is a biogenic sedimentary rock.

In vertical section many soils are characterized by various horizontal or near-horizontal layers of differing compositions, collectively known as a soil profile (Fig. 26.5). These are a consequence of the downward penetration of weathering into the underlying bedrock exceeding the upward accumulation of plant litter at the land surface. The main layers are:

- L layer: this is the litter layer of the upper surface of the soil, where most of the debris from plants and animals is deposited, and is composed of partially or completely decayed residues.
- A horizon (top soil): this is the uppermost horizon, containing mineral matter and some organic matter transported from the L layer.
- B horizon (sub-soil): this lies beneath the A horizon and has a lower organic matter content.
- C horizon: this is the horizon from which those overlying it have developed, i.e. part of the underlying parent rock from which the soil was derived.

For most natural soils the above profile sub-division is simplistic and an enlarged glossary, known as the horizon notation, is required if precise soil type identification is needed. Soil identification is further complicated by the fact that different names for the same soil type are used in different countries.

Organic matter – soils with lower organic matter content will generally be paler in colour. If you are not sure whether organic matter is present in a soil or sediment add a few drops of a strong oxidizing agent such as dilute (10% v/v) hydrogen peroxide (H_2O_2). In the presence of organic matter a vigorous reaction will occur as CO_2 is given off. Take care not to spill H_2O_2 on your skin or clothing as they will bleach.

KEY POINT　Colour is an important property in the identification and differentiation of soil horizons. Standardized descriptions should be made by reference to the Munsell Soil Colour Chart System.

Table 26.4 Textural characteristics of soil as determined by hand

Soil texture	Characteristics when wet
Sand	Not sticky: feels 'gritty'
Sandy loam	Not sticky: can be rolled into a thread which breaks up
Loam	Not sticky: will roll into a thread
Clay loam	Sticky: will roll into a thread easily
Clay	Very sticky: will mould into any shape

Table 26.5 The Udden-Wentworth particle size scale

Particle types	Particle size range (mm)
Boulders	>256
Large cobbles	128–256
Small cobbles	64–128
Very large pebbles	32–64
Large pebbles	16–32
Medium pebbles	8–16
Small pebbles	4–8
Granules	2–4
Very coarse sand	1–2
Coarse sand	0.5–1.0
Medium sand	0.25–0.5
Fine sand	0.125–0.25
Very fine sand	0.0625–0.125
Silt	0.004–0.0625
Clay	<0.004

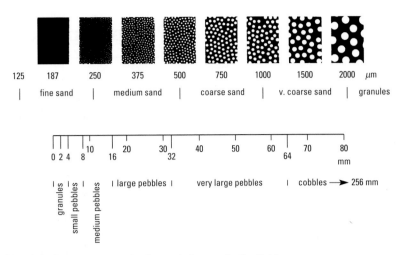

Fig. 26.6 Comparator grain size scale for use in the field.

Table 26.6 Approximate estimation of $CaCO_3$ content in soils and sediments by HCl reaction (adapted from Briggs, 1977)

Test observations	$CaCO_3$ content (%)	Soil/sediment description
No reaction	<0.1	Non-calcareous
Just audible	0.1–0.5	Very slightly calcareous
Audible	0.5–1.0	Slightly calcareous
Distinctly audible, just visible	1.0–5.0	Fairly calcareous
Easily audible and visible	5.0–10.0	Calcareous
Easily audible, strong effervescence	>10.0	Very calcareous

A quick and easy way to determine soil texture is to roll a wetted sample between your hands and refer to Table 26.4.

Particle size of fragmental sediments is conventionally expressed according to the Udden-Wentworth Scale (Table 26.5). Visual comparator grain size scales (Fig. 26.6), laminated for use in the field, are a useful means of estimating dominant particle size ranges and therefore fragmental sediment type. Note that soil scientists use <2 μm (<0.002 mm) as the definition of clay size particles whereas geologists use <4 μm (<0.004 mm).

KEY POINT **The audibility and visibility of reaction of a soil or sediment to the application of a few drops of dilute HCl is a useful approximate measure of $CaCO_3$ content in the field (Table 26.6).**

Trudgill (1989) provides an excellent field identification guide to soil types in Britain. The wall chart by Lof and van Baren (1987) presents colour photographs of 106 soil profiles labelled according to the national classifications of the USA, Canada, England and Wales, France, Germany and Australia, and is an important aid to detailed soil type identification.

Photography and imaging

Photography and imaging are valuable techniques used primarily for:

- documentation and validation of observations for projects, reports or publications;
- preparation of material for illustrating talks;
- preparation of poster displays;
- producing 'hard copy' of various observations, from microscopy to satellite images.

As a student, you may be able to request professional technical assistance for some or all of this type of work but there is an important role for you in defining your requirements precisely. A basic understanding of the key factors which affect the final product will help you do this.

Photography

Photography is usually carried out in one of three general situations:

- laboratory or studio environments where conditions are under your control and problems relatively easily overcome;
- field situations where many factors may be difficult to control;
- using specialized equipment such as photo-microscopes or electron microscopes, where the scope for your control of the photographic process is very limited and largely managed by the instrument's operating system.

Types of photographic film

There are four important decisions to make when choosing a film:

- what size of film you require in terms of both negative size and number of negatives on the film – this depends upon the camera system used;
- whether to use colour or black and white film;
- whether to use transparency (slide or reversal) film or negative film;
- what speed of film to use.

Film is classified by its sensitivity to light (its 'speed') and this is measured in either ISO (=ASA) or DIN units: do not confuse them. Black and white films and colour negative films use an emulsion which contains crystals and, therefore, have 'grain'. Table 27.1 summarizes the relationship between speed, grain and definition for such films. Colour transparency films, although classified using the same speed criteria, are based upon colour dyes and are effectively grainless. Slow film is used when fine detail and/or saturated colour is required, such as in microphotography, or when considerable enlargement may be required. Slow films have inherently more contrast than fast films. Use fast film when light levels are low, but remember that this results in reduction of contrast and detail. Films faster than 200 ISO (24 DIN) are not recommended for use except in exceptional circumstances.

The choice of film is often a compromise between speed and detail and a good general choice is film of about 100–160 ISO (21–23 DIN). There are many subtle differences between different makes of film, particularly with respect to colour balance, saturation and contrast, and choice is a matter of personal preference and cost.

Definitions

Saturation – the term used to describe the intensity of a colour – a saturated colour is an intense colour.

Contrast – the degree of gradation between colours or the number of grey shades in black and white film: the higher the contrast, the sharper is the gradation.

Table 27.1 The speed and grain relationship in film

Speed of film	ISO number	DIN number	Grain	Definition
Slow	25–64	15–19	Very fine	Very sharp
Medium	64–200	19–24	Fine	Sharp
Fast	200–400	24–27	Medium	Medium
Extra fast	4000–1600	27–32	Coarse	Poor to medium

- Black and white films – all the usual types of modern film are panchromatic, i.e. sensitive to ultraviolet light and all the colours of the visible spectrum. Special films are available which respond only to selected wavelengths (such as infra-red or X-ray) or are orthochromatic, responding only to blue, green and yellow but not to red light; such films are often used in copying and graphics work.
- Colour films – the main classification is into positive (reversal) film and negative film: the former is used to produce slides (transparencies) and the latter to produce colour prints. Prints can be produced from transparencies and slides from negatives but the former is the better process. Most negative films are colour masked giving them an overall orange tint when developed – this makes the colours purer when printed. Colour films must be balanced for the colour temperature of the light source used. Colour temperature is measured in kelvin (K; see Fig. 27.1). There are two main types of film: (a) daylight film is balanced for daylight conditions (5400 K) and for electronic flash; and (b) artificial light types A (3400 K) or B (3200 K), designed for studio lighting conditions. Filters must be used if colour temperature corrections are necessary.

Type of lighting

The quantity and quality of the light is a critical factor in all photography except in electron microscopy. The quantity of light is measured by a photographic light meter which may be external or built-in. The more light there is, the smaller the lens aperture you can use (larger 'f' number), and the greater will be the depth of field (= depth of focus). Therefore, the more light available, the better! By using the camera on a tripod, you can use slow shutter speeds and allow larger 'f' numbers to be used to maximize depth of focus. The use of an electronic flash system to provide some or all of the lighting makes this even easier since the effective shutter speed with electronic flash is extremely short (1 ms). Modern electronic flash systems are computerized making them easy to use.

The quality of light affects the colour balance of the film being used, even for black and white film. This is important under artificial light conditions when the spectrum can be different from that of sunlight. Always be sure to know the quality of light required for your film.

Remember that your choice of lighting arrangement will affect the quality of the picture: shadowless lighting is appropriate in some situations, but often shadows help to give three-dimensional form to the objects. In general, the use of more than one light source is advisable to prevent hard shadows.

Using colour film – colour film is highly sensitive to environmental factors such as heat and humidity which cause changes in film speed and colour rendition. Make sure that your film has a sufficiently long expiry date. Store film for extended periods in a refrigerator or freezer: if stored in a freezer, allow a 24 h thawing period before use.

Knowing how your camera operates – there are many camera types and modes of operation; for any camera new to you, read the instructions carefully before using it.

Tips for better photography –

Use your camera on a tripod whenever possible, and use high shutter speed to minimize the effect of movements.

Use electronic flash wherever possible as it provides uniformity of colour balance. Unless you want shadowless lighting, do not place the flash on the camera (hot-shoe) connection.

Shadowless lighting of smaller objects is usefully obtained through a ring-flash system.

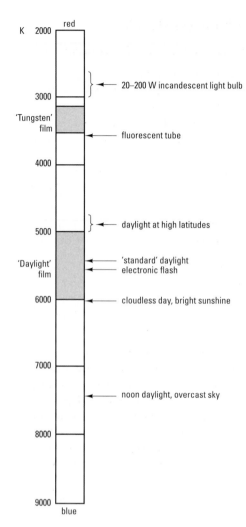

Fig. 27.1 Colour temperature and the kelvin scale in relation to sensitivity of film type.

KEY POINT To use a camera properly, you need to understand the relationship between aperture (f-number), shutter speed and depth of field. For moving objects, give fast shutter speed priority by opening the lens aperture (small f-number). Where depth of field is required, close the lens aperture (high f-number); this will result in slower shutter speeds, so take care to avoid camera shake. Bracket your exposures (plus or minus 1 f-number at same shutter speed) to ensure good results.

Film development (black and white)

Remember that the image quality is influenced not only by the conditions under which the film was exposed, but also by development conditions: the main factors include the type of developer used, the temperature and the duration of development. It is possible, therefore, to modify development when it is known that a film has been exposed under less than ideal light conditions and thus maximize the quality of the negative produced. If this is necessary, tell the photographer exactly what the conditions of exposure were so that adjustment of the development process can be considered. Do this only with the help of a professional photographer, however, as it is just as easy to ruin a film as it is to improve it!

Photomicrography

This requires the use of special equipment mounted on a microscope. Consult the manual(s) for the particular system you are using since most of the operations will be semi-automatic. The important operations for successful photomicrography are outlined below:

1. Carefully prepare the object: ensure thorough cleanliness of any slides or coverslips used.
2. Choose the correct film type and any filters required for alteration of colour balance, depending upon the type of light source available.
3. Decide on the magnification to be used: make sure that you know how this relates to the magnification of the negative/transparency.
4. Carefully focus the object onto the film plane: there will be a system-specific method for doing this but sometimes it requires practice to get it right.
5. Make extra exposures above and below the one indicated (called 'bracketing'), even when using an automatic exposure system: exposures of at least +1 and −1 stop are recommended, especially for colour photography.
6. Include a photograph of a stage micrometer so that the final magnification can be calculated and shown on the photograph.

Type of print

The type of print used depends upon its purpose. Glossy finish prints generally appear sharper than matt or other finishes and are usually required for publication: the addition of lettering and scales is often only possible on the smooth surface of a glossy print. However, if preparing prints for display on a poster, the matt/velvet finishes are often preferable. The contrast of the image is determined by the choice of paper, which comes in a variety of grades of contrast. If your photo has too much contrast, reprint using a 'softer' grade of paper. You may be able to learn to develop and print your own black and white films but colour printing is particularly difficult and best left to professionals.

Fig. 27.2 Use of white areas for labelling dark prints, illustrated by an SEM micrograph of a stellate hair on a leaf surface.

Adding scales and labels to photographic prints

Having acquired a suitable print, it is often necessary to add information to it.

- Use transfer letters to add lettering, scales and labels.
- Choose a simple font type that will not distract and a size which is legible but not overpowering: prints for publication should be prepared bearing in mind any reductions which may take place during subsequent operations.
- An 18 point label usually works well since published text is usually 10 point.
- Do not mix font types in related sets of prints.
- Choose an appropriate part of the photograph for the lettering, i.e. a black area for a white letter. If this is too variable, add a background label on which to place the letters (see Fig. 27.2).

Storing and mounting photographs

Both slides and negatives should be stored and maintained in good condition and be well organized. Avoid dampness, which is very destructive to all photographic materials: use silica gel desiccant in damp climates/ environments. Record-keeping should be done carefully and include all relevant details, both of the subject and of the relevant processing procedures.

- Transparencies (slides) should be mounted in plastic mounts but not between glass, as this often causes more problems than it solves. Beware of cheap plastic filing materials as some contain residual chemicals which can damage transparencies over long time periods. Labelling of transparencies is best done on the mount, using small, self-adhesive labels.
- Negative strips should be stored in transparent or translucent paper filing sheets. Obtain a set of contact prints for each film and store this with the negatives for easy reference.
- Prints should be stored flat in boxes or in albums. When used for display, mount on stiff board either with modern photographic adhesives or dry-mounting tissue.

Digital imaging

An alternative to photography is digital imaging, the production of an electronically stored image in digital format, for use by computer systems. These are usually produced using either a scanning device from a pre-existing image, or some form of digital camera (still or video). The image is held as a series of discrete units called pixels (Fig. 27.3); the greater the number of pixels per unit surface area, the better is the potential resolution of the image and the better the detail captured. The image may be in black/white, greyscale or colour. Image size and resolution are constrained by the amount of memory available for recording – file sizes can be very large. The quality may also depend on the printer available to you.

Generally, digital images tend to be of lower quality than a photograph, but they have the advantages of speed and ease of production, since a developing stage is avoided. The image file can be stored on disks and manipulated using programs such as Adobe Photoshop Pro™. This form of image is very suitable for use in computer-based applications, such as Web pages or a computer graphic presentation, but for high definition images, traditional photography remains the best option.

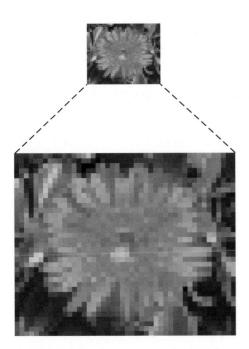

Fig. 27.3 Pixel structure in a digital image.

Environmental analysis

28 Ecological analysis and demographics

Definitions

Sample – a finite part of a statistical population whose properties are studied to gain information about the whole.

Population – a group of units comprising a discrete component that is definable.

Definition

Abundance – a measure of the number of individuals, whilst **cover** is the proportion of ground that is occupied. For plant populations, this includes the perpendicular projection of the aerial parts of individuals down onto the substrate: usually expressed as a percentage.

Definition

Modular organism – one which develops by repeatedly producing sub-units (modules) rather than developing into a complete (unitary) organism with fixed number of parts. Good examples are plants, fungi and many colonial animals such as corals.

Demography is a broad social science discipline concerned with the study of human populations, and demographers deal with the collection, presentation and analysis of data relating to people's basic life cycle experiences; birth, marriage, divorce, family structure, employment, ageing, migration and death. The discipline tends to emphasize the empirical investigation of population processes but with a view to deriving social and economic theories. This chapter, however, will not deal with expressly human characteristics but will refer to the general properties of populations and communities which form the subject of the broader environmental sciences.

The most commonly measured population parameters include:

- abundance/cover;
- population dispersion;
- tables (life and fecundity tables);
- age/size distribution.

Abundance/cover

One of the major field problems is the determination of population distribution, size and change in abundance. This will nearly always involve sampling (Chapter 15) to estimate the true population value, since most populations are too large to enumerate all component individuals.

Methods for analysing non-mobile animal and plant populations are numerous and require careful planning and statistical treatments. Choosing a method is beyond the scope of this text, but commonly used methods include using quadrats, sample plots, belt transects, line intercepts and point-frequency intercepts (Chapter 15 *et seq.*). An important early decision when studying such populations is whether to use abundance or cover as the measure. Abundance clearly implies a number of individuals, but for modular organisms, number does not necessarily reflect dominance or cover. Although separate and distinct properties, cover and abundance may be combined in a community description as the total estimate, but this is rather subjective and the data are difficult to analyse statistically.

The study of animal populations often involves considerably more difficulty than the study of plants, since animals are often not easy to see and are not usually stationary. The method of collection (Chapter 17) is very important as both the operator and the animal are liable to bias the results.

The methods of estimating animal numbers fall into three main categories:

1. The true census: this requires a direct count of all individuals in a given area and is similar to the human population census in principle. It is very difficult to do for most wild species but can be used where areas of concentration occur, e.g. waterfowl on wintering grounds, rookeries, roosts and breeding colonies of birds and mammals. Photography and subsequent image analysis is often appropriate for such studies.
2. The sampling estimate, derived from counts on sample plots. Sampling estimates (see Chapter 15) make two basic assumptions:
   - mortality and recruitment during the sampling period are negligible or can be accounted for;

- all members of the population have an equal chance of being sampled, i.e. there is no bias in the method being used.

   It is important, therefore, that the method employed is appropriate for the species, time, place and purpose of the study.

3. Indices: the use of different types of count such as faecal materials, counts of calls of vocal species, and other animal signs to determine trends in relative abundance. All data are relative and must be compared with data from other areas or other time periods. The results do not give estimates of absolute populations but can indicate trends.

The main methods of estimating animal populations include direct sampling methods such as trapping (live or dead) organisms, mark (see Box 28.1) and recapture methods and photography (e.g. of seabird or seal colonies).

Population dispersion

Population dispersion (distribution) may be uniform, random or clumped (Chapter 15) and data collected from quadrats, point quadrats and other

---

Box 28.1 Marking animals for study

Marking is necessary when you need to identify certain individuals at some future date, either for studies of behaviour or movement or to estimate populations by the mark–recapture method. In the mark–recapture method a proportion of the population is marked in some way, returned to the original population and then, after complete mixing, a second sample is taken. The method works on the principle that the number of marked individuals in the second sample will have the same ratio to the total number in that sample as the total of marked individuals originally released would have to the total population. Since the first three quantities are known, the total population can be easily calculated. It has the advantage over fixed-unit sampling methods in that its accuracy does not depend on an assessment of the number of sampling units available within the habitat. The detailed alternative methodologies and statistics are beyond the scope of this book. A basic pre-requisite for this method is that there is a method of marking individuals so that they can be released unharmed and unaffected back into the wild and can be recognized upon recapture. Such marked individuals can be used for a variety of studies such as dispersal, longevity and growth. The most widely used marking methods include:

- Paints and dyes: terrestrial snails are easily marked with quick-drying cellulose paint while aquatic species are best marked with marine paints. Mammalian fur and bird plumage can be marked by coloured dyes to permit individual recognition at a distance.

- Dyes and fluorescent substances in powder form may be appropriate for hairy insects but are relatively easily lost.
- Labels: fish are usually marked by tagging, typically through a fin. Birds are normally labelled by serially numbered aluminium bands (bird rings) often bearing colours which enable individual recognition in the field.
- Modification of body parts: small mammals, frogs, toads, salamanders and most lizards can be marked by some system of toe clipping which involves the removal of the distal part of one or more toes. Mammals may also be marked by notching of ears. Snakes and lizards can be marked by removing scales or patches of scales in particular combinations. Crabs and other crustaceans can have exoskeletal components modified.
- Radioactive isotopes are particularly useful for study of animals that are secretive in habit, live in dense cover, spend part or all of their life underground or have radically different phases in their life cycle. Animals are fed small amounts of gamma-emitting radioactive material which becomes incorporated into the tissues. However, their use requires particular care and special permissions.
- Photographs of individuals with identifiable markings, e.g. many whale species, may also allow individual recognition.

Note that arthropods, snakes, etc. shed their skin (moult) periodically and that this may affect the permanence of any external markings.

methods may be used to determine intra-population dispersion. Remember, however, that the analysis can be affected by the size of the sampling unit used. Where the density of individuals is low relative to the available surface area or volume, the Poisson method (Chapter 40) is useful to determine types of dispersion. The Poisson distribution provides values expected on the basis of a random dispersion pattern and approximates to an extremely asymmetrical distribution.

A further test for randomness is the ratio of the variance (s^2) to the mean (μ). In the Poisson distribution, the population mean (μ) is equal to the population variance (s^2), i.e. a ratio of 1. A ratio of much less than 1 would indicate a uniform distribution and a ratio much greater than 1 would indicate a clumped distribution.

Tables

A life table (e.g. Table 28.1) provides a clear and systematic picture of mortality and survival and was developed from studies of human populations by insurance companies. It consists of a series of columns, each of which describes an aspect of mortality statistics for members of a population according to age. Figures are presented in terms of a standard number of individuals all born at the same time (cohort). To construct a life table you must be able to determine the age of individuals and thus divide them into age classes or age intervals. Information is then needed on survival or mortality for each age class. They may be inaccurate or invalid if based upon sampling from a larger population.

There are three main types of life table:

- Horizontal (dynamic) life tables constructed by following a cohort of individuals all born within a short time period from birth to the death of the last individual.

> For insects and other organisms which have distinct stages to their life cycles, life tables are best divided into developmental stages rather than time intervals.

> The age interval used must be appropriate to the longevity of the organism.

Table 28.1 Life table for *Phlox drummondii* at Nixon, Texas (source: Leverlich and Levin, 1979)

Age interval (days) $x - x'$	No. surviving to day x N_x	Survivorship l_x	No. dying during interval d_x	Average mortality rate per day q_x	Mean expectation of life (days) E_x
0–63	996	1.0000	328	.0052	122.87
63–124	668	.6707	373	.0092	104.73
124–184	295	.2962	105	.0059	137.59
184–215	190	.1908	14	.0024	137.05
215–231	176	.1767	2	.0007	115.72
231–247	174	.1747	1	.0004	100.96
247–264	173	.1737	1	.0003	85.49
264–271	172	.1727	2	.0017	68.94
271–278	170	.1707	3	.0025	62.71
278–285	167	.1677	2	.0017	56.78
285–292	165	.1657	6	.0052	50.42
292–299	159	.1596	1	.0009	45.19
299–306	158	.1586	4	.0036	38.46
306–313	154	.1546	3	.0028	32.36
313–320	151	.1516	4	.0038	25.94
320–327	147	.1476	11	.0107	19.55
327–334	136	.1365	31	.0325	13.85
334–341	105	.1054	31	.0422	9.90
341–348	74	.0743	52	.1004	5.58
348–355	22	.0221	22	.1428	3.50
355–362	0	.0000			

- Vertical (static) life tables constructed by sampling the population and ageing the individuals to obtain a distribution of size classes at a particular moment. This type of table assumes that each age class is sampled in proportion to its numbers in the population, that the birth and death rates are constant and the population size is static: these assumptions are rarely adhered to and data may require adjustment or smoothing to minimize the effects.

- Dynamic-composite life tables record the same information as the dynamic tables but they take as the cohort a composite of a number of animals marked over a period of years rather than at just one birth period. An example would be the marking of each batch of newly hatched birds over a period of years and following the fate of each year's group. Data are then pooled and all marked animals are treated as a single cohort.

Both static and dynamic-composite tables are inevitably inaccurate because the assumptions of constancy from year to year are rarely valid. In spite of this, such tables may present a reasonable assessment of average population characteristics.

KEY POINT **Plant ecologists have adapted the use of life tables to study the dynamics of plant modules such as leaves that exhibit age-specific mortality.**

A fecundity table (e.g. Table 28.2) can be constructed if you know the reproductive productivity of each age class of females in a population. The productivity can be determined by counts of litter size, brood counts, young fledged or egg/seed production, depending upon the organism being investigated.

Age and size structure

The age structure of plant, animal and human populations determines, in part, population reproductive rates, death rates, vigour, survival and other

Table 28.2 Fecundity schedule for *Phlox drummondii* at Nixon, Texas, based on seed production (source: Leverlich and Levin, 1979)

$x - x^1$	N_x	l_x	$m_x{}^{seed}$	$l_x m_x$
0–299	996	1.0000	.0000	.0000
299–306	158	.1586	.3394	.0532
306–313	154	.1546	.7963	.1231
313–320	151	.1516	2.3995	.3638
320–327	147	.1476	3.1904	.4589
327–334	136	.1365	2.5411	.3470
334–341	105	.1054	3.1589	.3330
341–348	74	.0743	8.6625	.6436
348–355	22	.0221	4.3072	.0951
355–362	0	.0000	.0000	.0000
				$\Sigma = 2.4177$

$R_o = \Sigma l_x m_x = 2.42$ (per capita)

$R = \dfrac{\ln R_o}{365} = 0.0024$ (per capita per day)

Note: $x - x' =$ age interval; $N_x =$ no. surviving to day x; $m_x{}^{seed} =$ average no. of seeds per individual during interval; $l_x =$ survivorship. $l_x m_x =$ contribution to net reproductive rate during interval.

demographic attributes. The structure of populations can be characterized by:

- specific age categories such as years or months;
- life history stages, e.g. eggs, pupae, larvae and instars in insects;
- size classes where age is difficult to determine.

The use of age structure in studies of modular organisms such as plant populations is complicated by their modular nature and their extensive use of asexual reproduction. The use of size classes is therefore often substituted. This is because each module has its own age which is independent of the age of the genet.

KEY POINT **Modular species are composed of the genet (e.g. a tree), which is the product of the original zygote, and the modules (leaves, flowers, roots), units of construction each of which has its own birth, life and death, usually independently of the genet.**

Definitions

Zygote – the product of fertilization in a sexually reproducing species.

Genet – the term given to the genetic individual that results from the sexual reproduction of a modular species.

Box 28.2   Measuring age in organisms

Determining age in plants usually involves following a cohort of marked individuals over time or taking a sample and determining age by use of growth rings, bud scans or other measurements. Contrary to common expectation, growth rings are neither regular nor necessarily laid down annually: cambial rings may fail to be laid down or multiple rings may be produced by short-term changes in cambial activity during the growing season. Rings are usually laid down as a result of the interruption of growth by seasonal changes in temperature and/or light and should always be regarded with caution.

Ageing wild animal populations is not easy, although a number of techniques have been developed.

- Some fish can be aged using scales or ear stones (otoliths), both of which lay down growth rings which vary in spacing or density (Fig. 28.1).
- Any bony or calcareous structure which is laid down from the outside has the potential for possessing growth rings. Such structures have been proposed for echinoderm skeletal elements, molluscan and barnacle shells and vertebrae of fish.
- Length–frequency distribution of polymodal species can be useful, particularly where there is a very distinct and short reproductive and settlement phase. The statistical analysis of polymodal frequency distributions has been refined from commercial fish population studies but works well for many polymodal species.
- Ageing techniques for birds and mammals are less refined than those for fish but include the use of specific characteristics of body parts. For birds, plumage development is often used and for mammals, tooth characteristics can be useful.

(a)

(b)

Fig. 28.1 Structures used to age teleost fish: (a) scale of salmonid fish showing circuli; (b) otolith of flatfish showing annual rings.

Measuring community parameters

Some of the key parameters analysed for community structures are described below.

Interspecific association

Some species in a community may occur together more frequently than predicted by chance. Measurement of this association provides an objective way of recognizing natural groupings of species. Associations may be positive or negative, each providing information on the nature of interactions between the organisms considered, although the explanations for such associations may be complex. A commonly used measure is that of the coefficient of association (C) which varies from +1.0 for a maximum positive association to −1.0 for a maximum negative association: a value of 0 indicates no statistical association. Only presence or absence data sets are required and testing of the significance of a relationship requires application of the chi-squared test and the use of contingency tables (see Chapter 40).

Community similarity

We often need to compare the species composition of communities over space or time. The similarity of communities can be measured from data as basic as presence/absence of species or from more complex data sets such as those based on density or frequency. A variety of measures exist but you are advised to consult specialist texts if required to choose a particular statistical test: they include similarity coefficients, percentage similarity, and coefficient of community.

Community ordination

Ordination is the technique of arranging components in a uni- or multidimensional order in such a manner that the position of each component along the axis or axes conveys information about its composition or relationship to the other components.

Ordination is founded on the assumption that community composition varies gradually over a continuum of environmental conditions. It may be accomplished by two different approaches to deriving the axes:

- changes in the environmental conditions;
- changes in composition of the community.

When the axes are based on environmental changes, the relative position of the communities along the axes reflects changes in composition caused by the environment (gradient analysis). When based on community composition, their relative positions are based on similarities of species composition. Again the methods used are various and complex, though they have been simplified by the existence of computer programs. If you need to carry out an ordination, you should consult relevant statistical texts.

Species diversity

This can be quantified in a number of ways. The species richness is a simple measure of the number of species present in a community, but it takes no real account of the relative abundance of each species present. However, it is usually important to take relative abundance into account when measuring biodiversity. The two most widely used diversity indices are:

1. Simpson's Index
2. The Shannon–Weiner Index

but there are various other indices derived for use under particular conditions. Both of the above indices are sensitive to changes in the number of species and to changes in the relative abundance, but both are also affected by the sample size. If the indices are to be used to compare diversity between communities the sample sizes should be equal; or, if complete census data are available, the areas sampled should be of the same size.

KEY POINT **There is a great variety of indices available for community and population quantification, each with its own set of assumptions and requirements. Check the literature thoroughly before adopting any particular index and make sure that you are aware of its good and bad points.**

Care of maps – take good care of flat, unfolded copies of maps; do not bend, crease or tear them. If you take maps into the field always use a see-through map case or clear vinyl wallet to protect them. This allows you to consult your maps in any weather without risk of damage due to dampness.

Map symbols – different types of map (and different editions of the same map) often use different symbols for the various features and information shown. Always familiarize yourself with the 'key to symbols' given on a particular map; do not make assumptions as to what symbols might mean.

Photocopies – remember that many photocopiers cause image distortion, especially at the edges, so that the scale of any copy may be different from that of the original.

Definition

Spot height – a spot height is shown as an isolated number on a map indicating the height of a particular 'spot', e.g. the summit of a hill, above a specific datum. Spot heights provide important detail when the land is relatively flat lying, such that on much of the corresponding map its relief is depicted by very few, widely spaced contour lines.

Scales – do not confuse the scales of 1:10 560 and 1:10 000 maps, especially if you are using various editions to assess changes in an area.

KEY POINT To extract environmental information from a map or photograph you must first obtain the appropriate type or types for your chosen purpose.

Maps

There are many types of map available produced at a wide variety of scales. Among the ones you are likely to find most useful are:

- topographic maps;
- geological maps;
- hydrogeological maps (groundwater potential maps);
- soil survey maps;
- land use capability maps (agricultural potential maps);
- environmental geology maps (environmental potential maps);
- bathymetric maps (bathymetric charts).

KEY POINT Never write or draw directly onto a map or photograph; use tracing paper, acetate overlays or photocopies. If you use photocopies, make certain that you have copyright permission.

Topographic maps

These are produced at several scales, the most useful of which in practical environmental science are:

- 1: 50 000 = 2 cm: 1 km (superseding 1: 63 360 or 1 inch to 1 mile). This is an ideal general purpose scale of map for route navigation when motoring, locating roads, railways, cities, towns, villages, farms, specific areas of land, rivers, coastal features, antiquities, tourist attractions, etc. Topographic contours are drawn at 10 m intervals enabling mountain and hill peaks, valleys and other physical features of the landscape to be readily identified. Spot heights are included.
- 1: 25 000 = 4 cm: 1 km. These maps also have a contour interval of 10 m but generally provide greater detail of geomorphological, botanical (e.g. vegetation types), archaeological, historical and urban features than the 1: 50 000 scale. For example, the locations of footpaths, wells and springs are shown. They are useful for navigation when walking and for environmental surveys in which only a moderate level of positional accuracy is required.
- 1: 10 000 = 10 cm: 1 km (superseding 1:10 560 or 6 inches to 1 mile). With a contour interval of 5 m for urban and rural areas and 10 m in some mountain and moorland areas, these maps afford the optimum level of topographic detail. They should be used as the basis of field mapping of geological and geomorphological features and the accurate location of points in the field for many forms of environmental survey. In cities and towns the names of major streets are given and individual houses or blocks of houses identified. Such maps are therefore ideal for planning and property management purposes. Note that for remote, upland areas sheets at this scale may not be available and it could be necessary to use

the old 1: 10 560 maps with imperial contours at 100-foot intervals. For some locations very old editions are the only ones available. Note that these sometimes have spot heights only, lacking both contours and the National Grid.

There are many other types of specialist topographic map, including:

- Popular tourist and holiday areas at various scales. These show the detail of sites of recreational use and are helpful when assessing the environmental impact of leisure and recreation facilities.
- Reproductions of historical maps. These are useful for comparison with contemporary maps when assessing environmental change (e.g. in areas of coastal erosion or accretion) and land management/land use changes with time (e.g. urban development, woodland development or decline).
- Maps showing administrative boundaries, e.g. all levels of local authority (parishes, districts, counties, etc.) and parliamentary (e.g. British/ Westminster, European Union, etc.) boundaries.
- Large-scale, typically 1: 5000, maps of specific urban areas showing individual properties, names of roads/streets, schools, car parks and all aspects of urban infrastructure. These are useful when planning door to door questionnaire surveys.

In most countries maps are overprinted with a grid system delimiting 1 km × 1 km squares. On topographic maps of Britain produced by the Ordnance Survey (also shown on geological maps produced by the British Geological Survey) this is known as the National Grid (see also Box 16.1). Box 29.1 explains how to define the position of a point on a map on the basis of the National Grid. How to construct a topographic cross-section from a map is described in Box 29.2.

Geological maps

There are essentially two main types of geological map conventionally available at scales of 1: 250 000 and 1: 50 000:

- solid editions;
- drift editions.

Note that there are still areas of Britain for which 1: 50 000 geological maps are not available (1: 63 360 is the alternative scale), and some remote regions for which no comparable scale geological maps can be readily acquired.

Solid geological maps show, by means of colours, shading and symbols, the distribution of rock types at the surface of the Earth as they would appear if the veneer of superficial drift (i.e. glacial deposits, alluvium, peat, etc.) had been stripped away. Such maps include a detailed key to colours and symbols, and usually incorporate one or more cross-sections showing the sub-surface distribution of rocks along specific lines, together with a concise text summary of the geological history of the area and a few key references. Note that older editions of solid geological maps (typically at 1: 63 360 scale) incorporate information on the drift cover by means of symbols.

Drift geological maps show, by means of colours, shading and symbols, the distribution of Quaternary deposits (i.e. Recent and Pleistocene = last 2 000 000 years), including man-made deposits, reclaimed land, the locations of former shorelines and glacial channels, etc. No solid geological features are shown other than the occurrence of bedrock (rock type or age not

If you need up-to-date information about an area, make certain that you use the most recent edition of map available.

Further information – if you want to know more about the mapping of Britain by the Ordnance Survey and the availability of maps, consult their Web site at: http:// www.ordsvy.gov.uk.

Solid geological maps of Britain are also produced by the British Geological Survey at a scale of 1: 625 000. These cover the country in two sheets: North and South. Use them as a general guide to regional geology. Note that they are overprinted with a grid delimiting the areas of the individual 1: 50 000 and 1: 63 360 geological maps, so helping you to find the number of a specific sheet.

Fig. 29.1 A map measurer. This is a useful device for measuring distances to scale on any type of map. It consists of two pointers that record distance on two dials back-to-back, in kilometres and miles simultaneously, as a knurled wheel is run along the proposed route. The scale of the map must be known since this determines which reading of distance is read from the appropriate dial.

Bedrock – a solid geological map can give a false impression of the degree of bedrock exposure. Always consult both a solid and corresponding drift edition (if available) to get a true impression of the drift cover and distribution of rock outcrops in an area.

Hydrogeological maps provide valuable information on the vulnerability of aquifers to pollution.

Definitions

Aquifer – a body of permeable rock or drift saturated with groundwater and through which groundwater moves.

Aquiclude – a body of impermeable rock that acts as a barrier to groundwater migration.

Box 29.1 How to define the position of a point on a map

It is possible to define the position of a point to within 100 m on 1: 50 000 or 1: 25 000 scale maps and to 10 m on 1: 10 000 scale maps on the basis of the National Grid.

1. **Look at the sheet number of the map** (usually at the top right corner) and note the two capital letters which precede it (e.g. for sheet NS 78 NW these are NS).

2. **Locate the western edge of the grid square in which your point of interest lies** and read off the figures at either the northern or southern end of this line at the margins of the sheet (e.g. 72).

3. **With the aid of the 100 m divisions of the grid squares (at the margins of the map), estimate tenths eastward from the grid line to the point** (this three figure number, e.g. 724, is known as the Easting). Note that 100 m grid square divisions are not present on 1: 10 000 scale maps.

4. **Locate the southern edge of the grid square in which your point of interest lies** and read off the figures at either the eastern or western end of the line at the margins of the sheet (e.g. 85).

5. **With the aid of the 100 m divisions of the grid squares, estimate tenths northwards from the grid line to the point** (this three figure number, e.g. 856, is known as the Northing).

6. **The 100 m National Grid Reference** of the point is given by the two letters preceding the sheet number, followed by the Easting, followed by the Northing, i.e. NS 724856.

7. **Using a 1: 10 000 scale map you can define the position of a point to within 10 m by estimating tenth sub-divisions of the 100 m grid square divisions (e.g. NS 72418566).**

usually specified) at or near the land surface. A text summary of the Quaternary history of the area and a few key references are usually incorporated.

Hydrogeological maps

The availability of hydrogeological maps is usually restricted to those areas where the underlying rocks contain groundwater in economic quantities. They provide information on:

- distribution of aquifers and aquicludes;
- depth to water table;
- distribution of boreholes;
- groundwater yield from boreholes;
- groundwater quality (concentrations of major ions).

Soil survey maps

Soil survey maps are usually available at similar scales to geological survey maps. They show the distribution of soil types on the basis of classifications developed by soil scientists. They are most profitably used in conjunction with drift geological maps.

Land use capability maps

Also known as agricultural potential maps, these illustrate the suitability of soils for agriculture. In Britain (Soil Surveys of Scotland or England and Wales) this is on the basis of seven classes:

- Class 1: land with very minor physical or climatic limitations which do not interfere with the sustained production of cultivated field crops.
- Class 2: land with some physical or climatic limitations which under good management is capable of sustained production of field crops.
- Class 3: land with moderately severe limitations which restrict the choice of crops or require special cultivation practices.
- Class 4: land with severe limitations which restrict the choice of crops and/or require special cultivation practices.
- Class 5: land with very severe limitations which restrict its use to permanent pasture but mechanized improvement practices may be possible.
- Class 6: land with very severe limitations which restrict agricultural land use to rough grazing. Mechanized improvement is impossible.
- Class 7: land with extremely severe limitations, e.g. industrial waste tips, bare rock outcrops and unstable sand dunes.

> Land use planning – land use capability maps provide valuable information for the land use planner, more so than soil survey maps.

Environmental geology maps/environmental potential maps

There are several types of map that fall into these broad categories. As with hydrogeological maps they are usually available for specific regions only. All are designed to illustrate, usually by means of separate sheets, the relevant geological factors likely to influence planning, for example:

- foundation conditions;
- land susceptibility to land-slipping or subsidence;
- land susceptibility to flooding;
- distribution of mineral resources (e.g. sand and gravel) and workings.

> Environmental geology maps are presented in such a way that they are easy for non-geologists to understand.

KEY POINT Environmental potential maps are designed to facilitate the development of a multi-use plan of a particular area and to avoid one factor adversely affecting another.

Bathymetric maps

Also known as bathymetric charts since they are used for navigation purposes in coastal waters, these maps show contours and spot measurements of water depth *below* a datum. This is typically a local Chart Datum or Ordnance Datum (see Chapter 16) and is shown on the map as the 'zero' contour line. Usually shades of blue are used to indicate progressively deeper waters, whereas lands in the inter-tidal zone, such as sandbanks, are commonly indicated in yellow shades. Note that the depth information given for inter-tidal areas relates to drying heights, i.e. heights *above* the datum of the chart. To avoid confusion these are usually indicated with a line beneath the depth value. Thus 2.3 m indicates a drying height of 2.3 m *above* the datum of the chart, whereas 2.3 m indicates a water depth of 2.3 m *below* the datum of the chart. Other features shown include the locations of:

- navigation buoys, beacons and lighthouses;
- shipwrecks and other obstacles or hazards to navigation;
- pipelines and undersea telegraph cables;
- areas of seabed of different sediment type (e.g. mud, sand, gravel, shells).

> Water depths – all water depths on bathymetric charts are subject to natural variation. Such changes may be very rapid in dynamic environments. Always use the most up-to-date chart available.

Box 29.2 How to construct a topographic cross-section from a map

1. **Place a strip of paper with a cleanly cut edge along the line of interest on the map and mark the ends of the line on the paper as A and B**, for example, using a pencil.

Tip: use small pieces of masking tape to secure the strip of paper in place.

2. **Starting from A, mark off on the paper strip**, by means of a short line at right angles to the edge of the paper, the positions at which it intersects each contour line or spot height. Continue until B is reached.

3. **Against each mark on the paper strip, write the value of the contour height or spot height.**

4. **Transfer the paper strip to a piece of mm-graduated graph paper** and secure it beneath the horizontal (*x*) axis.

5. **Plot the height of the ground surface** as indicated by the marked values vertically above each point marked on the paper.

6. **To plot a true section you should use a vertical scale that is the same as the horizontal scale.** However, if the relief is small this may not be practical. Always make a note of the vertical exaggeration of your section as, for example $\times 2$, $\times 3$, etc.

7. **Join each of the plotted points by means of a smooth line.**

Tip: use a flexicurve (a flexible ruler) to help you to draw the profile of the land surface smoothly and neatly.

Copying photographs – modern photocopiers have a 'photo mode' facility that permits reasonably good quality copies of photographs to be made.

Photographs

There are two principal types of photograph:

- terrestrial;
- aerial.

Terrestrial photographs

Terrestrial photographs (see also Chapter 27) are taken for a wide range of purposes, typically to record field site information, but usually on an *ad hoc* basis. They may be taken by hand-held or tripod-mounted camera. Field photographs provide an important complement to field notes and sketches and are recommended as a means of recording the details of field sites, rock outcrops, etc.

Landforms may be photographed from the ground to produce a record of change through time (e.g. to record the progress of coastal erosion). Such a record may start from the present or make use of an old photograph of the feature. If a new record is begun, the location from which the photograph is taken should be meticulously chosen (fixed point photography) and noted so that return visits to the spot are simplified and can be undertaken by another person. Where an old photograph is used, it is easiest if a copy is taken to the site so that the same view may be obtained. In order that any changes can be quantified, an object of known dimensions should be incorporated into the photograph.

Old photographs – there are sometimes problems in identifying sites from which old photographs were taken. However, it is usually possible to find some identifying features from which measurements can be made.

Never under-estimate the value of old photographs as a source of historical data in studies of environmental change through time.

Aerial photographs

Aerial photographs are obtained for either:

- Reconnaissance purposes: these may be taken either obliquely or vertically and are used for interpretation purposes only. Several specialist firms carry out reconnaissance aerial photography and frames are available at a number of different scales.
- Survey purposes: these are taken vertically and are used primarily for topographic mapping, particularly for map revision (e.g. by the Ordnance Survey). Survey aerial photographs are taken with specialist cameras (equipped with low distortion lenses) and typically, in Britain, have a 230×230 mm (formerly 9×9 inch) format. Edge markings show the date and time that each frame was taken, together with the scale. For mapping purposes the Ordnance Survey uses the following scales of photograph according to the terrain:
  - Moorland, upland and mountainous areas: 1: 24 000;
  - Rural areas: 1: 7 500;
  - Urban areas: 1: 5 000.

Unlike maps, however, aerial photographs are seldom available at systematic scales and often the coverage of particular regions or countries is incomplete.

The Ordnance Survey can supply aerial photographs (mainly monochrome) covering most of England and much of Scotland and Wales and is the principal source of information on aerial photograph coverage of England from the 1940s to the present. The University of Cambridge holds one of the largest collections of both oblique and aerial photographs of Britain. Early frames (from the 1940s) are in a 5×5 inch format. Many recent plates are in colour. In Scotland, an extensive collection of aerial photographs, dating back to the 1940s, is held by the Royal Commission on the Ancient and Historical Monuments of Scotland (RCAHMS), Edinburgh.

Ideally, aerial photographs should be used in conjunction with reliable maps so that features can be identified with accuracy. Information that can be extracted from aerial photographs in this way includes:

- identification of anthropogenic and natural features;
- distribution of land use types and patterns;
- settlement and land use change;
- changes in fluvial and coastal configuration;
- crop markings (of potential archaeological significance).

For mapping purposes it is usually necessary to observe features on aerial photographs in three dimensions. A three-dimensional image is produced when adjacent overlapping photographs are optically superimposed by means of a stereoscope. The minimum overlap for such stereoscopic cover is 50%; survey aerial photographs are typically taken with a 60% overlap in the direction of flight. Note that a stereoscope produces a realistic though distorted view of Earth surface features. The corrections that must be applied for variations in height and topography, to provide the basis from which topographic maps can be made, are beyond the scope of this chapter.

Remote sensing

Remote sensing is a term used to describe any method by which information about the Earth, or objects on the Earth, is obtained without any physical contact between the subject of study and the sensor. Most commonly the

Viewing aerial photographs – if you wish to view one or more aerial photographs of an area you must know the National Grid References of the corners of the area or locational information such as the name of the town required. It is usually necessary to submit this information in advance and viewing is normally by appointment only (e.g. with the RCAHMS). It is always wise to view prior to purchase as the quality of older aerial photographs is variable. It is also quite possible that the feature you are interested in is obscured by cloud!

Crop markings – these are best observed on aerial photographs taken during the summer. They are visible as colour or tonal changes in crops caused by differential growth over buried features such as ditches which may define the sites of former settlements.

Studying coastlines – aerial photographs are particularly useful for the remote observation of coasts where the coastline is difficult to reach because of high cliffs with no beaches at their base.

If using aerial photographs to study coastal areas, it is important to know the date and time of day that the photograph was taken so that the state of the tide can be calculated.

Table 29.1 The radio wave to ultraviolet radiation portion of the electromagnetic spectrum

Wavelength (m)	Type of electromagnetic radiation
$> 1 \times 10^{-3}$	radio waves
1.5×10^3	long radiowaves
3×10^2	medium radiowaves
3×10^{-2}	microwaves
$8 \times 10^{-7} - 1 \times 10^{-3}$	infrared
$1 \times 10^{-5} - 1.2 \times 10^{-5}$	thermal infrared
$8 \times 10^{-7} - 4 \times 10^{-6}$	near infrared
$4 \times 10^{-7} - 8 \times 10^{-7}$	visible light
$5 \times 10^{-9} - 4 \times 10^{-7}$	ultraviolet

term is applied to the collection of data by instruments deployed from satellites or aircraft. Thus both aerial and terrestrial photography are forms of remote sensing, although the latter is often not thought of as such. There are many types of remote sensing device that record different forms of reflected electromagnetic energy from different parts of the electromagnetic spectrum (Table 29.1). The commonest are:

- Cameras: sensors that record reflected energy in the part of the electromagnetic spectrum that is detected by the human eye, i.e. visible light. For applications, see the section on photographs above.
- Infrared sensors: these record infrared radiation and create images showing temperature variations in an area (e.g. sea surface temperatures, detection of forest fires). In surveys of urban areas the locations of poorly insulated buildings and other structures with significant heat loss can be detected.
- Microwave sensors (e.g. radar): these transmit very long wavelength electromagnetic energy towards objects and record the resulting reflections. Such energy is capable of penetrating cloud cover (*cf.* visible light) and microwave sensors have important applications in geological mapping, the mapping of variations in soil moisture content and the extent and movement of sea ice. Synthetic aperture radar (SAR) may be used to monitor sea surface roughness and to detect and follow oil slicks.
- Multispectral scanners (e.g. the Thematic Mapper deployed from the Landsat satellite): such scanners produce images spanning both the visible and infrared parts of the electromagnetic spectrum. Computer processing of multispectral data, especially the use of 'false colours' (computer-generated), has led to numerous applications, e.g. land use management and planning, water quality assessment and the location of mineral deposits.

The spatial resolution (size of the smallest individual features or objects that may be seen or the closest separation of two objects) varies according to the type of system used. Generally camera-film or other systems, deployed either terrestrially or from the air, achieve the best spatial resolution. The Landsat Thematic Mapper, for example, permits observation of objects with an area of 30 m × 30 m, and other satellite-borne sensors produce still better spatial resolution. The technology of remote sensing is changing quickly and satellite-borne sensors capable of detecting features of a few m^2 in area are anticipated.

Geographical Information Systems (GIS)

A geographical information system, commonly abbreviated to GIS, is a powerful computer software system that is designed to record, store and analyse information about Earth surface features, permitting two- and three-dimensional visualization and manipulation of spatial data. Such systems are increasingly being used to overlay information in the form of 'layers'.

For example, individual layers could include the following information as derived from a variety of sources (Table 29.2):

- topography;
- solid geology;
- drift geology;
- soil types;

Definition

Layer – a layer in a GIS represents one particular type of geographical data, e.g. the vegetation cover of a region. A GIS database can include up to 100 layers.

Table 29.2 Principal sources of geographical data that may be accepted by a GIS

Maps
Aerial photographs
Satellite images
Statistical data
Printed text

- vegetation cover;
- land use/land capability;
- environmental geology (e.g. foundation conditions, flood risk, landslide risk).

A GIS is able to combine several layers into a single image. Thus, on the basis of the above example, the distribution of landslides in an area could be analysed in relation to its topography, geology and distribution of soil types. Similarly, the distribution of crimes of a particular class in an urban area may be viewed and analysed in terms of type of housing, district of the city, civic amenities, street names, postal code areas, etc.

Environmental impact assessment and environmental change

Definition

European Council EIA Directive 85/337/ EEC of 27 June 1985 applies the term **Environmental Impact Assessment** to the identification, description and assessment of the direct and indirect effects of a project on: human beings, fauna and flora, soil, water, air, climate and the landscape; the interaction of these factors; and on material assets, and the cultural heritage.

Definition

An **Environmental Impact Assessment** (EIA) is the name of the process undertaken to produce an **Environmental Statement** (ES).

Any proposed project or development that is likely to have an impact on the environment, e.g. the construction of a petrochemical factory, housing estate or leisure complex, the extraction of peat or coal, the installation of an effluent outfall into the sea, should be preceded by an Environmental Impact Assessment (EIA).

KEY POINT   EIA is a tool used for achieving sustainable development. It is intended to identify the environmental, social and economic impacts of a proposed development *before* decision making.

An EIA is carried out either by the developer or, more commonly, by a specialist firm of environmental consultants. You may be required to undertake, usually as part of a group, a hypothetical EIA as a training exercise. The procedures are identical and the end product is a report known as an Environmental Impact Statement (EIS), often abbreviated to Environmental Statement (ES). To play an effective part in an EIA, whether in the real world working for a consultancy firm or as part of a university group project, you should:

- Learn to think laterally.
- Use checklists and matrices (see below) as aids to identifying potential impacts.
- Consult widely with colleagues and experts in other fields of expertise.
- Carry out field visits: learn to collect and collate diverse data sets.

Stages involved in an environmental impact assessment

No two EIAs will be exactly the same but there is a generic series of stages that are normally followed. The stages are:

Public consultation – consider using a questionnaire survey (see Chapter 21) to gauge public opinion on a development as part of an EIA. Always involve the public as much as possible.

- Desk studies (also known as 'scoping') involving a combination of:
    - Collating pre-existing information about the site and the development proposal.
    - Identifying the key issues and concerns of the interested parties, in particular: who is concerned about the development? Why are they concerned about the development? What are their concerns about the development?

Beware of parties who have a vested interest in a development – always verify information that is made available to you (either verbally or in written form) by such parties.

- Field studies (e.g. geological, geomorphological, hydrological, hydrogeological, ecological).
- Review of appropriate legislation, e.g. planning regulations.
- Public consultation.
- Summation of potential environmental impacts and risks.
- Identification of mitigating measures and development alternatives.
- Production of ES as formal report.

Box 30.1 details the most important factors that should be considered in an EIA, but the relative emphasis on each of these will vary according to the project.

When beginning to identify potential impacts, construct simple checklists (e.g. Table 30.1).

Box 30.1   Key issues for consideration in an environmental impact assessment

- **Description** of the development: location, design, scale, whether industrial, commercial, residential, etc.
- **Topography and land use** of the site and its environs. History of land use: possible contamination (e.g. landfill gases) due to previous usage.
- **Proximity of the site to dwellings**, factories, schools, hospitals, etc.
- **Solid geology** of the site: underlying bedrock types and structure. History of natural hazardous events, e.g. seismicity.
- **Drift geology and geomorphology** of the site: nature and distribution of the superficial deposits. Risk of, e.g., subsidence and landsliding.
- **Hydrology** of the site: river drainage patterns and runoff, lakes, standing water, etc. Risk of flooding and surface water pollution.
- **Tide levels** and risk of flooding of coastal sites. Impact of potential sea level rise.

- **Hydrogeology** of the site: underlying aquifers and risk of groundwater pollution.
- **Microclimate** of the site.
- **Ecology** of the site: diversity and rarity of flora, fauna, endangered species and potential threats to these.
- **Archaeology** of the site and potential threats to disturbance of cultural heritage.
- **Historical significance** of the site, e.g. former battlefield.
- **Infrastructure**: projected traffic volume and environmental risk on roads leading to and from the site; access by emergency services; impact of traffic noise; impact of vehicle emissions.
- **Air and noise pollution** due to the development.
- **Aesthetics** of the development.
- **Economic impact** of the development.
- **Planning regulations** that may apply to the development site.

Table 30.1 An example of a checklist identifying environmental factors that may be affected by a development: case study of dredging for sand in an estuary

---

River flow
Sedimentation
Mineral aggregate (sand) replenishment
Wildlife and ecological interests
Fisheries interests
Commercial shipping
Underwater archaeology
Leisure and tourism

Even more helpful are matrices (e.g. Table 30.2). These are tables which plot environmental components against the individual development components. The latter can be considered under the headings of 'construction phase', 'operational phase' and, if appropriate, 'decommissioning phase'. A tick in the relevant box indicates that a particular development action, e.g. construction of buildings, will have an impact on a particular environmental component, e.g. fauna. The absence of a tick indicates no perceived impact. Such a simple matrix (e.g. Table 30.2) can be augmented by indicating the relative *magnitude* that an impact may have. This can be done by inserting numbers in the boxes in the range of, say, −5 to 0 to +5, which could represent the range from 'very large negative impact' to 'no impact' to 'very large positive impact'. Similarly, a matrix may be modified to incorporate the likely *timescale* in ranges of years over which an individual development action is perceived to have an impact on each environmental component.

The essential elements of an environmental statement

Just as no two EIAs are alike, neither are two ESs. The generic format of an ES, however, must include:

- A description of the development (see Box 30.1).
- A description of the likely environmental effects of the development (see Box 30.1).
- A review of mitigating measures, i.e. those measures which can be taken to avoid or minimize the potential adverse environmental impacts of a development, e.g. pollution prevention techniques.

KEY POINT   Note that mitigating measures could include modifying the development or abandoning it completely.

- A non-technical summary.

Table 30.2 An example of a matrix for identifying environmental impacts of a development. Note that a third set of development components under the heading 'decommissioning phase' could be added if appropriate

Environmental components	Development components							
	Construction phase				Operational phase			
	Services	Access roads	Buildings	Car parks	Access roads	Buildings	Car parks	Open spaces
Solid geology		✓	✓	✓				
Drift geology/soils	✓	✓	✓	✓				✓
Geomorphology	✓	✓	✓	✓				✓
Hydrology		✓	✓	✓				
Hydrogeology		✓	✓	✓				
Archaeology	✓	✓	✓	✓	✓			
Water quality			✓			✓		
Air quality			✓		✓	✓		
Flora	✓	✓	✓	✓				✓
Fauna	✓	✓	✓	✓				✓
Traffic levels	✓	✓	✓	✓	✓		✓	
Noise levels	✓	✓	✓	✓	✓	✓	✓	
Employment	✓	✓	✓	✓		✓		
Community structure					✓	✓	✓	✓

KEY POINT An ES must include a non-technical summary of its key points which can be readily understood by public officials, e.g. local councillors, and members of the general public.

Environmental change

An EIA is a formal means of identifying or predicting the environmental impacts resulting from a proposed development. However, it is often necessary to monitor environmental change continuously after completion to quantify the nature and extent of change, if any, which has actually taken place as a direct consequence of the development. This may, for example, involve surveying (Chapter 16), questionnaire surveys (Chapter 21), or sampling and analysis of biological materials (Chapter 17), soils or sediments (Chapter 18), solid geological materials (Chapter 19), or air or water (Chapter 20).

Studies of environmental change may also be undertaken without a specific association to an EIA, for example analyses of changes in rainfall, river discharge, wind velocity, air temperature or water temperature over time. In general, the longer the data record, the more significant the data set may be.

To monitor environmental change over time you must ensure:

- An appropriate time interval between sampling, measurements or observations. This may change with time from, e.g., one month immediately after completion of a development, to one or more years if the changes initially observed are minor.
- Measurements or observations are repeatable.
- Well established sampling procedures and protocols are adopted (see Chapter 15).
- Comparable surveying and analytical techniques are used.
- Unambiguous records are kept of all surveying, sampling and analytical procedures. This is particularly relevant in the event that you hand over all or part of the monitoring programme to someone else.

The study of environmental change epitomizes the complex and integrated nature of environmental science, as it is necessary to acquire, collate and interpret diverse data and information sets relating to a particular topic. The types of data and information may be either geological, geographical, biological, chemical or physical, or a combination of these. Box 30.2 illustrates these points using a case study.

Box 30.2   Case study of the assessment of the conservation status of a lake

A lake has been identified as potentially important as a conservation site. You have been asked to assess the status of the lake with a view to its subsequent management. The following stages guide you through the process to demonstrate the complexity and integrated nature of practical environmental projects.

KEY POINT   Remember that if you are to compare the present status of the lake with that of earlier times, then you will have to collect historical information and data.

Stage I. Review the existing knowledge of the system and the parameters that can influence the system

You may need to measure or estimate some or all of the following components:

Geological and geographical characteristics of the lake's catchment

- area, topography and relief
- solid geology
- drift geology, geomorphology
- soil types and vegetation
- land use, agricultural practices and industrial development, present and historical
- settlement types and distribution, present and historical
- climatic conditions

Hydrological characteristics of the lake's catchment

- water budget
  - precipitation
  - evaporation and evapotranspiration
  - infiltration to groundwater
  - surface runoff to rivers and streams
  - engineered transfer of water from other catchments
  - engineered transfer of water to other catchments
- inflow of water to the lake
- outflow of water from the lake

Physical characteristics of the lake basin

- morphometry
  - length
  - breadth
  - length of shoreline
  - surface area
- bathymetry
  - maximum depth
  - mean depth
  - volume
- residence time (= basin volume/volume of inflowing water per unit time)

Biological characteristics of the lake

- plankton
- nekton
- benthos
- macrophytes

Physical and chemical characteristics of the lake

- water chemistry
  - pH
  - electrical conductivity
  - concentrations of major ions
  - concentrations of specific ions (e.g. nitrate and phosphate)
- water temperature
  - vertical distribution
  - thermal stratification
- water circulation patterns
  - wind driven
  - river inflow driven
- suspended sediments
  - particle size
  - concentration
  - composition
  - distribution
- bottom sediments
  - particle size
  - composition
  - distribution
- sedimentation rate

Other characteristics of the lake

- recreational use
  - sailing
  - fishing
  - swimming
  - water-skiing
- tourism

Box 30.2 (continued)

KEY POINT You must take a pragmatic view of the above list. It will inevitably be necessary to prioritize the importance of the various parameters since it may not be practical, in a given time period, to acquire data and information relating to them all.

Stage II. Determine what measurements are needed in the light of the Stage I review (identify the gaps in knowledge)

Synthesize the data and information collected in Stage I and evaluate what additional data and information are required. On the assumption that field work will be necessary, read Chapter 5.

Stage III. Formulate a temporal and spatial sampling strategy and decide on the appropriate sampling devices and protocols

Before undertaking your sampling programme, read Chapters 15, 16, 17, 18, 19 and 20. You might need to use questionnaires, for example to find out the amount of fertilizer farmers apply to the land. If so, read Chapter 21.

Stage IV. Determine which analytical methods and protocols are to be used on any samples taken

Before undertaking your analytical programme, read Chapters 31, 32 and 33. Note that Chapter 34 may also be relevant if you consider airborne inputs to the lake to be of significance.

Stage V. Collate, analyse, present and interpret the information and data acquired, together with historical data

Begin by reading Chapters 35, 36 and 37. To optimize the statistical analysis of your data, refer to Chapters 39 and 40.

Stage VI. Establish conclusions, recommendations and, if relevant, mitigating measures in the light of Stages I–V

Begin by re-reading this chapter from the top!

Stage VII. Present the material from Stages I–VI in the form of a report

Read Chapters 46 and 48. A non-technical summary should be incorporated.

31 Chemical analysis of environmental materials

Our knowledge of the environment can only be as good as our knowledge of the identities and quantities of the diverse chemical and physical environmental parameters. After defining the information you wish to obtain and having decided on your general sampling strategy and methodology, a key factor in determining your protocol will be a proper understanding of the type of analysis to be undertaken. Although the methodologies of all potential chemical and physical procedures are well beyond the scope of this book, there are general features that need consideration. These include:

- Capabilities of the method chosen, e.g. range and precision (Fig. 31.1).
- Requirements for pre-treatments of sampling equipment.
- Sample treatment for transport and storage prior to analysis.
- Sources and scales of errors in the technique used, including contamination.
- Calibration of equipment and the use of reagent blanks.
- Protocol for the particular method.
- The nature of any special apparatus or reagents required.

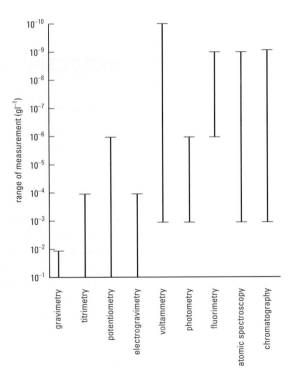

Fig. 31.1 Comparison of ranges of measurement for different analytical methods (after Schwedt, 1997).

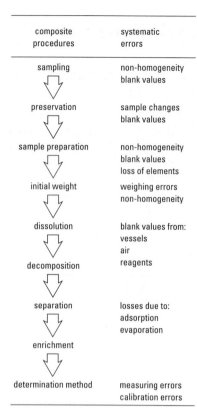

composite procedures	systematic errors
sampling	non-homogeneity blank values
preservation	sample changes blank values
sample preparation	non-homogeneity blank values loss of elements
initial weight	weighing errors non-homogeneity
dissolution	blank values from: vessels air reagents
decomposition	
separation	losses due to: adsorption evaporation
enrichment	
determination method	measuring errors calibration errors

Fig. 31.2 Sources of error in composite method analyses (after Schwedt, 1997).

Analytical techniques

Analysis of environmental materials may require either:

- **direct** procedures, where a sample can be analysed directly without any intermediate steps and usually with non-destructive methods. This includes the use of ion-sensitive electrode systems, particularly for testing aquatic systems.
- **composite** methods, typically required for complex or mixed materials: composite is the term given to the combination of methods and techniques for sample preparation, decomposing the sample, separating out interfering components, and final analysis. By virtue of the number of stages involved, such methods have diverse sources of potential error (Fig. 31.2).

If determinations are not to be made in the field, it may be essential to carry out pre-treatments on some samples as soon as they are taken to prevent changes in composition brought about by various agents (see Chapter 17). Commonly used techniques include:

- Cooling, filtration, freezing, or the addition of a biocide to minimize biological activities.
- Acidification to prevent metal precipitation or adsorption reactions.
- Filtration or centrifugation of aqueous samples where it is required to separately determine dissolved and particulate fractions.

Before the development of the sophisticated instrumentation available today, some analyses were done by classical methods requiring only balances, chemicals and basic glassware. The two major classical methods were:

- volumetric analysis, in which volumes of reagents are measured;
- gravimetric analysis, in which masses are measured.

Some classical methods are still relevant, and many have been adapted to instrumental and automated procedures.

KEY POINT Remember that the lower detection limits of many modern instruments may reduce the value of older data sets. The lower purity of reagents in the past may also be a complicating factor, particularly in studies of pollutants.

Modern methods are diverse and have significantly improved the sensitivity of the analyses (Fig. 31.1): the key ones that may be encountered by undergraduate students include:

- Colorimetric methods, in which reactions producing coloured reaction products are used to quantify substances.
- Spectrophotometric methods, including atomic absorption spectro-photometry (AAS) and X-ray fluorescence. Developed in the 1960s, AAS has become the method of choice for most metals analysed in environmental materials and is based upon measurement of absorption or emission spectra when samples are heated to a high temperature.
- Electrochemical sensor methods, which use ion-selective electrodes to quantify materials present in solution. Anodic-stripping voltammetry involves the deposition and subsequent stripping of metals on an electrode surface. This is used for the measurement of metals in solution.
- Chromatography, including gas–liquid chromatography (GLC) and high performance liquid chromatography (HPLC). These are methods based upon the principle that when a mixture of volatile (GLC) or soluble

Table 31.1 Summary of the main quantitative analytical approaches to environmental substances

Type of analysis	Methods
Gravimetric	Precipitation
	Electrodeposition
Titrimetric	Precipitate formation
	Acid–base
	Compleximetric
	Redox
Energy absorption	Molecular spectroscopy (UV–visible)
	Atomic absorption spectroscopy
	Infrared spectroscopy
Energy emission	Atomic emission spectroscopy
	X-ray fluorescence
	Electron spectroscopy (XPS, PES)
	Atomic and molecular fluorescence
Electroanalytical	Potentiometry
	Polarography
	Voltammetry
Chromatographic	Thin layer chromatography
	Gas–liquid chromatography
	High performance chromatography
Other	Mass spectrometry
	Radiochemical techniques
	Kinetic methods
	Thermal methods

(HPLC) substances transported by a carrier gas (GLC) or liquid (HPLC), is passed through a column containing an adsorbent material, each component will be partitioned between the carrier medium and the column material. Since different components will be retained to differing degrees, they will emerge from the column at different times. If a suitable detector is available, the quantities can be measured and the substances identified by the time required to pass through the system.

- Ion chromatography uses liquid chromatographic determination of certain ions and has enabled the measurement of chemical species that have been troublesome for water chemists. It is used for a diverse array of anions and for some cations also.
- Mass spectrometry is a method that depends upon the production of ions by an electrical discharge or chemical process, followed by separation based upon the charge-to-mass ratio and measurement of the ions produced.

Table 31.1 and Fig. 31.3 summarizes the methods generally available and their characteristics.

Choosing an analytical method

Several criteria influence the selection of the technique for any particular analysis.

- Accuracy: degree of agreement between a measured value and the true value.
- Precision: the degree of agreement between replicate measurements of the same quantity, i.e. reproducibility.
- Sensitivity (response of equipment per unit weight of determinant) and detection limit (minimum quantity of the analyte that can be confidently discriminated from zero).
- Amount of available sample.
- The selectivity (preference exhibited by a reaction or test towards the substance of interest over other [interfering] substances) or specificity required.
- Nature of the sample: whether solid, liquid or gas phase.
- Destructive or non-destructive techniques – limited or valuable samples may require non-destructive techniques.
- Reliability of the procedure, instrument or operator.
- Simplicity: the level of skill and practice required.
- Batch or continuous analysis.
- Time for analysis.
- Cost.

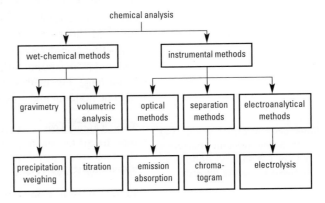

Fig. 31.3 A classification of analytical methods (after Schwedt, 1997).

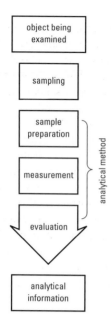

Fig. 31.4 The stages of an analysis (after Schwedt, 1997).

Avoiding contamination – remember that glassware and other containers used in the sampling and analysis phases may require chemical (e.g. acid) or physical (heat) pre-treatment to prevent adsorption and leaching problems which will alter or contaminate your analysis.

Chemical digestion – stronger acids may be required for some difficult materials but should not be considered lightly, as they pose considerable safety hazards.

The stages of an analysis

Fig. 31.4 presents a summary of the typical stages of an analysis. These are:

- sampling (considered in various chapters);
- preservation and pre-treatment (Chapter 17);
- sample preparation (separation and pre-concentration);
- measurement of analyte (technique-specific);
- expressing results (Chapters 35–40).

Sample pre-treatment techniques

Environmental samples tend to have either too high or too low a concentration of the substances to be analysed and will usually require either sample splitting or pre-concentration of the analyte before analysis is possible.

- Sample splitting: it is often possible to reduce the amount of a sample using a sample reduction procedure (see also Chapter 4). The important consideration here is that however it is done, the procedure must not introduce any bias into the sub-sample.
- Pre-concentration (also known as enrichment) may be required when it is known or expected that the concentration of the analyte in the raw sample is below the preferred sensitivity limit of the method being used. Such analytes are frequently referred to as trace materials. Pre-concentration procedures range from simple evaporation by heating to extraction and concentration procedures often involving phase conversions, i.e. extractions using a change from gas to liquid to solid phases, or the use of ion-exchange columns (sorption and solvent elution).

Another commonly required sample pre-treatment is the separation or extraction of the analyte from its matrix, from interfering compounds or from chemical complexes. Again, the methods are very much substance-specific; refer to the appropriate analytical sources.

KEY POINT Remember to use reagent blanks in each analysis to eliminate contaminants deriving from the chemicals used.

Ashing and digestion (decomposition) techniques are frequently used to convert complex materials into aqueous solutions containing the required analyte. Dry ashing involves the destruction of organic material by heating to about 500 °C (see also Chapter 33), leaving the non-volatile constituents in an easily soluble state. Losses due to partial volatilization of many elements has rendered this method prone to error. The most commonly used method for extracting non-degradable analytes such as metals from biological materials, soil, sediment and air filter samples is chemical digestion, also referred to as wet-ashing. The method typically uses a strong oxidizing acid to destroy the organic material and solubilize the analyte element.

KEY POINT The most commonly used acid is nitric acid, which may be added to the sample in a glass container and evaporated to near dryness on a hotplate. The residue is then dissolved in dilute acid for subsequent analysis.

Filtration is a commonly used form of pre-treatment for water samples because almost all natural waters contain both dissolved chemical and suspended particulate components. It is usual to separate these two phases and analyse them separately. The usual procedure is to use a $0.45 \mu m$ Millipore filter system to separate these phases into 'dissolved' and 'suspended' components, although it is accepted that such fractions are operationally defined and do not represent a real and significant physico-chemical division.

Calibration and use of standard solutions

Many instruments and protocols require a calibration phase in which the technique is tested using known amounts of the analyte, usually as standard solutions. The objective is to obtain a graphical relationship relating the known concentration of the standard to the instrument response so that unknown samples may be determined by reference to this relationship.

Where the analysis involves pre-treatments, tests of extraction efficiency should be carried out using spiked samples. These are samples of the environmental material with known amounts of the analyte added. It is important to know the effects of preservation, transport and pre-treatments on the analyte measurements. Always remember to run controls and reagent blanks to allow for impurities affecting your results.

Definition

Salinity – traditionally defined as the weight ratio between dissolved salts and water. It is often expressed as **practical salinity units (psu)**, where 1 psu = 1 part per thousand (ppt or ‰). Recently, practical salinity (S) has been redefined as the ratio of the conductivity of a water sample compared with that of a defined potassium chloride (KCl) solution. In practice S is calculated from the ratio of the conductivity of a water sample to that of International Association for Physical Sciences of the Ocean (IAPSO) Standard Seawater, batches of which are calibrated against the defined KCl solution. Since S is derived from a ratio, it is dimensionless.

Definition

The **electrical conductivity** (often abbreviated to conductivity) of a solution is a measure of its ability to conduct electricity. Electrical conductivity is the reciprocal of electrical resistivity and its units were formerly 'reciprocal ohms' (mhos) m^{-1}. Today the units used are $S\,m^{-1}$, where 1 S (Siemen) = 1 mho. For measurements in freshwater, the practical units are $\mu S\,m^{-1}$. The relationship between electrical conductivity, temperature and salinity is complex and will not be explored further here.

A simple threefold classification of aquatic environments can be made on the basis of salinity:

- freshwater (zero salinity);
- marine (salinity = c. 35 psu);
- estuarine (variable salinity between 0 and 35 psu).

The freshwater class may be further sub-divided into:

- rivers and streams (characterized by flowing water);
- lakes and ponds (characterized by relatively quiescent water).

Many analytical methods are common to all of the above environments (e.g. determination of suspended sediment concentration, Box 32.1, or pH) whilst others (e.g. measurement of river discharge) are environment-specific. For an introduction to chemical analytical approaches refer to Chapter 31. Your choice of analytical method(s) depends on what you want to measure and determines your sampling strategy (Chapter 15) and methods (Chapter 20).

KEY POINT Make certain that all field probes are well maintained and calibrated in accordance with manufacturers' instructions prior to field deployment.

Salinity, conductivity and temperature

A simple, though not very accurate, way to measure salinity is by evaporating a water sample of known weight to dryness, weighing the amount of salts that remain and expressing the latter as a ratio of the former. The classical laboratory procedure, however, involves the titration of a water sample with silver nitrate ($AgNO_3$) whereby:

$$NaCl + AgNO_3 \rightarrow NaNO_3 + AgCl \qquad [32.1]$$

The amount of halide halogen ion precipitated as AgCl from the sample is then compared with the precipitate from a Standard Seawater sample.

You are most likely to measure salinity using some form of field probe, often known as a salinometer. Such probes measure the electrical conductivity of the water and convert this to a salinity reading. The most versatile and recommended instruments measure electrical conductivity, salinity and water temperature, so can be used in both fresh and salt waters. In addition, the probes can be lowered over the side of a boat permitting measurements of these three parameters simultaneously at various depths (as determined from a graduated cable) in the water column.

pH determinations (see also Chapter 6)

There are many types of test kits and pH meters available for field and laboratory use. Meters are recommended. Those designed for field operation tend to have more robust probes but care must be taken not to damage them. In the field, they can be deployed in collected water samples (e.g. from specific depths in a lake) or directly into the water (e.g. the surface water of a lake). The general procedure for measuring pH is as follows:

1. Remove the protective cap from the probe.
2. Immerse the probe in the water (typically 2–3 cm).
3. Press the 'on' button.
4. Wait for the reading to stabilize; this may take c. 10–20 seconds.
5. Record the reading to the nearest 0.1 unit.
6. Repeat steps 2–5 for a second and third replicate.
7. Average the three pH readings and record to the nearest 0.1 unit.
8. Rinse the probe with distilled water from a wash bottle.
9. Replace the cap on the probe.

Box 32.1 How to determine suspended sediment concentration

Principle

A known volume of water is filtered under vacuum through a $0.45\,\mu m$ pore diameter filter paper (e.g. Whatman GF/C glass fibre filter papers of 47 mm diameter) and the dry weight of sediment collected is expressed as the suspended sediment concentration, typically in units of $mg\,l^{-1}$. The choice of pore diameter is somewhat arbitrary but it is now widely accepted that $0.45\,\mu m$ marks the division between solid and dissolved materials.

Procedure

KEY POINT Filter papers should be handled using flat-bladed tweezers only at all stages.

1. Either:
   - Write numbers on a series of filter papers. This should be done neatly at the margin (i.e. so that the number will not become obscured by sediment after filtration) using a drawing pen with a fine nib (0.2 mm) filled with waterproof ink. Allow the ink to dry. Or:
   - Use unlabelled filter papers in individually numbered petri dishes.

2. Pre-weigh the filter papers using a balance capable of a weighing accuracy of $1 \times 10^{-5}\,g$. This must be done after any numbers have been added to take account of the weight of the ink.
3. Record the initial weight as W_1.
4. Place the filter papers onto filter holders; attach the water containers above the filter holders and mount the assembly onto vacuum flasks attached to a vacuum pump (Fig. 32.1).
5. Agitate each water sample to ensure good dispersion of the particles prior to pouring them carefully into the containers. Do not spill any of the samples.

KEY POINT The amount of water to be filtered depends to a large extent on its suspended sediment concentration. For very low concentrations it may be necessary to filter several litres. For high concentrations less than 1 litre may prove sufficient. However, the volume of water filtered (V) must be accurately known. It is important that you do not try to filter so much water that the paper becomes clogged. This may cause a strain on the pump.

6. Filter the water samples under vacuum. It is usual to run several vacuum flasks from one pump.

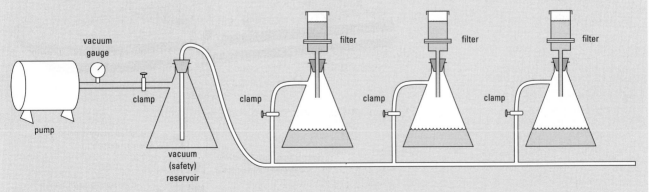

Fig. 32.1 A vacuum filtration system for the determination of suspended sediment concentration in water samples.

Box 32.1   (continued)

7. When all the water has been filtered, turn off the pump.

Tip: it is a good idea to include a water trap or safety reservoir between the vacuum line and the pump to avoid water being sucked back into the pump (Fig. 32.1).

8. Carefully remove the wet filter papers from the holders, taking care not to tear them or to lose any of the collected sediment.

9. Dry the filter papers on trays covered with aluminium foil in an oven at 105 °C, or air dry in individual petri dishes.

KEY POINT   Before reweighing the filter papers it is necessary to allow them to equilibrate with the atmosphere. Many clay minerals and organic matter are hygroscopic and so absorb moisture from the air. If you reweigh before equilibration is complete you will notice the weight of the filter paper plus sediment increasing as you observe at the scale of the balance.

10. Record the final weight as W_2.
11. Determine the suspended sediment concentration as

$$(W_2 - W_1)/V$$

and express in units of mg l^{-1}.

Water transparency

The Secchi disk

The Secchi disk provides an easy to use and inexpensive means of measuring water transparency or clarity. It consists of a circular disk, 20–30 cm in diameter, that is either white or is divided into alternating black and white quadrants. White Secchi disks are conventionally used for marine investigations, whereas black and white disks are usually used in studies of lake water quality. The disk is attached to a graduated rope and has a weight at its base to ensure vertical descent through a water column. The procedure for use is as follows (See also Fig. 32.2):

1. Slowly lower the disk from the side of a boat into the water until it disappears from view to the observer above. Record the depth from the graduated rope.
2. Carefully raise the disk until it just reappears in view. Record the depth.
3. The average of the two depth readings is known as the Secchi disk depth, often abbreviated to Secchi depth.

Deploying a Secchi disk – use a rope that will neither stretch nor shrink in contact with water.

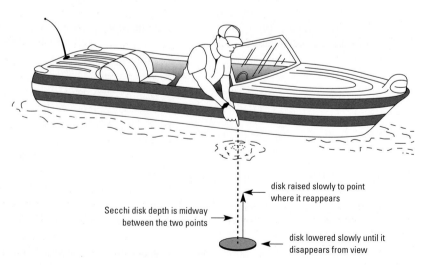

disk raised slowly to point where it reappears

Secchi disk depth is midway between the two points

disk lowered slowly until it disappears from view

Fig. 32.2 Field determination of Secchi disk depth.

An individual observer should always take Secchi depth measurements in the same manner each time (e.g. standing, sitting, with spectacles, without spectacles etc.). To further standardize procedures, always take measurements on the shady side of a boat.

The value recorded is a complex function of many factors:

- the reflection of light from the water surface;
- the light absorption characteristics of the water;
- water colour;
- suspended sediment concentration;
- concentration of algae.

However, it provides a simple and effective way of comparing the clarity of different waters or variations in clarity within the surface waters of a water body (e.g. a lake). Readings of Secchi disk depth can also provide rapid ground measurements to correlate with remote sensing observations (Chapter 29) of water bodies.

Optical instruments

Various optical methods are available to provide information on the characteristics and concentrations of materials suspended in water. These work either on the principle of light beam attenuation or light beam scatterance.

- Light attenuation instruments (transmissometers) – a beam of light is shone directly at a sensor; the greater the attenuation of the light, the higher the concentration of suspended materials. Note that one very large particle in the light path (e.g. a leaf) could produce the same attenuation as hundreds of suspended grains of silt.
- Light scatterance instruments – a sensor measures the light scattered (i.e. reflected and refracted) by particles suspended in the water column. The higher the scatterance, the greater the number of particles in suspension. Note, however, that scatterance is a complex function of particle size, particle shape and the reflective and refractive properties of the particles.

Water flow velocity

The easiest way to measure the velocity of flowing waters is to record, with a stop watch, the time it takes for a floating object to travel between two known points. Oranges or grapefruit act as ideal, partially submerged 'floats' for this purpose. Select, for example, a straight river reach with a minimum length of 100 m. To obtain an accurate flow velocity the minimum duration of float movement should be 20–25 s. The use of several floats across a river enables variations in flow velocity with distance from the banks to be determined, together with horizontal flow patterns. It is, however, important to note that this method measures the velocity of surface waters only.

To measure water flow velocity at depth below the surface it is necessary to use some form of current meter, of which there are many types available. The simplest type consists of a propeller, mounted at the upstream end of a streamlined, torpedo-shaped weighted body (Fig. 32.3). The number of revolutions of the propeller per unit time increases with increasing speed of water flow. Rotations are recorded, over fixed periods, either electronically or mechanically by a control box that can be installed on a boat for marine deployment or hand held by the operator for river measurements. An

Long-term monitoring – when deploying optical instruments to monitor materials suspended in water over long periods (as for example in a river), it is important to clean the sensor and light beam source covers regularly to prevent algal growth, which could erroneously be interpreted as high concentrations of suspended matter.

Choosing a float – current-following objects must not float high enough in the water to be influenced by wind; and must be clearly visible from the river bank.

Marking floats – use a black indelible felt pen to number oranges or grapefruits used as floats.

Definitions

Measurements of water flow by float tracking are known as **Lagrangian measurements**, whereas those made at a point in the water column using a current meter are known as **Eulerian measurements**.

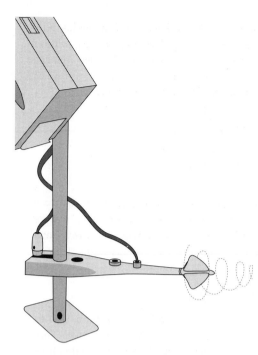

Fig. 32.3 A propeller type current meter mounted on a rod for measurement of flow velocity in a river.

On very large rivers, a current meter is deployed from a cable stretched across the river from which the meter can be lowered to chosen depths at specific distances.

Average flow velocity – in a river this occurs at approximately 0.6 × the water depth measured from the surface downwards. The velocity of flow of surface waters, as determined by float tracking, is, as a general guide, approximately equal to 1.25 × the average flow velocity of the river.

Units – the units of discharge (Q) are conventionally m³ s⁻¹, also written as cumecs.

instrument calibration curve enables the number of revolutions over a fixed time period to be converted to a flow speed. Current meters for marine use contain a compass within the body that enables flow direction (and therefore velocity) to be determined.

In rivers current meters are usually mounted onto a hand-held graduated rod that has a plate at its base. It is necessary to wade into the river and measure the current speed at known distances from the bank and known depths. Depth may be recorded by reference to the graduated rod, and distance from the bank by stretching a tape across the stream. In this way variations in flow rate with depth and distance from the banks may be determined.

Wear waders for current metering in streams and stand as far as possible downstream of the current meter propeller so as to cause minimal turbulence of the water. Take great care not to be swept away by powerful flows or to allow the water to overtop your waders. Ideally you should be roped from the waist to a colleague securely located on the bank. Avoid taking current meter measurements close to obstacles to flow, such as large boulders.

River discharge

To determine the volume of water per unit time (or discharge) passing through a particular cross-section of a river it is necessary to know the water velocity and area of cross-section. This is achieved at gauging stations where a river has been engineered to flow through a well-defined structure, for example a concrete flume, a rectangular weir or a V-notch weir. This enables cross-sectional area variations to be readily determined as the water level is continuously measured by some form of depth recorder.

The product of the flow velocity ($m\,s^{-1}$) and the cross-sectional area (m^2) at any time gives the instantaneous discharge (Q). In practice, a series of discharge measurements are made at various flow conditions over a period of years. This enables the construction of a stage–discharge relationship, or streamflow rating curve, where stage (h) is the river water level in m. A rating curve usually approximates to a straight line on a log–log scale (Fig. 32.4); thus the relationship is of the power function form:

$$Q = K(h)^n \qquad\qquad [32.2]$$

where K is a coefficient and n is an exponent.

At least 30 data points are needed to establish a good rating curve.

Once a good rating curve has been established, discharge can simply be determined by monitoring the water level and reading the corresponding value of discharge from the stage–discharge curve.

If you want to select your own site for river gauging, it is important that:

- The reach is straight and has relatively uniform cross-sectional area and slope angle.
- The water depth is sufficient for the immersion of a current meter.
- The channel is free from weed growth and obstacles such as large boulders or trees.
- The site chosen is not close to a tributary confluence.
- The banks and channel bed are stable and not subject to change during measurements.

Computation of cross-sectional area where the bed is irregular is problematic. You will find that it is necessary to measure water depth at several points

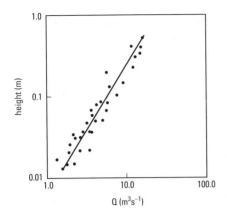

Fig. 32.4 Example of a stream flow rating curve.

> Calculating cross-sectional area – plot the cross-section of the stream to scale on graph paper. Work out the area represented by each 1 mm × 1 mm square. By counting the total number of squares, you can work out the cross-sectional area.

> Units – be careful not to confuse units when calculating suspended sediment discharge. Water discharge is conventionally measured in $m^3 s^{-1}$ and suspended sediment concentration in $mg l^{-1}$. For example, to express suspended sediment discharge in t day^{-1}, it is necessary to convert mg to t, litres to m^3 (see Chapter 9) and s to days.

across the channel using a graduated rod. The position and spacing between the points should be chosen so as to define the bed profile as accurately as possible.

A combination of water discharge measurements and determinations of suspended sediment concentration, as determined from the filtration of water samples (see Box 32.1), enables you to calculate the instantaneous suspended sediment discharge of a river as mass per unit time. Thus:

$$\text{suspended sediment discharge} = \text{water discharge} \times \text{suspended sediment concentration}$$

Collection of large numbers of samples over long periods of time permits a suspended sediment rating curve to be established, in which water discharge is plotted against suspended sediment discharge on a log–log scale. Thus, for a given water discharge, the suspended sediment discharge of a particular stream can be estimated.

Suspended biological materials – plankton

The collection of plankton, the assemblage of organisms that live suspended in the open waters of lakes and the sea, is usually qualitative and involves the use of nets of varying mesh size. In general, a plankton net consists of a cone of nylon mesh with a collecting vessel at the pointed end to retain the concentrated sample (Fig. 32.5). At the broad end of the net, the nylon is attached to a bridle hoop which has three attachment points to a rope. Nets of different mesh sizes (conventionally quoted as number of mesh per inch) are used to collect different types of plankton (see Table 32.1).

Always tow the plankton net slowly through the water. Tows can be horizontal or vertical. Tow speed is directly related to the gauge of the net mesh; the finer the gauge, the more slowly it must be towed. The duration of tow depends on the concentration of plankton in the water column and the size of sample you hope to collect. If you want to obtain quantitative plankton samples you should collect (see Chapter 20) and filter known volumes of water through meshes of the same gauge as those of the different plankton nets described above. Use water from a wash bottle to prevent plankton from adhering to the sides of the sample container. Such samples may require sub-sampling prior to identification and counting.

Free-swimming biological materials – nekton

Undergraduates rarely sample nektonic species, such as fish. Nets of various mesh apertures, towed behind a boat, are the conventional means of collection. However, specialized echo sounders, operating at high frequencies, that receive echoes from the bodies of fish, can be used to detect the presence of shoals in the water column. These provide a means of locating large numbers of fish and therefore can determine points at which it is best to sample. Analyses of nekton might include:

- Percentages of different species within a total catch.
- Body lengths (a measure of age) of individuals of the same species.
- Stomach contents, as a means of determining predator–prey relationships.

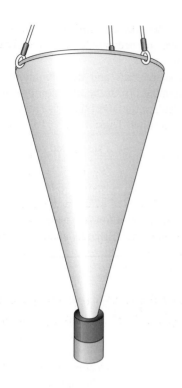

Fig. 32.5 A plankton net.

Table 32.1 Plankton net mesh sizes

Mesh size (mesh per inch)	Type of plankton collected
60	Coarse planktonic organisms
100	Zooplankton
200	Phytoplankton
up to 500	Ultraplankton

Definitions

Dissolved oxygen (DO) – the amount of gaseous oxygen (typically measured in $mg\,l^{-1}$ or as percentage saturation) that is dissolved in an aqueous solution.

Biological oxygen demand (BOD) – the amount of oxygen (typically measured in $mg\,l^{-1}$) required for the oxidation of organic matter by biological action under specific standard test conditions.

Chemical oxygen demand (COD) – the amount of oxygen (typically measured in $mg\,l^{-1}$) consumed under specific conditions in the oxidation of organic and oxidizable inorganic matter contained in water.

Bottom-dwelling biological materials – benthos

Benthic organisms are usually sampled by means of various forms of grab (see Chapter 18). Such samplers will collect both organisms living in the bottom sediment and the sediment itself. It is therefore necessary to separate the organisms from the sediment particles, prior to counting and identification. This can be done either on the boat or immediately after the samples have been returned to the laboratory, as follows:

1. Pass the sediment sample or a sub-sample through a stainless steel sieve (typically of 2 mm aperture) held over a bucket. Note that if you wish to collect a quantitative sample you must first measure the volume of sediment (e.g. using a measuring cylinder; this is best done in the laboratory).
2. Rinse with plenty of water from a wash bottle. Take care not to lose any of the sample at this stage.
3. After rinsing, the sieve should be placed on a large white tray, half filled with water, and gently agitated.
4. Any large pieces of inorganic (e.g. pebbles) or dead organic (e.g. shell fragments, twigs and leaves) particles should be carefully removed from the mesh using tweezers.
5. Benthic organisms retained on the sieve should be searched for with the naked eye and transferred, using tweezers, to a numbered collection jar containing 4% v/v buffered formaldehyde.
6. After all the organisms have been removed, the remaining sediment on the sieve can be discarded.
7. The material retained in the bucket can be similarly passed through a sieve of smaller aperture if you wish to obtain and analyse smaller benthic organisms.

Dissolved oxygen, biological (or biochemical) oxygen demand and chemical oxygen demand

Dissolved oxygen

There are several laboratory methods for determining dissolved oxygen (DO) but you are most likely to want to measure this parameter directly in the field. If you do return samples to the laboratory for DO analysis they should be chemically fixed on collection, typically using eight drops of manganous sulphate solution and eight drops of alkaline potassium azide, as a precursor to the iodometric or Winkler titration method of analysis.

The Winkler titration method is the most reliable laboratory method for the determination of DO. It uses iodine as a substitute for the oxygen dissolved in a fixed sample. Iodine is titrated with sodium thiosulphate to a clear endpoint. The amount of sodium thiosulphate required (in ml) is equivalent to $mg\,l^{-1}$ of DO.

In the field DO is measured using various types of DO probe which measure the rate of oxygen diffusion across a membrane. Note that such probes can also be used in the laboratory to determine BOD (see below). DO probes may be placed directly in water or into a water sample collected by bucket or water sampler from various depths in the water column. Follow the same general procedure for usage as for pH above, recording the DO concentration to the nearest $0.1\,mg\,l^{-1}$ or nearest 0.1% saturation.

Some DO probes include a thermistor which permits the simultaneous reading of DO and temperature. Many contain permanent membranes, eliminating the need for constant recalibration. An alternative is to measure DO in the field by one of the many DO kits commercially available. These operate on the basis of the Winkler titration.

BOD and COD

The determination of biological oxygen demand (BOD) (Box 32.2) is carried out on a replicate water sample after the initial determination of DO on the first sample.

You are less likely to measure chemical oxygen demand (COD) than BOD since COD is usually determined in industrial and municipal laboratories. COD is, however, commonly measured by adding water samples (typically 2 ml in volume) to small test tubes containing pre-measured reagents. The tubes are sealed and heated until digestion is complete (typically 2 h at 150 °C) and then cooled to room temperature. The COD level is then determined either using a colorimeter or a spectrophotometer (see *Practical Skills in Biology*, 2nd edn, Chapter 39 for details of these instruments).

Box 32.2 How to determine the BOD of a water sample

1. Collect two replicate water samples.
2. Measure the DO of one sample immediately, e.g. using a DO probe or test kit in the field.
3. Incubate the second sample in complete darkness for 5 days at 20 °C. If you do not have access to an incubator, wrap the sample bottles in aluminium foil and store at room temperature in complete darkness.
4. After 5 days measure the DO of the incubated water sample using the same technique/equipment as previously.
5. Subtract the second DO reading (day 5 reading) from the initial one (day 1 reading) to obtain the BOD ($mg\,l^{-1}$).

Analysis of soils and sediments

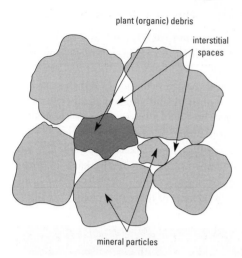

plant (organic) debris

interstitial spaces

mineral particles

Fig. 33.1 A mixed grade sediment/soil showing interstitial (pore) spaces.

X-ray diffraction – as X-rays pass into crystalline minerals they become diffracted from their original path at specific angles depending on the atomic structure of the material; the intensity of the diffracted beam depends on the nature of the atoms. A diffractogram, displayed on a computer screen, displays the positions and intensities of the various peaks. Minerals are identified by comparing the diffraction patterns with standards.

Stokes' Law states that the terminal fall velocity of a spherical particle (V) settling in a liquid (water) is directly proportional to the difference in density between the particle (ρ_s) and the liquid (ρ_w) and to the square of the particle diameter (d), and indirectly proportional to the viscosity of the liquid (μ):

$$V = [(\rho_s - \rho_w)gd^2]/18\mu$$

where g = acceleration due to gravity.

During or after the collection of soil or sediment samples (see Chapter 18) it is likely that you will wish to analyse them in some way. This chapter is largely concerned with physical methods of analysis; when considering chemical analyses start by reading Chapter 31. There are three main components to be considered in the study of soils and sediments (Fig. 33.1):

- the mineral component (the dominant particulate constituent);
- the organic component (living or dead materials);
- the interstitial component (air or water or both).

There are also summative properties of soils and sediments – properties affected by these components but which are measured as an overall property, e.g. bulk density.

Mineral components

The mineral component of soils and sediments is usually studied by an analysis of the particle size distribution of the particles: this is the most important characteristic since it determines most of the other significant properties of the matrix. The mineralogy of the constituent particles is a complex subject beyond the scope of this book, but is conventionally determined by X-ray diffractometry.

Particle size analysis

Since both soils and sediments are granular materials, their most fundamental property is particle size distribution. However, because component particle sizes may range through clay, silt, sand, granules, pebbles and cobbles to boulders (see Table 26.5), no single technique of particle size analysis is suitable.

KEY POINT **The technique selected to measure particle size must depend on the nature of the sediment or soil under consideration.**

The sizes of coarse particles can be measured directly, but for finer grained materials it is necessary to use indirect methods. Typically, direct methods are used for large pebbles and above (Box 33.1), sieving for medium pebbles to very fine sand (Box 33.2) and sedimentation or electronic sizing techniques for the silt and clay ranges.

Traditionally the particle size distribution of fine-grained materials was carried out by the 'pipette method'. This method is based on Stokes' Law and involves measuring the weight of sediment retained in suspension (as sampled by pipette) after known periods of settling. Today this time-consuming and labour-intensive technique has been superseded by a variety of rapid, automated, electronic methods. Some are based on the principle of Stokes' Law (e.g. SediGraph) whilst others measure particle size according to the degree of diffraction or scattering of a laser beam (e.g. Coulter Laser Particle Analyser).

Organic components

Measuring the organic content of soils is described under 'bulk properties' below. More detailed analyses will require sophisticated chemical procedures as outlined in Chapter 31.

Box 33.1 How to measure the grain size of pebbles or cobbles

1. **Hold the individual particle and determine the length of its longest axis** (*a* axis) using calipers.

2. **Rotate the pebble through 90°** so that the longest axis at right angles to the *a* axis can be measured. Record this as the *b* axis (intermediate axis).

3. **Rotate the pebble through a further 90°** and locate the longest axis mutually at right angles to the *a* and *b* axes. Record this as the *c* axis (short axis).

4. **Repeat for each particle in your sample.**

5. **Calculate the mean size of each particle** as $(a + b + c)/3$.

6. **Assign each particle to its appropriate size class** (see Table 26.5).

7. **Count or weigh the fraction in each size class** and express as a percentage of the total sample weight or number as appropriate.

8. **Plot results** as frequency histogram or cumulative percentage frequency curve showing percentage coarser.

9. **Describe statistics of grain size distribution** in terms of median grain size, mean, standard deviation, skewness and kurtosis.

Measuring the length of the *b* axis only can be used as a rapid assessment of the mean diameter of pebbles and cobbles.

Soil or sediment fauna requires extraction from the substrate before any analysis of species content or biomass can be made. There are a number of direct mechanical processes that can be used to separate animals from the soil and vegetable material: variations of sieving, flotation and elutriation (washing out) are the most common methods, particularly when the fauna has been killed or preserved before analysis begins. Live mobile material is usually extracted from substrates using some form of gradient, such as the heat gradient in the Berlese funnel (Fig. 33.2) for soil or litter samples, or ice gradients for aquatic sediment samples. Methods for identifying extracted organisms are discussed in Chapter 25.

If samples have to be hand-sorted, staining of organic materials with Rose Bengal stain is useful, but it does stain both living and dead organic material.

Interstitial components

The spaces between the particles may contain air, water and/or organisms belonging to the meiofauna or microbiota. Taking samples for gas or liquid analysis of the interstitial material is described in Chapter 18. Chemical analysis of the gas and liquid contents may be done by a variety of techniques ranging from simple colorimetric tests through to chromatographic analysis (Chapter 31).

The chemical composition of interstitial water is determined by the type of parent rock, the vegetation type, amounts of rainfall and average temperatures. The most important chemical characteristic of interstitial water is its pH (see Chapter 6) which can be measured *in situ* using a pH electrode system or in sampled soil water using colorimetric tests. A

Box 33.2 How to determine the grain size of sands by dry sieving

The following equipment is required:

- A set of stacked sieves with mesh sizes typically of 2 mm ($-1\,\phi$) to 62.5 μm ($4\,\phi$) at intervals of either 0.5 or 0.25 ϕ, together with a lid for the top of the stack and pan for the base (e.g. Endecott Test Sieve series). Note: grain size in ϕ (phi) $= -\log_2$ grain size in mm.
- A mechanical sieve shaker.
- A brass wire sieve brush for the coarse mesh sieves and a fine bristle sieve brush for the fine mesh sieves.
- A balance, capable of weighing to an accuracy of 0.01 g.

KEY POINT It is essential to dry and disaggregate the sample thoroughly before sieving.

Note that marine sediments should be washed to remove salts prior to drying. About three washings in 1 l of fresh water, with thorough stirring, are needed to remove the salt from 200 g of sediment. Take care not to lose fine particles through decantation.

Clay particles impart cohesion to sediment and soil samples. If significant amounts of clay are present in your sample, disaggregation will be necessary so that the primary particles are collected by the appropriate sieves, rather than aggregates of particles. The simplest method of disaggregation is to grind the sample in a pestle with a rubber-tipped mortar, but take care not to grind down the primary particles. An alternative is to use a chemical dispersing agent in water.

KEY POINT If aggregates are present it is important to note that these may reflect the true structure of the sediment in the natural environment. By destroying the aggregate structure to primary grains you may be making false assumptions about the actual grain size distribution of the sediment.

Method

1. **Weigh the initial sample or sub-sample.** This should be between 100 g and 500 g.
2. **Place the initial sample in the coarsest sieve at the top of the stack.**
3. **Mechanically agitate** for 15 minutes.
4. **Carefully remove all of the sediment retained by each sieve** using the appropriate brush, and weigh each fraction.
5. **Weigh the silt plus clay traction retained in the pan.**
6. **Express the weight in each size class as a percentage of the total sample weight.**
7. **Plot results** as a frequency histogram or cumulative percentage frequency curve showing percentage coarser.
8. **Describe statistics of grain size distribution** in terms of median grain size, mean, standard deviation, skewness and kurtosis.

Overloading of sieves must be avoided as this restricts the passage of particles through the meshes and may lead to distortion of the meshes. The load per sieve should be no more than 4–6 grains in thickness.

Note that it may be necessary to carry out sieving in several stages according to the number of sieve fractions you wish to measure and the number of sieves that the shaker will hold. In this case the material retained in the pan after the first sieving is transferred to the coarsest sieve of the second set, and so on.

KEY POINT Care must be taken to ensure that all grains are removed from each sieve by careful brushing. Never use a brass wire brush on a fine mesh sieve or you will tear it. Brass wire brushes should only be used on sieves above 2 mm in diameter – for lower mesh apertures use the bristle brush.

second important constituent is the oxygen concentration, which can be usefully measured using an electrode system (see p. 174 in *Practical Skills in Biology*, 2nd edn, Chapter 37); alternative, less convenient chemical methods can also be used.

Nutrients are the third most commonly measured constituents. They usually require at least the use of colorimetric tests, which are now available in kit forms.

Sampling for meiofaunal and microbiota samples is relatively straightforward and usually consists of taking small sub-samples or larger benthic samples or the taking of small cores where direct sampling is possible. The extraction and analysis of the organisms, however, is a very

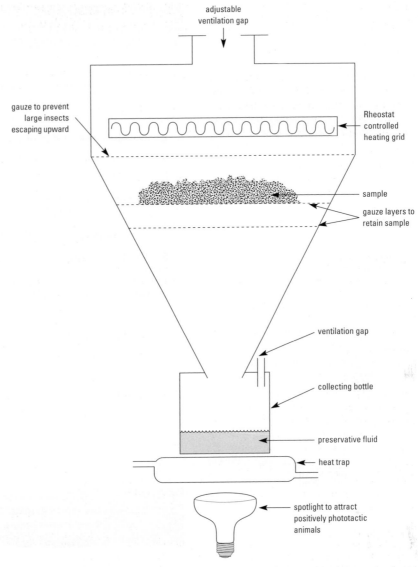

Fig. 33.2 A Berlese funnel for the extraction of invertebrates from soil or litter.

specialized task and is frequently species or group-specific. Consult specialized texts if you need to do such work.

Bulk properties

Bulk density

Bulk density is measured as the weight of soil or sediment per unit volume, usually expressed as $g\,cm^{-3}$. This represents two things: the proportions of mineral and organic matter, and the relative amount of void/pore space (interstitial space). The latter indicates the degree of compaction of the material. Mineral matter is very dense (typically 2.5–2.6 $g\,cm^{-3}$) compared with organic matter (typically 0.5 $g\,cm^{-3}$), so the density of the sample will indicate the relative proportions of mineral and organic constituents. As a general rule, soils and sediments decrease in

Analysis of soils and sediments

This method is difficult to use for wet sediments and soils because the materials will flow. It is also difficult to use in substrates containing pebbles or roots. Avoid using a hammer if possible.

Box 33.3 How to measure the bulk density of a soil or sediment

1. **Collect a sample using a soil corer** (a metal or plastic cylinder open at one end) by pushing it slowly and steadily (hammering it gently if absolutely necessary) into the soil/sediment to a measured depth.

2. **Measure the radius of the core.**

3. **The volume of the core** is now calculated as volume $= \pi r^2 h\,cm^3$, where r = radius (cm) and h = depth (cm).

4. **Transfer the material to an oven and dry to constant weight** at $105\,°C$.

5. **Bulk density = oven dry mass (g)/sample volume (cm^3).**

6. **Replicate samples** should be used.

The average bulk density of a mineral soil is about $1.5\,g\,cm^{-3}$ and of peat about $0.5\,g\,cm^{-3}$.

---

average particle density by $0.01\,g\,cm^{-3}$ for each 1% (by weight) increase in organic matter content.

Water content

Soil or sediment water content can be measured from the same sample by measuring the wet weight of the sample before Stage 4 (oven drying, Box 33.3). Soil water content as percentage by weight then equals:

Storing cores – if the soil or sediment core is to be used for measuring water content, it must be placed in a watertight container (e.g. plastic bag) during transportation and storage.

Remember that the measurement of organic content by loss on ignition (LOI) will include the living biota unless you have removed them (difficult). This makes it a very variable parameter and makes replication essential if a meaningful result is to be obtained. One earthworm present in a sample will make a very large difference!

Box 33.4 How to measure the organic content of soil and sediment samples using the loss on ignition (LOI) technique

This is an apparently simple technique based upon the loss in weight of a sample when organic matter is burnt off, converting it to carbon dioxide and water which are lost as gases.

KEY POINT Many authors have presented data indicating that the percentage weight loss on ignition of soil and sediment samples is approximately equal to twice their organic carbon (C) content.

There are, however, no standard conditions of temperature and time of combustion. For example, in the literature, quoted analytical conditions range through $375 \pm 5\,°C$ for 16 h, $500\,°C$ for 12 h, $550\,°C$ for 1 h, $600\,°C$ for 1 h, $800\,°C$ for 2 h, $850\,°C$ for 30 minutes, $1000\,°C$ for 20 minutes to $1100\,°C$ for 1 h! What you measure is therefore operationally defined and is very much dependent on the mineralogy of the sample.

For a pure quartz sand or silt the LOI will be a good approximation of the organic content. If clay minerals are present, water will be lost from their crystal lattices if combustion

If you do not have access to a furnace that permits control of combustion temperature, you can determine LOI approximately by heating the sample in a crucible over a Bunsen burner for 30 minutes.

Definitions

Organic matter (OM) – the total of organic molecules (i.e. containing C, H, O and N) in a soil or sediment sample, usually expressed as percentage LOI by weight.

Organic carbon (OC) – the carbon in a soil or sediment sample other than that in carbonates, usually expressed as percentage C by weight.

Box 33.4 (continued)

temperatures exceed about 550 °C. This could represent about 5–13% by weight of the clays according to their mineralogical type. Similarly, if $CaCO_3$ is present (e.g. in the form of shell fragments) it will break down at such temperatures to CaO with the loss of 44% by weight due to CO_2 release. Thus for calcareous samples a combustion temperature of 550 °C for 1 h has often been adopted.

You must, therefore, always specify your operational conditions. Only in this way can your results be compared with those of others. The general procedure is as follows:

1. **Take an aliquot of air-dried soil or sediment**, typically 2 g in weight, and grind using a mortar and pestle.

2. **Place the ground sample in a pre-weighed porcelain crucible and re-weigh to give combined weight.**

3. **Heat the sample and crucible** in a furnace for 1 h at 550 °C, for example.

4. **Allow to cool** in a desiccator and re-weigh when cold.

5. **Calculate organic content** as percentage weight loss by difference:

$$\% \text{ organic matter} = (W_2 - W_3)/(W_2 - W_1) \times 100$$

where W_1 = weight of crucible, W_2 = initial combined weight of sample plus crucible, and W_3 = final (after ignition) combined weight of sample plus crucible.

$$(W_1 - W_2)/W_1 \times 100\% \qquad [33.1]$$

where W_1 = wet weight of sample and W_2 = dry weight of sample.

Organic content

Soil organic content may be measured by the loss on ignition (LOI) technique (Box 33.4) or by measuring carbon content using chemical techniques or a CHO analyser. In addition, a strong oxidizing agent, such as hydrogen peroxide, is often used to quantify organic matter content by weight loss on digestion. However, it is important to note that H_2O_2 attacks colloidal or humified organic matter but not fibrous (cellulosic) residues, and therefore leads to an underestimation of the total organic content of samples.

There are many different reasons for wanting to analyse the chemical components of the atmosphere or for measuring the associated physical properties. The atmosphere and its sub-components are notoriously subject to spatial and temporal variation and it is vital that close attention be paid to the problems of obtaining representative samples (see Chapter 20).

The basic physical measurements are encompassed within the concept of meteorology, the study of weather. The total results of weather form the climate of an area. The main parameters studied in meteorology are:

- air pressure;
- temperature;
- humidity;
- precipitation;
- wind;
- cloud;
- solar radiation.

Microclimate – the atmospheric characteristics prevailing within a small space, usually in the layer near the ground that is affected by topographical or vegetational features of the surface.

It is important to recognize the various scales on which such parameters will vary, giving regional and local climates and microclimates. The frequency of sampling is project-dependent but is typically once or twice a day unless you have access to continuous data records obtained from chart recorders or computer data loggers.

KEY POINT Meteorological measurements are subject to very local effects caused by topographical features, trees and buildings. Ideally thermometers should be contained within a Stevenson Screen 1.2 m above the ground to provide a shaded and sheltered atmosphere. Associated equipment should be placed nearby.

KEY POINT Remember to check any instrument calibrations required at frequent and regular intervals.

Air pressure

Air pressure can be measured in three ways:

- Mercury barometer: uses the height of a column of mercury in a glass tube: the higher the column, the greater the atmospheric pressure. Uses tables or a calibrated scale to convert column height to pressure.
- Aneroid barometer: composed of a series of hollow discs within which is a partial vacuum. As air pressure changes, the discs expand or contract, moving an arm which indicates pressure on a calibrated scale.
- Barograph: an aneroid barometer connected to an arm and inked pen which records changes in pressure continuously on a slowly revolving drum.

Barometers are best kept indoors

Temperature

Temperature is typically measured in one of three ways:

- Thermometers: simple thermometers may contain either mercury or alcohol and can be obtained calibrated for different levels of precision

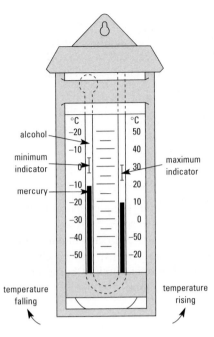

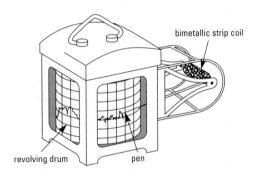

Fig. 34.1 Six's maximum–minimum thermometer.

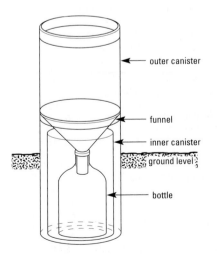

Fig. 34.2 A thermograph.

Fig. 34.3 A non-recording rain gauge.

and temperature ranges. Six's maximum–minimum thermometer (Fig. 34.1) uses metal indicators to allow recording of the maximum and minimum temperatures reached over a given period of time. Readings are taken from the bottom of the indicators, which must be reset using a magnet after a reading has been taken.

- Thermograph: a temperature-recording device which uses a bimetallic strip connected to an arm with a pen to measure temperature change. The pen writes on chart paper on a continuously revolving drum (Fig. 34.2).
- Electrical methods (thermistors and thermocouples): thermistors measure temperature as changes in the resistance of a temperature-sensitive substance. A thermocouple measures the electrical current produced between two wires made of different metals. Thermistors and thermocouples are usually available as professionally made instruments.

Humidity

Humidity can be measured in three ways:

- Wet and dry bulb hygrometer (psychrometer): a method requiring two simple thermometers, one of which is wrapped in muslin which is dipped in a reservoir of water to keep it damp. This is the wet bulb and by comparing the temperature shown by the wet and dry bulbs simultaneously, and by reference to tables, the humidity can be measured.
- Whirling psychrometer: comprises wet and dry bulb thermometers mounted on a frame which can be swung rapidly. Because evaporation rates are speeded up, the humidity can be measured rapidly.
- Hydrograph: an instrument which uses a specially treated hair, which changes in length with humidity change, to record changes in humidity using a pen and a slowly revolving recording drum.

Precipitation

Precipitation (rain, hail, snow) is measured in one of two ways:

- A non-recording gauge is simply a cylinder which collects rain as it falls (Fig. 34.3). The diameter of the funnel is standardized and the volume of water collected over a given period is measured using a calibrated glass container. Snow or hail falling in the gauge must be melted before taking any readings.
- A recording gauge records collected water level on a rotating drum and provides detailed information on timing and intensity. All have some emptying mechanism and tend to be expensive. They allow precipitation intensity to be recorded as mm h^{-1}.

Wind

Wind speed and direction can be determined in three main ways:

- A revolving cup anemometer consists of three revolving cups connected to a recording meter which counts the number of rotations in a given time period. The meter then converts this to wind speed. It may be fixed or hand held.

- A ventimeter (Fig. 34.4) is a calibrated tube over which wind passes, causing a reduction in pressure in the tube. This causes a pointer to rise in proportion to the wind speed. These are cheap and easy to use.
- By observation of the effects of the wind speed on objects. This method is based upon the Beaufort Scale (Table 34.1).

Wind direction is usually determined using a wind vane, which must be mounted away from obstacles that might locally affect the direction of the wind.

Cloud and solar radiation

Cloud amounts are usually recorded by estimating what proportion of the sky is covered by cloud. This is expressed in eighths covered (oktas).

Solar radiation is usually measured using a glass ball (lens) mounted on a frame. The ball focuses the sun on a specially treated paper behind it, burning a line along the paper as it moves. The total length of burnt line is a measure of the length of time for which the sun shone.

Chemical analyses

Most of the atmospheric gas and particle analysis in environmental science is related to the problem of airborne pollutants. Tests of emissions and ambient air masses are based on the assumption that the sample is representative (Chapter 20), perhaps the greatest problem in this area of study because of the complexity of the factors influencing spatial and temporal variability. Emitted materials are termed:

- Primary if they are emitted directly into the atmosphere from the source, e.g. carbonaceous particles from a diesel engine or sulphur dioxide from power stations.
- Secondary if they have been modified after emission in a primary form, e.g. sulphuric acid formed from sulphur dioxide emissions.

Sampled materials fall into three main categories for the purposes of analysis:

- Gas samples in containers: gaseous analytes must not react irreversibly with filter or sample container surfaces or with collected aerosol particles; usually analysed in the gas phase by, for example, chromatographic techniques.

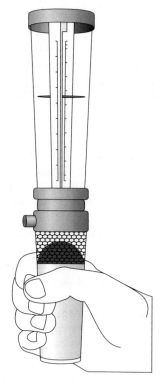

Fig. 34.4   A ventimeter.

Table 34.1   The Beaufort Scale of wind force

Beaufort number	Descriptive title	Effect on land features	Speed (m s^{-1})
0	Calm	Smoke rises vertically	< 0.3
1	Light air	Direction shown by smoke but not wind vanes	0.3–1.5
2	Light breeze	Wind felt on face; leaves rustle; vane moves	1.6–3.3
3	Gentle breeze	Leaves and twigs in constant motion	3.4–5.4
4	Moderate breeze	Raises dust and paper; small branches moved	5.5–7.9
5	Fresh breeze	Small trees begin to sway	8.0–10.7
6	Strong breeze	Large branches in motion; whistling in telephone wires	10.8–13.8
7	Near gale	Whole trees in motion	13.9–17.1
8	Gale	Breaks twigs off trees	17.2–20.7
9	Strong gale	Slight structural damage to roofs, etc.	20.8–24.4
10	Storm	Trees uprooted; considerable structural damage	24.5–28.4
11	Violent Storm	Widespread damage	28.5–32.6
12	Hurricane	Widespread devastation	>32.6

- Volatile and semi-volatile compounds adsorbed onto filter materials: these must be handled in ways that will minimize release or retention of analytes. However, it is difficult to prevent losses of volatile analytes collected on filters. Such substances usually require extraction and/or separation procedures prior to chemical analysis.
- Particulates and aerosols filtered from the air: filters must not be contaminated with materials that can convert to aerosols on the filter medium because this will lead to error.

The sampling of gaseous and semi-volatile materials is termed ambient air sampling unless it derives specifically from a point source of gaseous emissions. Once collected, the gaseous material sampled is then subject to the same chemical analysis processes and criteria as outlined in Chapter 31.

KEY POINT Sorbent sampling is fraught with problems of contamination, interferences, capture efficiency and recovery efficiency, but it is an important and valuable technique provided it is used with the appropriate controls and blanks.

Particulates

Particulate materials are very diverse in character. They include both organic and inorganic components with particle diameters from less than 10 nm to more than 100 μm. Due to particle interactions, physical measurements of the components of suspended particulate matter (aerosols) can be complex and variable.

A simple method for collecting particulates is to expose adhesive strips to the atmosphere, provided they can be protected from the direct effects of rain. Subsequent examination using a microscope allows an estimate of the size and number of particles to be made for qualitative and semi-quantitative assessments.

Quantitative measurement usually depends upon a gravimetric determination of particle mass after collection by filtration using a standardized aspiration technique. The most important derived value is termed the PM_{10}. Because it is determined gravimetrically, it includes both primary and secondary particles. Chemical analysis of the particulates usually requires solubilization and other pre-treatments of the filtered materials (Chapter 31).

KEY POINT Larger particles, by virtue of their inertia, are not readily able to enter the inlet of some samplers. Their measurement is therefore dependent upon both the orientation to the wind and the strength of the wind, both of which influence the efficiency of particle aspiration.

Acid rain

Some simple measurements such as the pH of rainwater can be informative in the context of acid rain. Here, atmospheric oxidation of gaseous nitrogen dioxide (NO_2) and sulphur dioxide (SO_2) causes formation of the strong acids nitric acid (HNO_3) and sulphuric acid (H_2SO_4). These are removed from the atmosphere with precipitation, giving rise to acid rain. Pure water in equilibrium with atmospheric carbon dioxide has a pH of about 5.6 but pH values of 4 and below may be observed as a result of gaseous pollution.

Definition

Aerosol – a dispersion of solid or liquid particles in a gas medium, e.g. smoke.

Definition

PM_{10} – the concentration (μg m^{-3}) of particulate materials with a particle diameter of 10 μm or less. This is the component thought to be most damaging to health.

Analysis and presentation of data

The process of discovering the meaning within your results can be fascinating! There are two main elements to this process:

- Exploratory data manipulation – this is used to investigate the nature of your results and suggest possible patterns and relationships within the data set. The aim is to generate hypotheses for further investigation. Exploratory techniques allow you to visualize the form of your data. They are ideal for examining results from pilot 'studies', but should be used throughout your investigations.
- Confirmatory analysis – this is used to test the hypotheses generated during the exploratory phase. The techniques required are generally statistical in nature and are dealt with in Chapter 40.

KEY POINT Spreadsheets are invaluable tools for data manipulation and transformation: complex mathematical procedures can be carried out rapidly and the results visualized almost immediately using the in-built graphing functions. Spreadsheets also facilitate the statistical analysis of data.

Organizing numbers

In order to organize, manipulate and summarize data, you should:

- Simplify the numbers, e.g. by rounding or taking means. This avoids the detail becoming overwhelming.
- Rearrange your data in as many ways as possible for comparison.
- Display in graphical form; this provides an immediate visual summary which is relatively easy to interpret.
- Look for an overall pattern in the data – avoid getting lost in the details at this stage.
- Look for any striking exceptions to that pattern (outliers) – they often point to special cases of particular interest or to errors in the data produced through mistakes during the acquisition, recording or copying of data.
- Move from graphical interpretations to well-chosen numerical summaries and/or verbal descriptions including where applicable an explanatory hypothesis.

After collecting data, the first step is often to count how often each value occurs and to produce a frequency table. The frequency is simply the number of times a value occurs in the data set, and is, therefore, a count. The raw data could be acquired using a tally chart system to provide a simple frequency table. To construct a tally chart (e.g. Fig. 35.1):

- enter only one tally at a time;
- if working from a data list, cross out each item on the list as you enter it onto the tally chart, to prevent double entries;
- check that all values are crossed out at the end and that the totals agree.

Summarizing your results – original, unsummarized data belong only in your primary record, either in laboratory books or as computer records. You should produce summary tables to organize and condense original data.

Colour	Tally	Total
Green	III	3
Blue	HHT III	8
Red	IIII	4
White	HHT HHT II	12
Black	I	1
Maroon	III	3
Yellow	II	2
		≤ 33

Fig. 35.1 An example of a tally chart.

A *neatly* constructed tally chart will double as a rough histogram.

Table 35.1 An example of a frequency table

Size class	Frequency	Relative frequency (%)
0–4.9	7	2.6
5–9.9	23	8.6
10–14.9	56	20.9
15–19.9	98	36.7
20–24.9	50	18.7
25–29.9	30	11.2
30–34.9	3	1.1
Total	267	99.8*

* ≠ 100 due to rounding error

stem	leaves
7	23
7	55
7	6
7	9
8	000
8	233
8	45555
8	77
8	888899
9	0000111111
9	2333333
9	44555555555
9	66677777
9	88888999
10	00

Fig. 35.2 A simple 'stem and leaf' plot of a data set. The 'stem' shows the common component of each number, while the 'leaves' show the individual components, e.g. the top line in this example represents the numbers 72 and 73.

Example Allometry involves a logarithmic transformation of data which reveals aspects of the relationship between the dimensions of organisms.

Convert the data to a formal table when complete (e.g. Table 35.1). Because proportions are easier to compare than class totals, the table may contain a column to show the relative frequency of each class. Relative frequency can be expressed in decimal form (as a proportion of 1) or as a percentage (as a proportion of 100).

Graphing data

Graphs are an effective way to investigate trends in data and can reveal features that are difficult to detect from a table, e.g. skewness of a frequency distribution. The construction and use of graphs is described in detail in Chapter 36. When investigating the nature of your data, the main points are as follows:

- Make the values stand out clearly; attention should focus on the actual data, not the labels, scale markings, etc. (contrast with the requirements for constructing a graph for data presentation, see p. 197).
- Avoid clutter in the graph; leave out grid lines and try to use the simplest graph possible for your purpose.
- Use a computer spreadsheet with graphics options whenever possible: the speed and flexibility of these powerful tools should allow you to explore every aspect of your data rapidly and with relatively little effort.

Displaying distributions

A visual display of a distribution of values is often useful for variables measured on an interval or ratio scale (p. 40). The distribution of a variable can be displayed by a frequency table for each value or, if the possible values are numerous, groups (classes) of values of the variable. Graphically, there are two main ways of viewing such data:

- histograms, (see p. 198), generally used for large samples;
- stem and leaf plots (e.g. Fig. 35.2), often used for samples of less than 100: these retain the actual values and are faster to draw by hand. The main drawback is the limitation imposed by the choice of stem values since these class boundaries may obscure some features of the distribution.

These displays allow you to look at the overall shape of a distribution and to observe any significant deviations from the idealized theoretical ones. Where necessary, you can use data transformations to investigate any departures from standard distribution patterns such as the normal distribution or the Poisson distribution.

Transforming data

Transformations are mathematical functions applied to data values. They are particularly valuable where your results are related to areas and volumes (e.g. leaf area, body mass).

The most common use of transformations is to prepare data sets so that specific statistical tests may be applied. For instance, if you find that your data distribution is unimodal but not symmetrical (p. 214), it is often useful to apply a transformation that will redistribute the data values to form a symmetrical distribution. The object of this exercise is often to find the

Using transformations – note that if you wish to conserve the *order* of your data, you will need to take negative values when using a reciprocal function (i.e. $-1/n^n$). This is essential when using a box plot to compare graphically the effects of transformations on the five number summary of a data set.

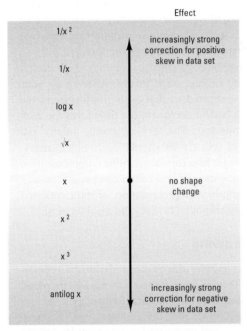

Fig. 35.3 Ladder of transformations (after J.W. Tukey).

Transforming by computer – transformation and graphical interpretation is quick and easy to perform with the help of a spreadsheet (Chapter 42), allowing you to use the full data set rather than working with summary statistics.

function that most closely changes the data into a standard normal distribution, allowing you to apply a wide range of parametric hypothesis testing statistics (see Chapter 40). A frequently used transformation is to take logarithms of one or more sets of values: if the data then approximate to a normal distribution, the relationship is termed 'log-normal'.

Some general points about transformations are:

- They should be made on the raw data, not on derived data values: this is simpler, mathematically valid, and more easily interpreted.
- The transformed data can be analysed like any other numbers.
- Transformed data can be examined for outliers, which may be more important if they remain after transformation.

Figure 35.3 presents a ladder of transformations which will help you decide which transformations to try (see also Table 40.1). Note that percentage and proportion data are usually arc-sine transformed which is a more complex procedure; consult Sokal and Rohlf (1994) for details.

Figure 35.4 illustrates the following 'quick-and-easy' way to choose a transformation:

1. Calculate the 'five-number summary' for the untransformed data (p. 212).
2. Present the summary graphically as a 'box-and-whisker' plot (p. 212).
3. Decide whether you need to correct for positive or negative skew (p. 214).
4. Apply one of the 'mild' transformations in Fig. 35.3 *on the five number summary values only*.
5. Draw a new box-and-whisker plot and see whether the skewness has been corrected.
6. If the skewness has been under-corrected, try again with a stronger transformation. If it has been over-corrected, try a milder one.
7. When the distribution appears to be acceptable, transform the full data set and recalculate the summary statistics. If necessary use a statistical test to confirm that the transformed data are normally distributed (p. 219).
8. If no simple transformation works well, you may need to use non-parametric statistics when comparing data sets.

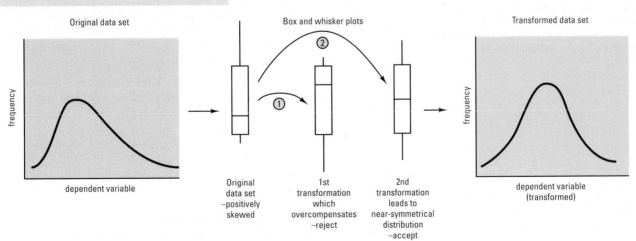

Fig. 35.4 Illustration of the processes of transforming a data set.

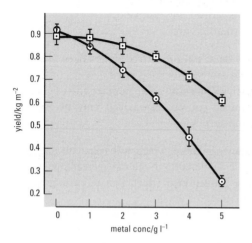

Fig. 36.1 Effect of soil metal concentrations on the yield of two plant species: ○ sensitive species; □ resistant species. Vertical bars show standard errors (*n* = 6).

Graphs can be used to show detailed results in an abbreviated form, displaying the maximum amount of information in the minimum space. Graphs and tables present findings in different ways. A graph (figure) gives a visual impression of the content and meaning of your results, while a table provides an accurate numerical record of data values. You must decide whether a graph should be used, e.g. to illustrate a pronounced trend or relationship, or whether a table (Chapter 37) is more appropriate.

A well-constructed graph will combine simplicity, accuracy and clarity. Planning of graphs is needed at the earliest stage in any write-up as your accompanying text will need to be structured so that each graph delivers the appropriate message. Therefore, it is best to decide on the final form for each of your graphs before you write your text. The text, diagrams, graphs and tables in a laboratory write-up or project report should be complementary, each contributing to the overall message. In a formal scientific communication it is rarely necessary to repeat the same data in more than one place (e.g. as a table and as a graph). However, graphical representation of data collected earlier in tabular format may be applicable in laboratory practical reports.

Practical aspects of graph drawing

The following comments apply to graphs drawn for laboratory reports. Figures for publication, or similar formal presentation are usually prepared according to specific guidelines, provided by the publisher/organizer.

KEY POINT Graphs should be self-contained – they should include all material necessary to convey the appropriate message without reference to the text. Every graph must have a concise explanatory title to establish the content. If several graphs are used, they should be numbered, so they can be quoted in the text.

- Consider the layout and scale of the axes carefully. Most graphs are used to illustrate the relationship between two variables (*x* and *y*) and have two axes at right angles (e.g. Fig. 36.1). The horizontal axis is known as the abscissa (*x* axis) and the vertical axis as the ordinate (*y* axis).
- The axis assigned to each variable must be chosen carefully. Usually the *x* axis is used for the independent variable (e.g. treatment) while the dependent variable (e.g. response) is plotted on the *y* axis (p. 56). When neither variable is determined by the other, or where the variables are interdependent, the axes may be plotted either way round.
- Each axis must have a descriptive label showing what is represented, together with the appropriate units of measurement, separated from the descriptive label by a solidus or 'slash' (/), as in Fig. 36.1, or brackets as in Fig. 36.2.
- Each axis must have a scale with reference marks ('tics') on the axis to show clearly the location of all numbers used.
- A figure legend should be used to provide explanatory detail, including the symbols used for each data set.

Handling very large or very small numbers
To simplify presentation when your experimental data consist of either very large or very small numbers, the plotted values may be the measured numbers

Selecting a title – it is a common fault to use titles that are grammatically incorrect: a widely applicable format is to state the relationship between the independent and dependent variables within the title, e.g. 'The relationship between enzyme activity and external pH'.

Remembering which axis is which – a way of remembering the orientation of the *x* axis is that *x* is a 'cross', and it runs 'across' the page (horizontal axis).

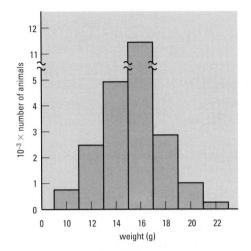

Fig. 36.2 Frequency distribution of weights for a sample of animals (sample size 24 085); the size class interval is 2 g.

Example For a data set where the smallest number on the log axis is 12 and the largest number is 9 000, three-cycle log-linear paper would be used, covering the range 10–10 000.

multiplied by a power of 10: this multiplying power should be written immediately before the descriptive label on the appropriate axis (as in Fig. 36.2). However, it is often better to modify the primary unit with an appropriate prefix (p. 43) to avoid any confusion regarding negative powers of 10.

Size

Remember that the purpose of your graph is to communicate information. It must not be too small, so use at least half an A4 page and design your axes and labels to fill the available space without overcrowding any adjacent text. If using graph paper, remember that the white space around the grid is usually too small for effective labelling. The shape of a graph is determined by your choice of scale for the x and y axes which, in turn, is governed by your experimental data. It may be inappropriate to start the axes at zero (e.g. Fig. 36.1). In such instances, it is particularly important to show the scale clearly, with scale breaks where necessary, so the graph does not mislead. Note that Fig. 36.1 is drawn with 'floating axes' (i.e. the x and y axes do not meet in the lower left-hand corner), while Fig. 36.2 has clear scale breaks on both x and y axes.

Graph paper

In addition to conventional linear (squared) graph paper, you may need the following:

- Probability graph paper. This is useful when one axis is a probability scale (e.g. p. 220)
- Log-linear graph paper. This is appropriate when one of the scales shows a logarithmic progression, e.g. the exponential growth of organisms. Log-linear paper is defined by the number of logarithmic divisions covered (usually termed 'cycles') so make sure you use a paper with the appropriate number of cycles for your data. An alternative approach is to plot the log-transformed values on 'normal' graph paper.
- Log-log graph paper. This is appropriate when both scales show a logarithmic progression.

Types of graph

Different graphical forms may be used for different purposes, including:

- Plotted curves – used for data where the relationship between two variables can be represented as a continuum (e.g. Fig. 36.3).
- Scatter diagrams – used to visualize the relationship between individual data values for two interdependent variables (e.g. Fig. 36.4) often as a preliminary part of a correlation analysis (p. 224).
- Three-dimensional graphs show the interrelationships of three variables, often one dependent and two independent (e.g. Fig. 36.5). A contour diagram is an alternative method of representing such data.
- Histograms represent frequency distributions of continuous variables (e.g. Fig. 36.6). An alternative is the tally chart (p. 191).
- Frequency polygons emphasize the form of a frequency distribution by joining the co-ordinates with straight lines, in contrast to a histogram. This is particularly useful when plotting two or more frequency distributions on the same graph (e.g. Fig. 36.7).
- Bar charts represent frequency distributions of a discrete qualitative or quantitative variable (e.g. Fig. 36.8). An alternative representation is the line chart (p. 219).
- Pie charts illustrate portions of a whole (e.g. Fig. 36.9).
- Pictographs give a pictorial representation of data (e.g. Fig. 36.10).

Using graphs

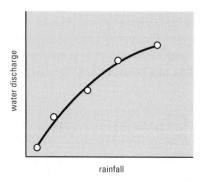

Fig. 36.3 Plotted curve: water discharge as a function of rainfall.

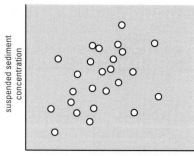

Fig. 36.4 Scatter diagram: suspended sediment concentration and Secchi disk depth.

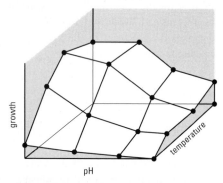

Fig. 36.5 Three-dimensional graph: growth of an organism as a function of temperature and pH.

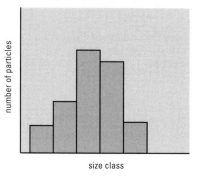

Fig. 36.6 Histogram: the number of sediment particles within different size classes.

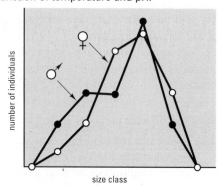

Fig. 36.7 Frequency polygon: frequency distributions of male and female animals according to size.

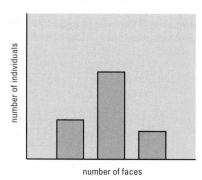

Fig. 36.8 Bar chart: number of faces per crystal.

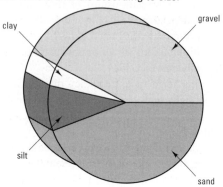

Fig. 36.9 Pie chart: relative abundance of particles sizes in a sediment sample.

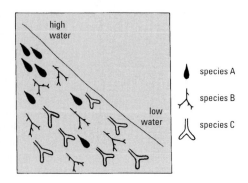

Fig. 36.10 Pictograph: distribution of plants on a rocky shore.

The plotted curve

This is the commonest form of graphical representation used in environmental science. The key features are outlined below and given in checklist form in Box 36.1.

Data points

Each data point must be shown accurately, so that any reader can determine the exact values of x and y. In addition, the results of each treatment must be readily identifiable. A useful technique is to use a dot for each data point, surrounded by a hollow symbol for each treatment (see Fig. 36.1). An alternative is to use symbols only (Fig. 36.3), though the co-ordinates of each point are defined less accurately. Use the same symbol for the same entity if it occurs in several graphs and provide a key to all symbols.

Statistical measures

If you are plotting average values for several replicates and if you have the necessary statistical knowledge, you can calculate the standard error (p. 213), or the 95% confidence limits (p. 223) for each mean value and show these on your graph as a series of vertical bars (see Fig. 36.1). Make it clear in the legend whether the bars refer to standard errors or 95% confidence limits and quote the value of n (the number of replicates per data point). Another approach is to add a least significant difference bar (p. 222) to the graph.

Interpolation

Once you have plotted each point, you must decide whether to link them by straight lines or a smoothed curve. Each of these techniques conveys a different

---

Box 36.1 Checklist for the stages in drawing a graph

The following sequence can be used whenever you need to construct a plotted curve: it will need to be modified for other types of graph.

1. **Collect all of the data values and statistical values** (in tabular form, where appropriate).
2. **Decide on the most suitable form of presentation**: this may include transformation of the data (p. 192) to convert the data to linear form.
3. **Choose a concise descriptive title**, together with a reference (figure) number and date, where necessary.
4. **Determine which variable is to be plotted on the x axis and which on the y axis.**
5. **Select appropriate scales for both axes** and make sure that the numbers and their location (scale marks) are clearly shown, together with any scale breaks.
6. **Decide on appropriate descriptive labels for both axes**, with SI units of measurement, where appropriate.
7. **Choose the symbols for each set of data points** and decide on the best means of representation for statistical values.
8. **Plot the points** to show the co-ordinates of each value with appropriate symbols.
9. **Draw a trend line for each set of points.**
10. **Write a figure legend**, to include a key which identifies all symbols and statistical values and any descriptive footnotes, as required.

Using graphs

Conveying the correct message – the golden rule is: 'always draw the simplest line that fits the data reasonably well and is scientifically reasonable'.

Extrapolating plotted curves – try to avoid the need to extrapolate by better experimental design.

In a histogram, each datum is represented by a column with an area proportional to the magnitude of y: in most cases, you should use columns of equal width, so that the height of each column is then directly proportional to y. Shading or stippling may be used to identify individual columns, according to your needs.

Using computers to produce graphs – never allow a computer program to dictate size, shape and other aspects of a graph: find out how to alter scales, labels, axes, etc. and make appropriate selections. Draw curves freehand if the program only has the capacity to join the individual points by straight lines.

message to your reader. Joining the points by straight lines may seem the simplest option, but may give the impression that errors are very low or non-existent and that the relationship between the variables is complex. Joining points by straight lines is appropriate in certain graphs involving time sequences (e.g. the number of animals at a particular site each year), or for repeat measurements where measurement error can be assumed to be minimal, (e.g. recording a patient's temperature in a hospital, to emphasize any variation from one time point to the next). However, in most plotted curves the best straight line or curved line should be drawn (according to appropriate mathematical or statistical models, or by eye), to highlight the relationship between the variables – after all, your choice of a plotted curve implies that such a relationship exists! Don't worry if some of your points do not lie on the line: this is caused by errors of measurement and by biological variation. Most curves drawn by eye should have an equal number of points lying on either side of the line. You may be guided by 95% confidence limits, in which case your curve should pass within these limits wherever possible.

Curved lines can be drawn using a flexible curve, a set of French curves, or freehand. In the latter case, turn your paper so that you can draw the curve in a single, sweeping stroke by a pivoting movement at the elbow (for larger curves) or wrist (for smaller ones). Do not try to force your hand to make complex, unnatural movements, as the resulting line will not be smooth.

Extrapolation

Be wary of extrapolation beyond the upper or lower limit of your measured values. This is rarely justifiable and may lead to serious errors. Whenever extrapolation is used, a dotted line ensures that the reader is aware of the uncertainty involved. Any assumptions behind an extrapolated curve should also be stated clearly in your text.

The histogram

While a plotted curve assumes a continuous relationship between the variables by interpolating between individual data points, a histogram involves no such assumptions and is the most appropriate representation if the number of data points is too few to allow a trend line to be drawn. Histograms are also used to represent frequency distributions (p. 191), where the y axis shows the number of times a particular value of x was obtained (e.g. Fig. 36.2). As in a plotted curve, the x axis represents a continuous variable which can take any value within a given range (e.g. plant height), so the scale must be broken down into discrete classes and the scale marks on the x axis should show either the mid-points (mid-values) of each class, or the boundaries between the classes.

The columns are adjacent to each other in a histogram, in contrast to a bar chart, where the columns are separate because the x axis of a bar chart represents discrete values.

Interpreting graphs

When you look at graphs drawn by other people, make sure you understand the axes before you look at the relationship. It is all too easy to take in the shape of a graph without first considering the scale of the axes, a fact that some advertisers and politicians exploit when curves are used to misrepresent information. Such graphs are often used in newspapers and on television. Examine them critically – many would not pass the stringent requirements of scientific communication and conclusions drawn from them may be flawed.

37 Presenting data in tables

A table is often the most appropriate way to present numerical data in a concise, accurate and structured form. Assignments and project reports should contain tables which have been designed to condense and display results in a meaningful way and to aid numerical comparison. The preparation of tables for recording primary data is discussed on p. 62.

Decide whether you need a table, or whether a graph is more appropriate. Histograms and plotted curves can be used to give a visual impression of the relationships within your data (p. 194). On the other hand, a table gives you the opportunity to make detailed numerical comparisons.

KEY POINT Always remember that the primary purpose of your table is to communicate information and allow appropriate comparison, not simply to put down the results on paper!

Preparation of tables

Title

Every table must have a brief descriptive title. If several tables are used, number them consecutively so they can be quoted in your text. The titles within a report should be compared with one another, making sure they are logical and consistent and that they describe accurately the numerical data contained within them.

Constructing titles – take care over titles as it is a common mistake in student practical reports to present tables without titles, or to misconstruct the title.

Structure

Display the components of each table in a way that will help the reader understand your data and grasp the significance of your results. Organize the columns so that each category of like numbers or attributes is listed vertically, while each horizontal row shows a different experimental treatment, organism, sampling site, etc. (as in Table 37.1). Where appropriate, put control values near the beginning of the table. Columns that need to be compared should be set out alongside each other. Use rulings to subdivide your table appropriately, but avoid cluttering it up with too many lines.

Saving space in tables – you may be able to omit a column of control data if your results can be expressed as percentages of the corresponding control values.

Headings and subheadings

These should identify each set of data and show the units of measurement, where necessary. Make sure that each column is wide enough for the headings and for the longest data value.

Table 37.1 Solar thermal power: some data on Central Receiver Systems. (From Jackson & Jackson, 1996).

Name	Location	Year completed	Electricity output/MW	Heat transfer medium
SSPS	Almeria, Spain	1981	0.5	Sodium
Eurelios	Adrano, Italy	1981	0.7	Steam
Sunshine	Nio, Japan	1981	0.8	Steam
Themis	Targasonne, France	1982	2.5	Molten salt
Solar One	Barstow, USA	1982	10.0	Steam
CESA 1	Almeria, Spain	1983	1.0	Steam

Presenting data in tables

Examples If you measured the width of a structure to the nearest one-tenth of a micrometre, quote the value in the form '52.6 μm'.

Quote the width of the structure as 52.6 (μm), rather than 0.000 052 6 (m) or 52.6 (10^{-6} m).

Saving further space – in some instances a footnote can be used to replace a whole column of repetitive data.

Using microcomputers and word-processing packages – these can be used to prepare high-quality versions of tables for project work (p. 237).

Numerical data

Within the table, do not quote values to more significant figures than necessary, as this will imply spurious accuracy (p. 41). By careful choice of appropriate units for each column you should aim to present numerical data within the range 0 to 1 000. As with graphs, it is less ambiguous to use derived SI units, with the appropriate prefixes, in the headings of columns and rows, rather than quoting multiplying factors as powers of 10. Alternatively, include exponents in the main body of the table (see Table 6.3, to avoid any possible confusion regarding the use of negative powers of 10.

Other notations

Avoid using dashes in numerical tables, as their meaning is unclear; enter a zero reading as '0' and use 'NT' not tested or 'ND' if no data value was obtained, with a footnote to explain each abbreviation. Other footnotes, identified by asterisks, superscripts or other symbols in the table, may be used to provide relevant experimental detail (if not given in the text) and an explanation of column headings and individual results, where appropriate. Footnotes should be as condensed as possible. Table 37.1 provides examples.

Statistics

In tables where the dispersion of each data set is shown by an appropriate statistical parameter, you must state whether this is the (sample) standard deviation, the standard error (of the mean) or the 95% confidence limits and you must give the value of n (the number of replicates). Other descriptive statistics should be quoted with similar detail, and hypothesis-testing statistics should be quoted along with the value of P (the probability). Details of any test used should be given in the legend, or in a footnote.

Text

Sometimes a table can be a useful way of presenting textual information in a condensed form.

When you have finished compiling your tabulated data, carefully double-check each numerical entry against the original information, to ensure that the final version of your table is free from transcriptional errors. Box 37.1 gives a checklist for the major elements of constructing a table.

Box 37.1 Checklist for preparing a table

Every table should have the following components:

1. **A title**, plus a reference number and date where necessary.

2. **Headings for each column and row**, with appropriate units of measurement.

3. **Data values**, quoted to the nearest significant figure and with statistical parameters, according to your requirements.

4. **Footnotes** to explain abbreviations, modifications and individual details.

5. **Rulings to emphasize groupings** and distinguish items from each other.

38 Hints for solving numerical problems

Environmental science often requires a numerical or statistical approach. Not only is mathematical modelling an important aid to understanding, but computations are often needed to turn raw data into meaningful information or to compare them with other data sets. Moreover, calculations are part of laboratory routine, perhaps required for making up solutions of known concentration (see p. 14 and below) or for the calibration of a microscope. In research, 'trial' calculations can reveal what input data are required and where errors in their measurement might be amplified in the final result (see p. 58).

KEY POINT **If you have a 'block' about numerical work, practice at problem-solving is especially important.**

Table 38.1 Sets of numbers and operations

Sets of numbers	
Whole numbers:	0, 1, 2, 3, …
Natural numbers:	1, 2, 3, …
Integers:	… −3, −2, −1, 0, 1, 2, 3, …
Real numbers:	integers and anything between (e.g. −5, 4.376, 3/16, π, $\sqrt{5}$)
Prime numbers:	subset of natural numbers divisible by 1 and themselves only (i.e. 2, 3, 5, 7, 11, 13, …)
Rational numbers:	p/q where p (integer) and q (natural) have no common factor (e.g. 3/4)
Fractions:	p/q where p is an integer and q is natural (e.g. −6/8)
Irrational numbers:	real numbers with no exact value (e.g. π)
Infinity:	(symbol ∞) is larger than any number (technically not a number as it does not obey the laws of algebra)
Operations and symbols	
Basic operators:	$+$, $-$, $\times$ and $\div$ will not need explanation; however, / may substitute for $\div$, $*$ may substitute for $\times$ or this operator may be omitted
Powers:	a^n, i.e. 'a to the power n', means a multiplied by itself n times (e.g. $a^2 = a \times a =$ 'a squared', $a^3 = a \times a \times a =$ 'a cubed'). n is said to be the index or exponent. Note $a^0 = 1$ and $a^1 = a$
Logarithms:	the common logarithm (log) of any number x is the power to which 10 would have to be raised to give x (i.e. the log of 100 is 2; $10^2 = 100$); the antilog of x is 10^x. Note that there is no log for 0, so take this into account when drawing log axes by breaking the axis. Natural or Napierian logarithms (ln) use the base e ($= 2.71828\ldots$) instead of 10
Reciprocals:	the reciprocal of a real number a is $1/a$ ($a \neq 0$)
Relational operators:	$a > b$ means 'a is greater (more positive) than b', $<$ means less than, $\leqslant$ means less-than-or-equal-to and $\geqslant$ means greater-than-or-equal-to
Proportionality:	$a \propto b$ means 'a is proportional to b' (i.e. $a = kb$, where k is a constant). If $a \propto 1/b$, a is inversely proportional to b ($a = k/b$)
Sums:	Σx_i is shorthand for the sum of all x values from $i = 0$ to $i = n$ (more correctly the range of the sum is specified under the symbol)
Moduli:	$|x|$ signifies modulus of x, i.e. its absolute value (e.g. $|4| = |-4| = 4$)
Factorials:	$x!$ signifies factorial x, the product of all integers from 1 to x (e.g. $3! = 6$). Note $0! = 1! = 1$

Hints for solving numerical problems

Practising at problem solving:

- demystifies the procedures involved, which are normally just the elementary mathematical operations of addition, subtraction, multiplication and division (Table 38.1);
- allows you to gain confidence so that you don't become confused when confronted with an unfamiliar or apparently complex form of problem;
- helps you recognize the various forms a problem can take.

Steps in tackling a numerical problem

The step-by-step approach outlined below may not be the fastest method of arriving at an answer, but most mistakes occur where steps are missing, combined or not made obvious, so a logical approach is often better. Error tracing is distinctly easier when all stages in a calculation are laid out.

Have the right tools ready

Scientific calculators (p. 4) greatly simplify the numerical part of problem-solving. However, the seeming infallibility of the calculator may lead you to accept an absurd result which could have arisen because of faulty key-pressing or faulty logic. Make sure you know how to use all the features on your calculator, especially how the memory works; how to introduce a constant multiplier or divider; and how to obtain an exponent (note that the 'exp' button on most calculators gives you 10^x, not 1^x or y^x; so 1×10^6 would be entered as $\boxed{1}\ \boxed{\text{exp}}\ \boxed{6}$, *not* $\boxed{10}\ \boxed{\text{exp}}\ \boxed{6}$).

Approach the problem thoughtfully

If the individual steps have been laid out on a worksheet, the 'tactics' will already have been decided. It is more difficult when you have to adopt a strategy on your own, especially if the problem is presented as a story and it isn't obvious which equations or rules need to be applied.

- Read the problem carefully as the text may give clues as to how it should be tackled. Be certain of what is required as an answer before starting.
- Analyse what kind of problem it is, which effectively means deciding which equation(s) or approach will be applicable. If this is not obvious, consider the dimensions/units of the information available and think how they could be fitted to a relevant formula. In examinations, a favourite ploy of examiners is to present a problem such that the familiar form of an equation must be rearranged (see Table 38.2 and Box 38.1). Another is to make you use two or more equations in series (see Box 38.2). If you are unsure whether a recalled formula is correct, a dimensional analysis can help: write in all the units for the variables and make sure that they cancel out to give the expected answer.
- Check that you have, or can derive, all of the information required to use your chosen equation(s). It is unusual but not unknown for examiners to supply redundant information. So, if you decide not to use some of the information given, be sure why you do not require it.
- Decide on what format and units the answer should be presented in. This is sometimes suggested to you. If the problem requires many changes in the prefixes to units, it is a good idea to convert all data to base SI units (multiplied by a power of 10) at the outset.
- If a problem appears complex, break it down into component parts.

A computer spreadsheet may be very useful in repetitive work or for 'what if?' case studies (see Chapter 42).

Table 38.2 Simple algebra – rules for manipulating

If $a = b + c$, then $b = a - c$ and $c = a - b$
If $a = b \times c$, then $b = a/c$ and $c = a/b$
If $a = b^c$, then $b = a^{1/c}$ and $c = \log a/\log b$
$a^{1/n} = \sqrt[n]{a}$
$a^{-n} = 1/a^n$
$a^b \times a^c = a^{(b+c)}$ and $a^b/a^c = a^{(b-c)}$
$(a^b)^c = a^{(b \times c)}$
$a \times b = \text{antilog}(\log a + \log b)$

Box 38.1   Example of using the rules of Table 38.2

Problem: if $a = (b - c)/(d + e^n)$, find e

1. Multiply both sides by $(d + e^n)$; formula becomes:

$$a(d + e^n) = (b - c)$$

2. Divide both sides by a; formula becomes: $d + e^n = \dfrac{b - c}{a}$

3. Subtract d from both sides; formula becomes: $e^n = \dfrac{b - c}{a} - d$

4. Raise each side to the power $1/n$; formula becomes:

$$e = \left\{ \frac{b - c}{a} - d \right\}^{1/n}$$

Present your answer clearly

The way you present your answer obviously needs to fit the individual problem. The example shown in Box 38.2 has been chosen to illustrate several important points, but this format would not fit all situations. Guidelines for presenting an answer include:

(a) Make your assumptions explicit. Most mathematical models require that certain criteria are met before they can be legitimately applied (e.g. 'assuming the sample is homogeneous . . .'), while some approaches involve approximations which should be clearly stated (e.g. 'to estimate the mouse's skin area, its body was approximated to a cylinder with radius x and height y . . .').

(b) Explain your strategy for answering, perhaps giving the applicable formula or definitions which suit the approach to be taken. Give details of what the symbols mean (and their units) at this point.

(c) Rearrange the formula to the required form with the desired unknown on the left-hand side (see Table 38.2).

(d) Substitute the relevant values into the right-hand side of the formula, using the units and prefixes as given (it may be convenient to convert values to SI beforehand). Convert prefixes to appropriate powers of 10 as soon as possible.

(e) Convert to the desired units step-by-step, i.e. taking each variable in turn.

(f) When you have the answer in the desired units, rewrite the left-hand side and underline the answer. Make sure that the result is presented with an appropriate number of significant figures (see p. 41).

Check your answer

Having written out your answer, you should check it methodically, answering the following questions:

- Is the answer of a realistic magnitude? You should be alerted to an error if an answer is absurdly large or small. In repeated calculations, a result standing out from others in the same series should be double-checked.
- Do the units make sense and match up with the answer required? Don't, for example, present a volume in units of m^2.
- Do you get the same answer if you recalculate in a different way? If you have time, recalculate the answer using a different 'route', entering the numbers into your calculator in a different form and/or carrying out the operations in a different order.

Show the steps in your calculations – most markers will only penalize a mistake once and part marks will be given if the remaining operations are performed correctly. This can only be done if those operations are visible!

Units – never write any answer without its unit(s) unless it is truly dimensionless.

Rounding off – do not round off numbers until you arrive at the final answer.

Hints for solving numerical problems

Some reminders of basic mathematics

Errors in calculations sometimes appear because of faults in mathematics rather than computational errors. For reference purposes, Tables 38.1–38.3 give some basic mathematical principles that may be useful. Eason *et al.* (1992) should be consulted for more advanced needs.

Exponents

Exponential notation is an alternative way of expressing numbers in the form a^n ('*a* to the power *n*'), where *a* is multiplied by itself *n* times. The number *a* is called the base and the number *n* the exponent (or power or index). The exponent need not be a whole number, and it can be negative if the number being expressed is less than 1. See Table 38.2 for other mathematical relationships involving exponents.

Example $2^3 = 2 \times 2 \times 2 = 8$

Box 38.2 Model answer to a typical environmental problem

Problem
Estimate the total length and surface area of the fibrous roots on a maize seedling from measurements of their total fresh weight and mean diameter. Give your answers in m and cm² respectively.

Measurements
Fresh weight[a] = 5.00 g, mean diameter[b] = 0.5 mm.

Answer
Assumptions: (1) the roots are cylinders with constant radius[c] and the 'ends' have negligible area; (2) the root system has a density of $1000\,kg\,m^{-3}$ (i.e. that of water[d]).

Strategy: from assumption (1), the applicable equations are those concerned with the volume and surface area of a cylinder (Table 38.3), namely:

$$V = \pi r^2 h \qquad [38.1]$$
$$A = 2\pi rh \text{ (ignoring ends)} \qquad [38.2]$$

where *V* is volume (m³), *A* is surface area (m²), $\pi \approx 3.14159$, *h* is height (m) and *r* is radius (m). The total length of the root system is given by *h* and its surface area by *A*. We can find *h* by rearranging eqn [38.1] and then substitute its value in eqn [38.2] to get *A*.

To calculate total root length: rearranging eqn [38.1], we have $h = V/\pi r^2$. From measurements[e], $r = 0.25\,mm = 0.25 \times 10^{-3}\,m$.

From density = weight/volume,

$$V = \text{fresh weight/density}$$
$$= 5\,g/1000\,kg\,m^{-3}$$
$$= 0.005\,kg/1000\,kg\,m^{-3}$$
$$= 5 \times 10^{-6}\,m^3$$

Total root length,

$$h = V/\pi r^2$$
$$5 \times 10^{-6}\,m^3/3.14159 \times (0.25 \times 10^{-3}\,m)^2$$

Total root length = 25.46 m

To calculate surface area of roots: substituting value for *h* obtained above into eqn [38.2], we have:

Root surface area

$$= 2 \times 3.14159 \times 0.25 \times 10^{-3}\,m \times 25.46\,m$$
$$= 0.04\,m^2$$
$$= 0.04 \times 10^4\,cm^2$$
(there being $100 \times 100 = 10^4\,cm^2$ per m²)

Root surface area = 400 cm²

Notes
(a) The fresh weight of roots would normally be obtained by washing the roots free of soil, blotting them dry and weighing.

(b) In a real answer you might show the replicate measurements giving rise to the mean diameter.

(c) In reality, the roots will differ considerably in diameter and each root will not have a constant diameter throughout its length.

(d) This will not be wildly inaccurate as about 95% of the fresh weight will be water, but the volume could also be estimated from water displacement measurements.

(e) Note conversion of measurements into base SI units at this stage and on line 3 of the root volume calculation. Forgetting to halve diameter measurements where radii are required is a common error.

Table 38.3 Geometry and trigonometry – analysing shapes

Shape/object	Diagram	Perimeter	Area
Two-dimensional shapes			
Square		$4x$	x^2
Rectangle		$2(x + y)$	xy
Circle		$2\pi r$	πr^2
Ellipse		$\pi[1.5(a + b) - \sqrt{a * b}]$ (approx.)	πab
Triangle (general)		$x + y + z$	$0.5zh$
(right-angled)		$x + y + r$ $\sin \theta = y/r, \cos \theta = x/r,$ $\tan \theta = y/x; r^2 = x^2 + y^2$	$0.5xy$

Shape/object	Diagram	Surface area	Volume
Three-dimensional shapes			
Cube		$6x^2$	x^3
Cuboid		$2xy + 2xz + 2yz$	xyz
Sphere		$4\pi r^2$	$4\pi r^3/3$
Ellipsoid		no simple formula	$\pi rab/3$
Cylinder		$2\pi rh + 2\pi r^2$	$\pi r^2 h$
Cone and pyramid		$0.5PL + B$	$BL/3$

x, y, z = sides;
a, b = half minimum and maximum axes;
r = radius or hypotenuse;
h = height;
B = base area;
L = perpendicular height;
P = perimeter of base.

Hints for solving numerical problems

Example Avogadro's number, $\approx 602\,352\,000\,000\,000\,000\,000\,000$, is more conveniently expressed as 6.02352×10^{23}.

Scientific notation

In scientific notation, also known as 'standard form', the base is 10 and the exponent a whole number. To express numbers that are not whole powers of 10, the form $c \times 10^n$ is used, where the coefficient c is normally between 1 and 10. Scientific notation is valuable when you are using very large numbers and wish to avoid suggesting spurious accuracy. Thus if you write 123 000, this suggests that you know the number to ± 0.5, whereas 1.23×10^5 might give a truer indication of measurement accuracy (i.e. implied to be ± 500 in this case). Engineering notation is similar, but treats numbers as powers of ten in groups of 3, i.e. $c \times 10^0$, 10^3, 10^6, 10^9, etc. This corresponds to the SI system of prefixes (p. 43).

A useful property of powers when expressed to the same base is that when multiplying two numbers together, you simply add the powers, while if dividing, you subtract the powers. Thus, suppose you counted 8 particles in a 10^{-7} dilution, there would be 8×10^7 in the same volume of undiluted solution; if you now dilute this 500-fold (5×10^2), then the number present in the same volume would be $8/5 \times 10^{(7-2)} = 1.6 \times 10^5 = 160\,000$.

Example (use to check the correct use of your own calculator)
102963 as a log = 5.012681 (to 6 decimal places)
$10^{5.012681} = 102962.96$
(Note loss of accuracy due to loss of decimal places).

Logarithms

When a number is expressed as a logarithm, this refers to the power n that the base number a must be raised to give that number, e.g. $\log_{10}(1000) = 3$, since $10^3 = 1000$. Any base could be used, but the two most common are 10, when the power is referred to as $\log_{10}$ or simply log, and the constant e (2.718282), used for mathematical convenience in certain situations, when the power is referred to as $\log_e$ or ln. Where a coefficient would be used in scientific notation, then the log is not a whole number.

To obtain logs, you will need to use the log key on your calculator, or special log tables (now largely redundant). To convert back, use

- the $\boxed{10^x}$ key, with x = log value;
- the $\boxed{\text{inverse}}$ then the log key; or
- the $\boxed{y^x}$ key, with $y = 10$ and x = log value.

If you used log tables, you will find complementary antilogarithm tables to do this.

There are many uses of logarithms in environmental science, including pH ($= -\log[H^+]$), where $[H^+]$ is expressed in $mol\,l^{-1}$ (see p. 27); the exponential growth of populations, where if log(number) is plotted against time, a straight-line relationship is obtained; and hydrology in relationships between mean annual flood and drainage density, channel slope and discharge or meander length and drainage area.

Hints for some typical problems

Calculations involving proportions or ratios

The 'unitary method' is a useful way of approaching calculations involving proportions or ratios, such as those required when making up solutions from stocks or as a subsidiary part of longer calculations.

1. If given a value for a multiple, work out the corresponding value for a single item or unit.
2. Use this 'unitary value' to calculate the required new value.

Example A lab schedule states that 5 g of a compound with a relative molecular mass of $220\,g\,mol^{-1}$ are dissolved in 400 ml of solvent. For writing up your Materials and Methods, you wish to express this as $mol\,l^{-1}$.
1. If there are 5 g in 400 ml, then there are 5/400 g in 1 ml.
2. Hence, 1000 ml will contain $5/400 \times 1000\,g = 12.5\,g$.
3. $12.5\,g = 12.5/220\,mol = 0.0568\,mol$, so [solution] $= 56.8\,mmol\,l^{-1}$ ($= 56.8\,mol\,m^{-3}$).

Calculations involving series

Series (used in e.g. dilutions, see also p. 14) can be of two main forms:

- arithmetic, where the *difference* between two successive numbers in the series is a constant, e.g. 2, 4, 6, 8, 10, ...
- geometric, where the *ratio* between two successive numbers in the series is a constant, e.g. 1, 10, 100, 1000, 10000, ...

Note that the logs of the numbers in a geometric series will form an arithmetic series (e.g. 0, 1, 2, 3, 4, ... in the above case). Thus, if a quantity y varies with a quantity x such that the rate of change in y is proportional to the value of y (i.e. it varies in an exponential manner), a semi-log plot of such data will form a straight line. This form of relationship is relevant for exponentially growing populations and radioactive decay.

Statistical calculations

The need for long, complex calculations in statistics has largely been removed because of the widespread use of spreadsheets with statistical functions (Chapter 42) and specialized programs such as Minitab™ (p. 239). It is, however, important to understand the principles behind what you are trying to do (see Chapters 39 and 40) and interpret the program's output correctly, either using the 'help' function or a reference manual.

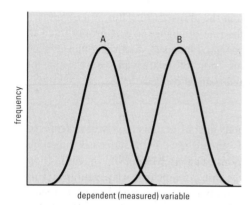

Fig. 39.1 Two distributions with different locations but the same dispersion. The data set labelled B could have been obtained by adding a constant to each datum in the data set labelled A.

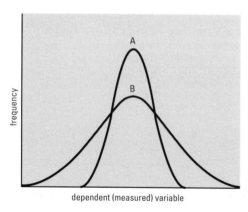

Fig. 39.2 Two distributions with different dispersions but the same location. The data set labelled A covers a relatively narrow range of values of the dependent (measured) variable while that labelled B covers a wider range.

Example Box 39.1 shows a set of data and the calculated values of the measures of location, dispersion and shape for which methods of calculation are outlined below. Check your understanding by calculating the statistics yourself and confirming that you arrive at the same answers.

---

39 Descriptive statistics

Whether obtained from observation or experimentation, most data in environmental science exhibit variability. This can be displayed as a frequency distribution (e.g. Fig. 36.6). Descriptive (or summary) statistics quantify aspects of the frequency distribution of a sample. You can use them to:

- condense a large data set for presentation in figures or tables;
- provide estimates of parameters of the frequency distribution of the population being sampled (p. 217).

KEY POINT The appropriate descriptive statistics to choose depend on both the type of data, i.e. quantitative, ranked, or qualitative, and the nature of the underlying population frequency distribution.

If you have no clear theoretical grounds for assuming what the underlying frequency distribution is like, graph one or more sample frequency distributions, ideally with a sample size >100. The tally system for recording data (see p. 191) can give an immediate visual indication of the frequency distribution as data are collected.

The methods used to calculate descriptive statistics depend on whether data have been grouped into classes. You should use the original data set if it is still available, because grouping into classes loses information and accuracy. However, large data sets may make calculations unwieldy, and are best handled by computer programs.

Three important features of a frequency distribution that can be summarized by descriptive statistics are:

- the sample's location, i.e. its position along a given dimension representing the dependent (measured) variable (Fig. 39.1);
- the dispersion of the data, i.e. how spread out the values are (Fig. 39.2);
- the shape of the distribution, i.e. whether symmetrical, skewed, U-shaped, etc. (Fig. 39.3).

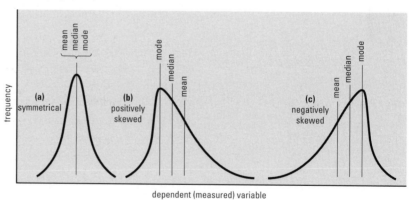

Fig. 39.3 Symmetrical and skewed frequency distributions, showing relative positions of mean, median and mode.

Measuring location

Here, the objective is to pinpoint the 'centre' of the frequency distribution, i.e. the value about which most of the data are grouped. The chief measures of location are the mean, median and mode. Fig. 39.4 shows how to choose among these for a given data set.

Box 39.1 Descriptive statistics for a sample of data

Value (Y)	Frequency (f)	Cumulative frequency	fY	fY²
1	0	0	0	0
2	1	1	2	4
3	2	3	6	18
4	3	6	12	48
5	8	14	40	200
6	5	19	30	180
7	2	21	14	98
8	0	21	0	0
Totals	$21 = \Sigma f\,(=n)$		$104 = \Sigma fY$	$548 = \Sigma fY^2$

In this example, for simplicity and ease of calculation, integer values of Y are used. In many practical exercises, where continuous variables are measured to several significant figures and where the number of data values is small, giving frequencies of 1 for most of the values of Y, it may be simpler to omit the column dealing with frequency and list all the individual values of Y and Y^2 in the appropriate columns. To gauge the underlying frequency distribution of such data sets, you would need to group individual data into broader classes (e.g. all values between 1.0 and 1.9, all values between 2.0 and 2.9, etc.) and then draw a histogram (p. 198). Calculation of certain statistics for data sets that have been grouped in this way (e.g. median, quartiles, extremes) can be tricky and a statistical text should be consulted.

Statistic	Value*	How calculated
Mean	4.95	$\Sigma fY/n$, i.e. 104/21
Mode	5	The most common value (Y value with highest frequency)
Median	5	Value of the $(n + 1)/2$ variate, i.e. the value ranked $(21 + 1)/2 = 11$th (obtained from the cumulative frequency column)
Upper quartile	6	The upper quartile is between the 16th and 17th values, i.e. the value exceeded by 25% of the data values
Lower quartile	4	The lower quartile is between the 5th and 6th values, i.e. the value exceeded by 75% of the data values
Semi-interquartile range	1.0	Half the difference between the upper and lower quartiles, i.e. $(6 - 4)/2$
Upper extreme	7	Highest Y value in data set
Lower extreme	2	Lowest Y value in data set
Range	5	Difference between upper and lower extremes
Variance (s^2)	1.65	$s^2 = \dfrac{\Sigma fY^2 - (\Sigma fY)^2/n}{n - 1}$ $= \dfrac{548 - (104)^2/21}{20}$
Standard deviation (s)	1.28	$\sqrt{s^2}$
Standard error (SE)	0.280	$s/\sqrt{n}$
Coefficient of variation (cov)	25.9%	$100s/\bar{Y}$

*Rounded to appropriate significant figures

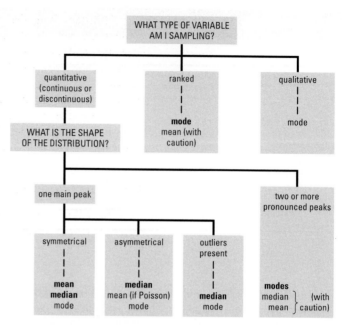

Fig. 39.4 Choosing a statistic for characterizing a distribution's location. Statistics written in bold are the preferred option(s).

Use of symbols – Y is used in Chapters 39 and 40 to signify the dependent variable in statistical calculations (following the example of Wardlaw, 1985, Sokal and Rohlf, 1994 and Heath, 1995). Note, however, that some authors use X or x in analogous formulae and many calculators refer to e.g. $\bar{x}$, Σx^2, etc. for their statistical functions.

Definition

An outlier – any datum which has a value much smaller or bigger than most of the data.

Definition

Rank – the position of a data value when all the data are placed in order of ascending magnitude. If ties occur, an average rank of the tied variates is used. Thus, the rank of the datum 6 in the sequence 1,3,5,6,8,8,10 is 4; the rank of each datum with value 8 is 5.5.

Mean

The mean (denoted $\bar{Y}$ and also referred to as the arithmetic mean) is the average value of the data. It is obtained from the sum of all the data values divided by the number of observations (in symbolic terms, $\Sigma Y/n$). The mean is a good measure of the centre of symmetrical frequency distributions. It uses all of the numerical values of the sample and therefore incorporates all of the information content of the data. However, the value of a mean is greatly affected by the presence of outliers. The arithmetic mean is a widely used statistic, but there are situations when you should be careful about using it (see Box 39.2 for examples).

Median

The median is the mid-point of the observations when ranked in increasing order. For odd-sized samples, the median is the middle observation; for even-sized samples it is the mean of the middle pair of observations. Where data are grouped into classes, the median must be estimated. This is most simply done from a graph of the cumulative frequency distribution, but can also be worked out by assuming the data to be evenly spread within the class. The median may represent the location of the main body of data better than the mean when the distribution is asymmetric or when there are outliers in the sample.

Mode

The mode is the most common value in the sample. The mode is easily found from a tabulated frequency distribution as the most frequent value. If data have been grouped into classes then the term modal class is used for the class containing most values. The mode provides a rapidly and easily found estimate of sample location and is unaffected by outliers. However, the mode is affected by chance variation in the shape of a sample's distribution and it may lie distant from the obvious centre of the distribution. Note that the mode is the only statistic to make sense of qualitative data, e.g. 'the modal (most frequent) eye colour was blue'.

The mean, median and mode have the same units as the variable under discussion. However, whether these statistics of location have the same or similar values for a given frequency distribution depends on the symmetry and shape of the distribution. If it is near-symmetrical with a single peak, all three will be very similar; if it is skewed or has more than one peak, their values will differ to a greater degree (see Fig. 39.3).

Measuring dispersion

Here, the objective is to quantify the spread of the data about the centre of the distribution. Figure 39.5 indicates how to decide which measure of dispersion to use.

Range

The range is the difference between the largest and smallest data values in the sample (the extremes) and has the same units as the measured variable. The range is easy to determine, but is greatly affected by outliers. Its value may also depend on sample size: in general, the larger this is, the greater will be the range. These features make the range a poor measure of dispersion for many practical purposes.

Semi-interquartile range

The semi-interquartile range is an appropriate measure of dispersion when a median is the appropriate statistic to describe location. For this, you need to determine the first and third quartiles, i.e. the medians for those data values

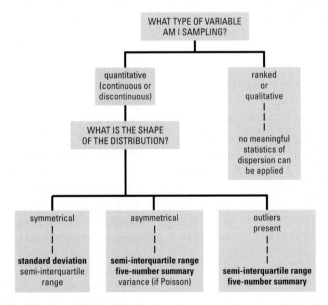

Fig. 39.5 Choosing a statistic for characterizing a distribution's dispersion. Statistics written in bold are the preferred option(s). Note that you should match statistics describing dispersion with those you have used to describe location, i.e. standard deviation with mean, semi-interquartile range with median.

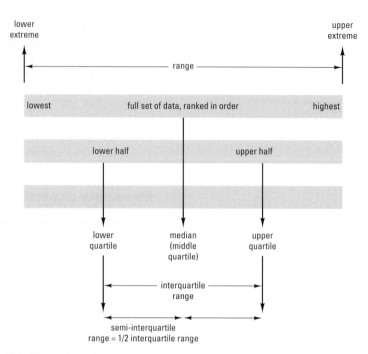

Fig. 39.6   Illustration of median, quartiles, range and semi-interquartile range.

ranked below and above the median of the whole data set (see Fig. 39.6). To calculate a semi-interquartile range for a data set:

1. Rank the observations in ascending order.
2. Find the values of the first and third quartiles.
3. Subtract the value of the first quartile from the value of the third.
4. Halve this number.

For data grouped in classes, the semi-interquartile range can only be estimated. Another disadvantage is that it takes no account of the shape of the distribution at its edges. This objection can be countered by using the so-called 'five number summary' of a data set, which consists of the three quartiles and the two extreme values; this can be presented on graphs as a box and whisker plot (see Fig. 39.7) and is particularly useful for summarizing skewed frequency distributions. The corresponding 'six number summary' includes the sample's size.

Variance and standard deviation

For symmetrical frequency distributions, an ideal measure of dispersion would take into account each value's deviation from the mean and provide a measure of the average deviation from the mean. Two such statistics are the sample variance, which is the sum of squares ($\Sigma(Y - \bar{Y})^2$) divided by $n - 1$ (where n is the sample size), and the sample standard deviation, which is the positive square root of the sample variance.

The variance (s^2) has units which are the square of the original units, while the standard deviation (s) is expressed in the original units, one reason s is often preferred as a measure of dispersion. Calculating s or s^2 longhand is a tedious job and is best done with the help of a calculator or computer. If you

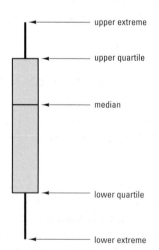

Fig. 39.7   A box and whisker plot, showing the 'five number summary' of a sample as it might be used on a graph.

don't have a calculator that calculates s for you, an alternative formula that simplifies calculations is:

$$s = +\sqrt{\frac{\Sigma Y^2 - (\Sigma Y)^2/n}{n-1}}$$

[39.1]

To calculate s using a calculator:

1. Obtain ΣY, square it, divide by n and store in memory.
2. Square Y values, obtain ΣY^2, subtract memory value from this.
3. Divide this answer by $n - 1$.
4. Take the positive square root of this value.

Take care to retain significant figures, or errors in the final value of s will result. If continuous data have been grouped into classes, the class mid-values or their squares must be multiplied by the appropriate frequencies before summation (see example in Box 39.1). When data values are large, longhand calculations can be simplified by coding the data, e.g. by subtracting a constant from each datum, and decoding when the simplified calculations are complete (see Sokal and Rohlf, 1994).

Coefficient of variation

The coefficient of variation (CoV) is a dimensionless measure of variability relative to location which expresses the sample standard deviation as a percentage of the sample mean, i.e.

$$\text{CoV} = 100s/\bar{Y}\,(\%)$$

[39.2]

This statistic is useful when comparing the relative dispersion of data sets with widely differing means or where different units have been used for the same or similar quantities.

A useful application of the CoV is to compare different analytical methods or procedures, so that you can decide which involves the least proportional error – create a standard stock solution, then base the comparison on the results from several sub-samples analysed by each method. You may find it useful to use the CoV to compare the precision of your own results with those of a manufacturer. The smaller the CoV, the more precise (repeatable) is the apparatus or technique (note: this does not mean that it is necessarily more *accurate*).

Measuring the precision of the sample mean as an estimate of the true value

Most practical exercises are based on a limited number of individual data values (a sample) which are used to make inferences about the population from which they were drawn. For example, the zinc content might be measured in soil samples from 100 sites and used as an estimate of the soil zinc content, with the sample mean ($\bar{Y}$) and sample standard deviation (s) providing estimates of the true values of the underlying population mean (μ) and the population standard deviation (σ). The reliability of the sample mean as an estimate of the true (population) mean can be assessed by calculating the standard error of the sample mean (often abbreviated to standard error or SE), from:

$$\text{SE} = s/\sqrt{n}$$

[39.3]

Using a calculator for statistics – make sure you understand how to enter individual data values and which buttons will give the sample mean (usually shown as $\bar{X}$ or $\bar{x}$) and sample standard deviation (usually shown as σ_{n-1}). In general, you should not use the population standard deviation (usually shown as σ_n).

Descriptive statistics

Strictly, the standard error is an estimate of the standard deviation of the means of n-sized samples from the population. At a practical level, it is clear from eqn 39.3 that the SE is directly affected by sample dispersion and inversely related to sample size. This means that the SE will decrease as the number of data values in the sample increases, giving increased precision.

Summary descriptive statistics for the sample mean are often quoted as $\bar{Y} \pm \mathrm{SE}\,(n)$, with the SE being given to one significant figure more than the mean. You can use such information to carry out a t-test between two samples (Box 39.1); the SE is also useful because it allows calculation of confidence limits for the sample mean (p. 223).

Describing the 'shape' of frequency distributions

Frequency distributions may differ in the following characteristics:

- number of peaks;
- skewness or asymmetry;
- kurtosis or pointedness.

The shape of a frequency distribution of a small sample is affected by chance variation and may not be a fair reflection of the underlying population frequency distribution: check this by comparing repeated samples from the same population or by increasing the sample size. If the original shape were due to random events, it should not appear consistently in repeated samples and should become less obvious as sample size increases.

Genuinely bimodal or polymodal distributions may result from the combination of two or more unimodal distributions, indicating that more than one underlying population is being sampled (Fig. 39.9). An example of a bimodal distribution is the height of adult humans (females and males combined).

A distribution is skewed if it is not symmetrical, a symptom being that the mean, median and mode are not equal (Fig. 39.3). Positive skewness is where the longer 'tail' of the distribution occurs for higher values of the measured variable; negative skewness where the longer tail occurs for lower values.

Kurtosis is the name given to the 'pointedness' of a frequency distribution. A platykurtic frequency distribution is one with a flattened peak, while a leptokurtic frequency distribution is one with a pointed peak (Fig. 39.8). While descriptive terms can be used, based on visual observation of the shape and direction of skew, the degree of skewness and kurtosis can be quantified and statistical tests exist to test the 'significance' of observed values (see Sokal and Rohlf, 1994), but the calculations required are complex and best done with the aid of a computer.

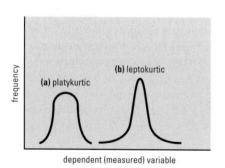

Fig. 39.8 Examples of the two types of kurtosis.

Fig. 39.9 Frequency distributions with different numbers of peaks. A unimodal distribution (a) may be symmetrical or asymmetrical. The dotted lines in (b) indicate how a bimodal distribution could arise from a combination of two underlying unimodal distributions. Note here how the term 'bimodal' is applied to any distribution with two major peaks – their frequencies do not have to be exactly the same.

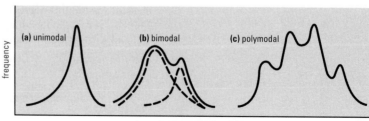

Box 39.2 Three examples where simple arithmetic means are inappropriate

Mean	n
6	4
7	7
8	1

1. If means of samples are themselves meaned, an error can arise if the samples are of different size. For example, the arithmetic mean of the means in the table shown left is 7, but this does not take account of the different 'reliabilities' of each mean due to their sample sizes. The correct weighted mean is obtained by multiplying each mean by its sample size (n) (a 'weight') and dividing the sum of these values by the total number of observations, i.e. in the case shown, $(24 + 49 + 8)/12 = 6.75$.

2. When making a mean of ratios (e.g. percentages) for several groups of different sizes, the ratio for the combined total of all the groups is not the mean of the proportions for the individual groups. For example, if 20 rats from a batch of 50 are male, this implies 40% are male. If 60 rats from a batch of 120 are male, this implies 50% are male. The mean percentage of males $(50 + 40)/2 = 45\%$ is *not* the percentage of males in the two groups combined, because there are $20 + 60 = 80$ males in a total of 170 rats $= 47.1\%$ approx.

pH value	$[H]$ $(mol\ l^{-1})$
6	1×10^{-6}
7	1×10^{-7}
8	1×10^{-8}
mean	3.7×10^{-7}
$-\log_{10}$ mean	6.43

3. If the measurement scale is not linear, arithmetic means may give a false value. For example, if three water samples had pH values 6, 7 and 8, the appropriate mean pH is not 7 because the pH scale is logarithmic. The definition of pH is $-\log_{10}[H]$, where $[H]$ is expressed in $mol\ l^{-1}$ ('molar'); therefore, to obtain the true mean, convert data into $[H]$ values (i.e. put them on a linear scale) by calculating $10^{(-pH\ value)}$ as shown. Now calculate the mean of these values and convert the answer back into pH units. Thus, the appropriate answer is pH 6.43 rather than 7. Note that a similar procedure is necessary when calculating statistics of dispersion in such cases, so you will find these almost certainly asymmetric about the mean.

Mean values of log-transformed data are often termed geometric means – they are sometimes used where log-transformed values for counts are averaged and plotted, rather than using the raw data values. The use of geometric means in such circumstances serves to reduce the effects of outliers on the mean.

This chapter outlines the philosophy of hypothesis-testing statistics, indicates the steps to be taken when choosing a test, and discusses features and assumptions of some important tests. For details of the mechanics of tests, consult appropriate texts (e.g. Wardlaw, 1985; Davis, 1986; Sokal and Rohlf, 1994; Heath, 1995; Walford, 1995). Most tests are now available in statistical packages for computers (see p. 239).

To carry out a statistical test:

1.   Decide what it is you wish to test (create a null hypothesis and its alternative).
2.   Determine whether your data fit a standard distribution pattern.
3.   Select a test and apply it to your data.

Setting up a null hypothesis

Hypothesis-testing statistics are used to compare the properties of samples either with other samples or with some theory about them. For instance, you may be interested in whether two samples can be regarded as having different means, whether the counts of an organism in different quadrats can be regarded as randomly distributed, or whether property A of an organism is linearly related to property B.

KEY POINT   **You can't use statistics to *prove* any hypothesis, but they can be used to assess *how likely* it is to be wrong.**

Statistical testing operates in what at first seems a rather perverse manner. Suppose you think a treatment has an effect. The theory you actually test is that it has no effect; the test tells you how improbable your data would be if this theory were true. This 'no effect' theory is the null hypothesis (NH). If your data are very improbable under the NH, then you may suppose it to be wrong, and this would support your original idea (the 'alternative hypothesis'). The concept can be illustrated by an example. Suppose two groups of subjects were treated in different ways, and you observed a difference in the mean value of the measured variable for the two groups. Can this be regarded as a 'true' difference? As Fig. 40.1 shows, it could have arisen in two ways:

● Because of the way the subjects were allocated to treatments, i.e. all the subjects liable to have high values might, by chance, have been assigned to one group and those with low values to the other (Fig. 40.1a).
● Because of a genuine effect of the treatments, i.e. each group came from a distinct frequency distribution (Fig. 40.1b).

A statistical test will indicate the probabilities of these options. The NH states that the two groups come from the same population (i.e. the treatment effects are negligible in the context of random variation). To test this, you calculate a test statistic from the data, and compare it with tabulated critical values giving the probability of obtaining the observed or a more extreme result by chance (see Boxes 40.1 and 40.2). This probability is sometimes called the significance of the test.

Note that you must take into account the degrees of freedom (d.f.) when looking up critical values of most test statistics. The d.f. is related to the size(s) of the samples studied; formulae for calculating it depend on the test

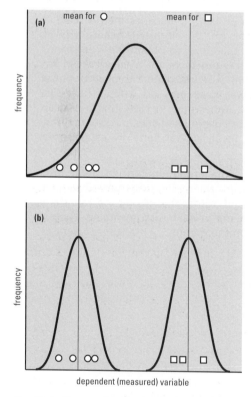

Fig. 40.1 Two explanations for the difference between two means. In case (a) the two samples happen by chance to have come from opposite ends of the same frequency distribution, i.e. there is no true difference between the samples. In case (b) the two samples come from different frequency distributions, i.e. there is a true difference between the samples. In both cases, the means of the two samples are the same.

Definition

Modulus – the absolute value of a number, e.g. modulus $-3.385 = 3.385$.

being used. Environmental scientists normally use two-tailed tests, i.e. we have no certainty beforehand that the treatment will have a positive or negative effect compared to the control (in a one-tailed test we expect one particular treatment to be bigger than the other). Be sure to use critical values for the correct type of test.

By convention, the critical probability for rejecting the NH is 5% (i.e. $P = 0.05$). This means we reject the NH if the observed result would have come up less than one time in twenty by chance. If the modulus of the test statistic is less than the tabulated critical value for $P = 0.05$, then we accept the NH and the result is said to be 'not significant' (NS for short). If the modulus of the test statistic is greater than the tabulated value for $P = 0.05$, then we reject the NH in favour of the alternative hypothesis that the treatments had different effects and the result is 'statistically significant'.

Two types of error are possible when making a conclusion on the basis of a statistical test. The first occurs if you reject the NH when it is true and the second if you accept the NH when it is false. To limit the chance of the first type of error, choose a lower probability, e.g. $P = 0.01$, but note that the critical value of the test statistic increases when you do this and results in the probability of the second error increasing. The conventional significance levels given in statistical tables (usually 0.05, 0.01, 0.001) are arbitrary. Increasing use of statistical computer programs is likely to lead to the actual probability of obtaining the calculated value of the test statistic being quoted (e.g. $P = 0.037$).

Note that if the NH is rejected, this does not tell you which of many alternative hypotheses is true. Also, it is important to distinguish between statistical and practical significance: identifying a statistically significant difference between two samples doesn't mean that this will carry any biological importance.

Comparing data with parametric distributions

A parametric test is one which makes particular assumptions about the mathematical nature of the population distribution from which the samples were taken. If these assumptions are not true, then the test is obviously invalid, even though it might give the answer we expect! A non-parametric test does not assume that the data fit a particular pattern, but it may assume some things about the distributions. Used in appropriate circumstances, parametric tests are better able to distinguish between true but marginal differences between samples than their non-parametric equivalents (i.e. they have greater 'power').

Choosing between parametric and non-parametric tests – always plot your data graphically when determining whether they are suitable for parametric tests as this may save a lot of unnecessary effort later.

The distribution pattern of a set of data values may be environmentally relevant, but it is also of practical importance because it defines the type of statistical tests that can be used. The properties of the main distribution types found in biology are given below with both rules-of-thumb and more rigorous tests for deciding whether data fit these distributions.

Binomial distributions

These apply to samples of any size from populations when data values occur independently in only two mutually exclusive classes (e.g. type A or type B). They describe the probability of finding the different possible combinations of the attribute for a specified sample size k (e.g. out of 10 specimens, what is the chance of 8 being type A). If p is the probability of the attribute being of type A and q the probability of it being type B, then the expected mean

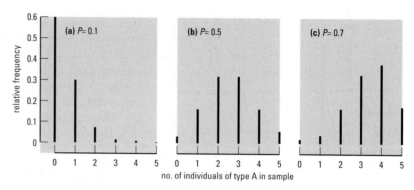

Fig. 40.2 Examples of binomial frequency distributions with different probabilities. The distributions show the expected frequency of obtaining *n* individuals of type A in a sample of 5. Here *P* is the probability of an individual being type A rather than type B.

sample number of type A is kp and the standard deviation is $\sqrt{kpq}$. Expected frequencies can be calculated using mathematical expressions (see Sokal and Rohlf, 1994). Examples of the shapes of some binomial distributions are shown in Fig. 40.2. Note that they are symmetrical in shape for the special case $p = q = 0.5$ and the greater the disparity between p and q, the more skewed the distribution.

Some examples of data likely to be distributed in binomial fashion are: whether an organism is infected with a microbe or not; whether an animal is male or female. To establish whether a set of data is distributed in binomial fashion: calculate expected frequencies from probability values obtained from theory or observation, then test against observed frequencies using a χ^2-test or a *G*-test.

Poisson distributions

These apply to discrete characteristics which can assume low whole number values, such as counts of events occurring in area, volume or time. The events should be 'rare' in that the mean number observed should be a small proportion of the total that could possibly be found. Also, finding one count should not influence the probability of finding another. The shape of Poisson distributions is described by only one parameter, the mean number of events observed, and has the special characteristic that the variance is equal to the mean. The shape has a pronounced positive skewness at low mean counts, but becomes more and more symmetrical as the mean number of counts increases (Fig. 40.3).

Some examples of characteristics distributed in a Poisson fashion are: number of plants in a quadrat; number of microbes per unit volume of medium; number of animals parasitized per unit time; number of radioactive disintegrations per unit time. One of the main uses for the Poisson distribution is to quantify errors in count data such as estimates of densities in dilute particle suspensions. To decide whether data are Poisson distributed:

- Use the rule-of-thumb that if the coefficient of dispersion ≈ 1, the distribution is likely to be Poisson.
- Calculate 'expected' frequencies from the equation for the Poisson distribution and compare with actual values using a χ^2-test or a *G*-test.

Tendency towards the normal distribution – under certain conditions, binomial and Poisson distributions can be treated as normally distributed:

- where samples from a binomial distribution are large (i.e. > 15) and p and q are close to 0.5;
- for Poisson distributions, if the number of counts recorded in each outcome is greater than about 15.

Definition

Coefficient of dispersion $= s^2 / \bar{Y}$. This is an alternative measure of dispersion to the coefficient of variation (p. 213).

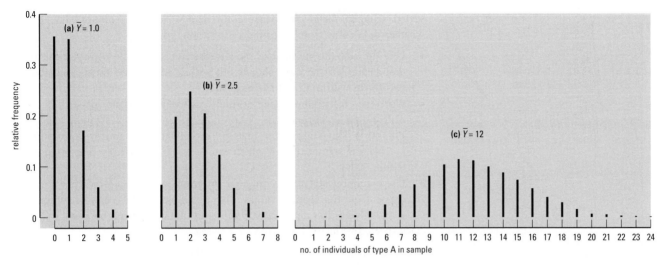

Fig. 40.3 Examples of Poisson frequency distributions differing in mean. The distributions are shown as line charts because the independent variable (events per sample) is discrete.

It is sometimes of interest to show that data are *not* distributed in a Poisson fashion, e.g. the distribution of parasite larvae in hosts. If $s^2/\bar{Y} > 1$, the data are 'clumped' and occur together more than would be expected by chance; if $s^2/\bar{Y} < 1$, the data are 'repulsed' and occur together less frequently than would be expected by chance.

Normal distributions (Gaussian distributions)

These occur when random events act to produce variability in a continuous characteristic (quantitative variable). This situation occurs frequently in environmental science, so normal distributions are very useful and much used. The bell-like shape of normal distributions is specified by the population mean and standard deviation (Fig. 40.4): it is symmetrical and configured such that 68.27% of the data will lie within ± 1 standard deviation of the mean, 95.45% within ± 2 standard deviations of the mean, and 99.73% within ± 3 standard deviations of the mean.

Some examples of data likely to be distributed in a normal fashion are: fresh weight of plants of the same age; linear dimensions of sand grains in a

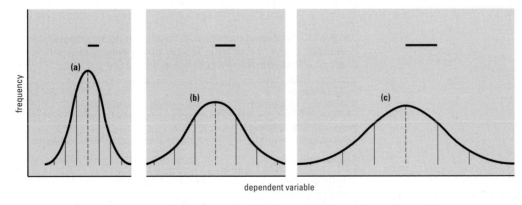

Fig. 40.4 Examples of normal frequency distributions differing in mean and standard deviation. The horizontal bars represent population standard deviations for the curves, increasing from (a) to (c). Vertical dashed lines are population means, while vertical solid lines show positions of values ± 1, 2 and 3 standard deviations from the means.

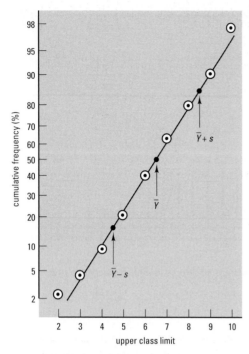

Fig. 40.5 Example of a normal probability plot. The plotted points are from a small data set where the mean $\bar{Y} = 6.93$ and the standard deviation $s = 1.895$. Note that values corresponding to 0% and 100% cumulative frequency cannot be used. The straight line is that predicted for a normal distribution with $\bar{Y} = 6.93$ and $s = 1.895$. This is plotted by calculating the expected positions of points for $\bar{Y} \pm s$. Since 68.3% of the distribution falls within these bounds, the relevant points on the cumulative frequency scale are $50 \pm 34.15\%$; thus this line was drawn using the points (4.495, 15.85) and (8.285, 84.15) as indicated on the plot.

sorted sediment height of either adult female or male humans. To check whether data come from a normal distribution, you can:

- Use the rule-of-thumb that the distribution should be symmetrical and that nearly all the data should fall within $\pm 3s$ of the mean and about two-thirds within $\pm 1s$ of the mean.
- Plot the distribution on normal probability graph paper. If the distribution is normal, the data will tend to follow a straight line (see Fig. 40.5). Deviations from linearity reveal skewness and/or kurtosis (see p. 214), the significance of which can be tested statistically (see Sokal and Rohlf, 1994).
- Use a suitable statistical computer program to generate predicted normal curves from the $\bar{Y}$ and s values of your sample(s). These can be compared visually with the actual distribution of data and can be used to give 'expected' values for a χ^2-test or a G-test.

The wide availability of tests based on the normal distribution and their relative simplicity means you may wish to transform your data to make them more like a normal distribution. Table 40.1 provides transformations that can be applied (see also Fig. 35.3). The transformed data should be tested for normality as described above before proceeding – don't forget that you may need to check that transformed variances are homogeneous for certain tests (see below).

A very important theorem in statistics, the Central Limit Theorem, states that as sample size increases, the distribution of a series of means from any frequency distribution will become normally distributed. This fact can be used to devise an experimental or sampling strategy that ensures that data are normally distributed, i.e. using means of samples as if they were primary data.

Choosing a suitable statistical test

Comparing location (e.g. means)

If you can assume that your data are normally distributed, the main test for comparing two means from independent samples is Student's t-test (see Boxes 40.1 and 40.2, and Table 40.2). This assumes that the variances of the data sets are homogeneous. Tests based on the t-distribution are also available for comparing paired data or for comparing a sample mean with a chosen value.

When comparing means of two or more samples, analysis of variance (ANOVA) is a very useful technique. This method also assumes data are

Table 40.1 Suggested transformations altering different types of frequency distribution to the normal type. To use, modify data by the formula shown; then examine effects with the tests described on p. 217–19.

Type of data; distribution suspected	Suggested transformation(s)
Proportions (including percentages); binomial	arcsine $\sqrt{x}$ (also called the angular transformation)
Scores; Poisson	$\sqrt{x}$ or $\sqrt{(x + 1/2)}$ if zero values present
Measurements; negatively skewed	x^2, x^3, x^4, etc. (in order of increasing strength)
Measurements; positively skewed	$1/\sqrt{x}$, $\sqrt{x}$, ln x, $1/x$ (in order of increasing strength)

Box 40.1 How to carry out a *t*-test

The *t*-test was devised by a statistician who used the pen-name 'Student', so you may see it referred to as Student's *t*-test. It is used when you wish to decide whether two samples come from the same population or from different ones (Fig. 40.1). The samples might have been obtained by selective observation or by applying two different treatments to an originally homogeneous population (Chapter 12).

The null hypothesis (NH) is that the two groups can be represented as samples from the same overlying population (Fig. 40.1a). If, as a result of the test, you accept this hypothesis, you can say that there is no significant difference between the groups.

The alternative hypothesis is that the two groups come from different populations (Fig. 40.1b). By rejecting the NH as a result of the test, you can accept the alternative hypothesis and say that there is a significant difference between the samples, or, if an experiment were carried out, that the two treatments affected the samples differently.

How can you decide between these two hypotheses? On the basis of certain assumptions (see below), and some relatively simple calculations, you can work out the probability that the samples came from the same population. If this probability is very low, then you can reasonably reject the NH in favour of the alternative hypothesis, and if it is high, you will accept the NH.

To find out the probability that the observed difference between sample means arose by chance, you must first calculate a '*t* value' for the two samples in question. Some computer programs (e.g. Minitab®) provide this probability as part of the output, otherwise you can look up statistical tables (e.g. Table 40.2). These tables show 'critical values' – the borders between probability levels. If your value of *t* exceeds the critical value for probability *P*, you can reject the NH at this probability ('level of significance').

Note that:

- for a given difference in the means of the two samples, the value of *t* will get larger the smaller the scatter within each data set; and
- for a given scatter of the data, the value of *t* will get larger, the greater the difference between the means.

So, at what probability should you reject the NH? Normally, the threshold is arbitrarily set at 5% – you quite often see descriptions like 'the sample means were significantly different (P < 0.05)'. At this 'significance level' there is still up to a 5% chance of the *t* value arising by chance, so about 1 in 20 times, on average, the conclusion will be wrong. If *P* turns out to be lower, then this kind of error is much less likely.

Tabulated probability levels are generally given for 5%, 1% and 0.1% significance levels (see Table 40.2). Note that this table is designed for 'two-tailed' tests, i.e. where the treatment or sampling strategy could have resulted in either an increase or a decrease in the measured values. These are the most likely situations you will deal with in environmental science.

Examine Table 40.2 and note the following:

- The larger the size of the samples (i.e. the greater the 'degrees of freedom'), the smaller *t* needs to be to exceed the critical value at a given significance level.
- The lower the probability, the greater *t* needs to be to exceed the critical value.

The mechanics of the test

A calculator that can work out means and standard deviations is helpful.

1. **Work out the sample means $\bar{Y}_1$ and $\bar{Y}_2$ and calculate the difference between them.**

2. **Work out the sample standard deviations s_1 and s_2.** (NB if your calculator offers a choice, chose the 'n-1' option for calculating s – see p. 213).

3. **Work out the sample standard errors $SE_1 = s_1/\sqrt{n_1}$ and $SE_2 = s_2/\sqrt{n_2}$; now square each, add the squares together, then take the square root of this** (n_1 and n_2 are the respective sample sizes, which may, or may not, not be equal).

4. **Calculate *t* from the formula:**

$$t = \frac{\bar{Y}_1 - \bar{Y}_2}{\sqrt{((SE_1)^2 + (SE_2)^2)}} \qquad [40.1]$$

The value of *t* can be negative or positive, depending on the values of the means; this does not matter and you should compare the modulus (absolute value) of *t* with the values in tables.

5. **Work out the degrees of freedom $= (n_1 - 1) + (n_2 - 1)$.**

6. **Compare the *t* value with the appropriate critical value (see e.g. Table 40.2).**

Box 40.2 provides a worked example – use this to check that you understand the above procedures.

Assumptions that must be met before using the test
The most important assumptions are:

- The two samples are independent and randomly drawn (or if not, drawn in a way that does not create bias). The test assumes that the samples are quite large.
- The underlying distribution of each sample is normal. This can be tested with a special statistical test, but a rule of thumb is that a frequency distribution of the data should be (a) symmetrical about the mean and (b) nearly all of the data should be within 3 standard deviations of the mean and about two-thirds within 1 standard deviation of the mean (see p. 223).
- The two samples should have equal variances. This again can be tested (by an F-test), but may be obvious from inspection of the two standard deviations.

Box 40.2   Worked example of a *t*-test

Suppose the following data were obtained in an experiment (the units are not relevant):

Control: 6.6, 5.5, 6.8, 5.8, 6.1, 5.9
Treatment: 6.3, 7.2, 6.5, 7.1, 7.5, 7.3

Using the steps outlined in Box 40.1, the following values are obtained (denoting control with subscript 1, treatment with subscript 2):

1. $\bar{Y}_1 = 6.1167$; $\bar{Y}_2 = 6.9833$:   difference between means $= \bar{Y}_1 - \bar{Y}_2 = -0.8666$

2. $s_1 = 0.49565$; $s_2 = 0.47504$

3. $SE_1 = 0.49565/2.44949 = 0.202348$
    $SE_2 = 0.47504/2.44949 = 0.193934$

4. $t = \dfrac{-0.8666}{\sqrt{(0.202348^2 + 0.193934^2)}} = \dfrac{-0.8666}{0.280277} = -3.09$

5. d.f. $= (5 + 5) = 10$

6. Looking at Table 40.2, we see that the modulus of this *t* value exceeds the tabulated value for $P = 0.05$ at 10 degrees of freedom ($= 2.23$). We therefore reject the NH, and conclude that the means are different at the 5% level of significance. If the modulus of *t* had been < 2.23, we would have accepted the NH. If modulus of *t* had been > 3.17, we could have concluded that the means are different at the 1% level of significance.

Table 40.2   Critical values of Student's *t* statistic (for two-tailed tests). Reject the Null Hypothesis at probability *P* if your calculated *t* value exceeds the value shown for the appropriate degrees of freedom $= (n_1 - 1) + (n_2 - 1)$

Degrees of freedom	Critical values for $P = 0.05$	Critical values for $P = 0.01$	Critical values for $P = 0.001$
1	12.71	63.66	636.62
2	4.30	9.92	31.60
3	3.18	5.84	12.94
4	2.78	4.60	8.61
5	2.57	4.03	6.86
6	2.45	3.71	5.96
7	2.36	3.50	5.40
8	2.31	3.36	5.04
9	2.26	3.25	4.78
10	2.23	3.17	4.59
12	2.18	3.06	4.32
14	2.14	2.98	4.14
16	2.12	2.92	4.02
20	2.09	2.85	3.85
25	2.06	2.79	3.72
30	2.04	2.75	3.65
40	2.02	2.70	3.55
60	2.00	2.66	3.46
120	1.98	2.62	3.37
∞	1.96	2.58	3.29

normally distributed and that the variances of the samples are homogeneous. The samples must also be independent (e.g. not sub-samples). The nested types of ANOVA are useful for letting you know the relative importance of different sources of variability in your data. Two-way and multi-way ANOVAs are useful for studying interactions between treatments.

For data satisfying the ANOVA requirements, the least significant difference (LSD) is useful for making planned comparisons among several means. Any two means that differ by more than the LSD will be significantly different. The LSD is useful for showing on graphs.

The chief non-parametric tests for comparing the locations of two samples are the Mann–Whitney *U*-test and the Kolmogorov–Smirnov test. The former assumes that the frequency distributions of the samples are similar,

Checking the assumptions of a test – always acquaint yourself with the assumptions of a test. If necessary, test them before using the test.

whereas the latter makes no such assumption. In both cases the sample's size must be $\geqslant 4$ and for the Kolmogorov–Smirnov test the samples must have equal sizes. In the Kolmogorov–Smirnov test, significant differences found with the test could be due to differences in location or shape of the distribution, or both.

Suitable non-parametric comparisons of location for paired data (sample size $\geqslant 6$) include Wilcoxon's signed rank test, which is used for quantitative data and assumes that the distributions have similar shape. Dixon and Mood's sign test can be used for paired data scores where one variable is recorded as 'greater than' or 'better than' the other.

Non-parametric comparisons of location for three or more samples include the Kruskal–Wallis H-test. Here, the number of samples is without limit and they can be unequal in size, but again the underlying distributions are assumed to be similar. The Friedman S-test operates with a maximum of 5 samples and data must conform to a randomized block design. The underlying distributions of the samples are assumed to be similar.

Comparing dispersions (e.g. variances)

If you wish to compare the variances of two sets of data that are normally distributed, use the F-test. For comparing more than two samples, it may be sufficient to use the F_{max}-test, on the highest and lowest variances. The Scheffé–Box (log-anova) test is recommended for testing the significance of differences between several variances. Non-parametric tests exist but are not widely available: you may need to transform the data and use a test based on the normal distribution.

Determining whether frequency observations fit theoretical expectation

The χ^2-test is useful for tests of 'goodness of fit', e.g. comparing expected and observed progeny frequencies in genetical experiments or comparing observed frequency distributions with some theoretical function. One limitation is that simple formulae for calculating χ^2 assume that no expected number is less than 5. The G-test ($2I$ test) is used in similar circumstances.

Comparing proportion data

When comparing proportions between two small groups (e.g. whether 3/10 is significantly different from 5/10), you can use probability tables such as those of Finney et al., (1963) or calculate probabilities from formulae; however, this can be tedious for large sample sizes. Certain proportions can be transformed so that their distribution becomes normal.

Placing confidence limits on an estimate of a population parameter

On many occasions, sample statistics are used to provide an estimate of the population parameters. It is extremely useful to indicate the reliability of such estimates. This can be done by putting a confidence limit on the sample statistic. The most common application is to place confidence limits on the mean of a sample from a normally distributed population. This is done by working out the limits as $\bar{Y} - (t_{P[n-1]} \times SE)$ and $\bar{Y} + (t_{P[n-1]} \times SE)$ where $t_{P[n-1]}$ is the tabulated critical value of Student's t statistic for a two-tailed test with $n-1$ degrees of freedom and SE is the standard error of the mean (p. 213). A 95% confidence limit (i.e. $P = 0.05$) tells you that on average, 95 times out of 100, this limit will contain the population mean.

Confidence limits for statistics other than the mean – consult an advanced statistical text (e.g. Sokal and Rohlf, 1994) if you wish to indicate the reliability of estimates of e.g. population variances.

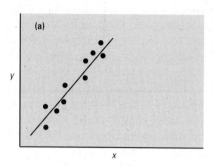

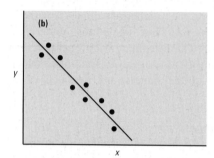

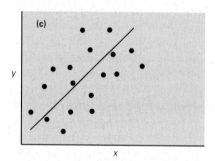

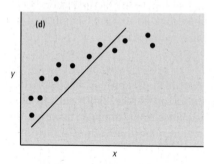

Fig. 40.6 Examples of correlation. The linear regression line is shown. In (a) and (b), the correlation between x and y is good: for (a) there is a positive correlation and the correlation coefficient would be close to 1; for (b) there is a negative correlation and the correlation coefficient would be close to −1. In (c) there is a weak positive correlation and r would be close to 0. In (d) the correlation coefficient may be quite large, but the choice of linear regression is clearly inappropriate.

Regression and correlation

These methods are used when testing relationships between samples of two variables. If one variable is assumed to be dependent on the other then regression techniques are used to find the line of best fit for your data. This does not tell you how well the data fit the line: for this, a correlation coefficient must be calculated. If there is no *a priori* reason to assume dependency between variables, correlation methods alone are appropriate.

If graphs or theory indicate a linear relationship between a dependent and an independent variable, linear regression can be used to estimate the equation that links them. If the relationship is not linear, try a transformation (see p. 192). For example, this is commonly done in analysis of ecoloxicology. However, 'linearizations' can lead to errors when carrying out regression analysis: take care to ensure (a) that the data are evenly distributed throughout the range of the independent variable and (b) that the variances of the dependent variable are homogeneous. If these criteria cannot be met, weighting methods may reduce errors. In this situation, it may be better to use non-linear regression but this involves complex calculations best handled by a suitable computer program.

Model I linear regression is suitable for experiments where a dependent variable Y varies with an *error-free* independent variable X and the mean (expected) value of Y is given by $a + bX$. This might occur where you have carefully controlled the independent variable and it can therefore be assumed to have zero error (e.g. a calibration curve). Errors can be calculated for estimates of a and b and predicted values of Y. The Y values should be normally distributed and the variance of Y constant at all values of X.

Model II linear regression is suitable for experiments where a dependent variable Y varies with an independent variable X which has an error associated with it and the mean (expected) value of Y is given by $a + bX$. This might occur where the experimenter is measuring two variables and believes there to be a causal relationship between them; both variables will be subject to errors in this case. The exact method to use depends on whether your aim is to estimate the functional relationship or to estimate one variable from the other.

A correlation coefficient measures the strength of relationships but does not describe the relationship. These coefficients are expressed as a number between −1 and 1. A positive coefficient indicates a positive relationship while a negative coefficient indicates a negative relationship (Fig. 40.6). The nearer the coefficient is to −1 or 1, the stronger the relationship between the variables, i.e. the less scatter there would be about a line of best fit (note that this does not imply that one variable is dependent on the other!). A coefficient of 0 implies that there is no relationship between the variables. The importance of graphing data is shown by the case illustrated in Fig. 40.6d.

Pearson's product-moment correlation coefficient (r) is the most commonly used correlation coefficient. If both variables are normally distributed, then r can be used in statistical tests to test whether the degree of correlation is significant. If one or both variables are not normally distributed you can use Kendall's coefficient of rank correlation (τ) or Spearman's coefficient of rank correlation (r_s). They require that data are ranked separately and calculation can be complex if there are tied ranks. Spearman's coefficient is said to be better if there is uncertainty about the reliability of closely ranked data values.

Information technology and library resources

The Internet and World Wide Web

Definitions

Browser – a program to display Web pages and other Internet resources.
FAQ – Frequently Asked Question; sometimes used as a file extension (.faq) for down-loadable files.
FTP – File Transfer Protocol; means of down-loading files.
URL – Uniform Resource Locator: the 'address' for WWW resources.

Making the most of information technology ('IT') requires skills related to the use of computers for finding, retrieving, recording, analysing and communicating information, especially via the developing global Internet environment. This includes using programs for:

- searching databases and Internet resources, e.g. using Web 'browsers' such as Netscape™;
- retrieving network resources, e.g. applying FTP to obtain copies of files;
- storing, modifying and analysing information, e.g. using databases, spreadsheets and statistical packages (see Chapters 42 and 44);
- communicating information, e.g. by e-mail, word processors, desk-top publishing packages and programs for making presentations (see Chapters 43 and 44).

The Internet as a global resource

The key to the rapid development of the Internet was the evolution and expansion of networks – collections of computers which can communicate with each other. They operate at various scales such as Local Area Networks (LANs) and Wide Area Networks (WANs) and these are connected to the Internet, which is thus a complex network of networks (Fig. 41.1). The Internet is loosely organized; no one group runs it or owns it. Instead, many private organizations, universities and government organizations pay for and run discrete parts of it. Private organizations include commercial on-line service providers such as America On-line™ and CompuServe™.

You can gain access to the Internet either through a LAN at your place of work or from home via a modem connected to a dial-in service provider over the telephone line. You do not need to understand the technology of the network to use it – most of it is invisible to the user. However, if you do wish to understand more, sources such as Gralla (1996) and Winship and McNab (1996) are recommended. What you do need to know are the options available to you in terms of using its facilities and their relative merits or disadvantages. You also need to understand a little about the nature of Internet addresses.

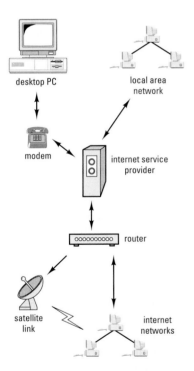

Fig. 41.1 Diagram of a network system.

desktop PC

local area network

modem

internet service provider

router

satellite link

internet networks

> **KEY POINT** Most material on the Internet has not been subject to peer review, vetting or editing. Information obtained from the WWW or posted on newsgroups may be inaccurate, biased or spoof; do not assume that everything you read is true or even legal.

Communicating on the Internet: e-mail and newsgroups

Using e-mail, you are able to send messages to anyone who is connected to the Internet, directly or indirectly. You can attach text files, data files, pictures, video clips, sounds and executable files to your messages. The messages themselves are usually only very simple in format but sufficient for most purposes: formatted material can be attached as a file if necessary. The uses that can be made of the system vary from personal and business-related

The Internet and World Wide Web

Examples Common domains and sub-domains include:

.com	commercial (USA mainly)
.edu	education (USA mainly)
.gov	government (USA only)
.mil	military (USA only)
.net	network companies
.org	organization
.au	Australia
.uk	United Kingdom

Newsgroups – these can be useful for getting answers to a specific problem: just post a query to the appropriate group and wait for someone to reply with an answer. You can find out about relevant newsgroups using your browser.

Locating information on the WWW – useful searching systems are located at the following URLs (some may be directly accessible from your browser):

http://www.altavista.com

http://www.goto.com/

http://www.lycos.com/

http://www.webcrawler.com/

http://www.yahoo.com

http://www.mamma.com/

http://www.go2net.com/search.htm/

to the submission of work to a tutor in an educational system. Note, however, that the system is not secure (confidential) and the transmission of sensitive information should be done with caution. Another downside of e-mail is the junk-mail that you may receive once your e-mail address is distributed, e.g. in newsletters.

Specific address information is required to exchange information and mail between computers. Although the computer actually uses a complex series of numbers for this purpose (the 'I.P.' address), the Domain Name System/Service (DNS) was developed to make this easier for users. Each computer on the Internet is given a domain name (= Internet address) which is a hierarchy of lists and addresses. Thus, 'dundee.ac.uk' is the DNS-registered name of Dundee University: the top (root) level domain is 'uk', identifying its country as United Kingdom, and the next is 'ac', identifying the academic community sub-domain. The final sub-domain is 'dundee' identifying the specific academic institute. For the purposes of e-mail, the names of individuals at that site may be added before the domain name and the @ sign is used to separate them. Thus, the e-mail address of the first author of this book is 'a.m.jones@dundee.ac.uk' and this is unique to him.

The Usenet Newsgroup service is an electronic discussion facility, and there are thousands of newsgroups representing different interests and topics. Any user can contribute to the discussion within a topic by posting his/her own message: it is like e-mail, but without privacy, since your message becomes available to all other subscribers. To access a newsgroup, your system must be running, or have access to, a newsgroup server and this must itself subscribe to the newsgroup. Obtain a list of newsgroups available on your system and search it for ones of interest, then join them. Contact your network administrator if you wish to propose the addition of a specific newsgroup. Be prepared for large amounts of information to be produced.

Internet tools

There are various facilities available for use on the Internet depending on your own system and method of accessing the system. The best way to learn how to use them is simply to try them out.

The World Wide Web (WWW) The 'Web' is the most popular Internet application. It allows easy links to information and files which may be located on computers anywhere in the world. The WWW allows access to millions of 'home pages' or 'Web sites', the initial point of reference with companies, institutes and individuals. Besides their own text and images, these contain 'hypertext links', highlighted words or phrases that you click on to take you to another page on the same Web site or to a completely different site with related subject material. Certain sites specialize in such links, acting like indices to other Web sites: these are particularly useful.

When using a Web browser program to get to a particular page of information on the Web all you require is the name and location of that page. The page location is commonly referred to as a URL (Uniform Resource Locator). The URL always takes the same basic format, beginning with 'http://' and followed by the various terms which direct the system to the resource pages. If you don't have a specific URL in mind but wish to find appropriate sites, use a 'search engine' within the browser: enter

Wide Area Information Systems – the WWW is an example of a WAIS, but there are others. Use Telnet to access other public WAIS systems on the Internet. 'Gophers' can be used to search one WAIS database at a time. Gophers are predecessors of Web browsers but use text only. They are menu-based and allow you to navigate through 'Gopher-space' using searching systems such as *Veronica*. This is much more powerful than using Telnet or Gopher alone.

appropriate and limited keywords on which to search and note the site(s) which may be of interest. There is so much available on the Web, from company products through library resources to detailed information on specialist biological and environmental topics, that much time can be spent searching and reading information: try to stay focused!

Telnet This is a simple system allowing connection between computers on the net so that they work as if you were directly connected to each. It is most frequently used to access structured collections such as a library catalogue or bibliographic database. You normally follow a pre-arranged connection routine involving log-in passwords, but some sites will allow limited access to users who log in as 'guest'. An easy way to discover the uses of Telnet is to log into *http://access.usask.ca* and type *hytelnet* at the log-in prompt.

FTP (File Transfer Protocol) and file transmission FTP is a method of transferring files across the Internet. In many cases the files are made available for 'anonymous' FTP access, i.e. you do not need previously arranged passwords. Log in as 'anonymous' and give your e-mail address as the password. Use your Web browser to locate the file you want and then use its FTP software to transfer it to your computer.

KEY POINT **The transfer of files can result in the transfer of associated viruses. Always check your files for viruses before running them.**

Archie This searching system keeps track of the main FTP servers on the Internet. Use it for locating a file by specifying the name of the file or search keywords, and it will locate the file or files for you. You can use Archie either by e-mailing your request to *archie@archie.doc.ic.ac.uk* with the message: 'find keyword/s' or by Telnet to an Archie site and typing the *find* command at the prompt. Use *quit* to finish.

Using the Internet as a resource

Traditional sources – remember that using the Internet to find information is not a substitute for visiting your university library. Internet resources complement rather than replace more traditional printed and CD-ROM sources.

A common way of finding information on the Internet is by browsing or 'surfing'. However, this can be time-consuming: try to restrict yourself to sites of known relevance to the problem being addressed. The most useful sites are often those which provide hypertext links to other locations. Good places to start might be the U.S. Geological Survey site at http://www.usgs.gov/ which covers most aspects of environmental science, or the Virtual Library: Science at http://www.vlib.org/Science.html.

Some of the main resources you can use on the WWW are:

Remembering useful Web sites – create a 'bookmark' for the ones you find of value, to make revisiting easy. This can be done from the menu of your browser program. Make a copy of your bookmark file occasionally, to avoid loss of this information.

- Libraries, publishers and commercial organizations – information on literature can be obtained from many sites (see below for some examples), and those such as BIDS (Bath Information and Database Services) provide access to abstracts of recent publications; use this *via* the WWW (http://www.bids.ac.uk) or Telnet to search for relevant literature for topics specified by keywords. Many publishers such as Pearson Education (http://www.pearsoneduc.com/catalogue.html) provide on-line catalogues.
- On-line journals – a number of traditional journals have Web sites. You can keep up to date by visiting *Nature* (http://www.nature.com/), *New*

The Internet and World Wide Web

Table 41.1 Examples of selected WWW sites of environmental interest

---

The World-Wide Web Virtual Library: Demography and Population Studies (http://coombs.anu.edu.au/ResFacilities/DemographyPage.html)

LSU Libraries Webliography: Environmental Science Internet Resources (http://www.lib.lsu.edu/sci/chem/internet/environmental.html)

Sea WiFS Project: (NASA) (http://seawifs.gsfc.nasa.gov/SEAWIFS.html)

Global Hydrology Links (http://www.hwr.arizona.edu/hydro_link.html)

The World-Wide Web virtual library: Earth Sciences (http://www.geo.ucalgary.ca/VL-EarthSciences.html)

Natural History Museum (UK) (http://www.nhm.ac.uk)

Access to all UK university library catalogues (http://www.niss.ac.uk/reference/opacs.html)

Note that the above URLs may change – make a keyword search using a search engine to find a particular web site if necessary.

Scientist (http://www.newscientist.com) and *Scientific American* (http://www.sciam.com/) Web sites. Journals published in electronic format are becoming available, e.g. *Radiation and Environmental Biophysics* at http://www.bio.net:80/bioarchives/BIO-JOURNALS/RAD_ENVIRON_BIOPHYS/) but they frequently require a subscription for access; check whether your institute is a subscriber.

- Data and pictures – archives of text material, video clips and photographs can be accessed, and much of the material is available for downloading using Telnet and anonymous FTP. Remember the copyright laws, however, if you intend using it for any form of publication or report.
- Institutions – many government departments, museums, research laboratories, zoos, culture collections and other institutions around the world are now on-line, providing various resources. Use their sites to obtain specific information and data sets. They frequently provide lists of other relevant sites or topics.
- Databases – many databases such as censuses and environmental measurements are accessible from the Internet. Databases of employment are available as are the prospectuses and course details of universities around the world.

When using information technology, including the Internet, always remember the basic rules of using computers and networks (Box 41.1).

Box 41.1 Important guidelines for using microcomputers and networks

Hardware
- Don't drink or smoke around the computer.
- Try not to turn the computer off more than is necessary.
- Never turn off the electricity supply to the machine while in use.
- Rest your eyes at frequent intervals if working for extended periods at a computer monitor.
- Never try to re-format the hard disk except in special circumstances.

Floppy disks
- Protect floppy disks when not in use by keeping them in holders or boxes.
- Never touch a floppy disk's recording surface.
- Keep disks away from dampness, excess heat or cold.
- Keep disks well away from magnets; remember these are present in e.g. loudspeakers, TVs, etc.
- Don't use disks from others unless first checked for viruses.
- Don't insert or remove a disk from the drive when it is operating (drive light on).
- Try not to leave a disk in the drive when you switch the computer off.

File management
- Always use virus-checking programs on imported files before running them.
- Make backups of all important files and at frequent intervals (say every half hour) during the production of your own work e.g. when using a word processor or spreadsheet.
- Periodically clear out and reorganize your file storage areas.

Network rules
- Be polite when sending messages.
- Never attempt to 'hack' into other people's files.
- Do not play games without approval – they can hinder the operation of the system.
- Periodically reorganize your e-mail folder(s). These rapidly become filled with acknowledgements and redundant messages which reduce server efficiency.
- Remember to log out of the network when finished: others can access your files if you forget to log out.

The Golden Rule – always make backup copies of important disks/files and store them well away from your working copies. Be sure that the same accident cannot happen to both copies.

42 Using spreadsheets

Definitions

Spreadsheet – a display of a grid of cells into which numbers, text or formulae can be typed to form a worksheet. Each cell is uniquely identifiable by its column and row number combination (i.e. its 2-D coordinates) and can contain a formula which makes it possible for an entry to one cell to alter the contents of one or more other cells.

Template – a pre-designed spreadsheet without data but including all formulae necessary for (repeated) data analysis.

Macro – a sequence of user-defined instructions carried out by the spreadsheet, allowing complex repeated tasks to be 'automated'.

KEY POINT **The spreadsheet is one of the most powerful and wide-ranging of all microcomputer applications. It is the electronic equivalent of a huge sheet of paper with calculating powers and provides a dynamic method of storing and manipulating data sets.**

Statistical calculations and graphical presentations are available in many versions and most have scientific functions. Spreadsheets can be used to:

- manipulate raw data by removing the drudgery of repeated calculations, allowing easy transformation of data and calculation of statistics;
- graph out your data rapidly to get an instant evaluation of results. Print-out can be used in practical and project reports;
- carry out limited statistical analysis by built-in procedures or by allowing construction of formulae for specific tasks;
- model 'what if' situations where the consequences of changes in data can be seen and evaluated;
- store data sets with or without statistical and graphical analysis. This is now common practice in ecology.

The spreadsheet (Fig. 42.1) is divided into rows (identified by numbers) and columns (identified by alphabetic characters). Each individual combination of column and row forms a cell which can contain either a data item, a formula, or a piece of text called a label. Formulae can include scientific and/or statistical functions and/or a reference to other cells or groups of cells (often called a range). Complex systems of data input and analysis can be constructed (models). The analysis, in part or complete, can be printed out. New data can be added at any time and the sheet recalculated. You can construct templates, pre-designed spreadsheets containing the formulae required for repeated data analyses.

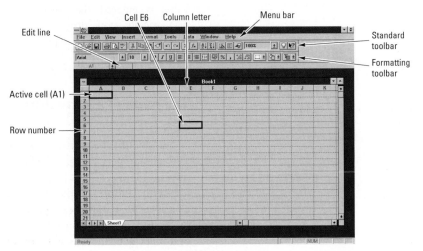

Fig. 42.1 A screen dump of a typical spreadsheet, showing cells, rows and columns, toolbars etc. Screen shot reprinted by permission from Microsoft Corporation.

Information technology and library resources **231**

Using spreadsheets

The power a spreadsheet offers is directly related to your ability to create models that are accurate and templates that are easy to use. The sequence of operations required is:

1. Determine what information/statistics you want to produce.
2. Identify the variables you will need to use, both for original data that will be entered and for any intermediate calculations that might be required.
3. Set up areas of the spreadsheet for data entry, calculation of intermediate values (statistical values such as sums of squares, etc.), calculation of final parameters/statistics and, if necessary, a summary area.
4. Establish the format of the numeric data if it is different from the default values. This can be done globally (affecting the entire spreadsheet) or locally (affecting only a specified part of the spreadsheet).
5. Establish the column widths required for the various activities.
6. Enter labels: use extensively for annotation.
7. Enter a test set of values to use during formula entry: use a fully worked example to check that formulae are working correctly.
8. Enter the formulae required to make all the calculations, both intermediate and final. Check that results are correct using the test data.

The spreadsheet is then ready for use. Delete all the test data values and you have created your template. Save the template to a disk and it is then available for repeated operations.

Data entry

Spreadsheets have built-in commands which allow you to control the layout of data in the cells. These include number format, the number of decimal places to be shown (the spreadsheet always calculates using eight or more places), the cell width and the location of the entry within the cell (left, right or centre). An auto-entry facility assists greatly in entering large amounts of data by moving the entry cursor either vertically or horizontally as data is entered. Recalculation default is usually automatic so that when a new data value is entered the entire sheet is recalculated immediately. This can dramatically slow down data entry so select manual recalculation mode before entering new data sets if the spreadsheet is large with many calculations.

The parts of a spreadsheet

Labels

These identify the contents of rows and columns. They are text characters, and cannot be used in calculations. Separate them from the data cells by drawing lines, if this feature is available. Programs make assumptions about the nature of the entry being made: most assume that if the first character is a number, then the entry is a number or formula. If it is a letter, then it will be a label. If you want to start a label with a number, you must override this assumption by typing a designated character before the number to tell the program that this is a label; check your program manual for details.

Numbers

You can also enter numbers (values) in cells for use in calculations. Many programs let you enter numbers in more than one way and you must decide which method you prefer. The way you enter the number does not affect the way it is displayed on the screen as this is controlled by the cell format at the point of entry. There are usually special ways to enter data for percentages, currency and scientific notation for very large and small numbers.

Formulae

These are the 'power tools' of the spreadsheet because they do the calculations. A cell can be referred to by its alphanumeric code, e.g. A5 (column A, row 5) and the value contained in that cell manipulated within a formula, e.g. (A5 + 10) or (A5 + B22) in another cell. Formulae can include a diverse array of pre-programmed functions which can refer to a cell, so that if the value of that cell is changed, so is the result of the formula calculation. They may also include limited branching options through the use of logical operators.

Functions

A variety of functions is usually offered, but only mathematical and statistical functions will be considered here.

Mathematical functions

Spreadsheets have program-specific sets of predetermined functions but they almost all include trigonometrical functions, angle functions, logarithms and random number functions. Functions are invaluable for transforming sets of data rapidly and can be used in formulae required for more complex analyses. Spreadsheets work with an order of preference of the operators in much the same way as a standard calculator and this must always be taken into account when operators are used in formulae. They also require a very precise syntax – the program should warn you if you break this!

Statistical functions

Modern spreadsheets incorporate many sophisticated statistical functions, and if these are not appropriate, the spreadsheet can be used to facilitate the calculations required for most of the statistical tests found in textbooks. The descriptive statistics normally available include:

- sums of all data present in a column, row or block;
- minima and maxima of a defined range of cells;
- counts of cells – a useful operation if you have an unknown or variable number of data values;
- averages and other statistics describing location;
- standard deviations and other statistics describing dispersion.

A useful function where you have large numbers of data allows you to create frequency distributions using pre-defined class intervals.

The hypothesis-testing statistical functions may be reasonably powerful (e.g. t-test, ANOVA, regressions) and they often return the *probability P* of obtaining the test statistic (where $0 < P < 1$), so there may be no need to refer to statistical tables. Again, check on the effects of including empty cells.

Using hidden (or zero-width) columns – these are useful for storing intermediate calculations which you do not wish to be displayed on the screen or printout.

Definition

Function – a pre-programmed code for the transformation of values (mathematical or statistical functions) or selection of text characters (string functions).

Example = sin(A5) is an example of a function in Microsoft® Excel®. If you write this in a cell, the spreadsheet will calculate the sine of the number in cell A5 (assuming it to be an angle in radians) and write it in the cell. Different programs may use a slightly different syntax.

Empty cells – note that these may be given the value 0 by the spreadsheet for certain functions. This may cause errors e.g. by rendering a minimum value inappropriate. Also, an error return may result for certain functions if the cell content is zero.

Statistical calculations – make sure you understand whether any functions you employ are for populations or samples (see p. 211).

Using spreadsheets

Copying

All programs provide a means of copying (replicating) formulae or cell contents when required and this is a very useful feature. When copying, references to cells may be either relative, changing with the row/column as they are copied or absolute, remaining a fixed cell reference and not changing as the formulae are copied. This distinction between cell references is very important and must be understood; it provides one of the most common forms of error when copying formulae. Be sure to understand how your spreadsheet performs these operations.

Naming blocks

When a group of cells (a block) is carrying out a particular function, it is often easier to give the block a name which can then be used in all formulae referring to that block. This powerful feature also allows the spreadsheet to be more readable.

Graphics display

Most spreadsheets now offer a wide range of graphics facilities which are easy to use and this represents an ideal way to examine your data sets rapidly and comprehensively (Chapter 44). The quality of the final graphics output (to a printer) is variable but is usually perfectly sufficient for data exploration and analysis. Many of the options are business graphics styles but there are usually histogram, bar charts, X-Y plotting, line and area graphics options available. Note that some spreadsheet graphics may not come up to the standards expected for the formal presentation of scientific data.

Printing spreadsheets

This is usually a straightforward menu-controlled procedure, made difficult only by the fact that your spreadsheet may be too big to fit on one piece of paper. Try to develop an area of the sheet which contains only the data that you will be printing, i.e. perhaps a summary area. Remember that columns can usually be hidden for printing purposes and you can control whether the printout is in portrait or landscape mode, and for continuous paper or single sheets (depending on printer capabilities). Use a screen preview option, if available, to check your layout before printing. The more sophisticated versions of spreadsheets are now WYSIWYG (What You See Is What You Get) so that the appearance on the screen is a realistic impression of the printout. A 'print to fit' option is also available in some programs, making the output fit the page dimensions.

Use as a database

Many spreadsheets can be used as databases, using rows and columns to represent the fields and records (see Chapter 44). For many biological purposes, this form of database is perfectly adequate and should be seriously considered before using a full-feature database program.

43

Word processors

Word processors

The word processor has facilitated writing because of the ease of revising text. Word processing is a transferable skill valuable beyond the immediate requirements of your course. Using a word processor should improve your writing skills and speed because you can create, check and change your text on the screen before printing it as 'hard copy' on paper. Once entered and saved, multiple uses can be made of a piece of text with little effort.

When using a word processor you can:

- refine material many times before submission;
- insert material easily, allowing writing to take place in any sequence;
- use a spell-checker to check your text;
- use a thesaurus when composing your text;
- produce high quality final copies;
- reuse part or all of the text in other documents.

The potential disadvantages of using a word processor include:

- lack of ready access to a computer, software and/or a printer;
- time taken to learn the operational details of the program;
- the temptation to make 'trivial' revisions;
- loss of files due to computer breakdown or disk loss or failure.

Word processors come as 'packages' comprising the program and a manual, often with a tutorial program. Examples are WordPerfect® and Microsoft® Word. Most word processors have similar general features but differ in operational detail; it is best to pick one and stick to it as far as possible so that you become familiar with it. Learning to use the package is like learning to drive a car – you need only to know how to drive the computer and its program, not to understand how the engine (program) and transmission (data transfer) work, although a little background knowledge is often helpful and will allow you to get the most from the program.

In most word processors, the appearance of the screen realistically represents what the printout on paper will look like (WYSIWYG). Word processing files actually contain large amounts of code relating to text format, etc., but these clutter the screen if visible, as in non-WYSIWYG programs. Some word processors are menu-driven, others require keyboard entry of codes: menus are easier to start with and the more sophisticated programs allow you to choose between these options.

Because of variation in operational details, only general and strategic information is provided in this chapter: you must learn the details of your word processor through use of the appropriate manual and 'help' facilities.

Before starting you will need:

- the program (ideally on a hard disk);
- a floppy disk for storage, retrieval and back-up of your own files when created;
- the appropriate manual or textbook giving operational details;

The computerized office – many word processors are now sold as part of an integrated suite, e.g. PerfectOffice® and Microsoft® Office, with the advantage that they share a common interface in the different components (word processor, spreadsheet, database, etc.) and allow ready exchange of information (e.g. text, graphics) between component programs.

Using textbooks, manuals and tutorials – the manuals that come with some programs may not be very user-friendly and it is often worth investing in one of the textbooks that are available for most word processing programs. Alternatively, use an on-line 'help' tutorial, available with the more sophisticated packages.

- a draft page layout design: in particular you should have decided on page size, page margins, typeface (font) and size, type of text justification, and format of page numbering;
- an outline of the text content;
- access to a suitable printer: this need not be attached to the computer you are using since your file can be taken to an office where such a printer is available, providing that it has the same word processing program.

Laying out (formatting) your document

Although you can format your text at any time, it is good practice to enter the basic commands at the start of your document: entering them later can lead to considerable problems due to reorganization of the text layout. If you use a particular set of layout criteria regularly, e.g. an A4 page with space for a letterhead, make a template containing the appropriate codes that can be called up whenever you start a new document. Note that various printers may respond differently to particular codes, resulting in a different spacing and layout.

Typing the text

Think of the screen as a piece of typing paper. The cursor marks the position where your text/data will be entered and can be moved around the screen by use of the cursor-control keys. When you type, don't worry about running out of space on the line because the text will wrap around to the next line automatically. Do not use a carriage return (usually the ENTER or ↵ key) unless you wish to force a new line, e.g. when a new paragraph is wanted. If you make a mistake when typing, correction is easy. You can usually delete characters or words or lines and the space is closed automatically. You can also insert new text in the middle of a line or word. You can insert special codes to carry out a variety of tasks, including changing text appearance such as underlining, **bolding** and *italics*. Paragraph indentations can be automated using TAB or ⇥ as on a typewriter but you can also indent or bullet whole blocks of text using special menu options. The function keys are usually pre-programmed to assist in many of these operations.

Editing features

Word processors usually have an array of features designed to make editing documents easy. In addition to the simple editing procedures described above, the program usually offers facilities to allow blocks of text to be moved ('cut and paste'), copied or deleted.

An extremely valuable editing facility is the search procedure: this can rapidly scan through a document looking for a specified word, phrase or punctuation. This is particularly valuable when combined with a replace facility so that, for example, you could replace the word 'test' with 'trial' throughout your document simply and rapidly.

Most WYSIWYG word processors have a command which reveals the normally hidden codes controlling the layout and appearance of the printed text. When editing, this can be a very important feature, since some changes to your text will cause difficulties if these hidden codes are not taken into account; in particular, make sure that the cursor is at the correct point before making changes to text containing hidden code, otherwise your text will sometimes change in apparently mystifying ways.

Using a word processor – take full advantage of the differences between word processing and 'normal' writing (which necessarily follows a linear sequence and requires more planning):

- Simply jot down your initial ideas for a plan, preferably to paragraph topic level. The order can be altered easily and if a paragraph grows too much it can easily be split.
- Start writing wherever you wish and fill in the rest later.
- Just put down your ideas as you think, confident in the knowledge that it is the concepts that are important to note; their order and the way you express them can be adjusted later.
- Don't worry about spelling and use of synonyms – these can (and should) be checked during a special revision run through your text, using the spelling checker first to correct obvious mistakes, then the thesaurus to change words for style or to find the *mot juste*.
- Don't forget that a draft printout may be required to check (a) for pace and spacing – difficult to correct for on a screen; and (b) to ensure that words checked for spelling fit the required sense.

Deleting and restoring text – because deletion can sometimes be made in error, there is usually an 'undelete' or 'restore' feature which allows the last deletion to be recovered.

Fonts and line spacing

Most word processors offer a variety of fonts depending upon the printer being used. Fonts come in a wide variety of types and sizes, but they are defined in particular ways as follows:

- Typeface: the term for a family of characters of a particular design, each of which is given a particular name. The most commonly used for normal text is Times Roman (as used here for the main text) but many others are widely available, particularly for the better quality printers. They fall into three broad groups: serif fonts with curves and flourishes at the ends of the characters (e.g. Times Roman); sans serif fonts without such flourishes, providing a clean, modern appearance (e.g. Helvetica, also known as Swiss); and decorative fonts used for special purposes only, such as the production of newsletters and notices.
- Size: measured in points. A point is the smallest typographical unit of measurement, there being 72 points to the inch (about 28 points per cm). The standard sizes for text are 10, 11 and 12 point, but typefaces are often available up to 72 point or more.
- Appearance: many typefaces are available in a variety of styles and weights. Many of these are not designed for use in scientific literature but for desk-top publishing.
- Spacing: can be either fixed, where every character is the same width, or proportional, where the width of every character, including spaces, is varied. Typewriter fonts such as Elite and Prestige use fixed spacing and are useful for filling in forms or tables, but proportional fonts make the overall appearance of text more pleasing and readable.
- Pitch: specifies the number of characters per horizontal inch of text. Typewriter fonts are usually 10 or 12 pitch, but proportional fonts are never given a pitch value since it is inherently variable.
- Justification is the term describing the way in which text is aligned vertically. Left justification is normal, but for formal documents, both left and right justification may be used (as here).

You should also consider the vertical spacing of lines in your document. Drafts and manuscripts are frequently double-spaced. If your document has unusual font sizes, this may well affect line spacing, although most word processors will cope with this automatically.

Table construction

Tables can be produced by a variety of methods:

- Using the tab key ⇥ as on a typewriter: this moves the cursor to predetermined positions on the page, equivalent to the start of each tabular column. You can define the positions of these tabs as required at the start of each table.
- Using special table-constructing procedures. Here the table construction is largely done for you and it is much easier than using tabs, providing you enter the correct information when you set up the table.
- Using a spreadsheet to construct the table and then copying it to the word processor. This procedure requires considerably more manipulation than using the word processor directly and is best reserved for special circumstances, such as the presentation of a very large or complex table of data, especially if the data are already stored as a spreadsheet.

Presenting your documents – it is good practice not to mix typefaces too much in a formal document; also the font size should not differ greatly for different headings, subheadings and the text.

Preparing draft documents – use double spacing to allow room for your editing comments on the printed page.

Preparing final documents – for most work, use a 12 point proportional serif typeface with spacing dependent upon the specifications for the work.

Graphics and special characters

Many word processors can incorporate graphics from other programs into the text of a document. Files must be compatible (see your manual) but if this is so, it is a relatively straightforward procedure. For highly professional documents this is a valuable facility, but for most undergraduate work it is probably better to produce and use graphics as a separate operation, e.g. employing a spreadsheet.

You can draw lines and other graphical features directly within most word processors and special characters may be available dependent upon your printer's capabilities. It is a good idea to print out a full set of characters from your printer so that you know what it is capable of. These may include symbols and Greek characters, often useful in biological work.

Tools

Many word processors also offer you special tools, the most important of which are:

- Macros: special sets of files you can create when you have a frequently repeated set of keystrokes to make. You can record these keystrokes as a 'macro' so that it can provide a short-cut for repeated operations.
- Thesaurus: used to look up alternative words of similar or opposite meaning while composing text at the keyboard.
- Spell-check: a very useful facility which will check your spellings against a dictionary provided by the program. This dictionary is often expandable to include specialist words which you use in your work. The danger lies in becoming too dependent upon this facility as they all have limitations: in particular, they will not pick up incorrect words which happen to be correct in a different context (i.e. 'was' typed as 'saw' or 'meter' rather than 'metre'). Beware of American spellings in programs from the USA, e.g. 'color' instead of 'colour'. The rule, therefore, is to use the spell-check first and then carefully read the text for errors which have slipped through.
- Word count: useful when you are writing to a prescribed limit.

Using a spell-check facility – do not rely on this to spot all errors. Remember that spell-check programs do not correct grammatical errors.

Printing from your program

Word processors require you to specify precisely the type of printer and/or other style details you wish to use. Most printers also offer choices as to text and graphics quality, so choose draft (low) quality for all but your final copy since this will save both time and materials.

Use a print preview option to show the page layout if it is available. Assuming that you have entered appropriate layout and font commands, printing is a straightforward operation carried out by the word processor at your command. Problems usually arise because of some incompatibility between the criteria you have entered and the printer's own capabilities. Make sure that you know what your printer offers before starting to type: although parameters are modifiable at any time, changing the page size, margin size, font size, etc., all cause your text to be re-arranged, and this can be frustrating if you have spent hours carefully laying out the pages!

Using the print preview mode – this can reveal errors of several types, e.g. spacing between pages, that can prevent you wasting paper and printer ink unnecessarily.

KEY POINT It is vital to save your work frequently to a hard or floppy disk (or both). This should be done every 10 min or so. If you do not save regularly, you may lose hours or days of work. Many programs can be set to 'autosave' every few minutes.

44

Databases and other packages

Databases

A database is an electronic filing system whose structure is similar to a manual record card collection. Its collection of records is termed a file. The individual items of information on each record are termed fields. Once the database is constructed, search criteria can be used to view files through various filters according to your requirements. The computerized catalogues in your library are just such a system; you enter the filter requirements in the form of author or subject keywords. Many are now available on the WWW (Internet).

You can use a database to catalogue, search, sort, and relate collections of information. The benefits of a computerized database over a manual card-file system are:

- The information content is easily amended/updated.
- Printout of relevant items can be obtained.
- It is quick and easy to organize through sorting and searching/selection criteria, to produce sub-groups of relevant records.
- Record displays can easily be redesigned, allowing flexible methods of presenting records according to interest.
- Relational databases can be combined, giving the whole system immense flexibility. The older 'flat-file' databases store information in files which can be searched and sorted, but cannot be linked to other databases.

Relatively simple database files can be constructed within the more advanced spreadsheets using the columns and rows as fields and records respectively. These are capable of limited sorting and searching operations and are probably sufficient for the types of databases you are likely to require as an undergraduate. You may also make use of a bibliography database especially constructed for that purpose.

Statistical analysis packages

Statistical packages vary from small programs designed to carry out very specific statistical tasks to large sophisticated packages (Statgraphics®, Minitab®, etc.) intended to provide statistical assistance, from experimental design to the analysis of results. Consider the following features when selecting a package:

- The data entry and editing section should be user-friendly, with options for transforming data.
- Data exploration options should include descriptive statistics and exploratory data analysis techniques.
- Hypothesis testing techniques should include ANOVA, regression analysis, multivariate techniques and parametric and non-parametric statistics.
- The program should provide assistance with experimental design and sampling methods.
- Output facilities should be suitable for graphical and tabular formats.

Some programs have very complex data entry systems, limiting the ease of using data in different tests. The data entry and storage system should be

Example Some useful databases for environmental science include:

HazDat Database –
http://atsdr1.atsdr.cdc.gov:8080/
hazdat.html
RTK Net Environmental Databases
http://www.rtk.net/www.rtknet/webpage/
databas3.html

Choosing between a database and a spreadsheet – use a database only after careful consideration. Can the task be done better within a spreadsheet? A database program can be complex to set up and usually needs to be updated regularly.

based upon a spreadsheet system, so that subsequent editing and transformation operations are straightforward.

KEY POINT Make sure that you understand the statistical basis for your test and the computational techniques involved *before* using a particular program.

Geographical Information Systems (GIS)

As described in Chapter 29, a geographical information system is a powerful computer software system that permits the manipulation and visualization of spatial data and enables new types of map to be generated. The first GIS was developed in the 1960s by the Canadian government to analyse land inventory data. Since that time, technological developments have led to large numbers of GIS software packages becoming commercially available. The data used in a GIS may be in the form of areas, lines, points or numbers (see Table 29.2). The lower cost of computers in the 1990s has contributed to the current widespread usage of GIS in industry and academia. GIS has now become an important tool in environmental impact assessment (see Chapter 30) where a spatial analysis of the interactions of several environmental variables is requied. Although many types of GIS are available, at a wide range of prices, they vary in their ease and speed of operation according to the computer operating system.

Choosing a GIS – before using a particular GIS always consult with others familiar with it to assess its user-friendliness and its applicability for your chosen purpose.

Graphics/presentation packages

Many of these packages are specifically designed for business graphics rather than science. They do, however, have considerable value in the preparation of materials for posters and talks where visual quality is an important factor. There is a variety of packages available for microcomputers such as Freelance Graphics®, Harvard Graphics® and Microsoft® PowerPoint®, which provide numerous templates for the preparation of overhead transparencies, slide transparencies and paper copy, both black and white and in colour. They usually incorporate a 'freehand' drawing option, allowing you to make your own designs.

Although the facilities offered are often attractive, the learning time required for some of the more complex operations is considerable and they should be considered only for specific purposes: routine graphical presentation of data sets is best done from within a spreadsheet or statistical package. There may be a service provided by your institution for the preparation of such material and this should be seriously considered before trying to learn to use these programs.

The most important points regarding the use of graphics packages are:

- Graphics quality: the built-in graphics are sometimes of only moderate quality. Use of annotation facilities can improve graphics considerably. Do not use inappropriate graphics for scientific presentation.
- The production of colour graphics: this requires a good quality colour printer/plotter.
- Importing of graphics files: graphs produced by spreadsheets or other statistical programs can usually be imported into graphics programs - this is useful for adding legends, annotations, etc., when the facilities offered by the original programs are inadequate. Check that the format of files

produced by your statistics/spreadsheet program can be recognized by your graphics program. The different types of file are distinguished by the three-character filename extension.

KEY POINT **Computer graphics are not always satisfactory for scientific presentation. While they may be useful for exploratory procedures, they may need to be re-drawn by hand for your final report. It may be helpful to use a computer-generated graph as a template for the final version.**

45 Finding and citing published information

The ability to find scientific information is a skill required for many exercises in your degree programme. You will need to research facts and published findings as part of writing essays, literature reviews and project introductions, and when amplifying your lecture notes and revising for exams. You must also learn how to follow scientific convention in citing source material as the authority for the statements you have made.

Sources of information

For essays and revision

You are unlikely to delve into the primary literature for these purposes – books and reviews are much more readable! If a lecturer or tutor specifies a particular book, then it should not be difficult to find out where it is shelved in your library, as most now have a computerized index system and their staff will be happy to assist with any queries. If you want to find out which books your library holds on a specified topic, use the system's subject index. You will also be able to search by author or by key words.

There are two main systems used by libraries to classify books: the Dewey Decimal system and the Library of Congress system. Libraries differ in the way they employ these systems, especially by adding further numbers and letters after the standard classification marks to signify e.g. shelving position or edition number. Enquire at your library for a full explanation of local usage.

The World Wide Web is an expanding resource for gathering both general and specific information (see Chapter 41). Sites fall into analogous categories to those in the printed literature: there are sites with original information, sites that review information and bibliographic sites. One considerable problem is that Web sites may be frequently updated, so information present when you first looked may be altered or even absent when the site is next consulted. Further, very little of the information on the WWW has been monitored or refereed. Another disadvantage is that the site information may not state the origin of the material, who wrote it or when it was written.

For literature surveys and project work

You will probably need to consult the primary literature. If you are starting a new research project or writing a report from scratch, you can build up a core of relevant papers by using the following methods:

- Asking around: supervisors or their postgraduate students will almost certainly be able to supply you with a reference or two that will start you off.
- Searching a computer database: these cover very wide areas and are a convenient way to start a reference collection, although a charge is often made for access and sending out a listing of the papers selected (your library may or may not pass this on to you).
- Consulting the bibliography of other papers in your collection – an important way of finding the key papers in your field. In effect, you are taking advantage of the fact that another researcher has already done all the hard work!

Browsing in a library – this *may* turn up interesting material, but remember the books on the shelves are those *not* currently out on loan. Almost by definition, the latter may be more up-to-date and useful. To find out a library's full holding of books in any subject area, you need to search its catalogue (normally available as a computerized database).

Example   The book *Environmental Science Methods* edited by Robin Haynes (1982, Chapman and Hall Ltd) is likely to be classified as follows:

Dewey decimal system: 303.3
where 301   refers to 'man and society'
301.3   refers to 'environmental science'

Library of Congress system: GB21.E58
where GB refers to Physical Geography
21 further identifies the subject area
E58 identifies the author

International Standard Book Number (ISBN)
0-412-23290-1 (pbk)

Computer databases – several databases are now produced on CD-ROM for open use in libraries (e.g. Geobase, Applied Science and Technology Index). Some databases can be accessed via the Internet, such as Cambridge Scientific Abstracts (which incorporates an Environmental Sciences and Pollution Management database) and BIDS (Bath Information and Data Service), a UK service providing access to information from over 7 000 periodicals (username and password required via your library). Each of these databases usually has its own easy-to-follow menu instructions. It is worthwhile to consider keywords for your search beforehand to focus your search and save time.

- Referring to 'current awareness' journals or computer databases: these are useful for keeping you up to date with current research; they usually provide a monthly listing of article details (title, authors, source, author address) arranged by subject and cross-referenced by subject and author. Current awareness journals cover a wider range of primary journals than could ever be available in any one library. Examples include:
  (a) *Current Contents*, published by the Institute of Scientific Information, Philadelphia, USA, which reproduces the contents pages of journals of a particular subject area and presents an analysis by author and subject.
  (b) *Current Advances*, published by Pergamon Press, Oxford, UK, which subdivides papers by subject within research areas and cross-references by subject and author.
  (c) *Geobase*, which contains citations, with abstracts covering worldwide literature on physical and human geography, geology, ecology, international development and their related disciplines. It forms the equivalent of the following print sources – *Geographical Abstracts*; *Ecological Abstracts*; *Oceanographic Literature Review*; *Geological Abstracts* and *International Development Abstracts*.

- Using the *Science Citation Index* (SCI): this is a very valuable source of new references, because it lets you see who has cited a given paper; in effect, SCI allows you to move forward through the literature from an existing reference. The Index is published regularly during the year and issues are collated annually. Some libraries have copies on CD-ROM: this allows rapid access and output of selected information.

For specialized information

You may need to consult reference works, such as encyclopaedias, maps and books providing specialized information. Many of these are now available on CD-ROM (consult your library's information service). Three books worth noting are:

- The *Handbook of Chemistry and Physics* (Lide and Frederikse, 1996): the Chemical Rubber Company's publication (affectionately known as the 'Rubber Bible') giving all manner of physical constants, radioisotope half-lives, etc.
- The *Merck Index* (Budavari *et al.*, 1996), which gives useful information about organic chemicals, e.g. solubility, whether poisonous, etc.
- The *Geigy Scientific Tables* (8th edition), a series of 6 volumes (Lentner, 1981; 1984; 1988; 1990; 1992; Lentner *et al.*, 1982) provides a wide range of information centred on biochemistry, e.g. buffer formulae, properties of constituents of living matter.

Obtaining and organizing research papers

Obtaining a copy

It is usually more convenient to have personal copies of key research articles for direct consultation when working in a laboratory or writing. The simplest way of obtaining these is to photocopy the originals. For academic purposes, this is normally acceptable within copyright law. If your library does not take the journal, it may be possible for them to borrow it from a nearby institute or obtain a copy via a national borrowing centre (an 'inter-library loan'). If the latter, you will have to fill in a form giving full bibliographic details of

Storing research papers – these can easily be kept in alphabetical order within filing boxes or drawers, but if your collection is likely to grow large, it will need to be refiled as it outgrows the storage space. An alternative is to keep an alphabetical card index system (useful when typing out lists of references) and file the papers by 'accession number' as they accumulate. New filing space is only required at one 'end' and you can use the accession numbers to form the basis of a simple cross-referencing system.

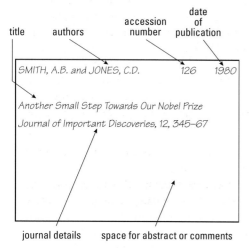

Fig. 45.1 A typical reference card. Make sure the index card carries all the bibliographic information of potential relevance.

the paper and where it was cited, as well as signing a copyright clearance statement concerning your use of the copy.

Your department might be able to supply 'reprint request' postcards to be sent to the designated author of a paper. This is an unreliable method of obtaining a copy because it may take some time (allow at least 1–3 months!) and some requests will not receive a reply. Taking into account the waste involved in postage and printing, it is probably best simply to photocopy or send for a copy via inter-library loan.

Organizing papers

Although the numbers of papers you accumulate may be small to start with, it is worth putting some thought into their storage and indexing before your collection becomes disorganized and unmanageable. Few things are more frustrating than not being able to lay your hands on a vital piece of information, and this can seriously disrupt your flow when writing or revising.

Card index systems

Index cards (Fig. 45.1) are a useful adjunct to any filing system. Firstly, you may not have a copy of the paper to file yet may still wish the reference information to be recorded somewhere for later use. Secondly, a selected pile of cards can be used when typing out different bibliographies. Thirdly, the cards can help when organizing a review (see p. 261). Fourthly, the card can be used to record key points and comments on the paper. The priority rule for storage in card boxes is again first author name, subsequent author name(s), date. Computerized card index systems simplify cross-referencing and can provide computer files for direct insertion into word-processed documents; however, they are very time-consuming to set up and maintain, so you should only consider using one if the time invested will prove worthwhile.

Making citations in text

There are two main ways of citing articles and creating a Bibliography (also referred to as 'References' or 'Literature Cited').

The Harvard system

For each citation, the author name(s) and the date of publication are given at the relevant point in the text. The Bibliography is organized alphabetically and by date of publication for papers with the same authors. Formats normally adopted are, for example, 'Smith and Jones (1983) stated that …' or 'it has been shown that … (Smith and Jones, 1983)'. Lists of references within parentheses are separated by semi-colons, e.g. '(Smith and Jones, 1983; Jones and Smith, 1985)', normally in order of date of publication. To avoid repetition within the same paragraph, a formula such as 'the investigations of Smith and Jones indicated that' could be used following an initial citation of the paper. Where there are more than two authors it is usual to write 'et al.' (or *et al.* if an italic font is available); this stands for the Latin *et alia* meaning 'and others'. If citing more than one paper with the same authors, put, for example, 'Smith and Jones (1987; 1990)' and if papers by a given set of authors appeared in the same year, letter them (e.g. Smith and Jones, 1989a; 1989b).

The numerical or Vancouver system

Papers are cited via a superscript or bracketed reference number inserted at the appropriate point. Normal format would be, for example: 'Analysis of soil samples[4,5] have shown that ...' or 'Jones [55,82] has claimed that ...'. Repeated citations use the number from the first citation. In the true numerical method (e.g. as in *Nature*), numbers are allocated by order of citation in the text, but in the alpha-numerical method (e.g. the *Annual Review* series), the references are first ordered alphabetically in the Bibliography, then numbered, and it is this number which is used in the text. Note that with this latter method, adding or removing references is tedious, so the numbering should be done only when the text has been finalized.

KEY POINT The main advantages of the Harvard system are that the reader might recognize the paper being referred to and that it is easily expanded if extra references are added. The main advantages of the Vancouver system are that it aids text flow and reduces length.

How to list your citations in a bibliography

Whichever citation method is used in the text, comprehensive details are required for the bibliography so that the reader has enough information to find the reference easily. Citations should be listed in alphabetical order with the priority: first author, subsequent author(s), date. Unfortunately, in terms of punctuation and layout, there are almost as many ways of citing papers as there are journals! Your department may specify an exact format for project work; if not, decide on a style and be consistent – if you do not pay attention to the details of citation you may lose marks. Take special care with the following aspects:

- Authors and editors: give details of *all* authors and editors in your bibliography, even if given as *et al.* in the text.
- Abbreviations for journals: while there are standard abbreviations for the titles of journals (consult library staff), it is a good idea to give the whole title, if possible.
- Books: the edition should always be specified as contents may change between editions. Add, for example, '(5th edition)' after the title of the book. You may be asked to give the International Standard Book Number (ISBN), a unique reference number for each book published.
- Unsigned articles, e.g. unattributed newspaper articles and instruction manuals – refer to the author(s) in text and bibliography as 'Anon.'.
- Unread articles: you may be forced to refer to a paper via another without having seen it. If possible, refer to another authority who has cited the paper, e.g. '... Jones (1980), cited in Smith (1990), claimed that ...'. Alternatively, you could denote such references in the bibliography by an asterisk and add a short note to explain at the start of the reference list.
- Personal communications: information received in a letter, seminar or conversation can be referred to in the text as, for example, '... (Smith, pers. comm.)'. These citations are not generally listed in the bibliography of papers though in a thesis you could give a list of personal communicants and their addresses.

Examples

Paper in journal
Smith, A. B., Jones, C.D. and Professor, A. (1998). Innovative results concerning our research interest. Journal of New Results, 11, 234–5.

Book:
Smith, A. B. (1998). Summary of my life's work. Megadosh Publishing Corp., Bigcity. ISBN 0-123-45678-9.

Chapter in edited book:
Jones, C. D. and Smith, A. B. (1998). Earth-shattering research from our laboratory. In: Research Compendium 1998 (ed. A. Professor), pp 123–456. Bigbucks Press, Booktown.

Thesis:
Smith, A. B. (1995). Investigations on my favourite topic. PhD thesis, University of Life, Fulchester.

Note that underlining used here specifies italics in print: use an italic font if working with a word processor.

Citing Web sites – there is no widely accepted format at present. We suggest providing author name(s) and date in the text if using the Harvard system, while in the bibliography giving the above, plus site title and full URL reference (e.g. Hacker, A. (1998). University of Cybertown homepage on aardvarks. http://www.myserver.ac.uk/homepage).

Communicating information

46 General aspects of scientific writing

Written communication is an essential component of all sciences. Most courses include writing exercises in which you will learn to describe ideas and results accurately, succinctly and in an appropriate style and format. The following are features common to all forms of scientific writing.

Organizing time

Making a timetable at the outset helps ensure that you give each stage adequate attention and complete the work on time. To create and use a timetable:

1. Break down the task into stages.
2. Decide on the proportion of the total time each stage should take.
3. Set realistic deadlines for completing each stage, allowing some time for slippage.
4. Refer to your timetable frequently as you work: if you fail to meet one of your deadlines, make a serious effort to catch up as soon as possible.

KEY POINT The appropriate allocation of your time to reading, planning, writing and revising will differ according to the task in hand (see Chapters 47 and 49).

Organizing information and ideas

Before you write, you need to gather and/or think about relevant material (Chapter 45). You must then decide:

- what needs to be included and what doesn't;
- in what order it should appear.

Start by jotting down headings for everything of potential relevance to the topic (this is sometimes called 'brainstorming'). A spider diagram (Fig. 46.1) will help you organize these ideas. The next stage is to create an outline of your text (Fig. 46.2). Outlines are valuable because they:

- force you to think about and plan the structure;
- provide a checklist so nothing is missed out;
- ensure the material is balanced in content and length;
- help you organize figures and tables by showing where they will be used.

Creating an outline – an informal outline can be made simply by indicating the order of sections on a spider diagram (as in Fig. 46.1).

In an essay or review, the structure of your writing should help the reader to assimilate and understand your main points. Sub-divisions of the topic could simply be related to the physical nature of the subject matter (e.g. zones of an ecosystem) and should proceed logically (e.g. low water mark to high water mark).

A chronological approach is good for evaluation of past work (e.g. the development of the concept of evolution), whereas a step-by-step comparison might be best for certain exam questions (e.g. 'Discuss the differences between lakes and streams'). There is little choice about structure for practical and project reports (see p. 256).

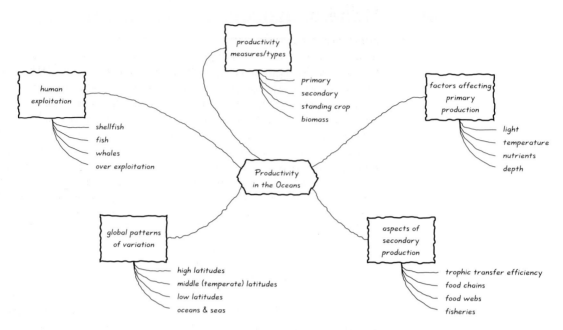

Fig. 46.1 Spider diagram showing how you might 'brainstorm' an essay with the title 'Productivity in the Oceans'. Write out the essay title in full to form the spider's body, and as you think of possible content, place headings around this to form its legs. Decide which headings are relevant and which are not and use arrows to note connections between subjects. This may influence your choice of order and may help to make your writing flow because the links between paragraphs will be natural. You can make an informal outline directly on a spider diagram by adding numbers indicating a sequence of paragraphs (as shown). This method is best when you must work quickly, as with an essay written under exam conditions.

Fig. 46.2 Formal outlines. These are useful for a long piece of work where you or the reader might otherwise lose track of the structure. The headings for sections and paragraphs are simply written in sequence with the type of lettering and level of indentation indicating their hierarchy. Two different forms of formal outline are shown, a minimal form (a) and a numbered form (b). Note that the headings used in an outline are often repeated within the essay to emphasize its structure. The content of an outline will depend on the time you have available and the nature of the work, but the most detailed hierarchy you should reasonably include is the subject of each paragraph.

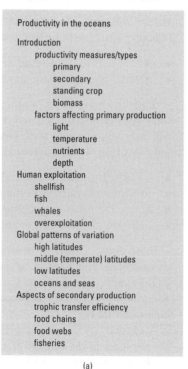

Productivity in the oceans

Introduction
    productivity measures/types
        primary
        secondary
        standing crop
        biomass
    factors affecting primary production
        light
        temperature
        nutrients
        depth
Human exploitation
    shellfish
    fish
    whales
    overexploitation
Global patterns of variation
    high latitudes
    middle (temperate) latitudes
    low latitudes
    oceans and seas
Aspects of secondary production
    trophic transfer efficiency
    food chains
    food webs
    fisheries

(a)

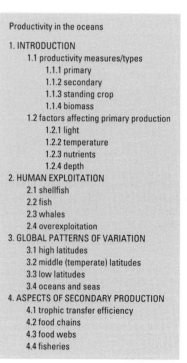

Productivity in the oceans

1. INTRODUCTION
    1.1 productivity measures/types
        1.1.1 primary
        1.1.2 secondary
        1.1.3 standing crop
        1.1.4 biomass
    1.2 factors affecting primary production
        1.2.1 light
        1.2.2 temperature
        1.2.3 nutrients
        1.2.4 depth
2. HUMAN EXPLOITATION
    2.1 shellfish
    2.2 fish
    2.3 whales
    2.4 overexploitation
3. GLOBAL PATTERNS OF VARIATION
    3.1 high latitudes
    3.2 middle (temperate) latitudes
    3.3 low latitudes
    3.4 oceans and seas
4. ASPECTS OF SECONDARY PRODUCTION
    4.1 trophic transfer efficiency
    4.2 food chains
    4.3 food webs
    4.4 fisheries

(b)

Writing

Adopting a scientific style

Your main aim in developing a scientific style should be to get your message across directly and unambiguously. While you can try to achieve this through a set of 'rules' (see Box 46.1), you may find other requirements driving your writing in a contradictory direction. For instance, the need to be accurate and complete may result in text littered with technical terms, and the flow may be continually interrupted by references to the literature. The need to be succinct also affects style and readability through the use of, for example, stacked noun-adjectives (e.g. 'restriction fragment length polymorphism') and acronyms (e.g. 'RFLP'). Finally, style is very much a matter of taste and each tutor, examiner, supervisor or editor will have pet loves and hates which you may have to accommodate.

Developing technique

Writing is a skill that can be improved, but not instantly. You should analyse your deficiencies with the help of feedback from your tutors, be prepared to change work habits (e.g. start planning your work more carefully), and willing to learn from some of the excellent texts that are available on scientific writing.

KEY POINT You need to take a long-term view if you wish to improve your writing skills. An essential preliminary is to invest in and *make full use of* a personal reference library (see Box 46.2).

Getting started

A common problem is 'writer's block' – inactivity or stalling brought on by a variety of causes. If blocked, ask yourself these questions:

- Are you comfortable with your surroundings? Make sure you are seated comfortably at a reasonably clear desk and have minimized the possibility of interruptions and distractions.
- Are you trying to write too soon? Have you clarified your thoughts on the subject? Have you done enough preliminary reading? Talking to a friend about your topic might bring out ideas or reveal deficiencies in your knowledge.
- Are you happy with the underlying structure of your work? If you haven't made an outline, try this. If you are unhappy because you can't think of a particular detail at the planning stage, just start writing – it is more likely to come to you while you are thinking of something else.
- Are you trying to be too clever? Your first sentence doesn't have to be earth-shattering in content or particularly smart in style. A short statement of fact or a definition is fine. If there will be time for revision, get your ideas down on paper and revise grammar, content and order later.
- Do you really need to start writing at the beginning? Try writing the opening remarks after a more straightforward part. With reports of

Box 46.1 How to achieve a clear, readable style

Words and phrases

- Choose short clear words and phrases rather than long ones: e.g. use 'build' rather than 'fabricate'; 'now' rather than 'at the present time'. At certain times, technical terms must be used for precision, but don't use jargon if you don't have to.
- Don't worry too much about repeating words, especially when to introduce an alternative might subtly alter your meaning.
- Where appropriate, use the first person to describe your actions ('We decided to '; 'I conclude that '), but not if this is specifically discouraged by your supervisor.
- Favour active forms of speech ('the solution was placed in a beaker') rather than the passive voice ('the beaker was filled with the solution').
- Use tenses consistently. Past tense is always used for materials and methods ('samples were taken from . . .') and for reviewing past work ('Smith (1990) concluded that . . .'). The present tense is used when describing data ('Fig. 1 shows . . .'), for generalizations ('Most authorities agree that . . .') and conclusions ('I conclude that . . .').
- Use statements in parentheses sparingly – they disrupt the reader's attention to your central theme.

- Avoid clichés and colloquialisms – they are usually inappropriate in a scientific context.

Sentences

- Don't make them over-long or complicated.
- Introduce variety in structure and length.
- Make sure you understand how and when to use punctuation.
- If unhappy with the structure of a sentence, try chopping it into a series of shorter sentences.

Paragraphs

- Keep short and restrict them to a distinct theme.
- Use repeated key words (same subject or verb) or appropriate linking phrases (e.g. 'On the other hand . . .') to connect sentences and emphasize the flow of text.
- The first sentence should introduce the topic of a paragraph and the following sentences explain, illustrate or give examples.

Note: If you're not sure what is meant by any of the terms used here, consult a guide on writing (see Box 46.2).

experimental work, the Materials and Methods section may be the easiest to start at.

- Are you too tired to work? Don't try to 'sweat it out' by writing for long periods at a stretch: stop frequently for a rest.

Revising your text

Wholesale revision of your first draft is strongly advised for all writing apart from in exams. If a word processor is available, this can be a simple process. Where possible, schedule your writing so you can leave the first draft to 'settle' for at least a couple of days. When you return to it fresh, you will see more easily where improvements can be made. Try the following structured revision process, each stage being covered in a separate scan of your text:

1. Examine content. Have you included everything you need to? Is all the material relevant?
2. Check the grammar and spelling. Can you spot any 'howlers'?
3. Focus on clarity. Is the text clear and unambiguous? Does each sentence really say what you want it to say?
4. Try to achieve brevity. What could be missed out without spoiling the essence of your work? It might help to imagine an editor has set you the target of reducing the text by 15%.
5. Improve style. Could the text read better? Consider the sentence and paragraph structure and the way your text develops to its conclusion.

Revising your text – to improve clarity and shorten your text, 'distil' each sentence by taking away unnecessary words and 'condense' words or phrases by choosing a shorter alternative.

Box 46.2 Improve your writing ability by consulting a personal reference library

Using dictionaries

We all know that a dictionary helps with spelling and definitions, but how many of us use one effectively? You should:

- Keep a dictionary beside you when writing and always use it if in any doubt about spelling or definitions.
- Use it to prepare a list of words which you have difficulty in spelling: apart from speeding up the checking process, the act of writing out the words helps commit them to memory.
- Use it to write out a personal glossary of terms. This can help you memorize definitions. From time to time, test yourself.

Not all dictionaries are the same! Ask your tutor or supervisor whether he/she has a preference and why. Try out the *Oxford Advanced Learner's Dictionary*, which is particularly useful because it gives examples of use of all words and helps with grammar, e.g. by indicating which prepositions to use with verbs. Specialized dictionaries of environmental science tend to be variable in quality, possibly because **the subject** is so wide and new terms are continually being coined. *The Dictionary of Environmental Science and Technology* (Wiley 1996) is a useful example.

Using a thesaurus

A thesaurus contains lists of words of similar meaning grouped thematically; words of opposite meaning always appear nearby.

- Use a thesaurus to find a more precise and appropriate word to fit your meaning, but check definitions of unfamiliar words with a dictionary.
- Use it to find a word or phrase 'on the tip of your tongue' by looking up a word of similar meaning.
- Use it to increase your vocabulary.

Roget's Thesaurus is the standard. Collins publish a combined dictionary and thesaurus.

Using guides for written English

These provide help with the use of words.

- Use a guide to solve grammatical problems such as when to use 'shall' or 'will', 'which' or 'that', 'effect' or 'affect', etc.
- Use it for help with the paragraph concept and the correct use of punctuation.
- Use it to learn how to structure writing for different tasks.

Recommended guides include the following:

Kane, T.S. (1983) *The Oxford Guide to Writing*. Oxford University Press, New York. This is excellent for the basics of English – it covers grammar, usage and the construction of sentences and paragraphs.

Partridge, E. (1953) *You Have a Point There*. Routledge and Kegan Paul, London. This covers punctuation in a very readable manner.

Tichy, H.J. (1988) *Effective Writing for Engineers, Managers and Scientists*. John Wiley and Sons, New York. This is strong on scientific style and clarity in writing.

The function of an essay is to show how much you understand about a topic and how well you can organize and express your knowledge.

Organizing your time

Most essays have a relatively straightforward structure and it is best to divide your time into three main parts (Fig. 47.1). For exam strategies, see Chapter 52.

Making a plan for your essay

Dissect the meaning of the essay question or title

Read the title very carefully and think about the topic before starting to write. Consider the definitions of each of the important nouns (this can help in approaching the introductory section). Also think about the meaning of the verb(s) used and try to follow each instruction precisely (see Table 47.1). Don't get side-tracked because you know something about one word or phrase in the title: consider the whole title and all its ramifications. If there are two or more parts to the question, make sure you give adequate attention to each part.

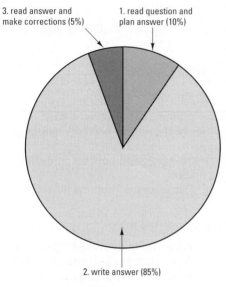

3. read answer and make corrections (5%)

1. read question and plan answer (10%)

2. write answer (85%)

Fig. 47.1 Pie chart showing a typical division of time for an essay.

Table 47.1 Instructions often used in essay questions and their meanings. When more than one instruction is given (e.g. compare and contrast; describe and explain), make sure you carry out *both* or your may lose a large proportion of the available marks

Account for:	give the reasons for
Analyse:	examine in depth and describe the main characteristics of
Assess:	weigh up the elements of and arrive at a conclusion about
Comment:	give an opinion on and provide evidence for your views
Compare:	bring out the similarities between
Contrast:	bring out dissimilarities between
Criticize:	judge the worth of (give both positive and negative aspects)
Define:	explain the exact meaning of
Describe:	use words and diagrams to illustrate
Discuss:	provide evidence or opinions about, arriving at a balanced conclusion
Enumerate:	list in outline form
Evaluate:	weigh up or appraise; find a numerical value for
Explain:	make the meaning of something clear
Illustrate:	use diagrams or examples to make clear
Interpret:	express in simple terms, providing a judgement
Justify:	show that an idea or statement is correct
List:	provide an itemized series of statements about
Outline:	describe the essential parts only, stressing the classification
Prove:	establish the truth of
Relate:	show the connection between
Review:	examine critically, perhaps concentrating on the stages in the development of an idea or method
State:	express clearly
Summarize:	without illustrations, provide a brief account of
Trace:	describe a sequence of events from a defined point of origin

Consider possible content and examples

The spider diagram technique (p. 250) is a speedy way of doing this. If you have time to read several sources, consider their content in relation to the essay title. Can you spot different approaches to the same subject? Which do you prefer as a means of treating the topic in relation to your title? Which examples are most relevant to your case, and why?

Construct an outline

Every essay should have a structure related to its title. Most marks for essays are lost because the written material is badly organized or is irrelevant. An essay plan, by definition, creates order and, if thought about carefully, can ensure relevance. Your plan should be written down (but scored through later if written in an exam book). Think about an essay's content in three parts:

1. The introductory section, in which you should include definitions and some background information on the context of the topic being considered. You should also tell your reader how you plan to approach the subject.
2. The middle of the essay, where you develop your answer and provide relevant examples. Decide whether a broad analytical approach is appropriate or whether the essay should contain more factual detail.
3. The conclusion, which you can make quite short. You should use this part to summarize and draw together the components of the essay, without merely repeating previous phrases. You might mention such things as: the broader significance of the topic; its future; its relevance to other important areas of environmental science. Always try to mention both sides of any debate you have touched on, but beware of 'sitting on the fence'.

KEY POINT Use paragraphs to make the essay's structure obvious. Emphasize them with headings and sub-headings unless the material beneath the headings would be too short or trivial.

Now start writing!

- Never lose track of the importance of content and its relevance. Repeatedly ask yourself: 'Am I really answering this question?' Never waffle just to increase the length of an essay. Quality rather than quantity is important.
- Illustrate your answer appropriately. Use examples to make your points clear, but remember that too many similar examples can stifle the flow of an essay. Use diagrams where a written description would be difficult or take too long. Use tables to condense information.
- Take care with your handwriting. You can't get marks if your writing is illegible! Try to cultivate an open form of handwriting, making the individual letters large and distinct. If there is time, make out a rough draft from which a tidy version can be copied.

Reviewing your answer

Don't stop yet!
- Re-read the question to check that you have answered all points.
- Re-read your essay to check for errors in punctuation, spelling and content. Make any corrections obvious. Don't panic if you suddenly realize you've missed a large chunk out as the reader can be redirected to a supplementary paragraph if necessary.

Essay content – it is rarely enough simply to lay down facts for the reader – you must analyse them and comment on their significance.

Using diagrams – give a title and legend for each diagram so that it makes sense in isolation and point out in the text when the reader should consult it (e.g. 'as shown in Fig. 1 ...' or 'as can be seen in the accompanying diagram, ...').

Learning from lecturers' and tutors' comments – ask for further explanations if you don't understand a comment or why an essay was less successful than you thought it should have been.

48

Writing reports

Table 48.1 Guidelines for giving advice in reports

Advice should be:
Focused on the issues
Clearly understandable
Simple but not simplistic
Contain an appropriate level of detail
Factually accurate
Carefully worded (if it can be misinterpreted, it will be)
Unequivocal and authoritative
Consistent – linked to previous advice
Provided on time

Options for discussing data – the main optional variants of the general structure include combining Results and Discussion into a single section and adding a separate Conclusions section.

- The main advantage of a joint Results and Discussion section is that you can link together different experiments, perhaps explaining why a particular result led to a new hypothesis and the next experiment.
- The main advantage of having a separate Conclusions section is to draw together and emphasize the chief points arising from your work, when these may have been 'buried' in an extensive Discussion section.

Practical reports, project reports, theses and scientific papers differ greatly in depth, scope and size, but they all have the same basic structure (Box 48.1).

Some variation is permitted, however (see Box 48.1), and you should always follow the advice or rules provided by your department.

Additional parts may be specified: for theses, a title page is often required and a List of Figures and Tables as part of the Contents section. When work is submitted for certain degrees, you may need to include certain declarations and statements made by the student and supervisor. In scientific papers, a list of Key Words is often added following the Abstract: this information may be combined with words in the title for computer cross-referencing systems.

Reports for outside bodies may require a Recommendations section to provide advice for non-scientific readers. Such advice should follow the guidelines in Table 48.1. Reports such as Environmental Statements (Chapter 30) should always include a 'Non-Technical Summary' (sometimes called an Executive Summary) that can be readily understood by non-experts.

KEY POINT Department or Faculty regulations may specify a precise format for producing your report or thesis. Obtain a copy of these rules at an early stage and follow them closely.

Practical and project reports

These are exercises designed to make you think more deeply about your experiments and to practise and test the skills necessary for writing up research work. Special features are:

- Introductory material is generally short and unless otherwise specified should outline the aims of the experiment(s) with a minimum of background material.
- Materials and methods may be provided by your supervisor for practical reports. With project work, your lab notebook (see p. 61) should provide the basis for writing this section.
- Great attention in assessment will be paid to presentation and analysis of data. Take special care over graphs (see p. 194). Make sure your conclusions are justified by the evidence.

Theses

Theses are submitted as part of the examination for a degree following an extended period of research. They act to place on record full details about your experimental work and will normally only be read by those with a direct interest in it – your examiners or colleagues. Note the following:

- You are allowed scope to expand on your findings and to include detail that might otherwise be omitted in a scientific paper.
- You may have problems with the volume of information that has to be organized. One method of coping with this is to divide your thesis into chapters, each having the standard format (as in Box 48.1). A General

Box 48.1 The structure of reports of experimental work

Undergraduate practical and project reports are generally modelled on this structure or a close variant of it, because this is the structure used for nearly all research papers and theses. The more common variations include Results and Discussion combined into a single section for convenience and Conclusions appearing separately as a series of points arising from the work. In scientific papers, a list of Key Words (for computer cross-referencing systems) may be included following the Abstract. Regarding variations in positioning, Acknowledgements may appear after the Contents section, rather than near the end. Department or faculty regulations for producing theses and reports may specify a precise format; they often require a title page to be inserted at the start and a list of figures and tables as part of the Contents section. These regulations may also specify declarations and statements to be made by the student and supervisor.

Part (in order)	Contents/purpose	Checklist for reviewing content
Title	Explains what the project was about	Does it explain what the text is about succinctly?
Authors plus their institutions	Explains who did the work and where; also where they can be contacted now	Are all the details correct?
Abstract/Summary	Synopsis of methods, results and conclusion of work described. Allows the reader to grasp quickly the essence of the work	Does it explain why the work was done? Does it outline the whole of your work and your findings?
List of Contents	Shows the organization of the text (not required for short papers)	Are all the sections covered? Are the page numbers correct?
Abbreviations	Lists all the abbreviations used (but not those of SI, chemical elements, or standard biochemical terms)	Have they all been explained? Are they all in the accepted form? Are they in alphabetical order?
Introduction	Orientates the reader, explains why the work has been done and its context in the literature, why the methods used were chosen, why the experimental organisms were chosen. Indicates the central hypothesis behind the experiments	Does it provide enough background information and cite all the relevant references? Is it of the correct depth for the readership? Have all the technical terms been defined? Have you explained why you investigated the problem? Have you explained your methodological approach to the problem?
Materials and Methods	Explains how the work was done. Should contain sufficient detail to allow another competent worker to repeat the work	Is each experiment covered and have you avoided unnecessary duplication? Is there sufficient detail to allow repetition of the work? Are proper scientific names and authorities given for all organisms? Have you explained where you got them from? Are the correct names, sources and grades given for all chemicals?
Results	Displays and describes the data obtained. Should be presented in a form which is easily assimilated (graphs rather than tables, small tables rather than large ones)	Is the sequence of experiments logical? Are the parts adequately linked? Are the data presented in the clearest possible way? Have SI units been used properly throughout? Has adequate statistical analysis been carried out? Is all the material relevant? Are the figures and tables all numbered in the order of their appearance? Are their titles appropriate? Do the figure and table legends provide all the information necessary to interpret the data without reference to the text? Have you presented the same data more than once?
Discussion/Conclusions	Discusses the results: their meaning, their importance; compares the results with those of others; suggests what to do next	Have you explained the significance of the results? Have you compared your data with other published work? Are your conclusions justified by the data presented?
Acknowledgements	Gives credit to those who helped carry out the work	Have you listed everyone that helped, including any grant-awarding bodies?
Literature Cited (Bibliography)	Lists all references cited in appropriate format: provides enough information to allow the reader to find the reference in a library	Do all the references in the text appear on the list? Do all the listed references appear in the text? Do the years of publications and authors match? Are the journal details complete and in the correct format? Is the list in alphabetical order, or correct numerical order?

Introduction can be given at the start and a General Discussion at the end. Discuss this with your supervisor.

- There may be an oral exam ('viva') associated with the submission of the thesis. The primary aim of the examiners will be to ensure that you understand what you did and why you did it.

Steps in the production of a report or thesis

Choose the experiments you wish to describe and decide how best to present them

Try to start this process before your lab work ends, because at the stage of reviewing your experiments, a gap may become apparent (e.g. a missing control) and you might still have time to rectify the deficiency. Irrelevant material should be ruthlessly eliminated, at the same time bearing in mind that negative results can be extremely important (see p. 55). Use as many different forms of data presentation as are appropriate, but avoid presenting the same data in more than one form. Graphs are generally easier for the reader to assimilate, while tables can be used to condense a lot of data into a small space. Relegate large tables of data to an appendix and summarize the important points. Make sure that the experiments you describe are representative: always state the number of times they were repeated and how consistent your findings were.

Make up plans or outlines for the component parts

The overall plan is well defined (see Box 48.1), but individual parts will need to be organized as with any other form of writing (see Chapter 46).

Write!

The Materials and Methods section is often the easiest to write once you have decided what to report. Remember to use the past tense and do not allow results or discussion to creep in. The Results section is the next easiest as it should only involve description. At this stage, you may benefit from jotting down ideas for the Discussion – this may be the hardest part to compose as you need an overview both of your own work and of the relevant literature. It is also liable to become wordy, so try hard to make it succinct. The Introduction shouldn't be too difficult if you have fully understood the aims of the experiments. Write the Abstract and complete the list of references at the end. To assist with the latter, it is a good idea as you write to jot down the references you use or to pull out their cards from your index system.

KEY POINT Never mix the reporting of data with data interpretation in the same section of a report. Present data/results first, then interpretations in a subsequent section.

Revise the text

Once your first draft is complete, try to answer all the questions given in Box 48.1. Show your work to your supervisors and learn from their comments. Let a friend or colleague who is unfamiliar with your subject read your text; they may be able to pinpoint obscure wording and show where information or explanation is missing. If writing a thesis, double-check that you are adhering to your institution's thesis regulations.

Repeating your experiments – remember, if you do an experiment twice, you have repeated it only once!

Presenting your results – remember that the order of results presented in a report need not correspond with the order in which you carried out the experiments: you are expected to rearrange them to provide a logical sequence of findings.

Prepare the final version

Markers appreciate neatly produced work but a well-presented document will not disguise poor science! If using a word processor, print the final version with the best printer available. Make sure figures are clear and in the correct size and format.

Submit your work

Your department will specify when to submit a thesis or project report, so plan your work carefully to meet this deadline or you may lose marks. Tell your supervisor early of any circumstances that may cause delay.

Producing a scientific paper

Scientific papers are the means by which research findings are communicated to others. They are published in journals with a wide circulation among academics and are 'peer reviewed' by one or more referees before being accepted. Each journal covers a well-defined subject area and publishes details of the format they expect. It would be very unusual for an undergraduate to submit a paper on his or her own – this would normally be done in collaboration with your project supervisor and only then if your research has satisfied appropriate criteria. However, it is important to understand the process whereby a paper comes into being (Box 48.2), as this can help you when interpreting the primary literature.

Box 48.2   Steps in producing a scientific paper

Scientific papers are the lifeblood of any science and it is a major landmark in your scientific career to publish your first paper. The major steps in doing this should include the following:

Assessing potential content
The work must be of an appropriate standard to be published and should be 'new, true and meaningful'. Therefore, before starting, the authors need to review their work critically under these headings. The material included in a scientific paper will generally be a sub-set of the total work done during a project, so it must be carefully selected for relevance to a clear central hypothesis – if the authors won't prune, the referees and editors of the journal certainly will!

Choosing a journal
There are many journals covering environmental science and each covers a specific area (which may change through time). The main factors in deciding on an appropriate journal are the range of subjects it covers, the quality of its content and the number and geographical distribution of its readers. The choice of journal always dictates the format of a paper since authors must follow to the letter the journal's 'Instructions to Authors'.

Deciding on authorship
In multi-author papers, a contentious issue is often who should appear as an author and in what order they should be cited. Where authors make an equal contribution, an alphabetical order of names may be used. Otherwise, each author should have made a substantial contribution to the paper and should be prepared to defend it in public. Ideally, the order of appearance will reflect the amount of work done rather than seniority. This may not happen in practice!

Writing
The paper's format will be similar to that shown in Box 48.1 and the process of writing will include outlining, reviewing, etc., as discussed elsewhere in this chapter. Figures must be finished to an appropriate standard and this may involve preparing photographs of them.

Submitting
When completed, copies of the paper are submitted to the editor of the chosen journal with a simple covering letter. A delay of one to two months usually follows while the manuscript is sent to one or more anonymous referees who will be asked by the editor to

Box 48.2 (continued)

check that the paper is novel, scientifically correct and that its length is fully justified.

Responding to referees' comments

The editor will send on the referees' comments and the authors then have a chance to respond. The editor will decide on the basis of the comments and replies to them whether the paper should be published. Sometimes quite heated correspondence can result if the authors and referees disagree!

Checking proofs and waiting for publication

If a paper is accepted, it will be sent off to the typesetters. The next the authors see of it is the proofs (first printed version in style of journal), which have to be corrected carefully for errors and returned. Eventually, the paper will appear in print, but a delay of six months following acceptance is not unusual. Most journals offer the authors reprints, which can be sent to other researchers in the field or to those who send in reprint request cards.

Writing literature surveys and reviews

The literature survey or review is a specialized form of essay which summarizes and reviews the evidence and concepts concerning a particular area of research.

KEY POINT A literature review should *not* be a simple recitation of facts. The best reviews are those which analyse information rather than simply describe it.

Making up a timetable

Figure 49.1 illustrates how you might divide up your time for writing a literature survey. There are many sub-divisions in this chart because of the size of the task: in general, for lengthy tasks, it is best to divide up the work into manageable chunks. Note also that proportionately less time is allocated to writing itself than with an essay. In a literature survey, make sure that you spend adequate time on research and revision.

Selecting a topic

You may have no choice in the topic to be covered, but if you do, carry out your selection as a three-stage process:

1. Identify a broad subject area that interests you.
2. Find and read relevant literature in that area. Try to gain a broad impression of the field from books and general review articles. Discuss your ideas with your supervisor.
3. Select a relevant and concise title. The wording should be considered very carefully as it will define the content expected by the reader. A narrow subject area will cut down on the amount of literature you will be expected to review, but will also restrict the scope of the conclusions you can make (and vice versa for a wide subject area).

Scanning the literature and organizing your references

You will need to carry out a thorough investigation of the literature before you start to write. The key problems are as follows:

- Getting an initial toe-hold in the literature. Seek help from your supervisor, who may be willing to supply a few key papers to get you started. Hints on expanding your collection of references are given on p. 242.
- Assessing the relevance and value of each article. This is the essence of writing a review, but it is difficult unless you already have a good understanding of the field (Catch 22!). Try reading earlier reviews in your area.
- Clarifying your thoughts. Sometimes you can't see the wood for the trees! Sub-dividing the main topic and assigning your references to these smaller subject areas may help you gain a better overview of the literature.

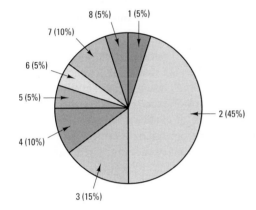

Fig. 49.1 Pie chart showing how you might allocate time for a literature survey:
1. select a topic;
2. scan the literature;
3. plan the review;
4. write first draft;
5. leave to settle;
6. structured review of text;
7. write final draft;
8. produce top copy.

Using index cards (see p. 244) – these can help you organize large numbers of references. Write key points on each card – this helps when considering where the reference fits into the literature. Arrange the cards in subject piles, eliminating irrelevant ones. Order the cards in the sequence you wish to write in.

Deciding on structure and content

The general structure and content of a literature survey is described below.

Introduction

The introduction should give the general background to the research area, concentrating on its development and importance. You should also make a statement about the scope of your survey; as well as defining the subject matter to be discussed, you may wish to restrict the period being considered.

Main body of text

The review itself should discuss the published work in the selected field and maybe subdivided into appropriate sections. Within each portion of a review, the approach is usually chronological, with appropriate linking phrases (e.g. 'Following on from this, . . .'; 'Meanwhile, Bloggs (1980) tackled the problem from a different angle . . .'). However, a good review is much more than a chronological list of work done. It should:

- allow the reader to obtain an overall view of the current state of the research area, identifying the key areas where knowledge is advancing;
- show how techniques are developing and discuss the benefits and disadvantages of using particular organisms or experimental systems;
- assess the relative worth of different types of evidence – this is the most important aspect. Do not be intimidated from taking a critical approach as the conclusions you may read in the primary literature aren't always correct;
- indicate where there is conflict in findings or theories, suggesting if possible which side has the stronger case;
- indicate gaps in current knowledge.

Conclusions

The conclusions should draw together the threads of the preceding parts and point the way forward, perhaps listing areas of ignorance or where the application of new techniques may lead to advances.

References, etc.

The References or Literature Cited section should provide full details of all papers referred to in the text (see p. 244). The regulations for your department may also specify a format and position for the title page, list of contents, acknowledgements, etc.

Balancing opposing views – even if you favour one side of a disagreement in the literature, your review should provide a fair description of all the published views of the topic. Having done this, if you do wish to state a preference, give reasons for your opinion.

Making citations – a review of literature poses stylistic problems because of the need to cite large numbers of papers; in the *Annual Review* series this is overcome by using numbered references (see p. 245).

50 Organizing a poster display

A scientific poster is a visual display of the results of an investigation, usually mounted on a rectangular board. Posters are used at scientific meetings, to communicate research findings, and in undergraduate courses, to display project results or assignment work.

In a written report you can include a reasonable amount of specific detail and the reader can go back and re-read difficult passages. However, if a poster is long-winded or contains too much detail, your reader is likely to lose interest.

KEY POINT A poster session is like a competition – you are competing for the attention of people in a room. Because you need to attract and hold the attention of your audience, make your poster as interesting as possible. Think of it as an advertisement for your work and you will not go far wrong.

Preliminaries

Before considering the content of your poster, you should find out:

- the linear dimensions of your poster area, typically up to 1.5 m wide by 1.0 m high;
- the composition of the poster board and the method of attachment, whether drawing pins, Velcro® tape, or some other form of adhesive; and whether these will be provided – in any case, it's safer to bring your own;
- the time(s) when the poster should be set up and when you should attend;
- the room where the poster session will be held.

Design

Plan your poster with your audience in mind, as this will dictate the appropriate level for your presentation. Aim to make your poster as accessible as possible to a broad audience. Since a poster is a visual display, you must pay particular attention to the presentation of information: work that may have taken hours to prepare can be ruined in a few minutes by the ill-considered arrangement of items (Fig. 50.1). Begin by making a draft sketch of the major elements of your poster. It is worth discussing your intended design with someone else, as constructive advice at the draft stage will save a lot of time and effort when you prepare the final version (or consult Simmonds and Reynolds, 1994).

Layout

Usually the best approach is to divide the poster into several smaller areas, perhaps six or eight in all, and prepare each as a separate item on a piece of thick card. Some people prefer to produce a single large poster on one sheet of paper or card and store it inside a protective cardboard tube. However, a single large poster will bend and crease, making it difficult to flatten out. In addition, photographs and text attached to the backing sheet often work loose.

Sub-dividing your poster means that each smaller area can be prepared on a separate piece of paper or card, of A4 size or slightly larger, making

(a)

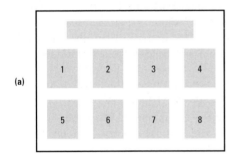

(b)

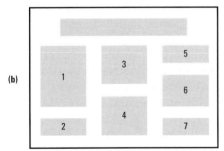

(c)

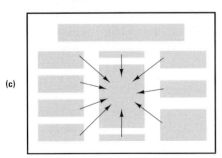

Fig. 50.1 Poster design. (a) An uninspiring design: sub-units of equal area, reading left to right, are not recommended. (b) This design is more interesting and the text will be easier to read (column format). (c) An alternative approach, with a central focus and arrows/tapes to guide the reader.

transport and storage easier. It also breaks the reading matter up into smaller pieces, looking less formidable to a potential reader. By using pieces of card of different colours you can provide emphasis for key aspects, or link text with figures or photographs.

You will need to guide your reader through the poster. It is often appropriate to use either a numbering system, with large, clear numbers at the top of each piece of card, or a system of arrows (or thin tapes), to show the relationship of sections within the poster (see Fig. 50.1). Make sure that the relationship is clear and that the arrows or tapes do not cross.

Title

Your chosen title should be concise (no more than eight words), specific and interesting, to encourage people to read the poster. Make the title large and bold – it should run across the top of your poster, in letters at least 4 cm high, so that it can be read from the other side of the room. Coloured spirit-based marker and block capitals drawn with a ruler work well, as long as your writing is readable and neat (the colour can be used to add emphasis). Alternatively, you can use Letraset®, or similar lettering. Details of authors, together with their addresses (if appropriate), should be given, usually in the top right-hand corner in somewhat smaller lettering than the title. At conferences, a passport-sized photograph of the contributor is sometimes useful for identification.

Text

Keep text to a minimum – aim to have a maximum of 500 words in your poster. Write in short sentences and avoid verbosity. Keep your poster as visual as possible and make effective use of the spaces between the blocks of text. Your final text should be double-spaced and should have a minimum capital letter height of 5–10 mm, preferably greater, so that the poster can be read at a distance of 1 m. One method of obtaining text of the required size is to photo-enlarge standard typescript (using a good-quality photocopier), or use a high-quality (laser) printer. It is best to avoid continuous use of text in capitals, since it slows reading and makes the text less interesting to the reader. Also avoid italic, 'balloon' or decorative styles of lettering.

Sub-titles and headings

These should have a capital letter height of 12–20 mm, and should be restricted to two or three words. They can be produced by photo-enlargement, by stencilling, Letraset® or by hand, using pencilled guidelines (but make sure that no pencil marks are visible on your finished poster).

Colour

Consider the overall visual effect of your chosen display, including the relationship between text, diagrams and the backing board. Colour can be used to highlight key aspects of your poster. However, it is very easy to ruin a poster by the inappropriate choice and application of colour. Careful use of two, or at most three, complementary colours will be easier on the eye and may aid comprehension. Colour can be used to link the text with the visual images (e.g. by picking out a colour in a photograph and using the same colour on the mounting board for the accompanying text). Use coloured inks or water-based paints to provide colour in diagrams and figures, as felt pens rarely give satisfactory results.

Making up your poster – text and graphics printed on good-quality paper can be glued directly onto a contrasting mounting card: use photographic spray mountant or Pritt® rather than liquid glue. Trim carefully using a guillotine to give equal margins, parallel with the paper. Photographs should be placed in a window mount to avoid the tendency for their corners to curl. Another approach is to trim pages or photographs to their correct size, then encapsulate in plastic film: this gives a highly professional finish and is less weighty to transport.

Content

The typical format is that of a scientific report (see Box 48.1), i.e. with the same headings, but with a considerably reduced content. Never be tempted to spend the minimum amount of time converting a piece of scientific writing into poster format. At scientific meetings, the least interesting posters are those where the author simply displays pages from a written communication (e.g. a journal article) on the poster board! Keep references within the text to a minimum – interested parties can always ask you for further information.

Introduction

This should give the reader background information on the broad field of study and the aims of your own work. It is vital that this section is as interesting as possible, to capture the interest of your audience. It is often worth listing your objectives as a series of numbered points.

Materials and Methods

Keep this short, and describe only the principal techniques used. You might mention any special techniques, or problems of general interest.

Designing the materials and methods section – photographs or diagrams of apparatus can help to break up the text of the Materials and Methods section and provide visual interest. It is sometimes worth preparing this section in a smaller typeface.

Results

Don't present your raw data: use data reduction wherever possible, i.e. figures and simple statistical comparisons. Graphs, diagrams, histograms and pie charts give clear visual images of trends and relationships and should be used in place of tabulated data (see p. 194). Final copies of all figures should be produced so that the numbers can be read from a distance of 1 m. Each should have a concise title and legend, so that it is self-contained: if appropriate, a series of numbered points can be used to link a diagram with the accompanying text. Where symbols are used, provide a key on each graph (symbol size should be at least 5 mm). Avoid using graphs straight from a written version, e.g. a project report, textbook, or a paper, without considering whether they need modification to meet your requirements.

Keeping graphs and diagrams simple – avoid composite graphs with different scales for the same axis, or with several trend lines (use a maximum of three trend lines per graph).

Conclusions

This is where many readers will begin, and they may go no further unless you make this section sufficiently interesting. This section needs to be the strongest part of your poster. Refer to your figures here to draw the reader into the main part of your poster. A slightly larger or bolder typeface may add emphasis, though too many different typefaces can look messy.

Listing your conclusions – a series of numbered points is a useful approach, if your findings fit this pattern.

The poster session

If you stand at the side of your poster throughout the session, you are likely to discourage some readers, who may not wish to become involved in a detailed conversation about the poster. Stand nearby. Find something to do – talk to someone else, or browse among the other posters, but remain aware of people reading your poster and be ready to answer any queries they may raise. Do not be too discouraged if you aren't asked lots of questions: remember, the poster is meant to be a self-contained, visual story, without need for further explanation.

Consider providing a handout – this is a useful way to summarize the main points of your poster, so that your readers have a permanent record of the information you have presented.

A poster display will never feel like an oral presentation, where the nervousness beforehand is replaced by a combination of satisfaction and relief as you unwind after the event. However, it can be a very satisfying means of communication, particularly if you follow these guidelines.

Giving an oral presentation

Most students feel very nervous about giving talks. This is natural, since very few people are sufficiently confident and outgoing that they look forward to speaking in public. Additionally, the technical nature of your subject matter may give you cause for concern, especially if you feel that some members of the audience have a greater knowledge than you have. However, this is a fundamental method of scientific communication and it therefore forms an important component of many courses.

The comments in this chapter apply equally to informal talks, e.g. those based on assignments and project work, and to more formal conference presentations. It is hoped that the advice and guidance given below will encourage you to make the most of your opportunities for public speaking, but there is no substitute for practice. Do not expect to find all of the answers from this, or any other, book. Rehearse, and learn from your own experience.

KEY POINT The three 'Rs' of successful public speaking are: reflect – give sufficient thought to all aspects of your presentation, particularly at the planning stage; rehearse – to improve your delivery; rewrite – modify the content and style of your material in response to your own ideas and to the comments of others.

Preparation

Preliminary information

Begin by marshalling the details needed to plan your presentation, including:

- the duration of the talk;
- whether time for questions is included;
- the size and location of the room;
- the projection/lighting facilities provided, and whether pointers or similar aids are available.

It is especially important to find out whether the room has the necessary equipment for slide projection (slide projector and screen, black-out curtains or blinds, appropriate lighting) or overhead projection before you prepare your audio-visual aids. If you concentrate only on the spoken part of your presentation at this stage, you are inviting trouble later on. Have a look around the room and try out the equipment at the earliest opportunity, so that you are able to use the lights, projector, etc., with confidence.

Audio-visual aids

Find out whether your department has facilities for preparing overhead transparencies and slides or for delivering computer-based presentations (e.g. Microsoft PowerPoint®). Check whether these facilities are available for your use and the cost of materials. Adopt the following guidelines:

- Keep text to a minimum: present only the key points, with up to 20 words per slide/transparency.
- Make sure the text is readable: try out your material beforehand.
- Use several simpler figures rather than a single complex graph.
- Avoid too much colour: blue and black are easier to read than red or green.
- Don't mix slides and transparencies as this is often distracting.
- Use spirit-based pens for transparencies: use alcohol for corrections.

Learning from experience – use your own experience of good and bad lecturers to shape your performance. Some of the more common errors include:

- speaking too quickly
- reading to notes and ignoring the audience
- unexpressive, impersonal or indistinct speech
- distracting mannerisms
- poorly structured material with little emphasis on key information
- factual information too complex and detailed
- too few visual aids

- Transparencies can be produced from typewritten or printed text using a photocopier, often giving a better product than pens. Note that you must use special heat-resistant acetate sheets for photocopying.

Audience

You should consider your audience at the earliest stage, since they will determine the appropriate level for your presentation. If you are talking to fellow students you may be able to assume a common level of background knowledge. In contrast, a research lecture given to your department, or a paper at a meeting of a scientific society, will be presented to an audience from a broader range of backgrounds. An oral presentation is not the place for a complex discussion of specialized information: build up your talk from a low level. The speed at which this can be done will vary according to your audience. As long as you are not boring or patronizing, you can cover basic information without losing the attention of the more knowledgeable members in your audience. The general rule should be: 'do not overestimate the background knowledge of your audience'. This sometimes happens in student presentations, where fears about the presence of 'experts' can encourage the speaker to include too much detail, overloading the audience with facts.

Content

While the specific details in your talk will be for you to decide, most oral presentations share some common features of structure, as described below.

Introductory remarks

It is vital to capture the interest of your audience at the outset. Consequently, you must make sure your opening comments are strong, otherwise your audience will lose interest before you reach the main message. Remember it takes a sentence or two for an audience to establish a relationship with a new speaker. Your opening sentence should be some form of preamble and should not contain any key information. For a formal lecture, you might begin with 'Mr Chairman, ladies and gentlemen, my talk today is about ...' then re-state the title and acknowledge other contributors, etc. You might show a transparency or slide with the title printed on it, or an introductory photograph, if appropriate. This should provide the necessary settling-in period.

After these preliminaries, you should introduce your topic. Begin your story on a strong note – this is no place for timid or apologetic phrases. You should:

- explain the structure of your talk;
- set out the aims and objectives of your work;
- explain your approach to the topic.

Opening remarks are unlikely to occupy more than 10% of the talk. However, because of their significance, you might reasonably spend up to 25% of your preparation time on them. Make sure you have practised this section, so that you can deliver the material in a flowing style, with less chance of mistakes.

The main message

This section should include the bulk of your experimental results or literature findings, depending on the type of presentation. Keep details of methods to the minimum needed to explain your data. This is *not* the place for a detailed description of equipment and experimental protocol (unless it is a talk about methodology!). Results should be presented in an easily digested format.

Giving an oral presentation

Allowing time for slides – as a rough guide you should allow at least two minutes per illustration, although some diagrams may need longer, depending on content.

Do not expect your audience to cope with large amounts of data; use a maximum of six numbers per slide. Present summary statistics rather than individual results. Show the final results of any analyses in terms of the statistics calculated, and their significance (p. 216), rather than dwelling on details of the procedures used. Remember that graphs and diagrams are usually better than tables of raw data, since the audience will be able to see the trends and relationships in your data (p. 194). However, figures should not be crowded with unnecessary detail. Every diagram should have a concise title and the symbols and trend lines should be clearly labelled, with an explanatory key where necessary. When presenting graphical data always 'introduce' each graph by stating the units for each axis and describing the relationship for each trend line or data set. Summary slides can be used at regular intervals, to maintain the flow of the presentation and to emphasize the key points.

Take the audience through your story step-by-step at a reasonable pace. Try not to rush the delivery of your main message due to nervousness. Avoid complex, convoluted story-lines – one of the most distracting things you can do is to fumble backwards through slides or overhead transparencies. If you need to use the same diagram or graph more than once then you should make two (or more) copies. In a presentation of experimental results, you should discuss each point as it is raised, in contrast to written text, where the results and discussion may be in separate sections. The main message typically occupies approximately 80% of the time allocated to an oral presentation.

Concluding remarks

Final remarks – make sure you give the audience sufficient time to assimilate your final slide: some of them may wish to write down the key points. Alternatively, you might provide a handout, with a brief outline of the aims of your study and the major conclusions.

Having captured the interest of your audience in the introduction and given them the details of your story in the middle section, you must now bring your talk to a conclusion. At all costs, do not end weakly, e.g. by running out of steam on the last slide. Provide your audience with a clear 'take-home message', by returning to the key points in your presentation. It is often appropriate to prepare a slide or overhead transparency listing your main conclusions as a numbered series.

Signal the end of your talk by saying 'finally ...', 'in conclusion ...', or a similar comment and then finish speaking after that sentence. Your audience will lose interest if you extend your closing remarks beyond this point. You may add a simple end phrase (for example, 'thank you') as you put your notes into your folder, but do not say 'that's all folks!', or make any similar offhand remark. Finish as strongly and as clearly as you started.

Hints on presentation

Notes

Many accomplished speakers use abbreviated notes for guidance, rather than reading from a prepared script. When writing your talk:

- Prepare a first draft as a full script: write in spoken English, keeping the text simple and avoiding an impersonal style. Aim to *talk* to your audience, not read to them.
- Use note cards with key phrases and words: it is best to avoid using a full script at the final presentation. As you rehearse and your confidence improves, a set of cards may be a more appropriate format for your notes.
- Consider the structure of your talk: keep it as simple as possible and announce each sub-division, so your audience is aware of the structure.

- Mark the position of slides/key points, etc.: each note card should contain details of structure, as well as content.
- Memorize your introductory/closing remarks: you may prefer to rely on a full written version for these sections, in case your memory fails.
- Use notes: write on only one side of the card/paper, in handwriting large enough to be read easily during the presentation. Each card or sheet must be clearly numbered, so that you do not lose your place.
- Rehearse your presentation: ask a friend to listen and to comment constructively on parts that were difficult to follow.
- Use 'split times' to pace yourself: following rehearsal, note the time at which you should arrive at key points of your talk. These timing marks will help you keep to time during the 'real thing'.

Using slides – check that the lecture theatre has a lectern light, otherwise you may have problems reading your notes when the lights are dimmed.

Image

Ensure that the image you project is appropriate for the occasion:

- Consider what to wear: aim to be respectable without 'dressing up', otherwise your message may be diminished.
- Develop a good posture: it will help your voice projection if you stand upright, rather than slouching or leaning over the lectern.
- Project your voice: speak towards the back of the room.
- Make eye contact: look at members of the audience in all parts of the room. Avoid talking to your notes, or to only one section of the audience.
- Deliver your material with expression: arm movements and subdued body language will help maintain the interest of your audience. However, you should avoid extreme gestures (it may work for some TV personalities, but it isn't recommended for the beginner!).
- Manage your time: avoid looking at your watch as it gives a negative signal to the audience. Use a wall clock, if one is provided, or take off your watch and put it beside your notes, so you can glance at it without distracting your audience.
- Try to identify and control any distracting repetitive mannerisms, e.g. repeated empty phrases, fidgeting with pens, keys, etc., as this will distract your audience. Practising in front of a mirror may help.
- Practise your delivery: use the comments of your friends to improve your performance.

Questions

Many speakers are worried by the prospect of questions after their oral presentation. Once again, the best approach is to prepare beforehand:

- Consider what questions you may be asked: prepare brief answers.
- Do not be afraid to say 'I don't know': your audience will appreciate honesty, rather than vacillation, if you don't have an answer for a particular question.
- Avoid arguing with a questioner: suggest a discussion afterwards rather than becoming involved in a debate about specific details.
- If no questions are forthcoming you may pose a question yourself, and then ask for opinions from the audience: if you use this approach you should be prepared to comment briefly if your audience has no suggestions. This will prevent the presentation from ending in an embarrassing silence.

Examples Commonly used abbreviations include:

∃	there are, there exist(s)
∴	therefore
∵	because
∝	is proportional to
→	leads to, into
←	comes from, from
⟶	involves several processes in a sequence
1°, 2°	primary, secondary (etc.)
≈, ≅	approximately, roughly equal to
=, ≠	equals, not equal to
≡, ≢	equivalent, not equivalent to
<, >	smaller than, bigger than
≫	much bigger than
[X]	concentration of X
∑	sum
f	function
#	number
∞	infinity, infinite

You should also make up your own abbreviations relevant to the context, e.g. if a lecturer is talking about photo-synthesis, you could write 'PS' instead.

You are unlikely to have reached this stage in your education without being exposed to the examination process. However, the following comments should help you to identify and improve on the skills required for exam success.

Information gathering

KEY POINT To do well in an examination, you need to do effective work long before you go into the examination hall and even before you start to revise. You need to base your revision on accurate, tidy notes with an appropriate amount of subject detail and depth.

Taking notes from lectures

Taking good lecture notes is essential if you are to make sense of them later. Start by noting the date, course, topic and lecturer. Number every page in case they get mixed up later. The most popular way of taking notes is to write in a linear sequence down the page; however, the alternative 'pattern' method (Fig. 52.1) has its advocates: experiment to see which you prefer.

Whatever method you use to take notes, you shouldn't try to take down all the lecturer's words, except when an important definition or example is being given, or when the lecturer has made it clear that he/she is dictating. Listen first, then write. Your goal should be to abstract the structure and reasoning behind the lecturer's approach. Use headings and leave plenty of space, but don't worry too much about being tidy at this stage – it is more important that you get down the appropriate information in a form that you at least can read. Use abbreviations to save time. Make sure you note down references to texts and take special care to ensure accuracy of definitions and numerical examples. If the lecturer repeats or otherwise emphasises a point, make a margin note of this – it could come in useful when revising. If there is something you don't understand, ask at the end of the lecture, and make an appointment to discuss the matter if there isn't time to deal with it then. Tutorials may provide an additional forum for discussing course topics.

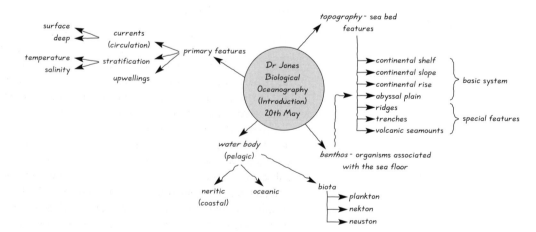

Fig. 52.1 An example of 'pattern' notes, an alternative to the more commonly used 'linear' format.

'Making up' your notes

As soon as possible after the lecture, work through your notes, tidying them up and adding detail where necessary. Add emphasis to any headings you have made, so that the structure is clearer. Compare your notes with material in a textbook and correct any inconsistencies. Make notes from, or photocopy, any useful material you see in textbooks, ready for revision.

Skimming texts

This is a valuable means of gaining the maximum amount of information in the minimum amount of time, by reading as little of a text as is required. It can be used to decide what parts to read in detail and to make notes of, perhaps when you have read the text in detail already.

Essentially, the technique requires you to look at the structure of the text, rather than the detail. In a sense, you are trying to see the writer's original plan and the purpose behind each part of the text. Look through the whole of the piece first, to gain an overview of its scope and structure. Headings provide an obvious clue to structure, if present. Next, look for the 'topic sentence' in each paragraph (p. 252), which is often the first. You might then decide that the paragraph contains a definition that is important to note, or it may contain examples, so may not be worth reading for your purpose.

Seeing sequences – writers often number their points (firstly, secondly, thirdly, etc.) and looking for these words in the text can help you skim it quickly.

Preparing for an exam

Begin by finding out as much as you can about the exam, including:

- its format and duration;
- the date and location;
- the types of question;
- whether any questions/sections are compulsory;
- whether the questions are internally or externally set or assessed;
- whether calculators are required.

Your course tutor is likely to give you details of exam structure and timing well beforehand, so that you can plan your revision: the course handbook and past papers (if available) can provide further useful details. Check with your tutor that the nature of the exam has not changed before you consult past papers.

Organizing and using lecture notes, assignments and practical reports

Given their importance as a source of material for revision, you should have sorted out any deficiencies or omissions in lecture notes/practical reports at an early stage. For example, you may have missed a lecture or practical due to illness, etc., but the exam is likely to assume attendance throughout the year. Make sure you attend classes whenever possible and keep your notes up to date.

Your practical reports and any assignment work will contain specific comments from the teaching staff, indicating where marks were lost, corrections, mistakes, inadequacies, etc. It is always worth reading these comments as soon as your work is returned, to improve the standard of your subsequent reports. If you are unsure about why you lost marks in an assignment, or about some particular aspects of a topic, ask the appropriate member of staff for further explanation. Most lecturers are quite happy to discuss such details with students on a one-to-one basis and this information may provide you with 'clues' to the expectations of individual lecturers that may be useful in exams set by the same members of staff. However, you should *never* 'fish' for specific information on possible exam questions, as this is likely to be counter-productive.

Revision

Begin your revision early, to avoid last-minute panic. Start in earnest about 6 weeks beforehand:

- Prepare a revision timetable – an 'action plan' that gives details of specific topics to be covered. Find out at an early stage when (and where) your examinations are to be held, and plan your revision around this. Try to keep to your timetable. Time management during this period is as important as keeping to time during the exam itself.
- Remember, your concentration span is limited to 15–20 min: make sure you have two or three short (5 min) breaks during each hour of revision.
- Make your revision as active and interesting as possible: the least productive approach is simply to read and re-read your notes.
- Include recreation within your schedule: there is little point in tiring yourself with too much revision, as this is unlikely to be profitable.
- Ease back on the revision near the exam: plan your revision, to avoid last-minute cramming and overload fatigue.

Active revision

The following techniques may prove useful in devising an active revision strategy:

- Prepare revision sheets with details for a particular topic on a single sheet of paper, arranged as a numbered checklist. Wall posters are another useful revision aid.
- Memorize definitions and key phrases: definitions can be a useful starting point for many exam answers.
- Use mnemonics and acronyms to commit specific factual information to memory. The dafter they are, the better they work!
- Prepare answers to past or hypothetical questions, e.g. write essays or work through calculations and problems, within appropriate time limits. However, you should not rely on 'question spotting': this is a risky practice!
- Use spider diagrams as a means of testing your powers of recall on a particular topic (p. 250).
- Try recitation as an alternative to written recall.
- Draw diagrams from memory: make sure you can label them fully.
- Form a revision group to share ideas and discuss topics with other students.
- Use a variety of different approaches to avoid boredom during revision (e.g. record information on audio tape, use cartoons, or *any* other method, as long as it's not just reading notes!).

The evening before your exam should be spent in consolidating your material, and checking through summary lists and plans. Avoid introducing new material at this late stage: your aim should be to boost your confidence, putting yourself in the right frame of mind for the exam itself.

The examination

On the day of the exam, give yourself sufficient time to arrive at the correct room, without the risk of being late (e.g. what if your bus breaks down?).

Preparing for an exam – make a checklist of the items you'll need (e.g. pens, pencils, sharpener and eraser, ruler, calculator, paper tissues, watch).

Final preparations – try to get a good night's sleep before an exam. Last minute cramming will be counter-productive if you are too tired during the exam.

The exam paper

Begin by reading the instructions at the top of the exam paper carefully, so that you do not make any errors based on lack of understanding. Make sure that you know:

- how many questions are set;
- how many must be answered;
- whether the paper is divided into sections;
- whether any parts are compulsory;
- what each question/section is worth, as a proportion of the total mark;
- whether different questions should be answered in different books.

If you are unsure about anything, ask! – the easiest way to lose marks in an exam is to answer the wrong number of questions, or to answer a different question from the one set by the examiner. Underline the key phrases in the instructions, to reinforce their message.

Next, read through the set of questions. If there is a choice, decide on those questions to be answered and decide on the order in which you will tackle them. Prepare a timetable which takes into account the amount of time required to complete each question and which reflects the allocation of marks – there is little point in spending one-quarter of the exam period on a question worth only 5% of the total marks! Use the exam paper to mark the sequence in which the questions will be answered and write the finishing times alongside: refer to this timetable during the exam to keep yourself on course.

Do not be tempted to spend too long on any one question: the return in terms of marks will not justify the loss of time from other questions (see Fig. 52.2). Take the first 10 min or so to read the paper and plan your strategy, before you begin writing. Do not be put off by those who begin immediately; it is almost certain they are producing unplanned work of a poor standard.

Providing answers

Before you tackle a particular question, you must be sure of what is required in your answer. Ask yourself 'What is the examiner looking for in this particular question?' and then set about providing a *relevant* answer. Consider each individual word in the question and highlight, underline or circle the key words. Make sure you know the meaning of the terms given in Table 47.1 (p. 254) so that you can provide the appropriate information, where necessary. Refer back to the question as you write, to confirm that you are keeping to the subject matter. Box 52.1 gives advice on writing essays under exam conditions.

It is usually a good idea to begin with the question that you are most confident about. This will reassure you before tackling more difficult parts of the paper. If you run out of time, write in note form. Examiners are usually understanding, as long as the main components of the question have been addressed and the intended structure of the answer is clear.

The final stage

At the end of the exam, you should allow at least 10 min to read through your script, to check for:

- grammatical and spelling errors;
- mathematical errors.

Using the exam paper – unless this is specifically forbidden, you *should* write on the question paper to plan your strategy, keep to time and organize your answers.

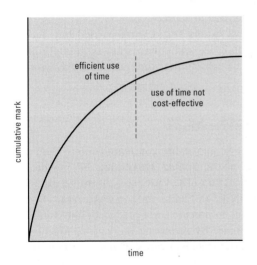

Fig. 52.2 Exam marks as a function of time. The marks awarded in a single answer will follow the law of diminishing returns – it will be far more difficult to achieve the final 25% of the available marks than the initial 25%. Do not spend too long on any one question.

Box 52.1 Writing under exam conditions

Never go into an exam without a strategy for managing the available time.

- **Allocate some time (say 5% of the total) to consider which questions to answer and in which order.**
- **Share the rest of the time among the questions.** Aim to optimize the marks obtained. A potentially good answer should be allocated *slightly* more time than one you don't feel so happy about. However, don't concentrate on any one answer (see Fig. 52.2).
- **For each question divide the time into planning, writing and revision phases** (see p. 254).

Employ time-saving techniques as much as possible.

- **Use spider diagrams** (p. 250) to organize and plan your answer.

- **Use diagrams and tables** to save time in making difficult and lengthy explanations.
- **Use abbreviations** to save time repeating text but *always* explain them at the first point of use.
- **Consider speed of writing and neatness** especially when selecting the type of pen to use – ball-point pens are fastest, but they can smudge. You can only gain marks if the examiner can read your script!
- **Keep your answer simple and to the point**, with clear explanations of your reasoning.

Make sure your answer is relevant.

- **Don't include irrelevant facts** just because you memorized them during revision as this may do you more harm than good. You must answer the specific question that has been set.
- **Time taken to write irrelevant material is time lost from another question.**

After the exam – try to avoid becoming involved in prolonged analyses with other students over the 'ideal' answers to the questions; after all, it is too late to change anything at this stage. Go for a walk, watch TV for a while, or do something else that helps you relax, so that you are ready to face the next exam with confidence.

Make sure your name is on each exam book and on all other sheets of paper, including graph paper, even if securely attached to your script, as it is in your interest to ensure that your work does not go astray.

Never leave any exam early. Most exams assess work carried out over several months in a time period of 2–3 h and there is always something constructive you can do with the remaining time to improve your script.

Practical exams: special considerations

The prospect of a practical examination may cause you more concern than a theory exam. This may be due to a limited experience of practical examinations, or the fact that practical and observational skills are tested, as well as recall, description and analysis of factual information. Your first thoughts may be that it is not possible to prepare for a practical exam but, in fact, you can improve your performance by mastering the various practical techniques described in this book. The principal types of question you are likely to encounter include:

- Manipulative exercises, often based on work carried out as part of your practical course.
- 'Spot' tests: short answer questions requiring identification, or brief descriptive notes on a specific item (e.g. a prepared slide).
- Numerical exercises, including the preparation of aqueous solutions at particular concentrations (p. 14) and statistical exercises (p. 216). General advice is given in Chapter 38.
- Data analysis, including the preparation and interpretation of graphs (p. 194) and numerical information, from data either obtained during the exam or provided by the examiner.
- Drawing a specimen, where accurate representation and labelling will be important (Chapter 11).

- Preparation of a specimen for examination with a microscope: this will test skills in light microscopy (p. 115).
- Interpretation of photographic material: sometimes used when it is not possible to provide living specimens, e.g. in relation to field work, or electron microscopy (Chapter 27).

Practical reports

You may be allowed to take your laboratory reports and other texts into the practical exam. Don't assume that this is a soft option, or that revision is unnecessary: you will not have time to read large sections of your reports or to familiarize yourself with basic principles, etc. The main advantage of 'open book' exams is that you can check specific details of methodology, reducing your reliance on memory, provided you know your way around your practical manual. In all other respects, your revision and preparation for such exams should be similar to theory exams. Make sure you are familiar with all of the practical exercises, including any work carried out in class by your partner (since exams are assessed on individual performance). Check with the teaching staff to see whether you can be given access to the laboratory, to complete any exercises that you have missed.

The practical exam

At the outset, determine or decide on the order in which you will tackle the questions. A question in the latter half of the paper may need to be started early on in the exam period (e.g. a leaf litter extraction procedure requiring an extraction period of several hours during a 3-h exam). Such questions are included to test your forward-planning and time-management skills. You may need to make additional decisions on the allocation of materials where particular items may be required for more than one question.

Make sure you explain your choice of apparatus and experimental design. Calculations should be set out in a stepwise manner, so that credit can be given, even if the final answer is incorrect (see p. 203). If there are any questions that rely on recall of factual information and you are unable to remember specific details, e.g. you cannot identify a particular specimen, or slide, make sure that you describe the item fully, so that you gain credit for observational skills. Alternatively, leave a gap and return to the question at a later stage.

References

Blomqvist, S. (1985) Reliability of core sampling of soft bottom sediment – an *in situ* study. *Sedimentology, 32*, 605–12.

Briggs, D.J. (1977) *Sources and Methods in Geography: Sediments.* Butterworth & Co., London.

Budavari, S., *et al.* (1996) *The Merck Index: An Encyclopedia of Chemicals, Drugs and Biologicals,* 12th edn. Merck & Co., Inc., Rahway, New Jersey.

Davis, J.C. (1986) *Statistics and Data Analysis in Geology,* 2nd edn. John Wiley & Sons, New York.

Eason, G., Coles, C.W. and Gettinby, G. (1992) *Mathematics and Statistics for the Bio-Sciences.* Ellis Horwood, Chichester.

Elliott, J.M. (1977) *Some Methods for the Statistical Analysis of Benthic Invertebrates,* 2nd edn. Freshwater Biological Association Publication No. 25, Windermere.

Fink, A. (ed). (1995) *The Survey Kit* (9 Volumes). Sage Publications, Thousand Oaks, California.

Fink, A. and Kosecoff, J. (1985) *How to Conduct Surveys: A Step-by-Step Guide.* Sage Publications, Newbury Park, California.

Finney, D.J., Latscha, R., Bennett, B.M. and Hsu, P. (1963) *Tables for Testing Significance in a 2 × 2 Table.* Cambridge University Press, Cambridge.

Fry, N. (1984) *The Field Description of Metamorphic Rocks.* Geological Society Handbook. Geological Society Publishing House, Bath.

Gralla, P. (1996) *How the Internet Works.* Ziff-Davis Press, Emeryville, California.

Gribble, C.D. (1988) *Rutley's Elements of Mineralogy,* 27th edn. Unwin Hyman, London.

Gribble, C.D. and Hall, A.J. (1985) *A Practical Introduction to Optical Mineralogy.* George Allen & Unwin, London.

Heath, D. (1995) *An Introduction to Experimental Design and Statistics for Biology.* UCL Press, London.

Holme, N.A. and McIntyre, A.D. (1984) *Methods for the Study of Marine Benthos,* 2nd edn. Blackwell Scientific Publications, Oxford.

Jackson, A.R.W. and Jackson, J.M. (1996) *Environmental Science,* Longman, Harlow.

Jones, H.G. (1992) *Plants and Microclimate: a Quantitative Approach to Environ-mental Plant Physiology,* 2nd edn. Cambridge University Press, Cambridge.

Leick, A. (1995) *GPS Satellite Surveying,* 2nd edn. John Wiley & Sons, New York.

Lentner, C. (ed.) (1981) *Geigy Scientific Tables, 8th edn, vol. 1: Units of Measurement, Body Fluids, Composition of the Body, Nutrition.* Ciba-Geigy, Basel.

Lentner, C. (ed.) (1981) *Geigy Scientific Tables, 8th edn, vol. 3: Physical Chemistry, Composition of Blood, Hematology, Somatometric Data.* Ciba-Geigy, Basel.

Lentner, C. (ed.) (1981) *Geigy Scientific Tables, 8th edn, vol. 5: Heart and Circulation.* Ciba-Geigy, Basel.

Lentner, C. (ed.) (1988) *Geigy Scientific Tables, 8th edn, vol. 4: Biochemistry, Metabolism of Xenobiotics, Inborn Errors of Metabolism, Pharmacogenetics, Ecogenetics.* Ciba-Geigy, Basel.

Lentner. C. (ed.) (1992) *Geigy Scientific Tables, 8th edn, vol. 6: Bacteria, Fungi, Protozoa, Helminths.* Ciba-Geigy, Basel.

Lentner, C., Diem, K. and Seldrup, J. (eds) (1982) *Geigy Scientific Tables, 8th edn, vol. 2: Introduction to Statistics, Statistical Tables, Mathematical Formulae.* Ciba-Geigy, Basel.

Leverlich, W.J. and Levin, D.A. (1979) Age specific survivorship and reproduction in *Phlox drummondi. Am. Nat.* **113**, 881–903.

Lide, D.R. and Frederikse, H.P.R. (eds) (1996) *CRC Handbook of Chemistry and Physics,* 77th edn. CRC Press, Boca Raton, Florida.

Lof, P. (1982) *Elsevier's Mineral and Rock Table.* Wall Chart. Elsevier Science, Amsterdam.

Lof, P. (1983) *Minerals of the World.* Wall Chart. Elsevier Science, Amsterdam.

Lof, P. and van Baren, H. (1987) *Soils of the World.* Wall Chart. Elsevier Science, Amsterdam.

Mudroch, A. and MacKnight, D. (eds) (1991) *CRC Handbook of Techniques for Aquatic Sediments Sampling.* CRC Press, Boca Raton, Florida.

Parsons, R. and Ogston, S.A. (1997) *Bio/Chem Lab Assistant Program.* Addison Wesley Longman.

Prys-Jones, O.E. and Corbet, S.A. (1987) *Naturalist's Handbook 6: Bumblebees.* Cambridge University Press, Cambridge.

Ritchie, W., Wood, M., Wright, R. and Tait, D. (1988) *Surveying and Mapping for Field Scientists.* Longman, Harlow.

Robinson, R.A. and Stokes, R.H. (1970) *Electrolyte Solutions.* Butterworth-Heinemann, London.

Schwedt, G. (1997) *The Essential Guide to Analytical Chemistry.* John Wiley & Sons, Chichester.

Simmonds, D. and Reynolds, L. (1994) *Data Presentation and Visual Literacy in Medicine and Science.* Butterworth-Heinemann, London.

Sokal, R.R. and Rohlf, F.J. (1994) *Biometry,* 3rd edn. W.H. Freeman & Co., San Francisco.

Stace, C. (1997) *New Flora of the British Isles,* 2nd edn. Cambridge University Press, Cambridge.

Thorpe, R.S. and Brown, G.C. (1985) *The Field Description of Igneous Rocks.* Geological Society Handbook. Geological Society Publishing House, Bath.

Tomkeieff, S.I. (1953) *Geological Magazine,* **90**, 406.

Trudgill, S. (1989) Soil types: a field identification guide. *Field Studies,* **7**, 337–63.

Tucker, M. (1996) *Sedimentary Rocks in the Field.* Geological Society Handbook. Geological Society Publishing House, Bath.

Tukey, J.W. (1977) *Exploring Data Analysis.* Addison-Wesley, Reading, Massachusetts.

Walford, N. (1995) *Geographical Data Analysis.* John Wiley & Sons, Chichester.

Wardlaw, A.C. (1985) *Practical Statistics for Experimental Biologists.* John Wiley & Sons, New York.

Winship, I. and McNab, A. (1996) *The Student's Guide to the Internet.* Library Association, London.

Wright, J. (1982) *Ground and Air Survey for Field Scientists.* Oxford University Press, Oxford.

Further reading

Briscoe, M.H. (1990) *A Researcher's Guide to Scientific and Medical Illustrations*. Springer Verlag, Berlin.

Ennos, R. and Bailey, S. (1995) *Problem Solving in Environmental Biology*. Longman, Harlow.

Fowler, J. and Cohen, L. (1990) *Practical Statistics for Field Biology*. John Wiley & Sons, Chichester.

Golterman, H.L., Clymo, R.S. and Ohnstad, M.A.M. (1978) *Methods for Physical and Chemical Analysis of Fresh Waters*. Blackwell Scientific Publications, Oxford.

Green, E.J. and Carritt, D.E. (1967) New tables for oxygen saturation of seawater. *Journal of Marine Research,* **25**, 140–7.

Grimestone, A.V. and Skaer, R.J. (1972) *A Guidebook to Microscopical Methods*. Cambridge University Press, Cambridge.

Hay, I. (1996) *Communicating in Geography and the Environmental Sciences*. Oxford University Press, Australia.

Haynes, R.M. (1982) *Environmental Science Methods*. Chapman & Hall, London.

Hodges, E.R.S. (ed.) (1989) *The Guild Handbook of Scientific Illustration*. Van Nostrand Reinhold, New York.

Jackson, A.R.W. and Jackson, J.M. (1996) *Environmental Science*. Longman, Harlow.

Jones, A.M. (1997) *Environmental Biology*. Routledge, London.

Jones, A.M., Reed, R. and Weyers, J. (1998) *Practical Skills in Biology,* 2nd edn. Longman, Harlow.

Keith, J.H. (1991) *Environmental Sampling and Analysis: A Practical Guide*. Lewis, Michigan.

Kneale, P. (1999) *Study Skills for Geography Students*. Arnold, London.

Lawrence, E., Jackson, A.R.W. and Jackson, J.M. (1998) *Longman Dictionary of Environmental Science*. Longman, Harlow.

Lennon, B.J. and Cleves, P.G. (1983) *Techniques and Fieldwork in Geography*. Unwin Hyman, London.

Manahan, S.E. (1991) *Environmental Chemistry*. Lewis, Michigan.

Merritts, D., de Wet, A. and Menking, K. (1998) *Environmental Geology*. W.H. Freeman, New York.

McGrew, J.C. Jnr and Monroe, C.B. (1993) *An Introduction to Statistical Problem Solving in Geography*. Wm. C. Brown, Dubuque.

Ott, W.R. (1995) *Environmental Statistics and Data Analysis*. CRC Press, Boca Raton, Florida.

Smith, R.L. (1996) *Ecology and Field Biology,* 5th edn. Harper Collins College Publishers, New York.

Wadsworth, R. and Treweek, J. (1999) *Geographical Information Systems for Ecology: An Introduction*. Longman, Harlow.

Watts, S. and Halliwell, L. (eds) (1996) *Essential Environmental Science: Methods and Techniques*. Routledge, London.

Index

Index

Index

Index

Index

Index